More Praise for
Planet Funny

"Ken Jennings hops aboard our thundering and does it like a pro. . . . *Planet Funny* is for the comedy geek in all of us."

—Maria Semple, author of *Where'd You Go, Bernadette*

"Ken Jennings has done the impossible: he's written an actually funny book about comedy. Ken is brilliant and incisive and the kind of guy with so many smarts that it makes you go, 'Man, that guy's really smart.' Fans of comedy will love *Planet Funny* and will undoubtedly wonder why I am not mentioned more."

—Michael Ian Black, author of *Navel Gazing*

"When did comedy become so serious and the daily news become so laughable? In his latest book, Ken Jennings provides excellent insight in detailing how comedy has infiltrated every corner of contemporary American culture—for better or for worse. *Planet Funny* is an illuminating take on that old cliché: 'Everybody's a comedian.' "

—Kliph Nesteroff, author of *The Comedians*

"America's biggest brain turns his attention to modern comedy—and delivers a book full of humor and insight. As a reader, I'm delighted . . . and as a comedy writer, I'm annoyed that he understands my field better than I do. Stay off my turf, Jennings!"

—Tim Long, writer and producer of *The Simpsons*

"Jennings's holistic, incisive argument presents a strong case that our comedy-first culture is resulting in too much of a good thing."

—*Booklist*, starred review

"This book is full of good sense and meaningful interviews, and it would be difficult to find a smarter or more satisfying treatment of a subject so evanescent and idiosyncratic as comedy."

—*Kirkus Reviews*, starred review

"An entertaining deep dive into culture . . . a highly entertaining yet genuinely scholarly look at the evolution of humor."

—*BookPage*

PLANET FUNNY

HOW COMEDY RUINED EVERYTHING

KEN JENNINGS

SCRIBNER   NEW YORK   LONDON   TORONTO   SYDNEY   NEW DELHI

Scribner
An Imprint of Simon & Schuster, Inc.
1230 Avenue of the Americas
New York, NY 10020

First Scribner trade paperback edition July 2019

SCRIBNER and design are registered trademarks of The Gale Group, Inc.,
used under license by Simon & Schuster, Inc., the publisher of this work.

For information about special discounts for bulk purchases,
please contact Simon & Schuster Special Sales at 1-866-506-1949
or business@simonandschuster.com.

The Simon & Schuster Speakers Bureau can bring authors to
your live event. For more information or to book an event, contact
the Simon & Schuster Speakers Bureau at 1-866-248-3049 or
visit our website at www.simonspeakers.com.

Interior design by Kyle Kabel

Manufactured in the United States of America

1   3   5   7   9   10   8   6   4   2

Library of Congress Control Number: 2018296934

ISBN 978-1-5011-0058-1
ISBN 978-1-5011-0060-4 (pbk)
ISBN 978-1-5011-0061-1 (ebook)

Planet Funny was previously published with the subtitle
How Comedy Took Over Our Culture.

There will never be enough comedy. Comedy is at a premium always.

—Phyllis Diller

America can be counted on to take any good idea, or any bad idea, and absolutely run it into the ground.

—George Carlin

CONTENTS

ONE

OUR FUNNY CENTURY

Stop me if you've heard this one before. A man walks into a sex ed class.

In my defense, I was supposed to be there. It was the first night of "For Boys Only," a popular four-hour seminar on puberty and sexuality given every month or so at Seattle Children's Hospital. The class, along with its "For Girls Only" counterpart, is the brainchild of a local nurse who thought parents shouldn't be outsourcing sex talk with their kids to elementary schools. "This is a relationship-building class," my registration e-mail told me, "so it will be important to your child to have you attend both sessions. Because class includes interactive exercises for the adult and child, our teachers request that you sit together." The classes have become so popular locally that they're virtually a rite of passage for Seattle-area fifth-graders and their helicopter parents, and the program has since spread to Oregon and California.

Retaking sex ed with a roomful of twelve-year-old boys wasn't my idea of a relaxing Monday evening. To make matters worse, my son, Dylan, discovered a week beforehand that two of his best friends from school had been signed up for the same session. So of course we all had to meet up beforehand for burgers, and then I had to sit through two hours of sex ed with my son's goofy friends *and their dads*. Also, right before the class was set to begin, a familiar-looking bearded man walked into the auditorium with his young son and sat down a few rows in front of us. It took me a few minutes to recognize him as longtime NBA coach P. J. Carlesimo. This is in no way relevant to the rest of the story, but you can't just go to sex class with P. J. Carlesimo and not mention it.

1

The instructor, Greg Smallidge, was exactly who I expected: a friendly-faced middle-aged white guy with receding brown hair, a vaguely professorial air, and an easel stacked with, I could only assume, the same grisly cross-sections of the human reproductive system that I remembered from fifth grade. But when Smallidge began the class, I couldn't believe what I was hearing. He was funny! In my day, sex ed wasn't funny. Maybe the girls' class was funny? I don't know, I still have no idea what went on in there. But the boys' class was only funny unintentionally, like when my friend Glenn asked the teacher, "What if pee comes out instead and you pee inside the lady?" and Mr. Jenkins explained that his wife liked morning sex and even when he *really* had to go, pee never came out when he ejaculated, and then everyone got incredibly uncomfortable and quiet.

Smallidge was a slow, careful talker, but what I had initially taken for unflappable dullness turned out to be a calculated deadpan, in the vein of Bob Newhart. He introduced the topic of masturbation by saying, "It's a very personal subject. It's not like a kid comes home one day and says, 'You know, I had a rough day at school. I'm going to go up to my room and masturbate for about ten minutes.'" He paused and let the laughter build, then added the topper. "'Dad, could you make me a sandwich?'"

Later, he asked the room to suggest slang terms for "penis" and jotted down a list on his big drawing pad. Many of the kids had obviously never been given license to yell anatomical slang in a crowded roomful of adults, and they jumped in with gusto, some of them possibly inventing terminology on the spot. "Old one-eyed Mr. Johnson!" shouted a boy two rows back, which I thought was a bit much. The room teetered on the brink of anarchy.* But Smallidge got them back! It was essentially a two-hour stand-up set for the most tentative of audiences, and it was masterful. I felt like applauding at the end.

"It's like Houdini," he told me later when I asked him about his crowd work. "How do you get out of this and survive?" Smallidge was

---

* When I asked Smallidge later about this interlude, he asked if he'd also done his "penis opera" bit at that point. "I don't know if I saw the penis opera," I replied. "You would remember it," he said. "Is there actually a singing penis?" I asked eagerly. Reader, there is not a singing penis, just a song *about* the penis.

a corporate trainer back in the 1990s when a friend at Seattle Public Schools called him out of the blue to see if he'd be interested in teaching puberty classes. He'd been a philosophy major in college and had no background in medicine, psychology, or education. He didn't even have any kids. "Sure, I'll do that," he said. He's now been a full-time sexuality curriculum guy for more than twenty years.

"It does feel like stand-up comedy," Smallidge said, but he disagreed with my assumption that "For Boys Only" is a tough room. No one is expecting the instructor in a hospital auditorium to be funny, he explained, so it's easy to beat low expectations. And he thinks the laughs are what makes it possible to spark real family conversations about sex. When parents come up against issues of sexuality with their kids, he said, the first response is usually discomfort and defensiveness. "But with humor, you don't have to be defensive for a few minutes, because you're laughing."

I told him that my childhood sex ed classes were never funny on purpose. "You could get in trouble for laughing."

"There's this one very conservative teacher, he always starts my introduction with, 'There will be no laughing! You know the rules!' Because they've gone over all the ground rules. 'I'm going to be watching you!' Very severe. It's sort of like having a bad opening act. I've got to undo that intro without offending him."

"Does that guy have a point? Are we giving kids a more casual view of sex because they got dick jokes with their puberty class?"

Smallidge smiled. "Something can be important without being serious," he said. "That's what it is for me."

In the Land of the Comedy Natives

One joke-heavy sex ed class isn't exactly headline news. My favorite schoolteachers were always the funny ones, and I'm sure that was true in my parents' and my grandparents' day as well. But it's part of a pattern, one that we sometimes fail to notice, the way a frog in simmering water doesn't notice each degree of temperature change.

Everything is getting funnier.

For millennia of human history, the future belonged to the strong. To the parent who could kill the most calories, in the form of regrettably cute, graceful animals, with rocks and sticks and things made out of rocks and sticks. To the child who could survive the winter or the scarlet fever epidemic. These were success stories.

The Industrial Revolution changed all that. Ideas replaced muscles. A century ago, we believed the future belonged to the efficient, those who had discovered the best ways to streamline a manufacturing process. Fifty years ago, our anointed were the best scientific minds. Slide rules and engineering know-how weren't just going to defeat Communism, they were eventually going to get us into flying cars and domed underwater cities.

Today, in a clear sign of evolution totally sliding off the rails, our god is not strength or efficiency or even innovation, but funny. Funniness.

If you assume that all modern institutions have always been as joke filled as they are now, you're part of the problem—and probably part of the rising generation. A 2012 Nielsen survey found that 88 percent of millennials say that their sense of humor is how they define themselves. Sixty-three percent of them would rather be stuck in an elevator with a favorite comedian than with their sports or music heroes. "We called them Comedy Natives," MTV research executive Tanya Giles told the *New York Times*. She's now the general manager at Comedy Central. "Comedy is so central to who they are, the way they connect with other people, the way they get ahead in the world. One big takeaway is that unlike previous generations, humor, and not music, is their number one form of self-expression."

Comedy, in other words, is no longer just a vehicle for selling nightclub drinks or ad time, something people passively consume because it's an "easier sit" than drama. More and more, we actively seek it out. We're connoisseurs. Instead of dozing off to a single late-night monologue, we stream highlights the next day from six or seven different late-night shows, assembling our own comedy *SportsCenter*. Instead of relistening to the same album or two by a favorite comedian, we use newer media like Twitter and podcasts to check in on them weekly or daily or even hourly. Instead of quoting the occasional comedy catchphrase with pals at work, we can consult Frinkiac, an online *Simpsons* search engine stocked with three million screengrabs, which will produce a *Simpsons* meme for almost any occasion. (Just found out your boss is out of the office this Friday? Time for a quick "Everything's coming up Milhouse!") Being this kind of obsessive comedy geek is now an avocation, and an increasingly mainstream one.

When *everyone* starts to turn into a comedy expert, very specific comic tropes and references can start to invade real life in surprising ways. The Kazakhstani government took out a four-page ad in the *New York Times* to rebut Sacha Baron Cohen's roasting of the Central Asian republic in his movie *Borat*. ("Nothing disturbing happens to me here," enthused a Turkish architect quoted in the puff piece.) Professional football players like Von Miller and Lance Moore have been flagged and fined for reenacting the touchdown dance of Hingle McCringleberry, a character from a *Key and Peele* sketch, in actual NFL games.* In 2011, Australian morning show host Karl Stefanovic, given a few minutes to interview the Dalai Lama, even tried to tell the Tibetan spiritual leader the classic joke about the Dalai Lama walking into a pizza shop. "Make me one with everything!" is the punch line. His Holiness just stared at Stefanovic blankly.

The most shocking comedy/reality crossover came in 2014, when Seth Rogen and his writing partner Evan Goldberg announced they were making *The Interview*, about two tabloid TV journalists who are recruited by the CIA to assassinate North Korean dictator Kim Jong-un. The premise didn't feel particularly edgy to me; it was a comfy throwback to the days when Leslie Nielsen would reenact Three Stooges smack-fights with Ayatollah Khomeini and Muammar Gaddafi in a *Naked Gun* movie, or Saddam Hussein would show up on *South Park*. You could even go back fifty years earlier. When Robert Benchley published a silly faux interview with Benito Mussolini, or Bugs Bunny terrorized Hitler and Goering, no one was actually afraid the dictators in question would seek revenge on comedy writers. (Even in the case of Charlie Chaplin's

---

* Keegan-Michael Key and Jordan Peele felt so bad about Miller's $11,000 fine that they wrote a check in that amount to his eye-care charity for children.

celebrated *The Great Dictator*, an international smash hit, there's no firm evidence that Hitler ever even saw it.)

But this time, things couldn't have gone more differently. Six months before *The Interview*'s planned release, North Korea's state-run media called the still-in-production movie "the most blatant act of terrorism and war" and vowed "merciless" retaliation. It was one thing to blow up the leader of North Korea in a fiery helicopter explosion *onscreen*, but now the moviemakers began to get cold feet: what if the carnage spilled over into real life? Sony asked Rogen and Goldberg if they'd consider rewriting the ending so Kim would survive. They refused, but writer Dan Sterling worried openly about his silly screenplay leading to "some kind of humanitarian disaster." "I would be horrified," he said. When North Korea threatened terrorist attacks at theaters that screened *The Interview*, Sony canceled its wide release in favor of a digital rollout—and was criticized by President Obama for capitulating to terrorism. In the end, the only real casualty of the threats turned out to be Sony cochair Amy Pascal, who stepped down after a massive data dump, almost certainly coordinated by North Korean hackers, revealed months of embarrassing studio secrets.

It was a rude awakening to open the newspaper one morning and realize that James Franco and Seth Rogen would probably be appearing in my kids' and grandkids' history textbooks. (That was the *best* case. Worst case was North Korea getting a missile that could reach the Pacific Northwest, and my kids and grandkids not existing to read history textbooks.) Stern, saber-rattling statements between two nuclear powers, followed by one of the biggest acts of cyberterrorism in history, had been provoked by a goofy stoner comedy. It was all almost as unfunny as the movie itself turned out to be.

What changed between *The Great Dictator* and *The Interview?* Sure, you could chalk it up to the unprecedented paranoia and strategic chaos practiced by the North Korean regime. But the real takeaway is that Kim probably wasn't wrong. North Korea has always survived by trading on larger countries' perception of its government as dangerous and unpredictable. Seth Rogen's painting "Supreme Leader" as a buffoon and then blowing him up for big movie laffs might have a real effect on how long his regime will last.

Today, we're savvy enough about the influence of comedy that we take it very, very seriously. Just ask Seth Rogen and James Franco, who were issued hulking round-the-clock studio bodyguards in 2014. Just ask advertisers paying five million dollars to show a goofy, cameo-filled comedy sketch during a Super Bowl time-out. Just ask ordinary people who have lost their jobs when the wrong joke attempt went viral on Twitter. Just ask the staff of *Charlie Hebdo*.

Comedians: Is There Anything They Can't Do?

But in the main, it's a good time to be in the business of being funny. Comedians, accustomed to their longtime roles of put-upon underdogs and insecure sideline snarkers, are adjusting slowly to their growing prestige. They should look to the United Kingdom, which got here first. In Britain, comedians are certified public intellectuals. The British have a whole TV genre that we don't: erudite panel shows on which quick-witted punsters with posh Oxbridge educations try to dazzle Stephen Fry or a Stephen Fry equivalent with their knowledge of current events and general knowledge. In 2008, Lancashire stand-up Jim Bowen made headlines for going onstage at a London comedy club and doing a full act of fourth-century Roman jokes, not a gambit you're likely to see on *Comedy Central Stand-Up Presents* anytime soon.* Or take the former members of Monty Python: Michael Palin is a past president of the Royal Geographical Society who has explored the poles and directed documentaries on World War I and Matisse. Terry Jones, an avid medievalist, tried to solve the death of Chaucer in a 2003 book. John Cleese has a species of lemur named after him, for his conservation work in Madagascar. In American post-comedy life, the closest thing we have to this is Steve Martin, who is now a passable banjo player.

But this is changing! Writing a book or two of funny essays is now a virtual requirement of comedy legitimacy and led to seven-figure publishing advances for hot commodities like Tina Fey, Aziz Ansari, and Lena

---

* Did you hear the one about the Kymaean who was selling his house? He carried around one of the building blocks to show what it was like. Boy, those Kymaeans, am I right, folks?

Dunham. This isn't a venerable trend in American publishing; it really only goes back to Jerry Seinfeld's 1993 bestseller *SeinLanguage*. Around the same time, we started putting legendary comedians on postage stamps: Jack Benny, Laurel and Hardy, and Abbott and Costello in 1991, then Bob Hope, Groucho, and Burns and Allen in 2009. Gloria Steinem and Amy Schumer started hanging out together at comedy clubs—and why not? They're both feminist icons. The unlikeliest comedy hangers-on were the fabulously good-looking ones. Celebrities like Jon Hamm and Justin Timberlake were among the biggest sex symbols in the world, but they were tired of lounging on beaches with supermodels. What they really wanted to do, apparently, was hang out with comedians! Only a Funny or Die director telling them how great that improv was on the last take would fill the comedy-shaped hole inside of them. It was the exact reverse of generations past, when an alpha dog like Frank Sinatra *might* let one comedy goofball—a Joey Bishop, say—join his gang. In 2014, *Esquire* even began a monthly feature where a rotating series of comedians were pressed into service as advice columnists. After all, is there a demographic more stereotypically famed for having their lives together than stand-up comics? Ask a comedian; they always know what to do.

And once comedy is done fixing your love life and roommate troubles, why not put it to work on public policy? The rise in comedy prestige was most notable on late-night TV, where a stand-up veteran like Jon Stewart, someone you might have seen on cable in 1992 telling jokes about "Just Say No" ads in a black leather jacket, acquired the moral authority of an éminence grise during his sixteen-year tenure on Comedy Central's *The Daily Show*. He was the closest thing millennials had to a Walter Cronkite, and his mere proximity had the power to create similarly endowed acolytes, a Legion of Substitute Stewarts that grew to include Stephen Colbert, John Oliver, Larry Wilmore, and Samantha Bee. Stewart knew that hosting an MTV talk show in the early Clinton era wasn't *exactly* the same journalistic training as covering the London Blitz, like Edward R. Murrow had, and was always the first to remind commentators that he was a comedian, not a reporter. But this was mostly just a (pretty transparent) way to preempt criticism.

Stewart's influence among young people was sometimes overstated in the press,* but in 2014, 12 percent of the country told Pew Research that they got their news from *The Daily Show*, roughly the same reach as *USA Today*. When you're a news source for as many people as the country's top-circulation newspaper, you're effectively a journalist, whether that's how you imagine your résumé or not. "My Comedy Channel Is Fox News. My News Channel Is Comedy Central," read the popular bumper sticker.

This change is often framed as a decline of traditional media, but to my mind, the real story was the new legitimacy and relevance of comedy. In the late sixties, when the Smothers Brothers were doing the edgiest, counterculture-friendliest comedy on TV, the network still carped about every joke that mentioned Vietnam, the most important news story of the day. (Pete Seeger was censored for singing "Waist Deep in the Big Muddy," a folk song that didn't even mention Vietnam.) It's not always remembered today that Tom and Dick Smothers *lost* their battle with CBS's Program Practices division: the show was repeatedly neutered and then, in 1969, abruptly canceled. That cemented the TV status quo for decades: jokes should not have a viewpoint on serious things. The rule worked mostly because the viewership was fine with keeping its news and its comedy in separate time slots. Satire just wasn't a mass-culture phenomenon; as George Kaufman famously said, it "closes on Saturday night."

That was all upended in the *Daily Show* era, when a comedy host could do an eight-minute tirade against the Iraq War, full of moral outrage—at a time when even the *New York Times* was banging the drum about Iraq's phantom weapons of mass destruction—and keep the full support of his network and his audience. In fact, they loved him for it. He was free to layer the editorial commentary in silly pop culture asides (when George Bush called Saddam Hussein "a deceiver, a liar, a torturer, and a murderer," Stewart asked if he was also "a picker, a grinner, a lover, and a sinner") and puns ("Mess O'Potamia!" read the chyron)

---

* In 2011, the show's average viewer was forty-one years old. And the evening network news (if you combined all three broadcasts) always drew more than twice as many twentysomething viewers as Jon Stewart did.

without anyone asking if war was too serious a subject for that sort of thing. He could even snipe at his own network. When President Bush said that the arguments over Iraq were like "a rerun of a bad movie, and I'm not interested in watching it," Stewart noted that, by an amazing coincidence, that was also the official slogan of Comedy Central. Instead of getting fired like the Smothers Brothers, he became the highest-paid performer on television.* Bush's successor secretly summoned Stewart to the White House twice to consult on policy, and petitioners tried to draft him to run for president himself in 2016.

Jon Stewart's vehement protesting-too-much that he was "just a comic" was always a reminder that he knew how influential his voice was. The *Daily Show* take on a policy matter or media skirmish could determine the opinion of millions of people, the same way Fox News's official line could. Was it any wonder that jokes began to receive more scrutiny and Monday-morning quarterbacking than ever before? It wasn't enough to be funny; every joke was held to strict ethical standards of fairness, civility, compassion. And why not? This was now serious business; comedy could quite literally change the world.

The Magic Spell of Khlebnikov

How did we get to this point? Our gradual descent into nonstop comedy started in the early decades of the twentieth century, and I'm going to blame it all on one man: an eccentric Russian futurist poet named Velimir Khlebnikov. The futurists, as the name of their movement implied, were young artists besotted with the speed and dynamism and violence of mechanized modernity, and eager to replace the tired old art of the past with experimental new forms in their new century. The most famous poem of the futurist movement is probably "Incantation by Laughter," which Khlebnikov wrote in 1909 while he was (nominally) studying mathematics at a Saint Petersburg university. It's a series of escalating nonsense riffs on the Russian word *smekh*, meaning "laughter." An English translation might look something like this:

---

* If you don't count syndication. Judge Judy made $47 million that year.

O, laugh, laughers!

O, laugh out, laughers!

You who laugh with laughs, you who laugh it up laughishly

O, laugh out laugheringly

O, belaughable laughterhood—the laughter of laughering laughers!

O, unlaugh it outlaughingly, belaughering laughists!

Laughily, laughily,

Uplaugh, enlaugh, laughlings, laughlings

Laughlets, laughlets.

O, laugh, laughers!

O, laugh out, laughers!

I don't know for sure what was on young Velimir's mind the day he wrote this poem, but his "Incantation by Laughter" turned out to be a pretty accurate look ahead at the twentieth century, with the simple command "laugh" endlessly branching and innovating into complex new forms, just as comedy itself would. The poem came true.

Am I implying that this little verse, scratched out over coffee and cigarettes in a bohemian Saint Petersburg cellar café, actually *was* some kind of magic futurist spell, invoking a new century of endlessly escalating laughs? You'd better believe I am. Khlebnikov saw himself as a prophet even as a teenager, and believed that he was destined to decipher the "laws of time" and predict the future. His essays imagine modern urban planning and even the internet with some accuracy, and he earned great fame for having predicted, in a 1912 pamphlet, the "fall of a state" in 1917—the year of the Russian Revolution. So why not make him a prophet of comedy as well? The secret history of the twentieth century is, after all, largely a history of humor. The old gods were dead, and what was left to us was the laughter of laughering laughers.

Let's be clear: this was not a complete break with the past. People have always made jokes, and most of them went unrecorded. But the culture of which jokes we tell, and when, and why, does change. Comedy's like any art form; it evolves over time. Yesterday's jokes influence today's, and if today's seem funnier, it's largely because we stand on the shoulders of giants.

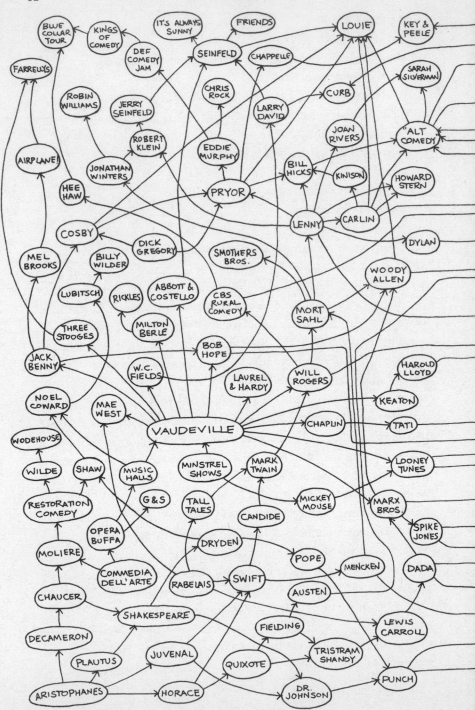

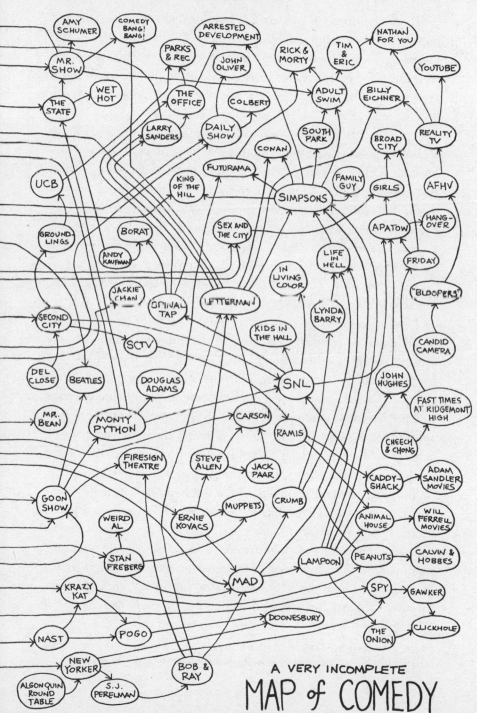

A VERY INCOMPLETE
MAP of COMEDY

The funnying-up of modern life has mostly been an organic and imperceptibly slow process, like a glacier inching toward the sea. But sometimes there are watershed moments on a cliff where the ice cracks all at once, and everyone on the cruise ship claps and the landscape in a certain place is changed forever. The glacier just doesn't flow back uphill.

April 9, 1917—seven years after Khlebnikov published his incantation—was such a date. On that day, New York's Society of Independent Artists rejected an entry for its first annual exhibit, a show that was supposed to be open to all artists. Unbeknownst to most of them, the sculpture had been submitted by one of the society's own board members, who later resigned in protest. The artist was Marcel Duchamp, and the work was the first of his "readymade" sculptures of found objects. It was a lavatory urinal, bought from a plumbing supply house, signed with a fanciful "R. Mutt" signature, and laid on its back. Duchamp called it *Fountain*.

Now, it's certainly possible to name older works of art that viewers found humor in. Paintings were primarily decor for centuries, and funny canvases sold because television hadn't been invented. If you're going to hang something pretty on the wall of your house, why not have a laugh as well?* That explains those sixteenth-century Arcimboldo portraits where some Saxon elector or naval hero is constructed entirely of fruit and fish, or those Jan Steen tableaux of merry domestic chaos, where chubby children are chasing each other around a table and the dog has just knocked over a platter of something.

But Duchamp's work was different. It didn't just have a mildly whimsical air to it; it *was* a joke, a joke you could "get." ("Hey, that's a sideways urinal!") With works like *Fountain* and *L.H.O.O.Q.* (the one where he painted a mustache and goatee on the *Mona Lisa*), Duchamp didn't just found the Dada movement. He started an avalanche of art that was incomplete without the laugh: the optical illusions of the surrealists, the soup cans and comic book panels and giant puffy hamburgers of

---

* Funny art has always been dangerous art, however. The Greek artist Zeuxis is said to have died laughing at his own painting of an old woman who had insisted on posing herself as the goddess Aphrodite.

the pop artists, the great pains taken by the photorealists to document something silly like a chrome car bumper or glass Automat window. The old masters still cast a long enough shadow that these new jokes could be powered by surprise at their mild subversion. That was their whole impact. Ha, someone made *that?* And someone else hung it up in their gallery?

The playful postmodern impulse eventually bled into all the other visual arts—even architecture, where it had been axiomatic since the days of the Bauhaus that function and efficiency were all that mattered. "A house," Le Corbusier had said, in one of the century's most depressing pronouncements, "is a machine for living in." There was only one possible future, and it was going to be defined by the clean, uniform glass-and-steel boxes of the International Style, dammit. It wasn't until the 1970s that architects woke from their reveries of rectilinear purity, squinted at their blueprints, and started to wonder *where the jokes were.* And so the pendulum swung back toward the winking neon of Charles Moore and the cheekily ornamented faux casinos of Michael Graves and the rippling titanium currents of Frank Gehry. As fans of John le Carré and James Bond spy fare know, even the British secret service, that least funny of all institutions, now operates out of a bizarrely kitschy postmodern Aztec temple on the Thames that employees call "Legoland." These new buildings aren't exactly hilarious, of course; it seems almost beside the point that no one in history has ever lol'ed at the sight of one of them. But it was enough that the architect seemed to have acknowledged *that fun exists.* As *Spy* magazine memorably asked, in a 1988 cover package on postmodernism, "For a building, is it funny?"

Muhammad Ali and Other Superheroes

Let's fast-forward from Marcel Duchamp's Paris to June 22, 1961. That's the day a young Cassius Clay did a morning radio interview in Las Vegas alongside the legendary wrestler "Gorgeous George" Wagner. In response to the host's questions about his upcoming bout against Duke Sabedong, just the seventh of his fledgling pro career, Clay was confident but restrained, in keeping with his public persona at the time. Then he watched George answer a similar question about his next match, against "Classy" Freddie Blassie. "I'll kill him! I'll tear off his arm!" the wrestler fumed. "If this bum beats me, I'll crawl across the ring and cut off my hair, but it's not gonna happen, because I'm the greatest wrestler in the world!" Clay was astounded at George's sheer force of personality and started to see how he could reinvent his persona as a boxer. "Keep on bragging, keep on sassing, and always be outrageous," Gorgeous George told him later when they met backstage after his wrestling match.

Sports heroes in those days were, almost to a man, not funny. They were sleepy-eyed white dullards with pomaded hair and beer bellies. When athletes got laughs back then, when Jim Thorpe told Gustav V of Sweden, "Thanks, King!" after receiving his Olympic medals or Yogi Berra issued one of his trademark cockeyed aphorisms, like "You can observe a lot just by watching," those quips were invariably unintentional or apocryphal. Or both, if that's even possible. It was all so dire that the funniest athlete of the 1930s—you can look this up—was actually Seabiscuit. Compare that to today's mischievous, smart-aleck sports heroes. The hinge on which that change turned was Gorgeous George strutting down the aisle in a satin robe, accompanied by a rose-water-spritzing valet, and his newest fan Cassius Clay sitting up tall in his seat and seeing an alternate future in his head: the self-aware boasting, the flirting with reporters, the well-rehearsed comic verse, all of it.*

Every sport didn't become funny overnight, of course. Even in my day as a young sports fan, everyone knew who the lone joker on the team roster was, the John Kruk or the Deion Sanders or the John Salley, the guy you knew you'd see in a booth someday. It wasn't like the modern locker room, where everyone is clowning and cheerfully trash-talking and angling for that postretirement analyst job. But every wisecracking modern athlete today of every race has the same model: Muhammad Ali. In 1964, it didn't immediately endear the cocksure young man to everyone in America, mostly because he was black and Muslim. But

---

* Even Ali probably didn't foresee what a weapon his comedic dexterity could be *within* the ring as well. Would he have been able to knock out Sonny Liston in 1964 if Liston hadn't been kept infuriated by months of Ali calling him "Big Ugly Bear"? "Liston even smells like a bear. I'm gonna give him to the local zoo after I whup him."

in hindsight, you could make a case that Ali was the most influential comedian of the twentieth century, and comedy wasn't even his day job.

Two months after sports got funny, a similar milestone, also spurred on by a single force of personality, changed another corner of pop culture: the lowly comic book. At the time, superhero comics were in a snoozy decline, still dominated, as they had been for decades, by Superman and Batman and the other square-jawed champions of DC Comics. Superman and Batman weren't the gritty, mutually suspicious rivals we see today on the big screen; in 1960 they were loyal chums who co-headlined *World's Finest Comics* every month. They both had dogs and boy sidekicks and secret clubhouses full of trophies, and planned each other surprise parties and treasure hunts every year for their birthdays.

The wake-up call was the November 8, 1961, publication of *The Fantastic Four* #1 by Jack Kirby and Stan Lee, the debut of an innovative new superhero line from Marvel Comics. Today, the conventional wisdom about Marvel is that their books took off because their superheroes were, unlike DC's demigods, human and relatable. The core dynamic of the Fantastic Four was that they weren't just a super-team but a *family*, with all the squabbles and growing pains and sentimental "mush" that entails. Spider-Man fought crooks in between long anxious thought balloons about his money troubles, or his sick Aunt May, or the kids who bullied him at his Queens high school. The Mighty Marvel Way was nothing more than grafting soap opera elements onto traditional superhero tropes, and the publisher would successfully stick with that human-interest formula for decades: Iron Man was an alcoholic, Daredevil was blind, the Hulk just wanted to be left alone, the teenage X-Men were battling both their hormones *and* society's bigotry. Soon, the rest of the industry was scurrying to catch up.

But what really made those early Marvel comics such a pleasure to read was that, despite all the adolescent angst, they were genuinely funny. For one thing, the heroes themselves were jokers. Ben Grimm, the Fantastic Four's rocky "Thing," spent his days in a perpetual vaudeville slow burn at the infuriating antics of his teammate the Human Torch, not to mention the pranks of the "Yancy Streeters," a gang of roughnecks from his Lower East Side neighborhood. "What a revoltin' development!" he would complain, in imitation of Jimmy Durante, or maybe William Bendix on *The Life of Riley*. Peter Parker, the amazing Spider-Man, had an even lighter comic touch, using wisecracks to mask his own teenage insecurities and surprising foes just as often with a snarky put-down as with his trademark webs. "Spider-Man!" Doctor Octopus or whoever would snarl. "Well it's not Dr. Kildare," Spidey would reply. Or "I sure ain't Albert Schweitzer!" Compared to the stodgy dads fighting crime over in DC's books, these were hip references.

Every issue was narrated in the knowing, irreverent voice of scripter-editor Stan Lee, immediately creating an over-the-top house style that defined Marvel for decades. "Like costume heroes?" Lee asked with a wink in the comic that introduced Spider-Man. "Confidentially, we in the comic mag business refer to them as 'long underwear characters'!" Marvel fans weren't just readers—they were in on the gag. This clubby relationship carried over into the letters pages, where Lee answered reader mail personally in an unidentifiable borderline-youthful patois of his own invention, somewhere in between "Greenwich Village hepcat" and "carnival barker." Every staffer and freelancer got credited with a nickname emphasizing just how fun it must be to goof around in the Marvel bullpen all day: "Smilin'" Stan Lee, "Jolly" Jack Kirby, "Cheerful" Chic Stone, "Merry" Marie Severin. Superhero comic books, for the first time in a long time, were actually *comic* books.

Laughing Through a Mouthful of Tapioca Foam

The dominoes kept falling as the twentieth century neared its end. The same wave of postmodernism that had turned architecture on its ear had long since become the language of fashion as well, with designers regularly praised for their "witty" new collections. With shelter and clothing taken care of, just one basic survival need remained stubbornly unamusing: food. Shout-out to food for providing us with the basic caloric content and nutrients needed to sustain life—but why wasn't it funnier?

In 1994, chef Ferran Adrià used a million-dollar investment from a Spanish philanthropist to expand and update the kitchen of his popular Catalonian restaurant elBulli. At the same time, he created an in-house "development squad" to focus on R & D for new culinary "concepts and techniques." The following year, a young Heston Blumenthal bought a run-down sixteenth-century pub in Berkshire and opened a soon-to-be-legendary bistro called the Fat Duck. These two events kick-started the avant-garde cooking movement now called "molecular gastronomy"—using science to prepare foods that no one had ever actually seen before. Not every newly possible dish was a culinary success—just because we have the technology to carbonate gravy or freeze bacon-and-egg ice cream doesn't mean it's a great idea—but for the most part, diners were delighted by the movement's chic novelties. Spherical mango "ravioli" would explode in your mouth like magic bubbles, and intricate little pocket watches of bouillon and gold leaf would melt, Salvador Dalí–style, into glass teapots of soup. The watchword was always surprise. Hey, these look like Oreos, but they're actually tapas made from black olive dough and sour cream! This mandarin orange is full of chicken liver parfait!

Just like a circus act, an avant-garde food menu is designed to elicit laughter and gasps in alternation—and sometimes in combination. I once had a three-hour dinner at Alinea, Grant Achatz's outpost of molecular gastronomy on Chicago's North Side, and the food, though delicious, was completely overshadowed by the showmanship of Achatz's "dinner as theater." The very first course, a butternut squash puree, was served *inside* a block of ice. A thick glass straw was the only utensil provided, so you couldn't get the puree down without producing a deafening slurping sound designed to draw stares from every other diner in the room. (We were the first table served, and got to enjoy the wave of periodic slurps that circuited the dining room over the next hour.) A hot potato soup was served in a wax cup punctured by a skewer; when the skewer was pulled out, five different cold garnishes would plop into the soup, which you could then down like a shot. Not every dish was slapstick comedy. Some were visual jokes, like the corn/corn-silk/corn-smut combo plated to match a painting hanging in the dining room. Others were semantic, like a "fish and chips" plate where the fish was trout and the chips were . . . crispier trout. Medallions of lamb served with an array of forty-eight different toppings—choose your own adventure!—seemed like a knowing parody of foodie excess. But nothing was over the top like dessert was over the top: first, a helium-filled balloon made of apple taffy that we were told to suck up in one breath, leaving us sticky and squeaky; next, Achatz's trademark "dark chocolate piñata," which you scoop off the table after a server freezes and then destroys it in front of you.

Does it sound gimmicky? It was absolutely gimmicky. Funny food can't literally *taste* funny. That wouldn't go over big in a Michelin-starred restaurant. So the humor in high-end cuisine has to come from something incidental to the way a dish tastes, like a surprising texture or the way it's plated. But even so, Achatz and his peers achieved the apparently impossible: wringing laughs from the simple, metabolically necessary act of eating. And that perception of "added value" helps when you want people to drop four to five hundred dollars apiece on dinner: laughs are included! At Alinea, that price also includes the wine pairing, which of course makes everything seem funnier.

It's interesting that there doesn't seem to be a single overarching cultural shift behind the race toward funny. In each of these four case studies, the push for more and more humor was powered by something completely different. In art, it was driven by mechanization. The invention of photography lifted from artists the responsibility of mimicking reality on canvas, and allowed them access to a broader palette of approaches and effects—humor among them. The change in sports came from technology as well, but this time from the invention of modern media culture. Mass media created an instant demand for athletes whose ability to entertain a home audience was just as important as whether they won or lost. The irreverent comic books of the same era were mostly a symptom of the growing cultural influence of youth. Baby boom America had just invented the teenager, and that new market demanded its own light entertainment, with comedic markers that would differentiate it from the routine, serious world of working adults. Funny food at the end of the century felt like something a little more ominous: a decadent sign of the fin de siècle, like Roman elites feasting on roast peacock and hummingbird tongues while civilization collapsed around them. But all these trends eventually converged into one spot: a rising tide of comedy, everywhere we looked.

A Stranger Here Myself

The world that has been delivered to us now seems to have the goal of packing in as many laughs into every second of the day as possible. "There were more jokes written in one minute on the web today than were written in all of the twentieth century," the *Onion*'s Joe Randazzo has observed, only halfway joking. Once you start noticing it, funny is everywhere—even the tiniest, dumbest places. The last time I waited on the phone for a corporate conference call to begin, the recorded hold music wasn't Vivaldi or smooth jazz; it was a faux-earnest novelty ditty about . . . the travails of being placed on hold. "Yes, I'm waiting on this conference call all alone / And I'm on hold, yes I'm on hold . . . I hope it's not all day!"* The yoga studio up the street from my house added a laughter yoga class. The corner drugstore has replaced its "Video Surveillance in Use" security notice with a sign that says "Smile! You're on *Candid Camera!*" The bag of organic dried mangoes sitting on my desk right now has "Tropical Humor!" as a label slogan. Not only has this company decided that the biggest selling point of dried mango snacks is how funny they are, they've decided to advertise the fact with a confusing pun!

So life is now a never-ending barrage of little micro-jokes, most so fleeting that they don't even register. One thing you don't see much is people wondering if they *should* make every joke that they can, if there are cases where humor might be pointless or even counterproductive. That kind of introspection usually only happens *after* a brand makes a joke that it shouldn't have and gets dragged for it online.† Online culture in particular seems to demand an even higher comedy quotient than real life. In 2014 I saw a *New York Times* story about an experimental new technique to save the life of trauma patients by injecting them with freezing salt water and inducing hypothermia—not a particularly hilar-

---

* The music was such a hit with users of the UberConference conferencing system that the company hired a YouTube-famous band to cover the song in ten different genres, from torch song to rap to samba.

† In hindsight, did Cinnabon *need* to mourn the 2016 death of actress Carrie Fisher with a tweet saluting her signature Princess Leia hairstyle as "the best buns in the galaxy"? I'd argue no.

ious topic, obviously. The headline in the print edition read, "Killing a Patient to Save His Life." On social media, the headline was, "A Chilling Medical Trial." Funnier! You have to admit, it's funnier.

I am not, generationally speaking, a Comedy Native. I'm an immigrant here. I come from a strange, topsy-turvy time when comedy had already acquired its cool cultural cachet, but—if you can imagine such a thing—*there wasn't actually enough of it.* We had to hoard what little of it we had on albums and cassettes and videotapes. The very first movie I ever saw on video (Betamax, specifically) was a comedy: *Airplane!*, at Michael Brewer's birthday party in third grade.* I grew up rewatching the same worn VHS comedy tapes over and over: *Raising Arizona, Ferris Bueller's Day Off, UHF*, David Letterman anniversary specials, *Tracey Ullman* episodes so we could fast-forward to the *Simpsons* sketches. I snuck *Mad* magazine home from friends' houses where it wasn't contraband. I reread *Peanuts* treasuries until the pages fell out. We weren't allowed to stay up late enough for *Saturday Night Live* for much of my youth, so my brother and I taped it and watched it the following day after church. (Once, my dad got wind at church that Robin Williams's monologue from the previous night's show had been *particularly* saucy, and the tape went missing when we got home. It's still the only episode from that season that I've never seen.) The scarcity of comedy meant that we watched or listened to things until we knew them letter-perfect. To this day, if you need an emergency transcript of anything from *This Is Spinal Tap, Monty Python Sings*, or the first season of *In Living Color*, I am your man. To this day, I can't even hear the word "lemonade" without mentally adding Eddie Murphy's brief Elvis impression from his *Comedian* record: "Lemonade! That cool, refreshing drink!" Sometimes people forget Eddie was a great impressionist.

I was a comedy geek. Not a first-generation one—those would be the kids about ten years older than me with George Carlin records and subscriptions to the *National Lampoon*. But our parents didn't understand

---

* The next time I saw *Airplane!* at somebody's house, it was in high school, and the girl's dad stayed in the room to sternly fast-forward through the scene where Julie Hagerty manually reinflates Otto the autopilot. Seeing fellatio simulated on a smiling inflatable dummy would apparently have been too much for our hair-trigger adolescent hormones to handle.

what we were laughing at, so it *felt* like we were breaking new ground. That was all that mattered.

This is largely hindsight, by the way. I don't remember ever identifying as a comedy geek at the time. Things were on; you watched them. If they were good, you taped them so you could watch them over and over. But being a funny kid *was* a big part of my identity, almost as far back as I can remember. Bothering grown-ups with riddles, asking them to explain the jokes you still didn't understand.* Do you remember? Making an adult genuinely laugh is a huge thrill when you're five or six and nobody really pays much attention to you.

I was the Smart Kid too, but it doesn't take long before reasonably self-aware Smart Kids start to see the ambivalence with which the world regards them, not just peers but adults as well. Funny Kid is a lot less lonely, as identities go. Not everyone can make people laugh, and children figure out pretty quickly who has the knack and egg them on. Not a week goes by when I don't think about Eric R., the kid in my kindergarten class who leaned over to me during the Pledge of Allegiance on the morning of May 19, 1980, and stage-whispered, "Mount St. Helens blew its penis yesterday!" This is still one of the top four or five funniest jokes I've ever heard. As George Carlin pointed out on his *Class Clown* record, elementary school classrooms are an amazing comedy venue, because "suppressed laughter is the easiest to get." The research bears out my childhood intuition on the benefits of being the Funny Kid. When psychologists ask fourth-graders to rate their class members on humor and popularity ("classroom social distance" is the nicer way to say this in the literature), the two variables are always closely linked—and the pattern of variances strongly suggests that popularity is predicted by funniness, not the other way around.

If you've met a few grade-school Smart Kids–turned–class clowns, or are one yourself, you won't be surprised to learn that this was also a preemptive measure for me. I wasn't the biggest kid in class or the best

---

* I distinctly remember my mom having to explain this joke to five-year-old me: "Waiter, this coffee tastes like dirt." "Well, it was just ground this morning." Even with the explanation, I thought it was pretty lame and told her so. Kindergartners don't pull punches.

soccer player; I was quiet and full of crippling self-doubt. That's not a *great* trade-off. In that situation, where all might be lost for others, at least the Funny Kid can tell jokes. You joke about your own bad haircut. Your bad skin. Your airball. The clothes your mom thought looked "sharp" at Mervyn's. Tell the joke you fear others might tell about you. It's a vaccination; you might get cowpox but you probably won't die of smallpox. You can also deflect by joking about literally anything else: the girls, the teacher, the bully trying to destroy you. As Harry Shearer once said to Marc Maron, "Comedy is controlling the reason people are laughing at you."

I never went anywhere close to comedy as a profession (see "crippling self-doubt," above) but I was always in its orbit. Nobody was quicker than me to jump into an argument over the worst "Weekend Update" anchor or the most underrated Judd Apatow movie (Kevin Nealon, *Walk Hard*, duh).* And after I became a professional ex–game show contestant and started to write for a living, I suddenly had a little online venue (blogs, then social media) to post things that cracked me up instead of just annoying my family and friends with them. The Internet is a seductive mistress for would-be comedians: personal enough for lots of strangers to tell you how funny they think you are, but impersonal enough that there's no humiliating silence (or silence-with-a-single-cough) when a joke misses. It's also a great place to buddy up to comedy writers and performers you have long admired, pretending to be one of the cool kids.

On paper, it seems like the modern funnying-up of America would be a golden age for a guy like me. Who doesn't like to laugh? Who would rather sit through an earnest, awkward sex ed class than a funny one? Who wants to go back to a time when if there was nothing funny on any of the three TV channels, our only options were a Dave Barry book or *Caddyshack* on video for the fiftieth time?

And yet, even in the midst of this embarrassment of riches, I have my doubts. In recent years, I have often found myself more bemused

---

* Once when I was running down a few of my beefs with the first *Anchorman,* my brother got frustrated enough to say, "Then you just don't like comedy!" This is seared into my memory as the single most hurtful thing anyone has ever said to me.

than delighted to find an endless stream of jokes everywhere I look, from politics to upscale dining to my kids' sex education. And it's made me think seriously about what this change might be doing to our institutions, our social relationships, our very brain chemistry.

Everything is funny now. Shouldn't we be happier?

Giggling Toward Gomorrah

In his 1985 book *Amusing Ourselves to Death*, Neil Postman worried that the trivialities of mass media were going to be the death knell for American culture. In his view, the West had successfully avoided the authoritarian dystopia of *1984* only to embrace the narcotized "soma" culture of Aldous Huxley's *Brave New World*. "An Orwellian world is much easier to recognize, and to oppose, than a Huxleyan," he wrote. "Everything in our background has prepared us to know and resist a prison when the gates begin to close around us . . . [but] who is prepared to take arms against a sea of amusements?" Postman, presciently describing information overload even before the dawn of the Internet, blamed our plight on a glut of celebrity culture, television commercials, and dumbed-down news. He longed for television that would stay in its lane, sticking harmlessly to "junk entertainment." Couldn't it leave commerce, news, culture, and education alone?

Decades later, we live in the exact culture Postman predicted. (He died in 2003, having seen his worst fears unfold before his eyes.) But even he underestimated the degree to which the thing that would "amuse us to death" would be amusement itself—laughter, comedy. Life is full of possible trivial distractions, but we have increasingly decided to while away our hours with the funny ones. Reality television is often just the dumbest excesses of Postman's celebrity culture, now molded into the shape of the classic sitcom. Television commercials once praised products; now that's almost incidental to telling jokes. On the Internet, with all of human knowledge at last available democratically to all, the most popular aggregation sites are usually topped by short-attention-span laughs: viral memes, TV screengrabs, funny animal videos. The smiling mannequins reading news and making light chitchat about it have been replaced, for millions of people, by actual comedians. If you can't get one of those comedy-news jobs—if you quit *Saturday Night Live* in 1995, for example, because you got passed over for the "Weekend Update" desk—you can still become a United States senator for nine years. If you get dropped from your reality show, but the crowds hoot and holler loudly enough at your campaign antics, you can even be elected president.

We are in uncharted waters here. No one really knows how a comedy-first culture might change comedy or culture. I agreed instinctively with Greg Smallidge's maxim, "Something can be important without being serious," but that doesn't mean that *nothing* should be taken seriously. I object to the nihilism of that, but I also object to the comedy construction. What would be our benchmark for comparison in a world where everything was funny?

My favorite part of Khlebnikov's "Incantation by Laughter" is the neologism that the translator renders as "laughterhood." It seems to encompass everything about a culture's funniness: not just the voice of its comedy, but its social clusters and media and genres and fan bases, its techniques and tropes, its lineage and influence. We don't really have a word like that in English. But even when they don't know what to call it, groups always have a laughterhood. Families have one, offices have one, online communities have one, ethnic groups have one. Zoom out and civilizations have one.

This book is an attempt to capture something ineffable: the comic mood of a moment. Today's jokes aren't just ubiquitous; they're also a new breed: faster, weirder, more complex, more self-aware than ever before. How did we get here? How is the new sensibility changing our laughterhood? How is it changing us? It seems to me that these are questions worth asking because we're not living through just *any* comic moment, subject to the usual shifting winds of fashion and circumstance. After a century of rising comedy saturation, our present society feels more like a culmination. In the same way that ecological doomsayers predict "peak oil," a point beyond which decline is inevitable, it may be that we are fast approaching "peak funny," the singularity of our current dizzying spiral toward never-ending hilarity.

There's something foreboding about all the funny buildings and desserts, the fifty new Twitter jokes per minute on my phone. Don't get me wrong, I'm still laughing, but it feels unsustainable, the same way tourists often feel amid the splendid excess of someplace like Vegas or Dubai. *This can't go on, right?*

When someone's telling a joke, you can usually sense when the punch line is coming.

TWO

FUNNY FOR NO REASON

Through all of recorded history, the basic structural and functional unit of humor has been the joke. But that's getting it backward. It would probably be more accurate to say that "joke" is the word we invented for any unitary thing that gets a laugh.

Consider all the different things that a joke can be. At its most formalized level, a joke is a little folktale—a one-act play with characters and a beginning, middle, and end.

> A grasshopper walks into a bar. The bartender says, "Wow, funny you should come in here. We have a drink named after you!" The grasshopper says, "You have a drink called Stanley?"*

The act of inventing a whole fictional setting and story to generate a laugh seems a little try-hard in our no-effort age. Today, a professional joke-teller is unlikely to start a joke, "So these three guys get on a train . . ." A "joke" in stand-up comedy is typically a first-person anecdote, or at least purports to be one. Here's Wanda Sykes on a cheap boyfriend:

> Whenever we go out, I pay all the tolls. Yeah—he backs up to the tolls so that the booth would be on my side.

---

* My brother tells this joke sometimes, and the grasshopper always has a British accent. *Why is the grasshopper British, Nathan?*

The anecdote usually leads to observations about life's little oddities. John Mulaney on ordering a chicken sandwich:

> "That comes with a choice of either salad or fries." Those were the choices: salad or fries, the two most different foods in the universe. "Oh, you're getting a chicken sandwich? Well, with that, you can go for a jog, or smoke crack cocaine."

In daily life, a "joke" is even less formal than that. It's situational humor, a quippy reaction. It's running into someone for the second time in the same day and saying, "Long time, no see!"

Books about humor always seem stodgy and square because they focus almost entirely on the first kind of joke, which all feel exactly fifty years old, even if they actually date back to ancient Greece or were written yesterday. They're usually full of midcentury things that don't really exist anymore: traveling salesmen, priests, golf. That's understandable, though. Before we entered our modern joke-savvy age, retold jokes *were* the most accessible form of humor to most people. They require no original thought, and they're hard to screw up even with lousy delivery. That makes them a perfect fit for academics who study humor—not always the world's most naturally funny people, you'll be shocked to learn. They also have the clinical virtue of sounding completely generic, from the culture itself rather than from any particular author or style of humor. But most importantly, academics prefer prepackaged jokes to situational humor for the same reason that geneticists prefer fruit fly DNA: simplicity. Fruit flies don't last long, they're easy to raise in captivity, they have only four chromosomes, and they're a universally recognized standard. Airless, formulaic joke scenarios—a crashing plane, a genie offering three wishes—allow "humor studies" experts to tease apart joke mechanics, either in theory or in a lab, without worrying that the experiment will be contaminated by any actual complexity or fun.

But not everything that's funny is a joke in any meaningful sense. Off the top of my head, here are some things I think are funny: tiki bars, murder mystery parties, vaping, water fluoridation, jigsaw puzzles, ska, egg salad sandwiches, "couponing," astronauts, tugboats, babies, calling

money "some serious coin," haiku, carpet sweepers, Hollywood movies
dubbed into Spanish, foot fetishists, those motorcycles with the weird high
handlebars, turtlenecks, elementary school plays, Costco, interventions,
Ken Burns, adults who don't know how to drive, local news shows, vegan
pizza, karaoke videos, state birds and minerals and whatnot, Henry and
Beezus but *not* Ramona, Wikipedia entries for regular stuff like "soup,"
time travel, Canada, those narcotic leaves that Somali pirates chew, public
radio, exotic pets, spelling words in the "NATO phonetic alphabet" with
lots of Romeos and Tangos, putting a pencil behind your ear, people who
own hot tubs, Roman numerals, CB radio lingo, supermarkets and snack
companies that have to call the Super Bowl "the Big Game" so they don't
get sued, those fancy Japanese toilet seats, the Chinese zodiac, media names
for blizzards, movies where somebody thinks they see the person they're
looking for but when they spin them around it's somebody totally different,
Weight Watchers "points," acronyms that were clearly reverse-engineered
to make words, podracing, at Christmas when the Wise Men are three
different races, soap opera comic strips in newspapers, Marilyn vos Savant,
the Boy Scouts of America, off-brand anything, Velcro, quesadillas, "dry
goods" stores, high school gym teachers, roller derby, that weird *Gnomes*
book from the seventies, "finger guns," moths eating holes in clothing,
mothballs, moths in general now that I think about it, the Amish, dogs
wearing bandannas, ghosts, forty-minute IMAX movies at science museums about coral reefs and airplanes and so forth, farmers' markets, Guam,
food that comes with "all the fixin's," Tom Cruise running, capitalizing
pronouns for God and Jesus, dockworkers and stevedores, those bird
stickers on glass doors, hot yoga, Will Shortz, pro wrestlers from the
1980s and early '90s *but no later*, the harpsichord, fabric stores, identical
twins, Betty Boop, homeschooling, elongated-penny machines, Korean
pop music, dolphins, dolphins talking, "dance floor lasso," personalized
license plates, 3-D printers, fire ants, when movie theaters show livecast
operas on weeknights for some reason, yogurt, sword stores in malls, Batman, prospectors, monocles, jukeboxes, gratitude journals, bubble wands,
Objectivism, being hydrated, spaghetti *and* meatballs (but neither of the
two separately), upside-down calculator words, owls, large novelty checks,
origami, the Irish, Irish Spring soap, nature walks, Roombas, Mount

Rushmore, mommy bloggers, churros, Kidz Bop, the word "bodacious," the Church of Satan, citizen's arrests, the Wiggles, fake search engines in movies, composting, Uno, the "tall tales" unit in elementary school, cavemen, buttermilk, auctioneer patter, T.J. Maxx, people leaning very close into table microphones, string cheese, little kids in sailor suits, white people saying they're part Cherokee, ten-foot party subs, when Darryl Dawkins used to name his dunks, revolving restaurants, Victorian euphemisms for sodomy, yearbook signatures, all Winter Olympic sports, when British people call dish soap "washing-up liquid," anything dogs or cats do with their butts or the butts of others, pudding, TV judges who say things like "I'll allow it, but you're on thin ice here, counselor," magnetic poetry, Kegels, the sign in my son's first-grade classroom that said "Use Furniture Correctly," swim diapers, the *Super Mario Bros.* music, shirtless driving, when hungry cartoon characters look at someone and they turn into a chicken leg, tetherball, hobo codes, "Polar Bear Plunge" dudes, the word "rollicking," backyard trampolines, raisins, Magic Eye posters, football announcers having to read plugs for tomorrow night's shows, atheists, sumo loincloths, boom boxes, Burt's Bees, "Battles of the Bands," Bob Balaban, calling a phone call "a jingle," the mini-pencils they have at the library, when you have a slight whistle in one nostril, *Wall Street Journal* stipple portraits, "infotainment," swear jars, sexting, fondue sets, the San Diego Chicken, Crispix, beatboxing, Jamaican slang, the warnings in movie ratings, Mad Libs, people who say "namaste," people who really love sports bloopers, pop-up calendar kiosks, Pilgrims, flossing, literally all anime, seersucker suits, libertarians, European cheek-kissing, the short urinal, Soviet art with lots of sturdy women on tractors, Ouija boards, shadow animals, "Mambo No. 5," people at spas with cucumbers on their eyes, square-dance callers, parkour, fake street drugs in sci-fi, cranberry bogs, Cyclopses, Jimmy Buffett fans, that creationist museum (or museums?) down south somewhere, koi ponds, cartoon suns wearing sunglasses, Garrison Keillor, "Coexist" bumper stickers, cursed Indian burial grounds, when Hooters had an airline, boxing kangaroos, stage magic, Temple Grandin "hug boxes," the NIT basketball tournament, wicker, folk dancing, books about briefly dead Christians or New Agers visiting heaven, coin-op massage chairs in airports, the "Kiss Cam," horses wearing floppy hats with ear holes and a flower on top, Jim Morrison's poetry, the word "sensual," Eeyore, harmonicas, muesli, gentleman callers sitting in the parlor, ships in bottles, quinceañeras, Christian Science reading rooms, "free sandwich" punch cards, and bow ties.

When I say that all those things are funny to me, it doesn't mean that I get paralyzed with laughter at the mere sight or mention of Crispix cereal or a harpsichord. That would be stupid. But each of them has at least a faint halo of amusement to me, if I look at them through comedy-nerd goggles. They're slightly funny as isolated concepts, but more importantly they're pregnant with possibility. They have, in joke terms, *potential energy.* And in the same way that a baseball stats guru might develop equations to compute how much better a given player is than a "replacement-level player," comedy writers get a sense for which breakfast cereals or musical instruments are better joke fuel than others. They'll just burn hotter. Crispix is funnier than Wheat Chex. Harpsichords are funnier than pianos. You might object that there's nothing *inherently* funny about a harpsichord, that my perception has been colored by media depictions of them (e.g., being played by foppish movie dandies in powdered wigs) or my own experiences with them (e.g., in the background of museum audioguides). That's true to a point, but look: *all* humor is a web of cultural associations. No elemental thing is *that* funny in a vacuum, as a pure Platonic ideal. But let me be clear: my list isn't just a collection of "things that I've learned are stock stand-up material or have been the punch line of a particularly memorable *Simpsons* gag." I don't think I've ever heard a joke about a cranberry bog in my life, or even seen a cranberry bog, but let's be honest: cranberry is a pretty funny kind of bog. For the most part, things don't become funny because joke-tellers seize on them. Joke-tellers seize on things that are already funny.

But breaking down the comedy atom into tiny spinning electrons of probabilistic funniness doesn't actually *explain* how humor operates—it just kicks the can farther down the road. The alchemy of where the laugh comes from remains mysterious and ineffable. It's the comedy equivalent of the unanswerable metaphysical question "Why is there something instead of nothing?" Why a laugh here but not here? What makes one story/quip/cartoon/breakfast cereal funny and another one not?

The Internet of Dead Frogs

To most of the world, the animals most closely associated with author E. B. White are a pig and a spider, because he wrote the universally loved 1952 children's classic *Charlotte's Web.** But in the rarefied world of humor studies, E. B. White's spirit animal is the frog. In the preface to a 1941 humor collection, White first used the simile later popularly paraphrased this way: "Analyzing humor is like dissecting a frog. Few people are interested, and the frog dies of it." The observation that explaining a joke is a singularly unfunny pursuit was not new to White; as early as 55 BC, Cicero was writing that "a man with any tincture of humor in him can discuss anything in the world more wittily than actual witticisms." But the analysis of humor was suddenly in vogue in the early twentieth century, with very serious Europeans like Freud and Bergson and Pirandello having turned their coolly appraising eyes and neatly trimmed beards to the subject. In 1937, Robert Benchley parodied the genre in one of his best *New Yorker* pieces, "Why We Laugh—or Do We?"

> In order to laugh at something, it is necessary (1) to know *what* you are laughing at, (2) to know *why* you are laughing, (3) to ask some people why *they* think you are laughing, (4) to jot down a few notes, (5) to laugh. Even then, the thing may not be cleared up for days.

White and Benchley were trivially correct: no joke becomes funnier once explained. But ask any biology teacher: Frog-dissecters aren't trying to save the frog. They're trying to see how frogs work.

Humor studies is a surprisingly new academic field, dating back to a 1976 conference on humor in Cardiff, Wales, which led to the creation of the World Humor and Irony Membership, or WHIM.†

* He also wrote *Stuart Little,* but it's wrong to associate him with mice because Stuart Little was not a mouse. White is very clear on this point. He was a human baby who was born to human parents but just happened to *look* exactly like a mouse, which is repulsive.

† WHIM published the annual *World Humor and Irony Membership Serial Yearbook,* or *WHIMSY.* Acronyms! So funny, right out of the gate.

The academic establishment had previously considered humor to be, by definition, too lightweight a subject for serious research, but by the 1970s, the slow creep of comedy into modernity was too obvious to be ignored. WHIM wisely abandoned its acronymic name when it was reorganized in 1989 as the International Society for Humor Studies, and today boasts more than five hundred members from universities on six continents, who work in dozens of different scholarly disciplines. Their quarterly journal, *Humor*, has all the solemn frog dissection you could ever hope for. A quick browse of the table of contents reveals articles with titles like "Why All Dictators Have Moustaches: Political Jokes in Contemporary Belarus" and "Poor Wee Souls and *Fraggle Rock:* The Visceral Humor of Nurse-Peers in a Non-Accomplishment Setting." Most university libraries don't subscribe to *Humor*, which is a tragedy because it's the only place you'll ever find a graph of René Thom's cusp function from catastrophe theory used to diagram a joke, or an eleven-column "Laugh Utterance" table recording all the glottal stops in the first laughter of a seventeen-month-old baby playing peekaboo. To the professional humor researcher, being funny is a deadly serious business.

I have no doubt that every single scholar who has ever published in *Humor* has the very drollest sense of humor in their department, and the selection of photocopied Gary Larson *Far Side* panels on their office door is impeccable, but you'd never know that from reading them. It's not just that their scholarship is unfunny, which you'd expect in any field. It's how weirdly divorced it feels from the way that professional funny people talk about their work—which they will do, incessantly. But real comedy people just aren't interested in the academic brand of analysis. In their 2014 book *The Humor Code*, humor researcher Peter McGraw and journalist Joel Warner tell an unbearably cringe-y story about landing a backstage interview with Louis C.K. before a show. In the dressing room, McGraw begins to explain his pet humor theory, but C.K. isn't interested, cutting him off with a grumbled objection that jokes can't be codified so simply. In the awkward silence that ensues, McGraw asks him if he has a small

penis. (A woman they'd met earlier in the lobby wanted to know.)*
The interview ends at this point.

My favorite thing about this story is *not* what an epic disaster of
both journalism *and* humor studies it is, blowing the chance to pick
the brain of a performer who was widely considered at the time to be
one of the most interesting comedy thinkers on the planet, though that
is pretty great.[†] It's Louis C.K.'s utter disinterest—almost bordering on
aversion—when it comes to the topic of what makes jokes funny.

"I've never known really funny people to be that interested in dissecting how it works," comedy writer George Meyer told me. That's largely
because it's such an unconscious and intuitive gift. "If you asked Robert
Plant after the show, 'Why did you say *ooh yeah* after that particular
bar?' or 'Why did you twirl the mike with your right hand?' he doesn't
know he's doing that so he can't tell you. He's just going with the flow."

But sometimes there's more to the aversion than that. People who
have based their livelihood (and self-image) on something as ineffable
as humor might think twice about looking under the hood. What if you
start overthinking it and it goes away, like an athlete with the "yips"?
"They're almost superstitious about it; they get freaked out," explained
Meyer. "Many of the people have no idea how they do it, and that's
how it should be."

Even if comedy professionals are hesitant, in general, to pierce the veil
of mystery, it's a favorite pastime in the peanut gallery of comedy nerds,
largely thanks to the power of the Internet. Pop culture sites rank and
taxonomize jokes endlessly, while the lawless frontier of social media and
message boards churns and froths over the comedy it collectively loves
and hates. Online wars can be waged for weeks over the interpretation of a
single Adult Swim gag. Are they just kibitzers, or could this kind of geekery

---

* 2014 was a simpler time, before Louis C.K.'s history of sexual misconduct was widely known. The woman in
the lobby had no idea that she could have asked any number of female comedians about the size of C.K.'s penis.

† I assume McGraw, a genuine comedy fan, was starstruck. When I spoke briefly to him for this book, he
was friendly and helpful and didn't ask me about my genitals once. He is the director of the University of
Colorado's Humor Research Lab, or "HuRL." *Again with these guys and their funny acronyms!*

be a gateway for the next generation of comedy talent? The results from the academic world aren't promising so far, but that's starting to change in our more comedy-savvy age. After all, every student who ever grew up to be a great neurologist or biochemist started out with frog dissection.

A Grand Unified Theory of Jokes

Cosmologists have spent the last century in search of a "theory of everything," a single framework that would explain all physical interactions in the universe. Things are much the same in the humor studies world: every scholar wants to be the one who unveils the One Overarching Secret that explains why we laugh. But the great minds who have weighed in on humor have described it so differently that to an outside observer, it's not even clear that they're thinking of the same phenomenon. It's the old fable of the blind men trying to describe an elephant, only the elephant is one of those elephant jokes from the sixties.

The ancient Greeks, back to Plato and Aristotle, originated what was the dominant humor theory for most of Western civilization: superiority theory. We make jokes to put others down. As Thomas Hobbes put it: "The passion of laughter is nothing else but a sudden glory arising from sudden conception of some eminency in ourselves, by comparison with the infirmities of others." Laughter, in other words, is always scorn.

The conflation of humor and ridicule meant that philosophers only wrote about humor to warn against it. Plato, his followers said, was an "intensely melancholy" man who "was never seen to laugh excessively," even as a youth. "As sad as Plato" went the proverb. Aristotle took such a hard line on jokes that he even wondered in his *Nicomachean Ethics* if they should be banned. "Most people delight more than they should in amusement and in jesting," he wrote. "Jest is a sort of abuse, and there are things that lawgivers forbid us to abuse; and they should, perhaps, have forbidden us even to make a jest of such." Joking about the gods should be just as illegal as vandalizing a temple, in other words. Making fun of a friend should be just as illegal as popping him in the mouth.

It's true that many jokes do have a target (or "butt," which is a funnier word), and that even today the undercurrent of hostility in a lot of comedy is underappreciated. Jokes end with *punch* lines, a witty remark is *sharp*. Both might *crack* us up. If enough people crack up, then the comedian *killed, knocked 'em dead*. If not, he *died*, she *bombed*. But ancient humor must have been pretty limited (or the philosophers overly concerned with one then-trendy and caustic strain of it) for no one to have thought of any counterexamples. Sure, superiority theory is easy to apply to political satire or insult comedy, but how does it explain puns?* How does it explain the epidemic of self-deprecation in modern comedy: Jim Norton on his sexual depravity, Bernie Mac on his hypocrisies as a parent, Amy Schumer on her looks, Tina Fey on her social awkwardness?† We don't laugh because we're mocking them—in fact, it's crucial to all these comic personas that we identify closely with them. If I'm laughing at a David Mitchell bit about his nerdy misanthropy because I also recognize it in myself, who exactly is feeling superior to whom? Comedy, in other words, can be powered by fellow feeling and empathy as well as by ridicule. Saying that superiority is the secret essence of humor is like hearing a few jokes set in restaurants and concluding that all comedy can be reduced to waiters.

In the twentieth century, superiority theory has been gradually eclipsed by dozens of other contenders, most notably relief theory and incongruity theory. Relief theory is usually traced back to English political theorist Herbert Spencer, best known as the guy who coined the phrase "survival of the fittest." When he studied "The Physiology of Laughter" in 1860, Spencer decided that it was an outlet for built-up psychic energy. "Nervous excitation always tends to beget muscular motion," he wrote. Sometimes we vent that energy via aggression or flight, but sometimes

---

* The argument is sometimes made by superiority theorists that the target of a pun is an implied dumber person who *isn't* so good at puns. Aren't we clever, to get the joke? That's not an insignificant part of comedy, as you know if you've ever seen an audience member laughing especially loudly at some highbrow joke, so everyone sees they got it. "Somebody should write a history of knowing self-congratulatory laughter, from Shakespeare down through watching Woody Allen on the Upper East Side," comedy writer Tim Long once suggested to me. But if we water the definition of superiority theory down this much (basically "anything, even a hypothetical, that makes us feel good about ourselves"), it could explain almost any human interaction.

† The history of perfectly attractive female comedians having to pretend in their acts that they are graceless, hideous Gorgons is a long and troubled one, to be revisited in chapter 10.

we laugh. This line of argument was given a big boost in the twentieth century by Sigmund Freud, who saw humor in much the same way he saw dreams. Both were ways to release all the pent-up strain of reality, particularly repressed hostility and—Freud being Freud—sexuality. Laughter was a primal pleasure satisfied, our mouths open wide in imitation of the release from our mothers' nipples as babies. The Freudian take on humor is a good match for the way laughter feels—liberating, a release—as well as the undeniable fact that edgy overtones of taboo subjects like sex or violence can make a laugh bigger. In 1968, a psychologist named Arthur Shurcliff conducted an experiment in which he told one group of subjects that they'd have to hold a mouse, a second group that they'd have to draw blood from a mouse, and a third group that they'd have to draw blood from an angry rat. In all three cases, the "rodent" was then revealed to be a stuffed toy. As Spencer and Freud would have predicted, laughter did correlate with relief. All the subjects laughed, and the ones who'd been feeling the most anxiety before the reveal laughed the most.

But relief theory doesn't explain the mechanics of jokes at all (just naming a taboo thing isn't funny: *necrophilia!*) and, again, it ignores all the things we laugh at that have no pent-up psychic energy behind them. An observational comic could tell a series of jokes on how much ducks love bread, but what would Freud say I'm laughing at there? What duck-related taboo is being violated? A sign that says "Please Don't Feed the Ducks"?

More popular today among scholars than relief theory is incongruity theory, the notion that we laugh when something violates the normal order of things, or when two mismatched concepts are juxtaposed: a monkey on roller skates, a bottle of shampoo in the fridge. It's often summed up using Immanuel Kant's 1790 declaration that "laughter is an affection arising from the sudden transformation of a strained expectation into nothing." Our mental patterns must quickly shift to adjust to some unexpected collision of concept with reality.

Many proponents of incongruity theory have followed in Kant's footsteps in focusing on that magical moment when the incongruity is resolved and humor is therefore produced: aha, "black and white and *read* all over," I get it! In fact, the theory is often called "incongruity resolution" in the literature. But a Swedish psychologist named Göran Nerhardt was unconvinced. In a famous 1970 experiment, he had subjects lift a series of small weights, then handed them one that was unexpectedly light or heavy. Participants invariably smiled or laughed when they picked up the odd weight—and their reaction varied in proportion with just how much the last weight varied from the earlier ones.* Nerhardt's implication was not that the true essence of humor is a man lifting a slightly-lighter-than-average weight—though I'd be willing to at least entertain the theory. He was pointing out that sometimes, *incongruity itself* can be funny. The humor is sometimes in the sheer oddity of something, not the neat resolution of it.

One frequent criticism of the incongruity theory is that it's so broad as to be almost tautological: things are funny (ha-ha) because they're funny (strange)—or they were but then they got resolved, which is funny too! Personally, I'm skeptical of the whole quest to find the One Fundamental Hidden Secret of Humor. What if there's a whole range of factors that contribute to pushing a certain joke or situation over the humor threshold? We cry for many reasons (sadness, happiness, pepper spray, *Brian's Song*). More to the point, even a single emotional response like "sadness" can be triggered by many different things: loss, guilt, loneliness, fear, disappointment, frustration, even music that swells in a certain way. Why should laughter and amusement be any different?

Even if the study of humor hasn't produced its grand unifying theory yet—and maybe never will—you have to be impressed by that cast! The bigwigs in the field aren't just associate professors at state universities with rubber chickens in their Facebook photos. They're Aristotle and Plato and Cicero and Hobbes and Descartes and Locke and Kant and Hegel and Schopenhauer and Kierkegaard and Darwin and Spencer and Freud and Bergson and Dewey. Even when humor wasn't accepted by the academy as a legitimate field of study, great thinkers just couldn't

---

* I've never been to a "humor research lab" like Peter McGraw's, but I picture them all looking something like Q's workshop in a James Bond movie: a long tracking shot where the background is a series of people bursting into nervous laughter at stuffed mice and dummy weights, while serious-looking scientists with white coats and clipboards look on.

stay away from it, whether they were writing about rhetoric or biology or knowledge or ethics.

But that also means that the most influential opinions on humor have, for centuries, come from people with no actual humor on their résumés. Do we really think that philosophers, orators, churchmen, political theorists, and scientists are the ideal people to be weighing in on how jokes work, especially when their numbers include famous sourpusses like Plato and Schopenhauer? It seems like asking a bunch of famous celibates to explain sexual pleasure. When do actual funny people get to weigh in?

The Laugh Reflex

A few years ago, I watched a web video of a Virginia family releasing back into the wild an adorable baby bunny they'd been feeding for a week. Maybe you've seen the video too. "We've got to let Kermit go, so he can find his mommy," Mom tells her cherubic little daughter. Then they see another rabbit watching from across their lawn. "There's your mommy, go get her!" she says, setting Kermit down on the edge of the driveway. He scampers off across the field but doesn't get more than sixty feet before a hawk swoops down and carries a screaming Kermit off in its talons, in full view of the shocked family—and, God help me, I burst out laughing. I laugh every time I see this video, and I've probably seen it twenty times.

The dad in the video, the one holding the camera, laughs immediately as well, even though he knows his daughter is probably traumatized for life. I laughed despite having said many a toilet-side eulogy for dead fish, and in one case having helped my teary-eyed daughter set up an incredibly elaborate backyard monument to a beloved golden retriever. We know that a child watching her pet die violently is sad, not funny. So why did we laugh? A superiority theorist would say we were laughing at the unfortunate rabbit, because Kermit's troubles made us feel good about *not* currently being carried off by a hungry hawk. A relief theorist would say we laughed to vent our own discomfort around that most taboo subject of all: death. An incongruity theorist might say we were laughing because the hawk entered the frame at such an unexpected and inopportune moment, violating everything we know about the bittersweet decorum of releasing a pet back into the wild.

None of those answers feels quite right—even taking into account Max Eastman's 1936 dictum "The correct explanation of a joke not only does not sound funny, but it does not sound like a correct explanation." My sudden, almost automatic bark of laughter at Kermit's painful death, as if it were just an exquisitely timed slapstick gag, didn't seem to reflect anything about my conscious persona or convictions. If anything, it reflected only the idea that some things are just ineffably funny, denying all explication. We laugh at first sight.

In support of this, you might be able to think of a joke that you once liked but then found less funny once you learned *why* it was actually funny. For example, one of my favorite running gags in the Beatles' *A Hard Day's Night* is that everyone who meets Paul's granddad, played by Irish actor Wilfrid Brambell, is impressed by how clean he is. ("Clean, though, isn't he?" John Lennon remarks to the band's road manager, Shake. "Oh, aye, he's very clean," agrees Shake.) I thought this was a hilarious non sequitur and laughed every time it recurred. But years later, I learned about the real genesis of the joke in a documentary. Brambell was, in 1964, famous for playing the grimy junkman Albert Steptoe in *Steptoe and Son*, the BBC sitcom on which *Sanford and Son* was later based. Just like Redd Foxx's Fred Sanford, Steptoe was often called a "dirty old man" by his son, and the filmmakers decided to have some fun with his casting as a more dapper type in the Beatles film. I was legitimately disappointed to learn that in seizing on the "clean old man" bit as an inspired bit of whimsy, I had actually misunderstood one of my least favorite kinds of joke: a wink at a then-contemporary pop culture reference. A sitcom catchphrase, of all things!*

I enjoy plenty of jokes about things that I've never actually seen—not just cranberry bogs but also conga lines, Murphy beds, Limburger

---

* Sometimes this goes for whole comedic works as well. *Don Quixote* and *Gulliver's Travels* are revered as milestone comic novels today, but modern readers probably have no clue that both were written as elaborate genre parodies (of chivalric romances and travelogues, respectively). They're *Scary Movie* installments, essentially—and possibly funnier today without that baggage.

cheese—and some about things that I don't think even exist, like poor people wearing barrels, or when a snootful of "alum" makes a cartoon character's mouth shrink. But the first scientific work on the funniness of nonexistent things was done in 2015, by an Alberta professor named Chris Westbury. Westbury had a computer generate almost six thousand nonsense words and went through them by hand to eliminate any that seemed dirty: "whong," "focky," "clunt." Then he had hundreds of students rate the nonwords' inherent funniness. Results were surprisingly consistent: some made-up letter strings ("himumma," "quaribbly," "subvick") immediately strike people as inherently funny, while others ("tessina," "crester," "mestead") do not. Westbury published his study as a victory for incongruity theory, because his funny nonwords tended to include lots of unusual sounds and letter combinations, violating expectations about language, while the least funny words all looked like very promising Scrabble racks. But if that's true, then it's a victory for the "deceptive weight" school of incongruity humor, where it's funny when something is strange and new, not when the newness gets explained away.

I'd go even further than that. Westbury's experiment inclines me to think that humor theory should resign the game and go home. It suggests that something completely incomprehensible and devoid of any cultural associations whatsoever—a "proffin," a "quingel"—can still strike hundreds of people as inherently funny. Explain that, Immanuel Kant.

"Sweaty" Republicans and Germans

Not everyone likes a joke that can't be explained. Humor researchers now believe this to be one of the few real ideological divides when it comes to comedy. Both sides of the political spectrum like to paint themselves as the ones who really *get* humor. To liberals, conservatives are nuance-challenged puritans too repressed (or even too dumb) to get a joke; to conservatives, liberals are dour pedants more likely to take offense at a joke than to laugh at it. Comedy is such a self-evidently crucial pillar of society now that no one can afford to be on the side of the aisle *without* it.

In fact, many studies have shown little difference between the humor appreciation of the Left and the Right—except in two areas. People who identify as conservatives are much less comfortable with risqué humor, and they're more likely to prefer tidy incongruity-resolution jokes. They want a punch line that "makes sense" in some way. Liberals go for nonsense humor, jokes with some leftover absurdity that doesn't get resolved.

This cultural gap shows up between nationalities as well. In 1940, Charles Addams drew perhaps the most famous of his bizarre *New Yorker* cartoons: a skier looks back down the slope quizzically at another skier, whose tracks have somehow diverged *around* the trunk of a pine tree. Today Addams's work seems quaintly charming, about as macabre as a middle school Halloween party, but its open absurdity was pretty edgy in its time. Addams's friend Wolcott Gibbs joked in the preface to one of his collections that these cartoons were being used in hospitals to diagnose incipient lunacy—if you thought a panel like "The Skier" made sense, "the lunacy is no longer incipient."

But when the "Skier" cartoon was reprinted in Germany, it created the opposite reaction. Where American readers smiled gently at the absurdity of the impossible ski tracks, a Heidelberg woman named Annemarie Hammer was bewildered. "I don't see how this is possible," she wrote the editors of *Heute* magazine. "Won't you please print the answer to the puzzle?" "From *Heute*'s literal-minded German readers came a flood of confident answers," *Time* reported. The skier had gone down the hill on one ski and back up on the other. He had slipped one foot out of his boot at just the right moment. Two amputees slid down the hill on one ski apiece. "A thoughtful Nürnberger suggested that it might be a kind of joke, [and] wrote six pages of tight Gothic script on the philosophy of humor." The nation of Schopenhauer!

Comedy that can be cleverly explained is not the trend today, possibly not even among conservatives or Germans. We like our comedy to be as pure and irreducible as one of Chris Westbury's nonsense words—funny for no reason, funny just because. "Himumma" and "proffin" really aren't that different from David Letterman saying the word "pants" until it's funny, or Charles Schulz using the word "Zamboni" until it's funny. It's not the article of clothing or the ice-smoothing machine; it's the word, the spell cast, the willing suspension of disbelief.

According to George Meyer, the reflexively funny joke appeals to comedy writers for its sheer grace. It's the opposite of what legendary *Saturday Night Live* writer Michael O'Donoghue used to call "sweaty" comedy, where the effort and laboriousness of manufacturing every joke is right there on the surface. The better jokes just alight on you effortlessly, like a butterfly. "That was considered, like, the acme of what we could do, if you came up with something like that," he told me. "If we could discuss, 'Why is that joke funny?'" And now that the audience for comedy is largely seen-it-all connoisseurs as well, the funny-for-no-reason joke is the Holy Grail, the last really impressive thing. You can't explain it. You can't teach or learn it as a matter of formula or craft.

Saying Funny Things vs. Saying Things Funny

A favorite in the *Simpsons* writing room, Meyer remembered, was a line from a 2000 episode structured like a *Behind the Music* parody. At one point, the melodramatic narrator intoned, "For the Simpsons, everything was coming up roses. But those roses contained *ready-to-sting bees.*" The joke came from former showrunner David Mirkin. "Such a bizarre line! We were always laughing at that. Why is that funny?"

Most funny-for-no-reason jokes rely on that thrill of exploration. In some cases, newfound comic potential is drawn from something that's never been joke fodder before, and the audience can sense the exciting novelty. But often the discovery can be as simple as an unexpected turn of phrase. The idea of metaphorical roses containing very concrete bees might be incongruous, like the real toads in Marianne Moore's imaginary gardens, but it isn't terribly *funny* at first blush. It's the bizarre phrasing—the bees aren't just ready to sting, they're adjectivally *ready-to-sting bees!*—that elevates the joke.

The first time I watched *Groundhog Day* with my kids, I was pleased to see them laughing at all the right places: "Watch the first step—it's a doozy!" "Morons, your bus is leaving." "Don't drive on the railroad track!" The movie, evidently, had aged well. But I'd seen it at least a dozen times over the years; I'd seen Bill Murray's alarm clock go off well over a hundred. I wasn't responding to entry-level stuff like "Needlenose

Ned" anymore. In fact, I found myself laughing the hardest at a line I'd never even noticed before. Late in the movie, when Murray is hoping to impress Andie MacDowell's character over drinks, he muses, "People place too much emphasis on their careers. I wish we could all live in the mountains . . . at high altitudes." At high altitudes! He later repeats the line. Maybe it's meant to echo his bored-weatherman shtick from earlier in the movie ("At high altitudes it will crystallize, and give us what we call snow") but mostly it's just a weirdly specific mismatch with the dreaminess of his utopian vision. The altitudes . . . they must be high. A mildly eccentric phrasing turned a slight joke into a very good one—if you've heard the other jokes so many times that you're desperate for novelty.

The notion that sometimes the funniest things *just sound funny* goes back at least to the English masters of nonsense poetry: Edward Lear with his Quangle Wangle and Jumblies and Scroobious Pip, Lewis Carroll with his borogoves and Jubjub bird. This is a strain of gleeful infantilism that we see in British language and comedy up through Monty Python's "Election Night Special" sketch, in which the candidates for the Silly Party have names that begin in Edward Lear territory and only escalate from there: Kevin Phillips-Bong, Mr. Elsie Zzzzzzzzzzzz, Tarquin Fintim-lin-bin-whin-bim-lin-bus-stop-F'tang-F'tang-Olé-Biscuitbarrel.*

But the modern phraseology of English-language comedy has more distinct American roots. The most influential British comedy voice, after all, is still the high-minded comedy of manners. It's the clever verbal jousting and elaborate social customs of a Sheridan play or Austen novel. When we appreciate a witty Dryden couplet or scathing Oscar Wilde comeback, we're not exactly laughing so much as we're admiring the intellect that went into its construction. The difference between witty and funny is *effort*. So even the airiest banter in this vein is going to feel, in Michael O'Donoghue's parlance, "sweaty."

In fact, high comedy takes *pride* in the fact that it doesn't produce belly laughs. As George Meredith sneered in the Victorian era, "We know the degree of refinement in men by the matter they will laugh at, and the ring of

---

* The last candidate in the sketch has a fifty-word name that also includes various sound effects, animal noises, song titles, and punch lines from other jokes, and is far too silly to reproduce here.

the laugh." When Samuel Johnson read the non sequiturs and shaggy-dog digressions in *Tristram Shandy*, a novel much funnier than anything he would ever write himself, he sniffed, "Nothing odd will do long."

For jokes that land a little lower on the brain stem, we have to turn to the American frontier. Artemus Ward, in his comic lectures (stand-up comedy, in its infancy, was a "lecture"), seems to have created out of whole cloth a new kind of silliness marked by simplicity and a casual eccentricity of wording. Explaining the landscape of the West to city slickers, he would say things like "The highest part of this mountain is the top" or "That beautiful and interesting animal is a horse. It was a long time before I discovered it." When he visited London in 1866, the British press immediately realized this was something new. "His jokes are of that true transatlantic type to which no nation beyond the limits of the States can offer any parallel," wrote the *Times*. "These jokes he lets fall with an air of profound unconsciousness." The *Spectator* noticed that Ward's naïveté of speech could not be as easy as it looked. "The art with which he gives the impression that he is floundering along in his choice of words, the victim of the first verbal association which strikes his memory, and yet just familiar enough with language to feel uncertain as to his ground, and to wish to get hold of some clearer term, is beyond praise."

The London papers were witnessing the birth of a new kind of humor writing, where the humor *is* the phraseology, the sheer rhythm of the words, and not the situational funniness of the nominal subject or story. Ward once told his contemporary Eli Perkins that you could even take something sad and beautiful, like Alexander the Great's famous line about weeping because he had no more worlds to conquer, and reword it to get a laugh: "He conkerd* the world and wept because he couldn't do it sum more." It's all in how you put the sentence together.

---

* Ward and his contemporaries went so far as to make their *spelling* funny, using comically misspelled words wherever possible. Ward's friend Josh Billings was quick to see the difference: he had no luck publishing his "Essay on the Mule," but when he rewrote it as "Essa on the Muel," it was a hit. Billings soon found he was locked into the device, which scholars call cacography. "I adopted it in a moment ov karlessness," he lamented, "and like a slip in chastity, the world don't let me back tew grace again." Today cacography is back in a big way on social media forums like Twitter, where nonstandard capitalization, punctuation, and spelling are commonly used to convey a casual-but-woke comic sensibility.

Sweet Free Association of Youth

The modern descendant of this frontier phrascology, filtered down through the random absurdities of the Dadaists and the Beats, is the voice of the stand-up who reinvents a familiar topic by finding a sillier, simpler way to talk about it. I always hear Bill Cosby's voice: kindergarten nonsense like calling adults "grown people" and saying things like "The food goes in the belly button!" with a weird cadence and expressionistic sound effects.* Today, comedians do it even when the subject isn't childhood reminiscence. Mike Birbiglia says "connect mouths" instead of "kiss"; Maria Bamford describes lube, in a singsong recess voice, as "jams and jellies and sauces." Louis C.K. paraphrases his doctor's order to lose some weight as "You gotta be less people. You can't be . . . so much." It's all carefully calibrated to sound awkward, unstudied. And it's grown into an entire genre of hit comedy movie built around Adam Sandler and Will Ferrell and Melissa McCarthy regressing into these childlike personas.

The trippy non sequiturs of modern comedy are often dismissed as diversions for "stoner culture"—and yes, it's certainly easier than ever before to get your hands on substances that will magically make the Seth Rogen movies and Cartoon Network shows playing in your dorm room much funnier, or at least drain your interest in changing the channel. Two thousand years ago, Pliny the Elder was already extolling the virtues of gelotophyllis, the mysterious "laughing leaf" of Central Asia—not coincidentally, perhaps, the same part of the world where cannabis plants originated. But why does every absurd bit of comedy have to be co-opted as a wink to potheads? In fact, lots of Adult Swim's more experimental programming requires such close attention that it seems guaranteed to bewilder or even panic the stoned.† Today's preference for out-of-left-field, why-am-I-laughing-at-this gags seems more closely linked to the guileless stage persona of Steven Wright:

* Back when we could listen to Bill Cosby records without feeling sad and angry.

† It's not particularly hard to tailor jokes to stoners. You know what kind of joke weed fans will laugh at? Any joke that mentions weed.

I went into a place to eat, it said, "Breakfast anytime." So I ordered French toast during the Renaissance.

Or the "Deep Thoughts" of *Saturday Night Live* writer Jack Handey:

If you ever drop your keys into a river of molten lava, let 'em go, because, man, they're gone.*

Their one-liners conjure up not the aimless profundities of getting blazed, but something more primal: the daydreams and flights of fancy of childhood.

Youth—or at least youthfulness—has always been the engine of comedy. In part, that's because the young brain seems to be wired for it. Networks know that television comedies attract an average viewer *decades* younger than their dramas and news programs.† English humorist Max Beerbohm admitted, "I protest that I do, still, at the age of forty-seven, laugh often and loud and long. But not, I believe, so long and loud and often as in my less smiling youth." Research backs him up: in a 2006 experiment, test subjects over sixty were unable to explain as many jokes or complete as many punch lines as younger folks. This is true of writers and performers as well. The original cast of *Saturday Night Live* was pretty much all under thirty;‡ ditto for *Monty Python's Flying Circus*. For every late bloomer like Rodney Dangerfield or Lisa Lampanelli, there are dozens of great comedians who calcified into Bob-Hope-telling-hippie-jokes mode in middle age or stopped performing altogether. So it goes in every generation for the angry young Turks who shake up comedy. Mark Twain died a bitter old coot; Thurber was an angry drunk.

---

* Oh man, is that Jack Handey "One thing that's funny . . ." diction ever deep in the comedy DNA now. *McSweeney's* wouldn't exist without it.

† In 2015, the median viewer of an episode of *Louie* was thirty-seven years old. The median *NCIS* viewer was sixty-one, and doesn't think you call home enough.

‡ Fine, Chevy Chase was thirty-one. The real outlier? Garrett Morris, who was a full decade older than his costars.

But the essential virtues of comedy are also young ones, regardless of the age of the teller or the listener. Why do you think we call a joke "kidding"? Children are still outsiders in the world; they come to it with fresh eyes. They can see the absurdities we don't, not just because their minds are flexible but also because they haven't been here so long. They are still tourists. When my daughter, Katie, asks me, "Why do we say 'tuna fish' but not 'chicken bird'?" I have no answer, because I am "grown people." I've been looking at things too long to see them anymore. The deeply funny never lose their sense of wonder, never stop playing. George Carlin at seventy seemed younger than most thirty-year-olds I know.

The inexplicably funny joke is the one most likely to crack up a room full of hardened comedy obsessives, but it's also the most childlike, because it trades in a deeply intuitive silliness that can't be diagrammed, that resists every theory. When my son, at the beach, whips off a pair of aviators to reveal a second pair of sunglasses underneath, he doesn't know he's reenacting an inspired gag from *Airplane!*, beloved by generations of comedy fans. It's just something goofy he thought up in the car.

Subjectivity on the Cob

When jokes were clear narratives with simple mechanics, their punch lines could be explained in a single sentence. These explanations might read like newspaper corrections:

> The bartender meant he served a sweet mixed drink called a grass-hopper.

> The headlines made by the corduroy pillows are literally "head lines."

> The man making the bet was Superman and knew all along he could fly.

Even humor theorists of competing schools could agree on explanations like these. And that's just not true anymore of many of the things that make us laugh. No one-sentence answer key can explain the slight aura of funniness around cranberry bogs or harpsichords. You can't defend or even pinpoint the rules that govern a silly verbal joke (why is "ready-to-sting" a funny way to describe a bee?) or an absurd non sequitur (why is this comedy special just a shot-for-shot reenactment of the *Simon & Simon* opening credits?). They just *are*.

People still try, though. Case in point: On a 2015 episode of Cartoon Network's hit sci-fi comedy *Rick and Morty*, Rick's family is on the run from the Galactic Federation, and they land on a likely-looking planet. The place has one seemingly charming eccentricity: strawberries and flowers grow "on the cob" there, like an ear of corn. But when Rick investigates the local fauna microscopically, he sees cobs even at the subatomic level. "Everything's on a cob! The whole planet's on a cob!" he says, panicking and rushing everyone back to the spaceship. "Go, go, go!"

Mystified viewers took to the Internet looking for someone to explain the joke to them. What exactly is so dangerous about a planet where everything is on a cob? Dozens of very serious answers were mooted. Because their lungs couldn't process air on the cob. Because they themselves would eventually grow on the cob. Because of the existential horror of recursive cob-ness: cobs within cobs within cobs. Because a planet of cobs would inevitably be eaten by some giant galactic eater of cobs. Everyone had a theory.

At Comic-Con the following year, a fan brought the swirling controversy to the show's creators, Justin Roiland and Dan Harmon. "Why are cobs so terrifying?" he asked. The panelists straight-facedly sketched out some of the possible downsides of a planet where everything was on the cob: mosquitoes on the cob, black widow spiders on the cob, arcade tickets that won't come out of the little slot because they're on the cob. ("The slots are on a cob! It's a mess!" added Harmon.) Staff writer Ryan Ridley joked, "We have a three-episode arc in season three that explains the origin of the cob and Rick's relationship to it."*

Justin Roiland came the closest to giving a serious answer to the question: "Well, as soon as we answer that, the joke dies, doesn't it?" I wonder if the nerds in the room thought that meant, "We know the

---

* In predictably bizarro Adult Swim fashion, the network posted a video of the exchange—but with the audio replaced by opera singers performing the dialogue to music.

answer, but telling it to you wouldn't be funny." To me, the joke was very clear: We weren't *supposed* to understand or even care why Rick is freaked out. We were meant to enjoy the silly idea that something that's not corn (indeed, everything that's not corn*) could grow on a cob, and the fun of using that to power a standard "We've got to get out of here!" sci-fi cliché.

Dan Guterman, the writer who pitched the cob planet idea, patiently confirmed this to me. "The lack of an explanation *is* the punch line to the joke. The only person who will ever know exactly why they needed to get off that planet is Rick, and the fact that only he knows it, knows it immediately, and won't risk taking the time to explain what he knows because of what he knows, is still hilarious to me. Really, it's a very simple joke."

Humor has always been a very individual quirk. A sign in the head writer's office on *The Carol Burnett Show* read, "There are few good judges of comedy. And they don't agree." According to writer Gene Perret, the writing staff used to argue about the sign, because a few of them thought "And *we* don't agree" would be funnier. The new, more nebulous comedy is even more subjective, because it's a quantum computer, not operating on principles that everyone can immediately measure the same way. Let's be honest: you were probably mystified by much of my list of random things that crack me up. If you were to make such a list, it might not overlap mine much, because it would be informed by your own experiences and comedy prejudices and not mine—my weakness for nostalgia, for example. I'm well aware that a focus group of average Americans might be able to agree on a dozen or more breakfast cereals that they collectively find funnier than Crispix. How could I argue with them? The people have spoken.

This is a perennial question in comedy circles: who is the ultimate arbiter of funny, the professional funny person or the audience? Generally, comedy writers are suspicious of audience laughter as a metric for funniness, knowing that it's possible (and even easy, once you clear a certain skill level) to get laughs with hacky material. Comedians are

---

* It's unclear whether corn exists on the cob planet.

more comfortable with the idea that the audience might know best, because they live and die with every response. They've all had to throw out a personal favorite joke because they just couldn't make it work live. I once watched a documentary about the making of a sketch show that David Cross and Bob Odenkirk put together for Netflix. In one segment, the duo is watching Paget Brewster rehearse an introduction to the blockbuster film "*Transformbots*, about transsexual robot performers." The line isn't working, and Cross is adamant that it's funnier shortened to "transsexual robots." He wants the flat, abrupt laugh of the twist. Odenkirk pitches the exact opposite idea: a meandering punch line that just keeps going. "*Transformbots*, about transsexual robots that can switch their sexual identity at will, and then switch back also, or not be robots either, even." The more convoluted the line gets, the bigger the laugh from onlookers. In the video, Cross is clearly not sold on the change, but he can't say anything, because the new line works. His comedy convictions have been trumped by forces beyond his control.

To me, the interesting viewers in the cob planet controversy aren't the confused ones, for whom the joke didn't land. Almost every joke has those. More revealing to me are the hundreds of others who thought the joke was funny—but, it turned out, couldn't agree on why. Like many ineffable jokes, it grabbed them immediately, and they laughed. But the joke was so elusive, even to them, that they couldn't walk back through the process. Like hypnotists' volunteers making chicken noises onstage, they were unable to explain what exactly they were doing.

Hothouse Flowers and Spanish Toast

The observation that dissection can kill a joke shouldn't surprise us; it's just one special case of the general truth that almost *anything* can kill a joke. At lunch one day, a friend and I started trading fondly recalled stories from the *Onion*. We quickly realized that neither of us was making the other laugh with our favorite headlines—because we weren't quite remembering them perfectly. You'd think that something as tight and elemental as an *Onion* headline ("Drugs Win Drug War," "New Dog Digs Up Old Dog," "Trophy Wife Mounted") would be idiot-proof, but no.

Even a conceptual joke like their famous 2008 Obama headline, "Black Guy Asks Nation for Change," needs to have every word just right, or there's really no point. "Black Candidate Wants"—no, wait. "Black Man Wants Change." "Black Guy Says He Needs Some—" Hold on. Shit.

The jokes seemed simple, but their simplicity had evidently been the result of long and careful effort. They were murdered by paraphrase. Everyone remembers E. B. White's frog comparison in "Some Remarks on Humor," but the very next sentence of the same essay is an even better analogy: he compares jokes to soap bubbles. Humor, he says, "won't stand much blowing up, and it won't stand much poking. It has a certain fragility, an evasiveness, which one had best respect."

When you think about how many different ways there are to kill a joke, it's a wonder that they evolved at all. Chaplin's famous dictum "Life is a tragedy when seen in close-up, but a comedy in long-shot" is essentially an admission that the exact same joke can succeed or fail depending on an accident of geography: how close to the subject you're standing. You can confirm this by watching any Jacques Tati movie, where gags line up precisely to the edge of the frame or some piece of the scenery. The viewer is watching the action from *the one point in the universe* where it's funny. Animator Chuck Jones once quantified the exact margin of error on one of his most famous jokes: Wile E. Coyote, when falling off a cliff, had to hit bottom exactly fourteen frames after he disappeared from sight. "It seemed to me that thirteen frames didn't work in terms of humor, and neither did fifteen frames. Fourteen frames got a laugh."

The implication is that one-twenty-fourth of a second, the flap of a hummingbird's wings, is enough to kill a joke. I was skeptical when I first read Jones tell an interviewer this; it seemed more like mystique-making than actual animation know-how. But I changed my mind after seeing the effect firsthand. One day after taping a *Jeopardy!* tournament on the Sony lot, I got a text from a friend, who happened to be doing the final sound mix for a *Simpsons* episode at a nearby stage.* I walked over to say hi on my way to dinner and ended up staying for over an hour,

---

* The *Simpsons* offices are on the Fox lot. On this day, they were mixing at the Sony lot for some reason.

mesmerized by the fine-tuning of an animated sitcom. A writer could suggest something like, "Can the music be more dramatic here but, like, twenty percent less ominous?" and I would roll my eyes in the dark. But then the engineer would do something to the bass and the drums, and when we watched it again, a miracle would occur: the scene would play funnier. Matt Groening himself was at the mix, which surprised the hell out of me, and at one point he quibbled about the sound made by an attacking Japanese-style robot. (Not a Transformbot, as far as I could tell.) "The lion's roar is good, but it should do it three times, in quick succession." Again, this seemed like gibberish, but the next time the robot attacked, the identical triplet ("ROAR! ROAR ROAR!") made me laugh out loud.*

If moving a camera one foot to the left or delaying a sound effect by a fraction of a second can hamstring humor, you can only imagine what the ravages of time and distance can do to a joke. At any performance of Shakespearean "comedy" today, you'll have a hard time mustering a genuine chuckle at the zany Elizabethan antics of the clown. "Aha, he's thrusting his hips and leering at the crowd! That must have been a sex joke!" It doesn't take five hundred years, either. Watch a typical sitcom from the 1950s, and then watch something from the same era that was dead serious when it was written—an advertisement for cream of wheat, an educational film about good hygiene. Guess which one gets bigger laughs today? It's not fair, but unintentional humor just has a longer shelf life than the intentional kind. Booth Tarkington summed up this Bizarro-world effect of old-timey humor perfectly: "Antique funnyings in print bring on a pleasant melancholy."

Translation across languages is an even more immediate way to see the fragility of humor. Steven Wright's "French toast during the Renaissance" isn't a complicated joke, but just try to tell it in Spanish. First of all, you face the problem that many Spanish-speaking cultures don't exactly have diners. Their closest analogue to a diner might not serve breakfast all

---

* You don't need access to a Culver City mixing stage to experiment with the limits of this phenomenon yourself. YouTube is a great place to sample *The Office* with a laugh track added, *Friends* with its laugh track removed, *The Big Bang Theory* with Ricky Gervais's laughter replacing the studio audience, and all manner of other comedy-killing abominations.

day. And their closest analogue to a diner that serves breakfast all day might not announce "Breakfast anytime" on a sign or menu. And *even if it did*, you're going to have a language problem. In English, we use the same word—"time"—to mean both "time of day" and "historical period," and the joke hinges on that ambiguity. But in Spanish, these are separate words: *hora* and *época*, respectively.*

In other words, the old maxim that "comedy is the universal language" could not be further from the truth. Jokes are the rainforest orchids of the artistic world, too delicate to survive most travel or transplantation. The great all-time international movie stars—Sophia Loren, Toshiro Mifune, Catherine Deneuve, Max von Sydow—are dramatic actors, because good looks and screen presence are near-universal, but every country seems to have some comedy superstar who is almost entirely unknown in the English-speaking world: Totò in Italy, Cantinflas in Mexico, Louis de Funès in France. The weird French embrace of a foreign-born Jerry Lewis or Woody Allen is the exception, not the rule. And the divide is culture as much as it's language: I've labored mightily to include non-American comedians among the examples in this book,† only to face the dispiriting fact that almost no non-American comedy is universal across the English-speaking world. Americans *say* they love that quirky British sense of humor, but they can name maybe five British comedy people tops, and one of them is Benny Hill.

When funniness gets lost in translation, I suspect that the fault often lies with lazy translators, who are too quick to boot a joke as "untranslatable" rather than cast about for a better alternative. As I was thinking about telling the French toast joke in Spanish, for example, I realized there *is* a single word that can be used to mean both kinds of time: *momento*. That might not be enough to save the joke, but it's a start. Sometimes, more radical surgery is required to get laughs to travel across boundaries of time and place. I saw a performance of *Macbeth* at London's Globe Theatre in 2016 where the famous "knocking at the

---

* Neither of them, interestingly, is *tiempo*, the dictionary translation for "time."

† In hopes of getting a book deal in the UK! I'm no dummy. It's like a parallel-universe America where people still buy and read books.

gate" scene, comic relief after the bloody murder of Duncan, broke with Shakespearean tradition by actually being funny. Every night, the actress playing the porter had been given free rein to improvise jokes about Donald Trump, Brexit, and whatever else was in the headlines. Watching her, I remembered reading an article about how Germans in the mid-1990s discovered a new favorite TV show: *Hogan's Heroes*. The thirty-year-old American sitcom, set in a Nazi POW camp, had never found an enthusiastic audience in Germany, *for some reason*. But in 1995, a German broadcaster commissioned a new dub, with broader, sillier humor nowhere to be found in the English-language original (and, naturally, less likely to bear any actual resemblance to World War II). In the newly christened *Ein Käfig voller Helden* ("A Cage Full of Heroes"), a plan to bomb London in one episode became a plot to drop condoms there, cutting off the British war effort via population control. The German Colonel Klink now made frequent references to Kalinka, a never-seen cleaning lady in his employ who worked in the nude. The reimagined show became a smash hit, drawing almost a million viewers a day. Are loose translations like these cheats? Or are they the only faithful way to translate comedy, because at least they preserve the laughs?

The observation that some jokes are "referential" and can survive translation, while others are "verbal" and cannot, goes back to Cicero. But referential humor can fail too, as soon as the references fade. Here's a joke that was insanely popular in Egypt in 1968.

A man narrowly misses a bus, and takes off down the street in pursuit. He's so fast that he catches up with the bus at the end of the block, and hops aboard. The conductor, seeing this feat, only charges him half fare.

That's it. That's the joke.

Feel free to close this book for a few hours or weeks or years and ponder the punch line—it will get you nowhere. I'm confident that you could spin theories about the bus joke indefinitely and never even get close to the gist of it. It's French toast during the Renaissance, specific to a single time and place. To understand it, you need three crucial pieces of information that Egyptians in 1968 would have known off the top of their heads:

1. Military personnel pay half fares on Egyptian city buses.
2. Egypt in 1968 had just lost the Six-Day War to Israel in decisive and demoralizing fashion.
3. As a result, jokes were often powered by the stereotype of the cowardly Egyptian soldier, the kind of jokes that got told about the Italians a century ago and are still heard about the French today.*

Now you can probably piece it together: the conductor saw how fast the man was running, realized that only a soldier who had recently been running away from the Israeli army could be so fleet of foot, and charged him the soldier's discount. Now you're laughing!

The fragility of comedy means that it's always transitory, and therefore doomed. The addition of a few catchy tunes can resurrect a timeworn piece of tragedy like Victor Hugo's *Les Misérables* or Hans Christian Andersen's "The Snow Queen" into a worldwide phenomenon, but that just doesn't happen to comedy. When comedy is dead, it's dead. No professionally funny person wants to face this truth, but their very best work, the stuff that left millions rolling in the aisles, will leave no legacy. At the time Booth Tarkington was lamenting "antique funnyings," he was perhaps the leading humorist in America, acclaimed as the successor to Mark Twain for his *Penrod* stories of Midwestern boyhood. Today, he's an antique funnying himself. The *Penrod* books have been out of print for decades.

Chasing Absurdity

In the 1970s, Andy Kaufman essentially invented a new kind of a laughter, the laugh of incredulity. He would do one of his oddball anticomedy set pieces—singing along with the *Mighty Mouse* theme, donning an Indian

---

* Did you hear about the new French tanks with fifteen gears? Fourteen are reverse, and one goes forward . . . in case the enemy attacks from behind.

headdress to revive an elderly woman who had collapsed onstage—and people would laugh because they couldn't quite believe what they were seeing. It was performance art.

Kaufman's act was iconic because it was completely unprecedented, but today, the incredulity laugh is everywhere in comedy. Now it's the mainstream. On *Saturday Night Live*, experimental sketches that would once have been quarter-to-one filler can go viral overnight and become water-cooler catchphrases by Monday morning. An uncategorizable and eccentric genius like Reggie Watts can be a beloved late-night sidekick. On *Conan*, Tig Notaro might stop telling jokes altogether and push a squeaky stool across the stage for two or three minutes. Comedians Kurt Braunohler and Kristen Schaal can go as long as *ten* minutes onstage with their endlessly repeating, increasingly maniacal "Kristen Schaal is a horse" hoedown dance.* Good luck trying to explain to your ninety-year-old grandpa, who fought in Korea, why you're in hysterics over a half-hour Adult Swim special where two comedians golf very badly. ("The one playing golfer John Daly is a comedian named Jon Daly, and the one playing golfer Adam Scott is a comedian named Adam Scott. That's what's so funny, Grandpa! They have the same name.") I don't think any particular historical theory of humor will ever explain all laughter, but the incongruity theory has never been more convincing. The "unresolved incongruity" joke, the kind that starts weird and stays weird, is now our default joke.†

The rise of the non sequitur is, in large part, just the hunger for novelty. We got so good at comedy that "well constructed" no longer seemed funny—it was "inspired" or nothing. But the jokes that match this new sensibility are more subjective and more fragile than ever before, because we scarcely know what we're laughing at ourselves. These new funny-for-no-reason jokes are even more vulnerable to the endless scramble for novelty, because they rely so much on a mysterious, reflexive response.

---

* The sketch can't really be described. You're going to have to find a clip.

† And it's only getting weirder. When the web video series *Lasagna Cat* began in 2008, straight-faced reenactments of old *Garfield* strips were cutting-edge weirdness. By the time the show returned in 2017, however, it took more to push the envelope. The new crop of *Garfield*-themed "comedy" videos included a five-hour recitation of real-life responses to a telephone sex survey, with a graphic horror-movie conclusion.

If you don't "get it," there's nothing to get. Cranberry bogs seem marginally funny to me today only because they are, in my experience, an *untapped* vein for comedy. (And also, in some cases, for cranberries.) If I were to run across an old *Family Guy* episode with sixteen cranberry bog jokes, that would about do it. From then on, it would probably take a different, more obscure kind of bog to crack me up.

But the modern taste for absurd jokes also says something about the times we live in. For centuries, religion provided people with a sense of meaning and order in a cruel, random world. It's not a coincidence that the rise of comedy and the decline of faith happened in the same century. Religion says of life, "This sucks, but it's God's will." Humor says, "This sucks, but look, at least it's funny." The effect is largely the same, but it's easier, and lowers the stakes considerably. (A lousy sense of humor might annoy your peers, but you won't burn forever in hell.) As Eric Idle sings during the crucifixion scene in *Life of Brian*, "life is quite absurd and death's the final word," but that doesn't mean you can't look on the bright side of life. And we shouldn't be surprised when that means making jokes that are just as inexplicable as the universe itself.

In Isaac Asimov's 1956 short story "Jokester," a computer scientist of the future becomes obsessed with the mystery of humor—where jokes come from, what makes things funny. He programs the world's jokes into a supercomputer and asks the computer to trace them back to their starting point. The answer that comes back is startling: "Extraterrestrial origin." According to the infallible computer, higher intelligences have seeded our culture with jokes as a psychological test, and once humanity discovers this fact, the experiment will become useless and therefore must be brought to a close. The computer scientist and his colleagues sit staring glumly at the results, and none of them can think of a single joke. "The gift of humor is gone," one of them realizes. "No man will ever laugh again."

In our alternate future, we also became hyper-savvy about the DNA of jokes, and developed abstruse academic disciplines to study them.* But for the most part, we dodged Asimov's bullet. The old joke forms

* Even, sometimes, using computers, as we will see in chapter 6.

did start to seem stale and joyless over time, but we found new, stranger stuff to laugh at. We started to see the humor that could be inherent in smaller things: an eccentric turn of phrase, an old-timey trope, a funny reference to some bit of cultural detritus. I'm not sure if this can continue indefinitely, if we can keep finding more and more unlikely things to laugh at. But so far we've come out smelling like roses—which may or may not contain ready-to-sting bees.

THREE

THE MARCH OF PROGRESS

In April 1965, a young Woody Allen took the stage at a Washington, D.C., nightclub called the Shadows, on M Street near Georgetown University. At the urging of his manager, Jack Rollins, the playwright and wunderkind TV joke writer had taken up touring as a stand-up comic, developing the gulping nebbish persona that would propel him into his film career. The set was recorded and released later that year as his second hit comedy album.

At one point in the set, Allen tried out a joke about "the pill," still a hot topic in 1965. "I must pause for one fast second and say a fast word about oral contraception," he said. "I was involved in an extremely good example of oral contraception two weeks ago. I asked a girl to go to bed with me, and she said no."*

Listening to the record today, the audience response is hard to believe. There's a second or two of silence before one guy gets the joke and guffaws loudly. It's fully three to five seconds before most of the crowd catches on and starts laughing along. But then the laughter goes on and on, giving Allen one of his best responses of the night.

What amazed me when I first heard the record was that moment of complete silence. I kept listening to the pause over and over: dead air, the sound of a joke making its way through a crowded room completely unnoticed. Here's the deal with the silence: *everyone is still waiting to hear what happened after the girl said no!* When, they wondered, is this going

---

* Yes, this is a Woody Allen joke about sexual consent, and you are correct to note the irony. It's harder to separate the art from the artist when the artist never tried particularly hard to keep them separate either.

to get back around to birth control pills? When one person finally gets the joke, the crowd, hearing him laugh, suddenly has to consider that they've missed the punch line. It takes them a second of backtracking to connect the "oral" in the setup to "she said no," but when they do, it's a cascade of laughter.

Today, a joke like this one would not be a hand grenade with a four-second fuse. The pause stood out to me because "she said no" immediately struck me as the punch line of a pretty well-constructed joke, and I couldn't believe it was being met with silence. A modern crowd, I thought, would catch on immediately. Some of the quicker comedy minds might even see it coming, based on other contraception jokes they've heard with a similar premise—like the old military joke of calling ugly frames "birth control glasses."

Funny doesn't just change; it evolves. It shambles out of the mire, learns to stand up straight, discovers new tricks and tools. Individual species branch off from the tree of comedy life and thrive and eventually die when there's no longer an ecological niche for them. When the "Tupac is still alive" trope caught on, "Elvis is alive" jokes went away. They were competing for the same resources, and we didn't need both. But the field as a whole advances as well. Woody Allen's birth control joke could blow minds in 1965; today it's old hat. This is true of all of yesterday's comedians, even the greats. David Brenner was one of the sharpest observational comics of all time, but in his 1971 *Tonight Show* debut, he did a full six minutes on how men don't like to ask for directions. On his landmark album *Class Clown*, George Carlin got big laughs and even applause for demonstrating how kids make farting sounds with their armpits. The routines are still funny, but today they immediately strike you as period pieces, like when you see a car or a hairstyle from the same era. They're a little quaint, even silly. They cover old ground.

In contrast, jokes today have evolved into forms that a 1965 audience would probably not even be able to identify as comedy. We've already seen how the endless hunger for novelty has pushed comedy into new frontiers of absurdity, but the advances in speed, sophistication, and complexity have been just as dramatic. Familiarity breeds contentment, at best. Laughter, on the other hand, comes from sudden discovery.

Monkey Puzzles

Many scientists today wonder if laughter's relationship to discovery could be evolutionary for humans as well—if we as a species might have been evolving along with the jokes. The ancient Greeks believed that the diaphragm muscle was the seat of humor appreciation, which is why the nearby armpits are the most ticklish part of the body. Our knowledge about the neurology of humor has advanced since then, but it's still rudimentary, because humor processing is so complex that it seems to encompass pretty much every part of human cognition. In 2001, a group of London scientists used MRIs to scan the brains of people listening to jokes, as well as those of a control group listening to unfunny jokelike constructions.* This study, and a similar one done at Stanford in 2003 using cartoons, found that there is no one "humor area" of the brain. Instead, when humor was processed, the whole brain lit up like Times Square. Neural activity rose in all four lobes of the cerebral cortex, though different areas were more involved in different types of jokes. Conceptual jokes led to activity in parts of the brain that process language semantically, while puns were handled by the part of the brain that interprets the sounds of speech. A UCLA neurosurgeon discovered in 1998 that he could make a patient feel enough amusement to laugh out loud, just by zapping a certain area in her frontal lobe. When the doctors asked her why she was laughing, she said, "You guys are just so funny, standing around."

Beneath all that, the MRIs found that emotional response to jokes was just as important. Funnier jokes led to bigger responses in the brain's pleasure centers—the neurons that fire when you eat a cookie, have sex, enjoy art you like, or shoot up heroin—as well as the parts of the prefrontal cortex that integrate reason with emotion. So you "get" a joke up in your smarty-pants frontal and temporal cortices, and then "enjoy" it deep down in your early-mammalian limbic system.

In 2004, a Tufts undergraduate named Matthew Hurley proposed an honors thesis on the evolutionary origins of humor. Because his thesis

---

* Jay Leno monologues. Kidding! Just kidding.

adviser was Daniel Dennett, the bestselling writer and philosopher, the thesis was later expanded into a book, *Inside Jokes*. In the book, Hurley, Dennett, and psychologist Reginald Adams argue that our ability to understand and survive the world is directly connected to what our brain finds funny. They propose that joking arose at some point in our primate past as a way to make sense of life's little weirdnesses, the juxtaposed incongruities at the core of Kant's humor theory. Your great-great-[130 full pages of "great"s omitted]-great-grandmother reached for a fish in a stream but was misled by the refraction of the water and grabbed her own foot instead. Your great-great-[same joke]-great-grandfather was standing too close to the cooking fire when the wind changed and got a lungful of smoke. The hominids who merely got frustrated with little glitches like these died out; the ones who could analyze them solved the problem and lived long enough to contribute to the gene pool. Evolution in action.

But this process only works if there's a short-term reward involved—in other words, if doing the "fittest" thing also feels good. So the pleasures of eating and sex evolved to make sure our dumb brains didn't die out from never feeling like eating and having sex. In the same way, amusement or mirth* evolved to make it pleasurable for us to notice the little absurdities and mistakes in our thinking, so we could understand and fix them. For immediately life-threatening stimuli (lightning, large snakes) we had already evolved good responses like "running away" and "hitting things with rocks," so the humor response was a finer-tuned thing, which evolved so we would enjoy figuring out mistaken assumptions too innocuous to be immediately harmful. Humor researcher Peter McGraw calls this the "benign violation" theory of humor: we laugh at things that are somehow wrong, but not *dangerously* so. A situation that's not quite wrong enough doesn't produce a laugh, but neither will a situation that's *too* wrong.

---

* Hurley et al. use these two words interchangeably for "the good feeling of finding something funny," which just goes to show that English doesn't really have a good word for that. "Amusement" is so detached and clinical; "mirth" sounds downright Dickensian. How can you feel "mirth" if you're not a large British man drinking spiced wine at a Victorian Christmas party? As a result, other humor researchers use "comedy" to mean "humor" (the stimulus) and "humor" to mean "amusement" (the response), which is even more confusing.

If Hurley's reasoning is correct, then we owe our brains—we owe our very civilization—to our sense of humor.

Formula and Novelty

Fast-forward one million years. Humor for modern humans is very different than it was in the Stone Age. Like the smartest rat in the lab, we learned how to get to the food dispenser without running the maze. We invented jokes.

When our primitive ancestors laughed because Ogg had tripped over a vine in the path, there was an evolutionary advantage there: we had to figure out how to avoid the vine. But today, organic, "in the wild" humor stimuli like that one are outnumbered by hundreds of examples of engineered humor, *designed* to get a laugh. Most of our modern jokes are cheats, ways for us to stimulate the amusement reflex without actually learning anything useful. In other words, our multibillion-dollar laff industry exists to *create* fake little bugs in our worldview, and then quickly demolish them.

If you open up Facebook and your dad has posted a joke like, "I bought the world's worst thesaurus yesterday. Not only is it terrible, but it's terrible," there's a moment where the brain has to close a loop. Not only is it terrible, but it's . . . *terrible?* That's literally the last adjective your brain expected to hear there. Oh *right*, "worst thesaurus"! Got it. The glitch has been understood, and you're rewarded with the little charge of mild amusement. In 1965, Woody Allen stood silently on a nightclub stage for over three seconds while he waited for this same evolutionary process to finish.

But that little short circuit only works once. The next time it hears a similar joke, the brain will already know the trick, and the trigger to our reward system won't be so intense. That explains our insatiable appetite for the *new* in comedy. I can watch *It's a Wonderful Life* twenty Christmases in a row and get a little weepy every time, but the same jokes in *Groundhog Day* weren't laugh-out-loud funny to me anymore on a second or third rewatch. For a testament to the short shelf life of funny, check out the "Humor" section of any used-book store, the endless rows of old P. J. O'Rourke books and *Garfield* collections. Whether they've aged well or not, the owner never wanted to reread them. For the most part, jokes are a single-use item, like Kleenex.

There have always been more people who wanted to tell jokes than people who could think up good ones. The stereotype of the unoriginal jokester goes back to the Roman playwright Plautus, who in his comedy *Stichus* introduced the character Gelasimus ("laughable"). Gelasimus is a social parasite who uses a book of prewritten jokes to wangle invitations to things, the ancestor of the twentieth-century traveling salesman trying to close a deal with tired jokes and saucy French postcards. In fact, many of the ancient world's gags still circulate today, to judge by *Philogelos*, the fourth-century Roman text that's the world's oldest surviving joke collection. Here's one excerpt from the *Philogelos*: "When the garrulous barber asks him, 'How shall I cut your hair?' a quick wit answers, 'Silently.'" The same joke was still being told about the notorious British politician Enoch Powell well into the 1980s.

So Mark Twain was right in *A Connecticut Yankee in King Arthur's Court* when he speculated about the ancient origins of today's old-chestnut jokes. The time-traveling Yankee, listening to a medieval after-dinner speech by a knight of the Round Table, says,

> I think I never heard so many old played-out jokes strung together in my life. He was worse than the minstrels, worse than the clown in the circus. It seemed peculiarly sad to sit here, thirteen hundred years before I was born, and listen again to poor, flat, worm-eaten jokes that had given me the dry gripes when I was a boy thirteen hundred years afterwards. It about convinced me that there isn't any such thing as a new joke possible. Everybody laughed at these antiquities—but then they always do; I had noticed that, centuries later.

Twain noticed that comedy audiences would put up with old material, though I imagine no one liked it much. There was just no other game in town. In the vaudeville era, even the best comedians cycled through the same quasi–public domain trove of sketches and routines—you could go years without having to write a joke. Abbott and Costello made their

"Who's on First" routine a hit when they performed it on Kate Smith's radio show in 1938, but it was based on a standard baseball routine that had been making the rounds in burlesque for almost a decade. Milton Berle lifted so many bits from other performers that he would even joke about his own joke theft in his act.*

But with literally thousands of comedy outlets available today, recycled jokes don't get far. Whole art forms have largely vanished in the rush for novelty. Take newspaper comics, which lean heavily on repetition and familiarity. Even a genuinely inspired strip like George Herriman's *Krazy Kat* could repeat the same simple setup—a mischievous mouse trying to throw a brick at a deeply flattered cat—every single day for thirty years. Critic Gilbert Seldes loved *Krazy Kat*, but that didn't prevent him from quipping, "According to my records, the last time a grown man laughed at a comic strip was in February of 1904, but that may be a typographical error. So far as I know, no child, male or female, has ever laughed at the funny pages. Something is wrong. Perhaps with the comics. Perhaps with the name."

Or consider the midcentury sitcom, which would often repeat the same formulaic plots week after week. Beaver gets into trouble and needs some sage advice from Pop. Samantha's magical powers screw up Darrin's important business whatever. Familiar stories would even recur on show after show, like Aristotle's six basic plots: a power outage, two dates at once, an egg babysitting assignment. In the sitcom, everything is okay: all families are happy, and all problems get resolved in twenty-five minutes. It's not exactly what you'd call the funniest take on life, but it was the dominant comedic form in America for decades.

I always associate the decline of the sitcom formula with Paul Feig and Judd Apatow's short-lived teen comedy *Freaks and Geeks*, because I still bear the scars of its unforgettable sixth episode, the one where Jason Segel's character Nick pursues his dreams of rock stardom as a drummer. Nick's hardcase father is threatening him with the army, but then his friend Lindsay sees a flyer about a top local band in need of a drummer. This is it, a way out! Years of TV watching had taught me, I

---

* Berle's peers nicknamed him the "Thief of Bad Gags," which was a funny and topical pun in the 1940s.

believed, where this was going. But then I got to the painful audition scene, where Nick flames out behind the drum kit and everyone—the band, Lindsay, the viewer, Nick himself—realizes at the same time that he'll never be a professional musician. As is true for most of us, his enthusiasm for something he loves outstrips his talent. It was the first time I'd ever seen a TV comedy subvert the familiar sitcom life lesson with such honest, brutal abandon.

In hindsight, we can see that unsurprising, conservative genres like newspaper comics and three-camera family sitcoms were perfect at what they were designed to do: not offend anyone enough for them to cancel their subscription or change the channel. In an era of little choice, comedy didn't actually have to be *funny*. As soon as there was more interesting competition—*Mad* magazine was funnier than *Blondie*, David Letterman was funnier than *Happy Days*—they hurriedly adapted, produced a late flowering of great art (*The Far Side* and *Calvin and Hobbes*, *Frasier* and *Roseanne*), and faded away.

Mockumentaries and Callbacks

When we move on from old jokes and forms, the replacement can't be merely different. The next joke has to be a little more advanced in some way: a little more complex, a little more subtle, a little more outré. As Jim Downey, the veteran *Saturday Night Live* writer, said of comedy, "Advances are made, and we must always move forward, never backward. . . . Once something has been done, it should perhaps be built upon, but never repeated."

These might be advances in structure. Gone are the days when a comedy routine was just a series of one-liners, maybe grouped into chunks by topic if the comic had two or three good lines that could be linked up. Mike Birbiglia's solo comedy shows have the joke density of a modern stand-up routine, but cleverly shaped into a single virtuoso monologue, an overarching whole. *My Girlfriend's Boyfriend*, his second one-man show, jumps back and forth in time from a 2007 car crash to his courtship of his wife, Jen Stein, to his romantic misadventures in adolescence. Flashbacks are nested within flashbacks, and the routine is packed with comic asides on subjects from airport Cinnabon stalls to unsafe carnival rides, but the audience is so invested in Birbiglia's relationship history that it never loses its place. If you were to graph the routine, it would look something like this:

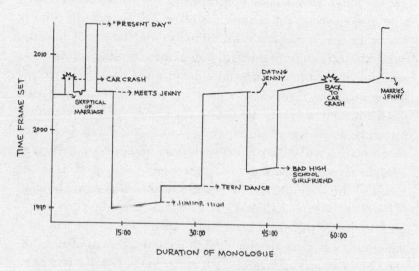

There are entire *genres* today that no one would have even recognized as comedy a few decades ago. When Albert Brooks created his ersatz "Famous School for Comedians" in a 1971 *Esquire* article and subsequent short film,* the "mockumentary" didn't really exist yet. As a result, the magazine got thousands of real letters inquiring about admission to the fictional comedy school. Likewise, I once rented *This Is Spinal Tap* in high school and couldn't figure out why my friend's date wasn't laughing. After the movie, we found out she thought it was a real documentary about a real band.† It's hard to believe if you grew up on Christopher

---

* Sample fill-in-the-blank question from the school's Comedy Talent Test: "Knock knock." "Who's there?" "Sam and Janet." "Sam and Janet who?" "Sam and Janet _____." A. evening B. (comma) the Bloomfields C. (comma) you know, Jimmy's friends.

† For decades, I couldn't get over this. *Even the exploding drummer?* But then I read an interview with Noel Gallagher of Oasis in which he admitted that his brother Liam—an actual rock star!—thought for years that Spinal Tap was a real band.

Guest movies and *Larry Sanders* and *Modern Family*, but audiences needed years of training to process fake documentaries.

Old devices might stick around, but they need to adapt. The callback, for example, has long been a staple of comedy in almost every medium. The canonical callback is a simple reference to a joke earlier in the act, a little joke encore. For example, on Hannibal Buress's first comedy record, he does a couple absurd minutes on an unusual Christmas present he just bought for himself: a set of metal prosthetic arms. "You never know when you're gonna lose an arm, and I want to be prepared for the situation." He describes some of the advantages of owning spare metal arms and moves on. But then, half an hour later, as he's finishing his set, he does a joke about insulting his one-year-old nephew who's always playing with his computer keyboard: "You can't type!" He then imagines his nephew growing up to get revenge by cutting off his Uncle's hands. "Naw, *you* can't type!" When the laughter dies down, he adds, "I'll be like, 'Whatever, dude, I got these metal arms right over here.'" Huge audience response! Buress hasn't actually mined any new jokes out of the metal-arms premise; he's just reminded the crowd about the good times we had laughing about it earlier in the evening. It's like we have a little in-joke with him now! The satisfying sense of closure makes it a good way to finish up an act.

But too many of those can start to seem formulaic, so the callback had to mutate in increasingly baroque ways. In his Netflix specials, Bill Burr has tried callbacks to favorite bits from *other* routines, and sure enough, the audience remembered. In March 2016, John Oliver interrupted a *Last Week Tonight* monologue about a Mexican border wall to talk seriously about ladder shopping for a moment. "Avoid Werner," he said. "Do yourself a favor and get a DeWalt ladder. And I'm not being paid to say that!" This might sound like nothing more than a committed bit of ladder-brand silliness, but hard-core fans remembered that this was a callback to a quick 2015 joke on college basketball, when Oliver had complained that Werner, despite being the official ladder of the NCAA, was "pure shit." "I'm a DeWalt man," he had assured the audience. "I'm not a ladder idiot." The *Last Week Tonight* writers had waited a full year to do the callback. Now that's commitment.

But nobody played twelve-dimensional chess with callbacks like Mitchell Hurwitz, the creator of the cult single-camera comedy *Arrested Development*. Taking advantage of the shift in TV watching to DVRs and DVDs, Hurwitz and the show's writers filled each episode of the series to the brim with tiny micro-gags and odd bits of business that might only make sense with repeated viewings. If these were Easter eggs, they were as finely filigreed as a Fabergé. Hurwitz's most extravagant innovation was probably the "call-forward": dropping in references to jokes that *hadn't even happened yet*. For example, the first half of the show's second season is filled with perplexing little gags about the left hand of Tony Hale's character Buster. Then, in episode eleven, he loses that hand when a seal bites it off. The call-forwards don't even rise to the level of jokes (at one point, Buster sits down on a bench that reads "Army Surplus Office Supply," covering most of the ad so the only visible letters read "Arm Off")—*except in retrospect*. Only on a second viewing, or to higher-dimensional beings who can see all of time and comedy as a single geometric solid, do they get a laugh.* When the show was revived on Netflix in 2013, Hurwitz took advantage of the new streaming video paradigm to push the weird comedy math as far as it would go. Each episode followed different characters through interwoven, overlapping timelines, so that in theory the season could be watched in any order at all. The plan didn't quite come off, but it was certainly ambitious. Long stretches of early episodes were virtually incomprehensible until later episodes circled back and filled in the plot gaps.

This Place Has Everything

As comedy structures branched into increasingly intricate fractals, the jokes they held had to become more complex and delicate as well. Improv guru Del Close used to tell his students to wait for their third thought— they could avoid stereotypes and obvious comebacks and hackery by

---

* The *Arrested Development* writers sometimes even wrote call-forwards to jokes that would *never* get made. The series drops repeated hints that David Cross's character, Tobias, is not Caucasian at all, but rather a black man with a skin condition—but no actual joke or plot twist ever results. Was this an extremely deft hidden-ball play, or just a plotline abandoned due to the vagaries of serialization?

not using the first joke idea that came to mind, even if it was funny. Heighten the idea, refine it. Today the air is even more rarefied. Every week, the staff of the *Onion* generates about five hundred headlines for every one that actually gets published, the comedy version of a sushi chef using only the single fattiest part of the tuna belly and throwing the rest of the hundred-pound carcass into the chum bucket. The image of the lone comedy genius scratching away at a notepad or hunched in front of a typewriter is out of fashion, because no one writer can produce the joke density and novelty that a modern audience expects. Sitcoms and even movies now have *rooms* like NASA Mission Control has rooms, places where a dozen of the sharpest comedy minds available can sit for days rewriting and polishing every facet of a script.

"Reference humor" was a relative novelty when Dennis Miller made his reputation on it in the 1990s. Lenny Bruce and Woody Allen had discovered that you could make a joke funnier by adding a current newsmaker or brand name ("Bobby Breen"! "Fresca"!), but Miller's tortured similes made the reference itself the whole joke. "The current tax code is harder to understand than Bob Dylan reading *Finnegans Wake* in a wind tunnel," he would smirk, and the laughs would be laughs of self-congratulation: "I understood the gist of that thing he said!" Not to laugh would be tantamount to a confession: I'm a big bonehead. Miller showed that a sufficiently confident head-waggle and hair-preen could put over *any* reference, no matter what tiny percentage of the crowd had actually seen the *Partridge Family* episode in question. (A 1999 *Simpsons* joke called one-in-a-million odds the "Dennis Miller Ratio," for this very reason.) His HBO "rants" briefly propelled him to comedy superstardom, before 9/11 converted him into a deeply frightened conservative pundit almost overnight.

The intensification of twenty-first-century comedy upped the ante on references as well. If Dennis Miller is using *Moby-Dick* and James Lipton as punch lines—well, you don't want to seem less hip than a *Monday Night Football* color guy, right? So the comedy/folk duo Garfunkel and Oates dropped rhymes about Hashimoto's thyroiditis and the decline of the Whig Party after Millard Fillmore's presidency, and Bill Hader imagined Dan Cortese club-hopping with the principal from *Kindergarten*

Cop as *Saturday Night Live*'s "Stefon."* *Family Guy* hoped that everyone remembered the 1997 drunk driving arrest of Ukrainian figure skater Oksana Baiul. *Community* even introduced a major character, Danny Pudi's Abed, whose entire shtick was his ability to see quirky pop culture comparisons in every show's plotline.

Does it all seem a little lazy, getting laughs by merely mentioning a topic instead of having to, you know, think up an actual joke about it? Maybe. But my jaw dropped when I heard Patton Oswalt name-check "the short stories of Tillie Olsen" on a 2007 album—I felt an instant, visceral connection to the material that I hadn't before. It's nice to sometimes be on the right side of the Dennis Miller Ratio, feel like one of the cool kids. If nothing else, there's nostalgic pleasure in thinking about a pop-cultural footnote for the first time in years, like paging through a high school yearbook. Hey, look, Dan Cortese!

The Soul of Wit

If people a generation or two ago were brought to the present and, for some reason, forced to watch television comedy, the first thing they would notice—well, the first thing would probably be the cell phones. But the *second* thing they'd notice would be the pacing. For evidence of this, put on a show that's aged a bit but that you still think of as "modern." Watch an early *Seinfeld*. It all feels so leisurely now! In the first act of the show, whole scenes sometimes go by without a laugh, just to introduce or advance the relationship or social ambiguity that the plot turns on. Characters cross paths in Jerry's apartment and just putter aimlessly for a few minutes, like in real life.

The first speed revolution in humor was a transatlantic one: Americans loved to gloat over how pithy and direct their jokes were, in comparison to the snoozy stuff that passed for "humour" in the mother country. "An Englishman wants hiz fun smothered deep in mint sauce, and he iz willing

---

* On that October 2014 show, guest star Bill Hader "broke" no fewer than three times over the reference to 1990s MTV stud Dan Cortese. Writer John Mulaney would often add new jokes to Stefon bits between *SNL*'s dress rehearsal and the live broadcast, in hopes of cracking up Hader on-air when he saw the altered cue cards for the first time.

tew wait till next day before he tastes it," wrote Josh Billings. (There's that hilarious frontier spelling again.) "If you tickle or convince an Amerikan, yu hav got tew do it quick. An Amerikan luvs tew laff, but he don't luv tew make a bizzness ov it; he works, eats and hawhaws on a canter." The Canadian humorist Stephen Leacock noticed the difference immediately: "Mark Twain can be quoted in single sentences, Dickens mostly in pages."*

At the turn of the century, Wilbur Nesbit, who wrote a humor column for the *Baltimore News-American* as "Josh Wink," complained that the American joke speed-up was making his job much harder. "To-day the joke, or the humorous article, is funny all the way through. In other days it was enough to write on and on, with minute and detailed description, leading up to the comic denouement in the last two lines. Now the risibilities of the reader must be aroused with the opening line." What's wrong with these kids today, who won't sit through pages of "detailed description" to get to a punch line?

But American jokes really kicked into high gear with the 1925 debut of the *New Yorker*. In a prospectus that appeared on posters all over New York City, and was reprinted in the magazine's first issue, founding editor in chief Harold Ross famously wrote, "*The New Yorker* will be the magazine which is not edited for the old lady in Dubuque." It's hard to believe now, but in the early twentieth century, the dominant voice in American humor was rural. A full third of the country still lived on farms, and jokes were droll and folksy, yarns spun by slow talkers. (It's no accident that old-fashioned jokes are still called "corny," literally springing from the cornfields.) At the turn of the century, no New York paper even had a humor columnist—that was a Midwestern thing, a regional phenomenon centered in Chicago.

No longer! Today the reputation of the *New Yorker* is mostly built on its highbrow cultural commentary, but for its first decade or two, it was read first and foremost for laughs. As early as the second issue, Ross was purporting to be "astonished and alarmed as much as anybody else at the tone of levity and farce that seemed to pervade it . . . above all we don't

---

* The Victorian satirist Samuel Butler felt, in return, that Canada fell on the wrong side of this divide, opining that Canadian jokes were, "like their roads, very long and not very good." Shots fired!

want to be taken as a humorous magazine." But these faintly disingen-
uous protests were to no avail. The *New Yorker* ushered in a new era in
American humor writing, one in which the jokesters—Thurber, Benchley,
Clarence Day, S. J. Perelman—were contemporary and sophisticated.
Timelessness was out. The new tone reflected the blithe, world-weary
conviviality of Manhattan society, and the pace reflected the rapid-fire
immediacy of big-city talk in general and Jewish humor in particular.
The magazine's "Talk of the Town" section captured city life in vivid,
witty little snapshots, with the camera lens moving on to the next theater
opening or nightspot before the reader could tire of the last. Cartoons,
which had begun as full-page, elaborately captioned engravings in *Punch*
and then shrank to strips in *Life*, were now just a single panel, often
doodled as simply as possible to convey the joke. "Its essence lies in its
brevity," wrote Stephen Leacock of modern humor. "It must be as short
as possible, and then a little shorter still."

This new economy wasn't forced upon jokes; it was a natural fit for
them. If, as Ricky Gervais once said, a joke is "the minimum amount
of words to get to a punch line," then by definition each setup needs
to convey all the information necessary for the laugh, *but no more*. Any
additional detail isn't just extraneous—it's actively confusing to the listener. ("But why did the first salesman have to be Catholic?") It's a plot
hole, an undropped shoe. This is why jokes sometimes even come with
their own clipped syntax, like a telegram, dropping any article or linking
verb that might delay the punch line by even a syllable. Man walks into
a bar. Your momma so ugly. The smallness of jokes is so essential that
comedy routines are even *called* "bits."*

---

* Comedy also needs brevity because it doesn't sustain the way other art forms do. There's a reason why
no comedian will do a set the length of a Springsteen concert: the audience would burn out. The modern TV
convention of "half hour = comedy, hour = drama" isn't new. Even in ancient Athens, the satyr plays were
much shorter than the tragedies. The twelve Shakespeare plays listed as tragedies in the First Folio are, on
average, 3,242 lines long. The fourteen comedies average out to just 2,570 lines apiece. (Interestingly, the
most common chronology has the Bard's work getting longer and more serious as he got older, sort of like
an Elizabethan Judd Apatow. After alternating comedies and dramas for many years, he followed *Measure
for Measure* with seven heavy tragedies in a row. Then he finished his career with three "romances," which
are structured like comedies but aren't funny. Like *Funny People* with Adam Sandler.)

Brevity even explains the comic "rule of three" principle, which holds that groupings of three items are funnier than those of any other size. Like this: Frank Drebin in *The Naked Gun* telling a woman, "Jane, since I've met you, I've noticed things that I never knew were there before: birds singing, dew glistening on a newly formed leaf, stoplights." Note that there's nothing inherently magical or mathematically perfect about the number three. Three is funny only because it's the shortest list that can set up a pattern and then break it with a surprising final item. A set of two is just a pair; there's no rhythm. A set of four works in theory, but it feels cluttered, because the audience can sense that it's *one more example than you actually needed.*

One casualty of the new comedy pace was the double act, the familiar comedy duo of the straight man and the clown. Once the dominant form in comedy (Laurel and Hardy, George and Gracie, Abbott and Costello, Lewis and Martin), the double act had a hard time competing in a faster comedy ecosystem. "Why is half the material here coming from someone whose role is *not* to be funny?" an audience member could be forgiven for wondering. "Do we need that guy? Would this have twice as many laughs without him?" Solo comedians, by contrast, can make a playground out of joke brevity. Steven Wright, who constructs sets out of a seemingly endless series of non sequitur one-liners, got delighted applause out of a seven-word joke: "Today, I was . . . no, that wasn't me." But even that is a rambling shaggy-dog story compared to George Carlin's famous three-word joke, "Tonight's forecast: dark." Robin Williams sped up comedy without lowering the word count, zipping through a manic flail of voices and poses so fast that his manager once had to hire a court stenographer to transcribe the material. Williams had made the same discovery as the Marx Brothers: speed is *inherently* funny. In *Duck Soup*, Groucho notes that Chico "may look like an idiot and talk like an idiot, but don't let that fool you. He really is an idiot." Slow it down and that's not actually a clever line. The turn doesn't make any logical sense—but the rat-a-tat sells the joke. Similarly, when Robin Williams switched from a Jamaican accent to a Yiddish one in the middle of his Pacino impression, it didn't even matter what the joke was. You were laughing at the sheer dexterity, the hyperactive whir of it.

Faster than Life

The *New Yorker* brought humor into the twentieth century, but the real speed explosion came with radio and television. The surprising torpor of early *Seinfeld*—a show that otherwise still feels very contemporary—inspired me to take a closer look at the rising pace of sitcoms over the past fifty years. I watched a sample episode of a popular sitcom from each of the last six decades (the second-season premiere of each, for uniformity) and counted laughs—not just places where *I* necessarily laughed out loud, or the laugh track did, but every point where an actor or writer might reasonably hope to amuse. Just for kicks, I tacked the fastest-paced contemporary comedy I could think of—Netflix's *Unbreakable Kimmy Schmidt*—onto the end of the graph. Here's how the LPM (laughs per minute) changed over time.

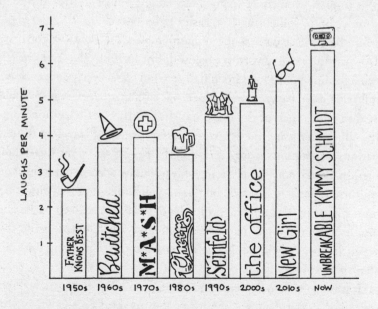

This isn't an exhaustive survey, of course. The upward trend might have been a little less clear if my 1950s sitcom episode had been a frantic *I Love Lucy* instead of a sedate *Father Knows Best*,* or if I'd used the

---

* Especially since *Lucy*'s second-season premiere was the "chocolate conveyor belt" episode.

joke-rich *Friends* for the 1990s and followed that up with two decades of more organically paced semi-mockumentaries (*Curb Your Enthusiasm*, *Modern Family*). But there's no getting around it: twenty-first-century comedies can pack in two to three times the jokes that our grandparents were accustomed to.

The speedup wasn't just a result of shorter attention spans in the post-war era—it helped create them. Accelerated comedy had to be invented. Ernie Kovacs discovered that the abruptness of a joke could be the whole point, like his famous sight gag in which a used-car dealer taps the roof of a car, only to have it fall through the pavement. (This six-second bit cost $12,000, to the annoyance of Kovacs's sponsors.) Then *Laugh-In* discovered you could construct an entire hour of quick blackouts like these.* Monty Python discovered that sketches didn't need to end with a neat capper—you could wring a few laughs out of an idea and then just move on to something else. Faster faster faster.

But the game changer, without question, was *The Simpsons*. Today it's a TV institution, timeworn yet beloved, but in 1989 *The Simpsons* felt like a lightning bolt. Matt Groening's creation was a pretty conventional family sitcom on paper. But because it was animated, *The Simpsons* could dispense with much of the tiresome "shoe leather" of television comedy—all that crossing the set, rummaging for props, traveling to new locations, explaining offstage action in dialogue—and draw instead on a seemingly bottomless well of new ideas: cutaway gags, parodies, non sequiturs, impossible slapstick, blink-and-you'd-miss-it puns. Animation meant that even fundamental principles of the universe like physics and causality were no longer barriers to comedy. "*The Simpsons* made you do a little bit of work," longtime writer-producer Tim Long told me. "There was a lot going on."

"It was just culturally dense and firing in so many brand-new directions," added Matt Selman, about to enter his third decade writing for

---

* Like many great discoveries in other sciences, this one was accidental. In 1963, George Schlatter was pulling together a TV special for Jonathan Winters, but the gut-punch of the Kennedy assassination meant that no one felt like writing or rehearsing. At the last minute, he edited together a full half hour from quick vignettes of Winters clowning around with Art Carney. The network was confused ("That's *not* a television show!" one exec told Schlatter) but the special won an Emmy, and the fast-paced *Laugh-In* style was born.

the show. "Every week you had to turn it on and see what they were going to do. And it said to a generation, 'Oh, TV can be better,' more than any other show."

The secret to the brisk pace of *The Simpsons* was, above all, the one thing the show didn't have: a studio audience. It's hard to overstate how much sitcom time and propulsion have been lost over the decades to the laugh track, or to actors shifting in their seats waiting for audience applause to end. George Meyer, the *Simpsons* writer who's probably more responsible for the show's comic DNA than any other, grew up watching staid three-camera sitcoms, but he always preferred the comedies that tried something a little less claustrophobic, a little more ambitious: *I Dream of Jeannie* and *Get Smart* and *Batman*. "Actors would almost always prefer being in front of a live audience, and that's one reason that form persisted as long as it did," he told me. "There was almost a moral superiority to performing it straight through."

"Sometimes they would even reassure you at the top of the show," I remembered. "'Filmed before a live studio audience.'"

"Your seal of quality! Yes, the audience imposes their own lame pace on stuff."

The *Simpsons* influence on animated TV is obvious: the legacy of *South Park* and *Family Guy*, Cartoon Network and Adult Swim. But when you look at television comedy overall during the last three decades, what you're largely seeing is shows trying to recapture in live action what *The Simpsons* did in animation. The flashbacks and cutaways on *Arrested Development* and *How I Met Your Mother*,* the screwball tempo of *30 Rock* and *Kimmy Schmidt*, the sprawling supporting casts of *Gilmore Girls* and *Parks and Recreation*, the *whoosh*-ing whip pans of *Malcolm in the Middle* and *Scrubs*, even the heightened reality of *Louie* and *Atlanta*—they all reflect the cartoonification of the sitcom into its current breakneck, single-camera form.

The accelerating pace of modern life in general has not been an

---

* Also their narrators. It's hard to overstate how much a narrator speeds up a sitcom. On *Arrested Development*, one quick line from Ron Howard ("And Tobias had found the perfect wardrobe for his leading man: the red dress he discovered in the attic crawl space. Assuming Michael had found and returned it, Lindsay called her mother hoping to get money for a new one") could replace five minutes of plot.

unalloyed good. Anxiety has been on a steady upswing for most of the twentieth century, and forty million American adults—almost one in five—have been diagnosed with an anxiety disorder. Heart disease is up; so are attention disorders. And there's even evidence that speed is bad for the soul. In 1973, two Princeton seminarians reenacted the Christian parable of the Good Samaritan on campus. They instructed subjects to head over to a different building to participate in a study but planted in their path a man slumped in an alley, who would moan and cough twice as they passed. Sixty-three percent stopped to help the man. But if participants were told that they were already late for their appointment and had to hurry, only 10 percent stopped. Sometimes, all it takes to turn a caring person into a callous one is a ticking clock.

The stakes may be lower when it comes to jokes, but the fever pitch we've achieved might be just as unhealthy for comedy—and maybe just as unsustainable. At 6.38 jokes per minute, a show like *Unbreakable Kimmy Schmidt* already feels breathless to me. It's as sharply written as anything on television, but you almost can't laugh at it—there's no time. No joke can be savored, because it's probably just a setup for a new joke. Emotional beats tend to feel a little tacked-on and even unwelcome, because they cause a jarring lull in the joke barrage. Most importantly, the audience *knows* that no one in real life tells a joke every nine seconds, so it's very hard for a show this fast to feel *real*, for the characters to seem lifelike and empathy-worthy. The viewer is constantly aware of how "written" it all feels—and there's nothing wrong with an ornate little operetta of a sitcom, but that's not the only thing (or the most interesting thing) that comedy can do.

Is there a mathematical limit to the speedup? I asked the *Simpsons* writers. A comedy singularity that we are asymptotically approaching, like the event horizon of a black hole?

"I don't think you can go that much faster than people are going now," was Tim Long's opinion.

Matt Selman agreed. "There have been shows on Adult Swim that are so dense with comedic chaos that for anyone over the age of thirty, it's almost hard to watch." I imagined a comedy moving so fast that it couldn't maintain its own structural integrity anymore—a fighter jet losing its wings and tail to air resistance, a space capsule shedding heat tiles as it attempts reentry.

Metamorphosis into Metacomedy

The faster and more sophisticated the jokes got, the more complex their structures and esoteric their references, the more removed they felt from the universal roots of humor buried deep in our midbrains. It was harder to suspend disbelief that any of these capital-J Jokes bore much resemblance to the everyday things that made us laugh in life. Funny people were more conscious of this than anyone and couldn't resist embracing it with a postmodern twist. Metahumor was born.

Just as metafiction is fiction about fiction, metahumor encompasses jokes about jokes. The idea of breaking the "fourth wall" in comedy performance isn't new. Roman playwrights like Plautus loved that sort of thing. In his comedy *Persa*, one slave asks another, "Where am I going to get a disguise?" "Ask the stage manager," the other replies. But in the twentieth century, the device was always reserved for the broadest and silliest kind of comedy: Groucho waggling his eyebrows at the camera; Bugs Bunny tormenting Elmer Fudd and confiding to the audience, "I do this kind of stuff to him all through the picture"; Bob Hope warning us that Bing Crosby was about to sing, "Now's the time to go out and get the popcorn."

This is funny when it's surprising, but over the following decades, it grew from a rule-breaking device to the reigning sensibility in a lot of comedy. You can trace this in the works of Mel Brooks: no metajokes in *The Producers*, a handful in *Blazing Saddles*, and by *Spaceballs* the movie is wall-to-wall with them.* The characters in *Spaceballs* even spend a couple minutes watching *themselves* watch themselves on-screen, the first infinitely regressing metajoke in cinema history.

A metajoke doesn't have to show you the sprockets of the film stock; there are softer ways to wink at the audience. For example, it has become

---

* Literally. The movie's very first joke is a title crawl that reads "Chapter Eleven"; the last line is the Yoda character, Yogurt, saying, "God willing we'll all meet again in *Spaceballs II: The Search for More Money*."

commonplace for characters to recognize and comment on the silliness of the comedy in which they find themselves. Ron Burgundy's "That escalated quickly!" in *Anchorman* might be the canonical example, but you also saw it when *The Simpsons's* Superintendent Chalmers said, "What an odd remark!" to Principal Skinner, or Michael Bluth on *Arrested Development* responded to one of Tobias's increasingly improbable homoerotic double entendres by saying, "There's got to be a better way to say that." These jokes are tempting in the writers' room: not only do they liberate the comedy to speak to the audience directly, but they can double the pace—a second free follow-up joke for the price of one. But they come at a cost: less emotional investment in a scenario that viewers realize the show might step back from at any second.

You might think that metahumor only works in comic fictions like plays and TV and movies. How can stand-up comedy, for example, break the fourth wall? By definition, a stand-up's whole routine is delivered to the audience. Exhibit A would be veteran comic Andy Kindler, probably best known for his acting roles on *Bob's Burgers* and *Everybody Loves Raymond*, but who also put on a clinic in self-aware stand-up in his frequent appearances on David Letterman's show. It was always easy to see why nobody ever wrote about Kindler without calling him a "comic's comic." His sets, even to Letterman's huge national audience, were full of insider-y jokes about the career of comedy ("I'm currently on my Half-a-House Tour! I refuse to sell more than half the available tickets in any venue!") or joke construction ("When I started comedy, you had to walk twenty miles just to get to the premise!") or comic patter ("If Huey Lewis was a comedian, the name of his band would be Huey Lewis and . . . What Else Is in the News?"). But he could usually get a bigger laugh by stepping outside the jokes to comment on them. "Look, I don't write any of this," he would tell a crowd. Or "I was so hoping that Huey Lewis would have a career resurgence by tonight, so that joke would work better." The act was an elaborate dance with comedy, right down to comically exaggerated gestures and facial expressions, with Kindler keeping up a running commentary on everything: the jokes, the audience, sometimes even his own commentary. "Yes!" he would say to greet applause. "I agree with your reaction!"

Engineered for the Savvier Audience

"Twenty years ago, I made a breakthrough," Kindler told me. "I've noticed that whenever I say what I'm thinking in the moment, the more I would really be able to tell the truth." He used to plan every aside; then he realized he could just make his inner monologue the act. Sometimes he stripped away the skin of a joke so you could see the anatomy, like Penn and Teller doing a magic trick with transparent props. "And then a third example!" he might finish a bit, nodding to the "rule of three" without actually thinking up a funny third example. Or ". . . and a funnier joke, and then a funnier joke, and then the kicker!" If you didn't understand comedy norms and history, it was probably mystifying.

But, more and more, the audience *was* in on the joke.

In 1991, Kindler wrote an article for the *National Lampoon* called "The Hack's Handbook" in which he outlined, with devastating accuracy, how easy it was to become an untalented club comic at the tail end of the 1980s comedy boom. The starter kit provided sample hack jokes about recommended topics including Dan Quayle, Madonna, TV commercials, Yugos, and gays. ("An effeminate voice is always a crowd pleaser.") The organizers of Montreal's Just for Laughs comedy festival invited Kindler to present a live version of the article onstage, and the popular show eventually grew into an annual "State of the Industry" speech in which Kindler gave a scathing rundown of the comedy year in review. By its twentieth year, the show was one of the festival's undisputed highlights, always selling out its six-hundred-seat room. Kindler gleefully roasted everyone who mattered, returning time and again to expected targets (Ricky Gervais is insufferable, Jimmy Fallon isn't funny, Adam Sandler just doesn't care) but also declining to spare comedians whose work he admired (pre-scandal Louis C.K. was pretentious, Jerry Seinfeld is out of touch).

The most interesting thing about the "State of the Industry" is that it's become a mainstream phenomenon, eagerly downloaded by fans and dissected in a thousand-word *New York Times* piece. This is the state of comedy now: it's increasingly performed not for casual Saturday-night drinkers or TV-channel-flippers looking for a laugh, but for an audience of aficionados. The end of the mass-market comedy boom in the

1990s created a more experimental "alternative comedy" scene on both coasts, with smaller but *much* more devoted fan bases. The mainstays of that scene—Patton Oswalt, Sarah Silverman, David Cross, Bob Odenkirk, Marc Maron, Louis C.K.—eventually shed the "alternative" label and became the biggest names in comedy, full stop. But they brought their cannier, comedy-mechanics-obsessed audience with them into the mainstream.

In the past, comedy superfan anecdotes were mostly origin stories told by comedians—no one else they knew growing up even cared. Billy Crystal would bring home every comedy record from his dad's 42nd Street music store. Marc Maron used to scour *Parade* magazine for its "My Favorite Jokes" column, the only place he could read about stand-up as a kid. Judd Apatow was so obsessed that he would arrange to interview big-name comedians for his ten-watt high school radio station, hoping publicists wouldn't catch on that the "reporter" was going to be a sixteen-year-old with a giant green tape recorder. Most of his interviews never even aired.

But today, comedy fandom *is* mass culture. Mourners leave doughnuts with receipts on the grave of the late Mitch Hedberg, in honor of a single stand-up joke he used to do.* *The Aristocrats*, about a filthy joke that comedians have been telling each other since vaudeville, became one of the most successful documentaries of all time. No detail, it seemed, was too inside-baseball for this new comedy audience. *My Name Is Earl* frequently used the TV comedy shibboleth "Who Jackie?" in dialogue as an inside joke among the writers. ("Who Jackie?" is funny for reasons that are too complicated to go into in this parenthetical but probably fit in a footnote.†) But when *Unbreakable Kimmy Schmidt* named an Asian

---

* "I'll just give you the money, and you give me the doughnut. End of transaction. We don't need to bring ink and paper into this. I just can't imagine a scenario where I would have to prove that I bought a doughnut."

† The story, much beloved in comedy circles, concerns a stand-up hired for the *Roseanne* writers' room despite having no writing experience. After two quiet years on the job, he finally spoke up to pitch a bizarre story idea—one in which Roseanne would play her own sister. "We already have Jackie," someone pointed out. (Laurie Metcalf had just won the second of her three consecutive Emmys for playing Roseanne's younger sister, Jackie, a major character on the show.) "Who Jackie?" asked the clueless writer. As the story goes, he went on to suggest that his pitch would still work if Jackie were to die, become a ghost, and fly around the room.

character "Hu Zha Qi" in 2015 in honor of the trope, it could do so fully aware that some nonzero percentage of the audience would understand.

Too Smart to Laugh

The sophistication of modern comedy and the savviness of the audience have grown up symbiotically, a game of evolutionary leapfrog. Do you think Woody Allen's nightclub crowd, the ones having trouble with a punch line about birth control, could have followed the speed of *30 Rock*, the chronology of *My Girlfriend's Boyfriend*, the cadence of Andy Kindler?

The extraordinary result is that today, most very good comedy is popular, and vice versa. This, to put it mildly, has not always been the case. During the last comedy boom, in the 1980s, mass-market popularity killed experimentation, because every comic was angling for the exact same brass ring: the late-night spot, the sitcom deal. And because comedy has often been a comparatively narrow cultural niche, its history is filled with genuinely great art that no one seemed to like very much. Buster Keaton's masterpiece *The General* was an expensive flop that ended Keaton's career as an independent moviemaker and plunged him into fifteen years of alcoholic despair. The Monty Python movies only got made when the Pythons wheedled their rock musician friends into kicking in money; George Harrison mortgaged his house to fund *Life of Brian*. The original *The Office* received some of the lowest focus group scores the BBC had ever seen, just ahead of women's lawn bowling. Viewers voted Andy Kaufman off of *Saturday Night Live*. *Freaks and Geeks* got canceled.

But in just thirty years, we went from a near-total lack of smart mass-culture comedy to an incredible glut of it. Producer James L. Brooks was an Oscar-laden Hollywood powerhouse in 1989 when he was developing *The Simpsons* with Matt Groening and Sam Simon, while Fox was barely even a network. That gave him the clout to negotiate a very unusual contract giving network executives almost no input into the show's creative side. As a result, as Mitch Hurwitz has observed, "The most successful TV show in the history of the medium has never received a single note from any executive." When everyone realized that a single creative vision, unspoiled by committee, could be a massive hit, the landscape started to transform. A more knowledgeable audience and a dizzying variety of new media options (independent film, basic cable, premium cable, streaming video) changed the math as well—suddenly making comedy that would *stand out* in a crowded culture was more important than making sure it fit in.

But now that we're getting so much good comedy, are we enjoying it as much? Many professionally funny people have noticed that, paradoxically, the audience that knows the most about comedy might not be the *best* audience. Stand-up comedian and writer Jen Kirkman told me about a comedy show at which she used to perform regularly in Los Angeles. The show moved from its original home, a bar and lounge, to the Upright Citizens Brigade Theatre, and suddenly the audience was different: less diverse, less relaxed, more serious young men in their twenties with a definite whiff of improv classes about them. "I remember having a harder time suddenly getting them to laugh at things that had done well on the road," she said. "At the time the debate backstage was, 'Are they too comedy-savvy? Is the problem that they are so well trained in watching comedy that they know when a punch line is coming, and they don't laugh?'"

Funny people get into comedy because it's everything to them, but once it's your job, that relationship can change. "I still love stand-up—I just love it in a different way," comedian Moshe Kasher told me. "I'm still a fan of the art form. I just know a little too well where the numbers are that the paint got splattered on." His friend Chelsea Peretti (*Brooklyn Nine-Nine*) has described it as being like one of the characters in *The Matrix* who gets unplugged but can still keep an eye on the matrix world via the stream of text on their computer monitors. They understand what's going on, but they're not immersed in the same way as someone who's never been woken up from the simulation. "I would say that I laugh at comedy probably ninety-nine percent less than a regular person at a comedy show," Kasher said. "Mostly because, yeah, I know the mechanics of what they're doing."

When an entire society buries itself in comedy, we can start to experience the same problem. We haven't just become a culture of comedy geeks. We essentially became a culture of comedy writers. Our brains, which have evolved to ferret out all the twists and incongruities that make humor possible, keep racing ahead of the performer or the script, eager to make that next connection, "get" the next joke. No modern audience will ever be as heartbroken as I was when Nick from *Freaks and Geeks* watched his rock dreams slip away from him. Subverting sitcom formula was surprising then, but today it's what every show does. We've been trained for whiplash story twists; we even expect them. In writers' rooms across Hollywood, so many late nights and recreational drugs must get poured into staking out zigzaggy third-option endings that are neither easy tropes nor simple reversals.

And when we see all the tricks, we can get jaded. In Tim Long's view knowledgeable comedy audiences don't actually seem to be enjoying their favorite thing all that much. "In the era of vaudeville, everyone was wrapping their belly and slapping their knee. Now I see a lot of people going"—he switches to a completely deadpan voice—"'*That's funny.*' This is the golden age of people in a very straight-faced way saying, 'That's funny.'" In other words, an MRI of the modern comedy geek might show the cerebral cortex sparking away brilliantly over jokes that are ever more complicated and abstruse—but at the expense of the dark pleasure centers beneath. When we connoisseurs applaud a joke, we're applauding the degree of difficulty, like Olympic judges watching a platform dive or gymnastics routine. We don't say that funny things "tickle" us anymore. That sounds too involuntary. Today, we *decide* to laugh.

There's a danger, I think, that becoming coolly jaded comedy customers starts to make us jaded to everything else as well. The emotional underpinning of comedy isn't just amusement. Becoming fixated on the mechanics, like we imagine the professionally funny to be, means that we're less invested emotionally. Tina Fey famously described that difference this way: "If you want to make an audience laugh, you dress a man up like an old lady and push her down the stairs. If you want to make comedy writers laugh, you push an actual old lady down the stairs."

I've thought about that quote many times while watching modern comedy, where the pace is so fast and the jokes so elaborate and finessed that empathy for the characters is almost an afterthought—you want them to have funny shenanigans (involving, where possible, a flight of stairs) more than you actually want them to get what *they* want. Fey's Liz Lemon is Exhibit A that real, rounded, beloved characters can still survive a milieu of dense, frenzied comedy writing, but she's the exception, not the rule. Nobody cares about Michael Bluth quite the way they did about Mary Richards. Nobody feels Ron Burgundy's pain the way they did Bud Baxter's in *The Apartment*.

Sometimes I even miss the laugh track. Whether you were laughing along with a live studio audience or canned guffaws from a sound man's Laff Box,* it was a communal experience. You were laughing on behalf of society, together with the other people watching *Cheers* or whatever all at the same time, not because you were smart or special but because everyone else was too. Now I laugh less often, in the quick breaths allowed me before the show races on, before I hurry on to the next episode in my binge. It feels a little superior, like a judgment: *This joke, unlike that last one, has pleased me.* Now we laugh alone.

---

* For decades, inventor Charley Douglass had a near-monopoly on the business of canned television laughter. His giant Laff Box device was a padlocked secret; only Douglass and his close family members knew how to operate it. It was stocked with laughs he'd collected from all manner of live and televised performances over the years. (Marcel Marceau mime shows were good, because there'd be no talking overlapping the laughs.) When you listened to the canned laughter in a lot of twentieth-century sitcoms, you were hearing (at least in part) the chuckles of the dead.

FOUR

NOTES FROM AN EPIDEMIC

Funny is like a virus. Once it adapts to a new vector, or colonizes a new host, or spreads to a new population, it's almost impossible to eradicate.

The Northwest Ice and Cold Storage building in downtown Portland, Oregon, was an abandoned warehouse for decades, but in 1999 the advertising agency of Wieden + Kennedy remodeled it into a new headquarters the size of a city block. Today the office is a puzzle box of bridges and partial floors surrounding a central atrium, full of quirky "creatives"-work-here touches around every corner. There's an eight-foot plywood beaver standing in the main entrance, and one hundred thousand pushpins stuck into a wall upstairs spelling out the agency's motto, "Fail Harder." The conference room on the top floor is a giant nest, made by sculptor Patrick Dougherty from thousands of sticks gathered from the Columbia River Valley and woven together without a single fastener of any kind. (The nest is not, however, the basket of a giant hot-air balloon, as depicted in a 2011 *Portlandia* sketch.)

What is one of the world's most influential ad agencies doing in Portland? In a word, Nike. Wieden + Kennedy made the up-and-coming shoe company's first national TV ads back in 1982, and the two home-grown Oregon companies have been very good to each other over the years. W+K cofounder Dan Wieden coined the iconic "Just Do It" slogan in 1988,* and for decades, the ad agency's reputation was based

---

* Inspired by, of all people, executed murderer Gary Gilmore. When Utah prison guards brought Gilmore before the firing squad in 1977, they asked if he had any last words. "Let's do it," he replied.

on its muscular, motivational TV campaigns for Nike, the kind of spot that for thirty seconds could make you believe you might want to run a triathlon, or at least look into a gym membership.

But the W+K brand is no longer just about pumping up sweaty strivers. When I met there with creative director Eric Baldwin, he had just returned from a pro wrestling match in Austin, Texas, where he'd been shooting the agency's latest commercial. Mike "the Miz" Mizanin, dressed in a yellow chicken suit as the fictional "Puppers Cluckers" mascot, was absolutely destroyed in the ring by KFC's Colonel Sanders, played on this occasion by wrestling superstar Dolph Ziggler. Did the *WWE SmackDown Live* audience mind the interruption of their show by a live ad break? I wondered. "They lost their shit," Baldwin told me. "The chant of 'Colonel Sanders!' started the minute he came out."

Wieden + Kennedy was the agency responsible for the KFC campaign in which a series of beloved comedians (Darrell Hammond, Norm Macdonald, Jim Gaffigan) traded off impersonating the venerable restaurateur, who had died in 1980, in a series of ridiculous wigs and false beards. It took guts to try a comedic Colonel Sanders reboot in 2015. His last appearance on American televisions was a cringeworthy campaign in which Randy Quaid voiced a sassy animated Sanders. "Go Colonel! Go Colonel!" the cartoon pitchman would chant while doing the Cabbage Patch with his cane, just like the real Sanders probably used to. But the new campaign was a hit. "Sales are through the roof for them," said Baldwin. "They couldn't be happier."

As the ad-viewing public became savvier than ever before, this brand of self-aware, winking weirdness (Dolph Ziggler as an elbow-dropping Colonel, Rob Riggle as one who owns a chicken-themed pro football team, George Hamilton as an "extra crispy" one) became central to the Wieden + Kennedy playbook. "If you're taking yourself too seriously as a brand, people are just going to turn off and walk away," explained Baldwin. "But if you can poke fun at yourself, and say, 'This is an ad, that's what it is, and we're going to try to make you laugh,' being very straightforward with that, people find it refreshing and are more willing to let it wash over them."

"It's the acknowledgment that we're in a relationship together," added his colleague Jason Kreher. "I'm trying to make you eat this chicken. I've interrupted your experience to tell you about eating this chicken. So instead of giving you thirty seconds of facts about chicken, I am going to entertain you."

That was a surprisingly recent discovery for the advertising industry. "Be serious. Don't use humor or fantasy," wrote ad guru David Ogilvy in his 1963 book *Confessions of an Advertising Man*. "Good copywriters have always resisted the temptation to entertain."* For decades, advertising was built on this truism: anything fun or showy might distract from the brand. Even if customers laughed at the joke, it didn't mean they'd try the product. You can look at thousands of print and broadcast ads from the first half of the twentieth century—the same time frame when comedy was making millions for movies, radio, and TV—and you'll find a chuckle-free wasteland. You will be instructed to buy, say, Kraft mayonnaise not by a jovial mascot or a punny tagline, but by two columns of tiny type describing the brand's many nutritional and textural advantages. The copy might suggest how much happier your household will be once you switch brands, or inform you that singer Rosemary Clooney uses the stuff, but it will all be in deadly earnest. Back then, a boundary-pushing ad slogan was something like Morton Salt's "When it rains, it pours!"—slightly clever, but still a straightforward salute to Morton's big game-changing innovation in the salt world, the addition of a chemical called magnesium carbonate so its salt wouldn't cake in wet weather. The only vintage ads that would get a laugh today are unintentionally funny, like ones that use the word "gay" in its original sense. The pinnacle of this genre is a 1945 magazine ad featuring a negligee-clad girl-next-door type brushing her hair in her boudoir. "To Wake Up GAY in the Morning!" teases the headline, "Just Try This at Bedtime Tonight!"†

---

* Ogilvy's book was a touchstone for *Mad Men* producer Matthew Weiner in creating the world of 1960s adman Don Draper. Draper, like Ogilvy, is deeply skeptical of humor in advertising. When shown the ironic 1960 "Lemon" ad for the Volkswagen Beetle, one of the most influential "funny" campaigns in history, Draper says, "I don't know what I hate about it the most: the ad or the car."

† Sorry about the clickbait. "Drink a warm cup of Ovaltine," is the answer.

But when Madison Avenue let radio comics read their commercials, that soon started to change. Like a chameleon, advertising adapted to its surroundings. Bob Hope used to annoy his sponsors by ad-libbing around their copy. "I've been chewing Beech-Nut gum for twenty-five years," he would say. "Its price has never changed." Then, unable to resist, he would look up from the script. "It's either a big bargain now or it was a big gyp then!"

Fathering the Funny Commercial

In 1957, a comic named Stan Freberg debuted his satirical radio show on CBS as a summer replacement for Jack Benny. Freberg's show featured ads for fake products like "Puffed Grass" cereal, and like Bob Hope, he liked to rewrite his sponsors' copy so the real ads would be as funny as the rest of the show. "We have agencies to do that," his CBS producer told him. "Yes, I've seen their work," replied an unimpressed Freberg.

The edgy parodies on Freberg's show often targeted corporate America, as in the famous "Gray Flannel Hat Full of Teenage Werewolves" sketch, in which a vapid Madison Avenue adman leads a secret double life as a werewolf. Perhaps not coincidentally, the show had a hard time attracting advertisers. Two different cigarette companies offered to sponsor the show, but Freberg refused to shill for tobacco. On the show's last original episode, Freberg drolly read commercials that advertised . . . himself. When CBS canceled the series the next week, ending the last network comedy show of the Golden Age of Radio, Freberg decided that if you can't beat 'em, you join 'em. Preparing a stack of business cards that read "*Ars Gratia Pecuniae*"—"Art for Money's Sake"—he opened Freberg Ltd. (But Not Very), his very own ad agency.

As a result, Stan Freberg, who in his seventy-year show business career did everything from voicing Looney Tunes characters to writing for *Mad* magazine to releasing million-selling comedy records,* left

* His most famous records include "John and Marsha," in which the two lovebirds do nothing but coo each other's names for 2:28 over a bed of soap opera organ music (and which the BBC banned under the theory that John and Marsha might conceivably be in the throes of sexual passion), and the *Billboard* number one hit "St. George and the Dragonet," a *Dragnet* parody in a medieval setting.

behind a surprising legacy. In the words of his 2015 *New York Times* obituary, he was above all "the father of the funny commercial." Over a forty-year second career in the advertising world, Freberg produced an endless stream of dazzlingly high-concept sixty-second mini-masterpieces. In Freberg-world, Ann Miller's suburban kitchen opened up into a Broadway stage so that she could lead a twenty-dancer chorus line in a mock Busby Berkeley number praising Heinz's Great American Soup. ("Emily, why do you always have to make such a big production out of everything?" her husband complains.) Science fiction author Ray Bradbury appeared on a giant *Fahrenheit 451* view-screen to predict a futuristic world in which Sunsweet prunes would be wrinkle free. The Lone Ranger and Tonto crashed a dinner party to protest the use of the "William Tell Overture" in Jeno's Pizza Rolls ads. None of this would be surprising today, but in 1960, winking at the customer was downright subversive. But clients couldn't quibble when their sales went up. Freberg's groundbreaking commercials won him twenty-one Clio awards and bought him a shag-carpeted stucco mansion in Beverly Hills complete with Olympic-sized swimming pool. He called it "Stan Simeon."

Freberg's most innovative trademark came from his early days as a parodist: he loved to make ads that made fun of advertising. "Nine out of ten doctors recommend Chun King chow mein," read one print ad. The photo showed nine Asian men wearing stethoscopes . . . and one white one. (Okay, you probably couldn't get away with that today, but it's a pretty solid joke.) In his last iconic campaign, Freberg reinvented *Encyclopaedia Britannica*'s image in 1987 with a savvy spoof of infomercials. A squeaky, jean-jacketed teen* sparred winningly with a big-voiced announcer ("Let's have that 800 number. Excellent!") over the virtues of a good home library. As a result, Britannica sold an all-time-high 120,000 encyclopedias in a single year.

The spots were explicit about creating a new advertising dynamic in an age of more jaded viewers with shorter attention spans. "Sorry for the interruption," the kid-with-the-report-due-on-space said at the top of one ad.

---

* Played by Freberg's own son, Donavan.

"The what?" asked the worried announcer.

"Well, that's what a commercial is, basically, right?"

"Uh, don't tell them that."

"This *is* a commercial," the kid insisted. "Hold on," he added, leaning into the camera. "Don't zap me yet."

"I usually zap the commercials," said a bored-sounding child's voice, offscreen.

"I understand. But you can really use these books." This infomercial was different, we were given to understand. It was on our side. It knew that infomercials are dumb. With that out of the way, we could get down to some straight talk.

The Ad Your Ad Could Sell Like

Wieden + Kennedy dipped its toes into the water of cutting-edge humor with its long-running "This Is *SportsCenter*" campaign for ESPN. These ads predicted the mockumentary boom of the *Office* era by imagining the cable channel's dreary Connecticut headquarters as a playground where bajillionaire athletes goofed around at the water cooler with reporters and staff. But the real turning point for the agency debuted during the 2010 Super Bowl and starred an athlete who had never made it off the practice squad. In the first of the award-winning "Smell Like a Man, Man" spots for Old Spice, a shirtless hunk bragged to female viewers about how superior he was to their husbands and boyfriends, because he used a more masculine body wash. Everyone was talking about the ad's in-camera visual trickery, which moved the Old Spice Man from a bathroom to a boat deck to the back of a horse, all in one seamless take.* But what gave the ad its staying power was the crisply written monologue ("What's in your hand? It's an oyster with two tickets to that thing you love!") and the cheerfully over-the-top performance of former wide receiver Isaiah Mustafa. The ad was viewed thirteen million

---

* Over a three-day shoot, W+K only got three usable versions of the intricately choreographed shot. The one in the commercial is take fifty-seven of the final day.

times on YouTube in its first six months, and Old Spice sales doubled. "We had to run the ad less because people would go to the stores and there'd be no product left," said Craig Allen, who co-wrote the ad with Eric Kallman.

The calculus was changing. Though David Ogilvy famously recanted his "no humor" rule in 1982, he wasn't entirely wrong. The research is still mixed on exactly how persuasive a funny ad can be, because many viewers do indeed remember the joke and forget the product. When Taco Bell abruptly ended its "Yo quiero Taco Bell!" campaign in 2000, word quickly spread that their Chihuahua mascot had died. In fact, that was an urban legend. The Chihuahua was alive and prospering, but same-store sales numbers at Taco Bell franchises were not. The company learned that ad viewers loved their quippy mascot but weren't buying the gorditas.

But technology marched on, and by 2010, that was a problem that a sufficiently entertaining ad could easily overcome. A funny commercial that went viral would be passed around to a vastly larger audience than would ever see it otherwise. As of 2017, the first "Smell Like a Man, Man" ad had been viewed over fifty million times online, not by people who were waiting to get back to their TV show, but by people who *chose* to watch it. By *fans*. They were so delighted by the ad that they wanted to pass it on to friends and family. And none of this cost Old Spice a cent in television airtime! With numbers like that, it doesn't matter if some, or even most, of the viewers don't remember what product the "I'm on a horse" guy was plugging. The sheer number of eyeballs captured can make the funny ad more influential than a much "stickier" earnest one.

"The CEO of Procter and Gamble told everyone that 'Old Spice is now an entertainment brand. It's not a deodorant brand,'" Jason Kreher bragged. Think about that for a second: Old Spice—the eighty-year-old product that smells like your grandpa's undershirts, a stodgy brand so threatened by Axe in 2009 that P&G executives discussed changing the name to "Spice"—is now a hip, digital-era entertainment property. The aftershaves and stuff could go away tomorrow, and "Old Spice" would still exist as an intangible metaphysical concept—an attitude, a comic sensibility. It wouldn't smell like anything, but it would be cool.*

Wackiness at Nine Million Dollars Per Minute

Years after the Old Spice Man made his debut, the industry was still chasing his chiseled, towel-clad glutes. It wasn't just KFC. Every advertiser wanted that whimsical wink at the viewer, that confidently ridiculous pitchman, that slightly absurd sense of humor. Watching the Super Bowl in 2016, I could almost sense the sweaty desperation of a child beauty pageant from every commercial. Not every ad can go viral, after all. Which would it be? Clearly, the advertisers all had the same theory: it would be the surprising one, the one that pushed the envelope of outlandishness and visual trickery just far enough. A horrifying science-project-gone-wrong called "PuppyMonkeyBaby" broke into an apartment and forced Mountain Dew Kickstart on a trio of confused roommates, while repeating its name in a rhythm that PepsiCo clearly hoped would become an unstoppable earworm. Steven Tyler sang a duet with his own Skittles portrait.

But the whiff of Old Spice was strongest in the first quarter, when a hammy Jeff Goldblum promoted Apartments.com by singing the *Jeffersons* theme as he and his grand piano were hoisted up the outside of a high-rise to a "deluxe apartment in the sky." (This ad's absurd kicker wasn't a horse; it was . . . literally a kicker. Lil Wayne place-kicked a football between the uprights of a miniature gridiron atop the penthouse, for no discernible reason.) Goldblum was the perfect twenty-first-century spokesperson, combining old-school gravitas with modern ironic cachet. "Guess they couldn't get Christopher Walken," I commented at our Super Bowl party. Not too long after, there was a cranky Willem Dafoe, dressed as Marilyn Monroe for a Snickers commercial. "Walken turned down Snickers too!" I said, impressed. Harvey Keitel, currently America's

---

* A few years after Craig Allen helped mastermind the new Old Spice campaign, he was talking to a W+K account manager just back from a Nike shoot in China. At a store in Beijing that sold fashion-forward Western clothing, there was a series of Old Spice deodorant sticks lined up on the counter. "Why do you have these?" the account man asked. "It's Old Spice!" the clerk told him. "It's a cool American thing!"

third-string Christopher Walken, showed up in a Mini car commercial. I had just about given up. But in the third quarter, there he suddenly was in all his eccentric glory: Christopher Walken hiding in a suburban man's "Walken closet" (get it?) so he could criticize his drab, beige wardrobe and talk him into a choice with a little more "pizzazzzzzz": the all-new Kia Optima.

The epidemic of "funny" Super Bowl ads escalated so quickly that now it's big industry news when an ad agency tries to run a different play during the big game: an adorable wordless story about the Budweiser Clydesdales, for example. Once the competition has Jeff Goldblum scaling skyscrapers, you don't want to be the brand looking to the past with irony-free, Goldblum-free content. Once a certain kind of humor becomes cultural shorthand for hipness and youth and smarts, literally anything else risks looking square and old and dumb.

According to Millward Brown, in 2013, 52 percent of all advertising in North America was "funny or light-hearted" in nature, more than any other part of the world. Humor is a more obvious ad technique for a $4 stick of deodorant than it is for weightier purchasing decisions, like a car or a refrigerator. But that was changing as well. Take auto insurance. In 1998, Geico controlled just 2.5 percent of the car insurance market. Then, under the new ownership of Warren Buffett's Berkshire Hathaway Inc., the company went on an unprecedented advertising blitz, with annual expenditures eventually topping one billion dollars. A Screen Actors Guild strike made it impossible to hire a celebrity for their new campaign, so the company settled for an animated gecko. The Cockney lizard was an unexpected hit, and over the next decade, as Geico's market share tripled, insurance advertising changed. The sedate testimonials of years past were replaced with an endlessly wacky parade of ducks, cavemen, nutty professors, humming quarterbacks, and peppy salespeople. Even Allstate's Dennis Haysbert had to take a backseat to a madman called "Mayhem," played by *30 Rock*'s Dean Winters, who barely survived a series of catastrophic *Jackass*-style stunts. Nationwide spoofed the trend—and succumbed to it—by introducing their own cocky equivalent of the Old Spice Man, the "World's Greatest Spokesperson in the World." It was an arms race.

"I don't think that any product is off-limits for humor if you do it correctly," Jason Kreher told me. "I don't think there's one client I've ever worked on where I haven't *tried* humor, to see how it goes." He had recently pitched Weight Watchers on its first funny campaign—not the usual testimonial from a dieter proudly checking herself out in new jeans, but a clever and sympathetic mini-symphony about the universal temptation of snacking. W+K followed this up with a more ambitious Super Bowl spot, a densely edited montage lampooning American excess, consumerism, and the tropes of food advertising itself. "That was the perfect example where, if you did it wrong, you would be completely destroyed. But if you did it right, people would react really well."

When even dieting and insurance were fair game for funny ads, it was hard to imagine the pendulum ever swinging back. The ad right before Kreher's "All You Can Eat" Weight Watchers spot at the 2015 Super Bowl was from Nationwide, but they'd ditched their "World's Greatest Spokesperson" in favor of a daring pushback against the grain: a sweet ad about childhood in which the cherubic narrator dramatically revealed, at the thirty-second mark, "I couldn't grow up, because I died from an accident." A sad white curtain blew through the open second-story window behind him, perhaps marking the scene of the tragedy. America's collective jaw dropped. Was Nationwide lauded for using the biggest TV audience of the year to air a potentially life-saving PSA about household safety? They were not! Sixty-four percent of social media reactions were negative, and the chief marketing officer who oversaw the ad left Nationwide three months later.*

That's an extreme example, but it shows the difficulty of weaning advertisers and viewers off the comedy teat. The slide from serious to funny was easy because surprise, the unlooked-for laugh, is so essential to humor. But once audiences *expect* that infusion of jokes every thirty seconds, anything else falls flat. Internet advertising, for example, is universally hated, by the same people who will watch funny TV commercials

---

* The ad was equally unpopular in the halls of Weight Watchers and Wieden + Kennedy. "Everyone was saying, 'Oh my God, did that f—king kid die?' for the first twenty seconds of our commercial," groused Jason Kreher. "So that didn't work out great."

on YouTube for hours. It's no coincidence that Internet pop-ups are also the only ads that never figured out how to be funny.

There's also the question of what modern ads could even fall back on to replace humor. Craig Allen explained that old-school ad gurus of David Ogilvy's generation preferred factual product rundowns to jokes for a very good reason: there were just fewer products then. "They didn't have to differentiate themselves very much. They actually had something to talk about." Back when there were only three kinds of mayonnaise, you could convince a consumer just by demonstrating that your brand was creamier, or lasted longer on the shelf, or used real lemon juice, or something. No jokey distraction required. "I don't know why you would *need* to make a joke if you have something like that in your back pocket," Allen told me. "I pray for briefs that have that clear of a product benefit." That's why cell phone and car ads can still be lengthy, fact-filled encomia to higher-resolution cameras and better fuel mileage: the product is still improving. Mayonnaise, in the absence of new advances in the condiment field, has to resort to making you laugh. Laugh about mayonnaise.

The Pocket Joke Factory

Advertising is just one world that's been overrun by the joke virus—and it's no longer the most ubiquitous one. If the average American sees 362 paid media ads a day, as one study found, and over half use humor, that's almost two hundred jokes a day. Writing about advertising humor in 2014, professor Fred K. Beard opined that "humorous advertisements may be the most frequent way that many come into contact with intentional humor," dwarfing more traditional delivery methods like stand-up or sitcoms. But within a few years, Beard was exponentially out of date. In the age of social media, a two-hundred-joke day seems downright sedate, a relic of a simpler time.

Twitter was founded almost accidentally in 2007, spun out of a failing podcasting company called Odeo. It was a hybrid technology that filled a need no one actually had: to send messages with the enforced brevity of texts to one's entire social network. "From early on, we didn't know what it was," cofounder Evan Williams admitted in 2015. "'Microblogging' was a thing a lot of people called it."

I was bemused every time someone tried to explain Twitter to me: Facebook but shorter? That's more or less what people thought. It was a toy, a way to shout out important updates like "Just finishing lunch!" or "FINALLY, THE WEEKEND" into the digital ether. I remember thinking that maybe it would be good at zoos. "OMG the tiger is actually awake now and just moved its legs a little, get over there!!!"

Someone at my publisher eventually talked me into getting on Twitter, but I soon learned that just because I'd been on TV at one point, that didn't make people interested in hearing me hype a book release or reminisce about quiz shows. Nobody even noticed. Frustrated, I started posting jokes just to amuse myself—and immediately started getting responses. I still remember the moment I gave up on real trivia and started tweeting made-up facts instead.

Ken Jennings @KenJennings
DID YOU KNOW! If you laid all Alex Trebek's Perry Ellis suits on the ground end to end . . . HE WOULD BE ANGRY. They are fancy & very expensive!

Suddenly, sixty retweets! For that! Not bad. In hindsight, I shouldn't have been surprised. What would you rather pass around to your friends, a new joke, or PR? Twitter's 140-character limit, it turned out, was crippling for lots of the things the company hoped you would use it for: political discussion, customer service, marketing.* But it was perfect for one-liners.

Clicking "Follow" on a selection of the most entertaining Twitter feeds turns your phone or laptop into a real-time joke factory of pitiless efficiency. Within a year of joining, I was following about five hundred accounts, which is actually small potatoes by Twitter standards. But that was, on an average weekday, enough to provide me with an unending fire hose of comedy, a new joke or two every single minute. In the early days I would feel guilty if I missed any tweets in my timeline and tried to "catch up" every time I opened Twitter. But eventually it's just too much. You have to stop struggling and let the waves wash over you.

---

* Twitter recognized this fact in 2017, controversially doubling its character limit to 280.

Let's Get Small

Everything about Twitter was miniaturized: the character limit, the little glowing screen you probably read it on, the small daily concerns of the quipsters there.* And that makes sense. The modern proliferation of funny into everyday life has been driven, in large part, by the shrinking scale of the jokes themselves.

It's difficult to construct a historical narrative of humor, because the vast majority of jokes ever told in human history were never written down. We can assume that medieval peasants liked to tell earthy stories about horny damsels and farting monks, but there's no way to be sure.† The history of jokes is like the history of sexuality: the most important stuff was never written down. In fact, when the brothers Grimm changed the history of folklore by compiling written records of popular tales, they deliberately left out funny stories in order to keep the scope of their project manageable.

But when jokes started to get published, their subjects tended to be unlikely, larger than life. Think of all of Shakespeare's cross-dressing heroines and their improbable love polygons, or the delusional escapades of Don Quixote. It might have been farce, or satire, but it certainly didn't remind readers much of everyday life. This was especially true in America, where the homegrown mode of humor was based in the "tall talk" of the frontier. The new landscape of the West was jaw-droppingly big and strange: the plains, the canyons, herds of buffalo a million strong, whatever the Mormons were up to. So the jokes were big too. Humor almanacs with names like *The Rip Snorter* and *Whim Whams* filled their pages with cheerful braggadocio about corn that grew so fast it caused an earthquake, men so tall they had to climb a ladder to shave, rain so hard that you'd shoot fifteen feet in the air out of your shrinking buckskins.

That's a strain of bravado you still see on the American scene today,

---

* A Twitter update from *The State* comedian Michael Ian Black: "Had some soup already today. Later I'm going to have a salad. It's like a soup and salad combo but spread out over a few hours. Thx."

† Even in the absence of documentation, scholars tend to believe there was plenty of such joking. Sociologist Christie Davies points out that for decades there was no written record of antigovernment joking in the Soviet Union, but émigrés and defectors assured us that such jokes were common.

from pro wrestling to hip-hop, but it's no longer the dominant voice of comedy. We might think of observational comedy as an early-eighties genre pioneered by stand-ups like David Brenner and Jerry Seinfeld: "*What's* the *deal* with socks in the dryer?" But that all began in the 1920s, with humorists like James Thurber, S. J. Perelman, and the incredibly influential Robert Benchley. Benchley was a cofounder of the wisecracking Algonquin Round Table, along with famous friends like Dorothy Parker and Robert Sherwood. In his essays for *Vanity Fair* and the *New Yorker*, Benchley created a new kind of epic, detailing his furious struggle with the smallest annoyances of modern life: hay fever, a broken shoelace, trying to read a newspaper on a crowded bus. When he described waiting in a long post office line only to realize at the counter that your package isn't in fact ready to mail, he got a new kind of laugh—a laugh of *recognition*—that could never be earned by a tall tale about Davy Crockett putting a rifle ball through the moon. "That's funny because it could never happen!" was replaced by "That's funny because it happens to me all the time!"

Benchley and his contemporaries also reversed the notion of humor as the province of the masterful. No longer would joke-tellers be either swaggering Falstaffs or wise court jesters. The new comic type was the hapless neurotic, the nebbish, the loser. As Thurber wrote in his 1933 autobiography, twentieth-century humorists led "an existence of jumpiness and apprehension"; they "talked largely about small matters and smally about great affairs." Their muses were the modern men who, in Thurber's words, "look so swell, and go to pieces so easily." Benchley, who became a household name during the Great Depression playing himself as a lovably befuddled everyman in a series of short films for MGM, was in reality a much more complicated, troubled soul. His older brother, Edmund, had died in the Spanish-American War when Robert was only eight years old. When his mother received the telegram informing her of the tragedy, she was at a public Fourth of July picnic. "Why couldn't it have been Robert?" she shouted, with her stunned younger son at her side. The story, for obvious reasons, became a town legend in Worcester, Massachusetts, for decades afterward. Later in life, Benchley became a kind of World War II–era Eddie Murphy, lured away from his early comic genius by big Hollywood paychecks, neutered by the system. His column was dropped by the *New Yorker*, and when his movie and radio career stalled, he turned to alcohol and pills. He died unexpectedly of a brain hemorrhage, complicated by cirrhosis of the liver, in 1945.

Today Benchley is a fairly obscure figure compared to fellow *New Yorker* humor luminaries like Thurber and E. B. White. But without the comic archetype he helped create, the put-upon "Little Man," we'd never have a Woody Allen or Charlie Brown or Liz Lemon. And the comic sensibility he built, where big laughs can be mined from small, commonplace occurrences, opened the door for comedy to infiltrate every part of modern life. Jerry Seinfeld became the biggest comedian in the world with a show, as he described it, "about nothing," gripes and quips about the most inconsequential minutiae possible, because that was part of the joke. Shirt buttons could be funny. Junior Mints could be funny. The jokes were so small they could trickle down into any part of society. Every nook and cranny could be filled. Anything could be funny.

Comedy Abhors a Vacuum

The sheer joke density of contemporary life suggests that "peak funny" could very well be, like "peak oil," a sign of depletion. What if we're running out? On any given day, a breaking news event will be inevitably followed on Twitter by many, many people simultaneously making the same jokes about it. A new Indiana Jones movie has been announced? Brace yourselves for hundreds of variations on the premise that his new adventures might be a little different because Harrison Ford—wait for it—is very old! Congressional leaders propose a tariff on Mexican imports? Here comes a tidal wave of guacamole jokes! Even a celebrity death can become a ghoulish, nerdy rap battle on Twitter, with thousands of aspirants mining the deceased's show-biz résumé for good one-liner material.

I've had to delete dozens of tweets after a follower pointed out that someone else had told the exact same joke thirty seconds or thirty minutes earlier.* And the professionals aren't immune. Late-night talk show and comedy news hosts are now competing with the Internet equivalent of a million monkeys with typewriters. They know that unless a monologue joke idea is very, very good, it probably made the rounds on Twitter hours ago. Outlets with longer lead times like *Saturday Night Live* and the *Onion* have it even worse: they need to scavenge for comic takes that days of Twitter users *and* late-night writers have somehow left on the vine.

Late-night TV is, in fact, one of the best examples of comedy colonizing a new frontier and immediately changing it forever. In July 1953, when Steve Allen began a live local comedy show on New York's WNBT every night at 11:20, late-night television didn't exist. After the local news at eleven, stations would generally play the national anthem and sign off until morning. But in 1957, NBC decided to air Allen's show nationally, renaming it *Tonight.* The new time slot was a complete vacuum, desperate for content, and Allen filled it with a new type of program that emerged from his head like Athena, fully formed: the bandleader, the announcer, the opening monologue, the celebrity interviews, the comedy bits, the musical guests. Once comedy had planted its flag in late night, it prospered there for sixty years, with Allen's template shoving aside news and late movies until it spanned all four networks. For a few decades, *Nightline* swam upstream against Leno and Letterman, but by 2013, the acclaimed news show couldn't even survive as counterprogramming anymore. ABC pushed it back to 12:35, so that Jimmy Kimmel, a perfectly pleasant white man, could do his reliable Steve Allen–derived hour against two or three other pleasant white men doing the same thing.

Almost fifty years later, another new frontier opened. The YouTube website made its public debut in May 2005 with cofounder Jawed Karim's classic video "Me at the zoo," a nineteen-second test shot of elephants at the San Diego Zoo. The site was in beta-test mode for over six months, establishing itself as a place for teens to share videos of their bedroom rants or acoustic guitar performances, and it launched officially on December 15, 2005. Just two days later, on December 17, someone uploaded a copy

---

* Generally, this is how you know your joke was easy or "hack" in some important way. Presumably people who are better at jokes than I am can actually tell this in advance.

of a new *Saturday Night Live* digital short: Andy Samberg and Chris Parnell's "Lazy Sunday." This was a rap parody based on the premise that, as rappers go, Samberg and Parnell were anything but "hard," two middle-class slackers spitting rhymes about Magnolia Bakery cupcakes and an Upper West Side matinee of the first *Chronicles of Narnia* movie. It was one joke, but it was a pretty funny joke. The video went viral, generating a then-unprecedented five million views before NBC Universal finally pulled the clip. YouTube's reputation had been made: this was now *the* destination to catch new copyrighted content, either with the permission of rights holders or before they could respond. Just a month later, YouTube overtook Yahoo Video, then the web's leading video-sharing site, in traffic numbers, and was soon acquired by Google for $1.65 billion.

Two days! Two days was all it took for comedy to find a nascent medium and terraform it into a completely new ecosystem.

Sitcom Land in Bad Decline

The new omnipresence of comedy explains one puzzling outlier: the seeming decline in popularity of television comedy. This chart shows the number of top-rated television series that were comedies for every TV season since 1951.

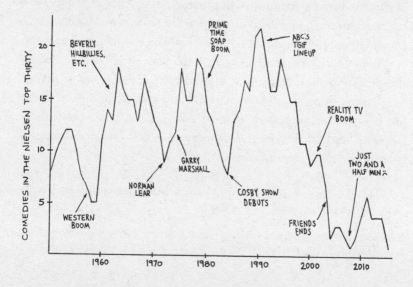

In an age when comedy is ascendant in nearly every facet of modern life, and sometimes takes as little as two days to conquer new ones, what's going on here? In just a quick glance at the chart, you can see multiple eras when comedy was the most popular thing on the television dial. In 1974, the year of my birth, every single one of the seven top-rated programs on TV was a sitcom.* The all-time pinnacle of the genre was 1991, when Brandon Tartikoff's sitcom revival at NBC, led by *The Cosby Show, Cheers*, and *The Golden Girls*, was in full swing. "Must See TV" so transformed the broadcast landscape that an unprecedented twenty-two of the top thirty shows were comedies.

But that collapsed pretty abruptly a decade later. In fact, by 2016, *The Big Bang Theory* was the lone comedy left in the Nielsen top thirty.† In just fifteen years, even though the Platonic ideal of "funniness" was more influential than ever in popular culture, network comedy collapsed to a tiny fraction of its onetime greatness relative to other genres. What happened?

"Now you have more of *everything*," *New York Times* television critic James Poniewozik explained when I went to him for answers. "That allows more diversity, more voices. Everything becomes more niche.

"Comedy isn't unpopular. It's huge! There are a lot more comedies. More late-night shows. Sketch comedies on cable. Comedy Central, premium cable, Netflix. And then you have a dispersal of the energy and audience of comedy into different forms of programming. A lot of reality TV is, essentially, comedy. Ambitious dramas like *The Sopranos* or *Mad Men* or *The Good Wife* were all among the funniest shows on the air any given week."

"But why didn't drama balkanize in the same way?" I asked. "Why is the same monolithic bloc still sticking with *NCIS* and *Criminal Minds*?"

"I think that goes to how personal and specific humor is. People just divide more on comedy than they do on, say, police procedurals. Comedy becomes a niche thing more easily, because sitcoms depend more on personal identification."

---

* *All in the Family, Sanford and Son, Chico and the Man, The Jeffersons, M*A*S*H, Rhoda*, and *Good Times*. Then *The Waltons* breaks the streak.

† If you don't count ties. The single-camera family comedy *Life in Pieces* was tied with two NBC procedurals for the thirtieth slot. In on a technicality!

There's also the demographic trend involved. Procedural dramas skew to an older audience that's more likely to watch the same stuff as each other, the same stuff they got used to watching five years ago. But young people are suckers for the new heat, the new destination. "Including stuff that's not on TV," Poniewozik points out, citing YouTube and other short viral-video media that are much better at delivering laughs than drama.

In other words, the apparent ratings disadvantage of network comedy is a direct result of the funniness explosion. There are now so many options if you want to laugh—why would anyone settle for the genre that gave us *The Facts of Life* and *Full House*?

The Charms of Deltalina

The ad world was the first industry to learn that humor was a reliable way to increase the attention, comprehension, and persuasion of just about any audience. Then *Sesame Street* brought the same approach to the world of education, teaching generations of children letters and numbers using the 1960s sketch comedy playbook of *Laugh-In*. More recently, in one of the oddest comedy developments of our time, the airline industry has been trying out the same technique.

Over the past decade, the simple preflight safety demonstrations of yore—here's how the seat belts work, here's where the life vests are—metastasized into full-blown comedies, with lavish musical production numbers and absurdist modern in-jokes. I lived in two different cities that were Delta hubs during this era, so I could watch the progress of the disease on the world's largest airline. Their first new-wave safety video, in 2008, attracted media attention for what Delta announced as "bits of humor and unexpected twists," but the staid five-minute video really had only two light touches: a digital twinkle added to the smile of one flight attendant demonstrating how to use seat cushions as flotation devices, and a sassy "No smoking!" finger wag from Katherine Lee, the redheaded flight attendant who narrated the video. Lee became a particular favorite with Delta's passengers (mostly the male ones, presumably), who nicknamed her "Deltalina" and set up Internet fan pages in her honor. As she returned to reprise her trademark gesture in future updates (now created by—who else?—Wieden + Kennedy), the comedy gradually took over the videos. The 2012 update to the video included silly throwaway gags like a robot powering himself down for takeoff and a man stowing a noisy accordion under his seat.

At first there was an illicit little thrill in seeing jokes sprinkled into a serious—and federally mandated—ritual of air travel. What a fun bonus! But then the videos proliferated in a half-dozen new variations. There was a special holiday-themed video every December, in which Ebenezer Scrooge refused to sit in an exit row ("Bah!") and Santa put his own oxygen mask on first before helping an elf. (Santa flies commercial?) There was an eighties-themed video complete with cameos from ALF, Teddy Ruxpin, Gerald Casale from Devo stowing his red "energy dome" hat under the seat in front of him, and in the copilot's seat, Kareem Abdul-Jabbar. Get it? It was funny because he also played the airline copilot in the funny movie.

By 2015, the once-refreshing Delta safety videos had descended into comic anarchy. One new version of the video was themed around Internet memes and featured briefly popular online "celebrities" like Keyboard Cat, Double Rainbow Guy, and Overly Attached Girlfriend. ("What is going on here?" I once heard an older passenger ask her husband while this video played.) In the next installment, Delta swallowed its own tail with a safety video *about Delta safety videos*. Highlights from past videos were replayed as winners of a spoof awards show called "the Safetys" (*sic*). If you hadn't been watching the evolution of the art form since 2008, you would have been very, very confused.

This is the twenty-first-century love affair with humor in a nutshell: take something funny, a small delight, and *absolutely wear it out*. Strip-mine it for every penny, every eyeball, every chuckle, until there's nothing left. Salt the earth so no one can ever laugh at tray tables and overhead compartments again.

The Bottomless Appetite

"What happens if the all-you-can-eat buffet runs out of food?" my daughter, Kate, asked when she was six or seven. Like many kids that age, she was obsessed with jokes and trying to figure out how they work.

"I give up. What happens if it runs out?"

"It can't!" she said. "It's an all-you-can-eat buffet!"

"That's a good one."

"Get it? 'All you can eat.'" I didn't really get it, but she seemed very pleased with herself.

The funny boom has turned daily life into an endless smorgasbord of comedy, more than you can ever consume. "Thirty-three percent of the American economy is now comedy," Conan O'Brien has said to his writers. It was a joke, but it didn't seem too far off.

Jokes are a little like soda pop, or porn. As an occasional treat, the way they started out, they hardly even counted as a vice. Who would begrudge the thirsty teen her tall, sweet cherry Coke from a soda fountain after school, or the bachelor-party rowdies their scratchy, worn-out stag film? But when high-fructose corn syrup or Internet porn began to *saturate* the culture, when they became the meal and not the dessert, we became grimly aware of their downsides. It was difficult not to wonder if the Big Gulps might be fueling an obesity epidemic, if the hours of online porn-watching might be warping the way people think about real-life sex.

When jokes come at us in dozens of YouTube videos and late-night monologues and hundreds of ads and thousands of tweets per day, they also start to feel less and less like a treat. They're just a constant low-level hum in the bed of the culture. As our baseline advances, we can become victims of what psychologists call the "hedonic treadmill," needing the steady flow of jokes just to keep from feeling unhappy, and ever needing more stimuli, and more novel ones, to feel real amusement.

Why does everything have to be funny anyway? It's hard to imagine anything that lends itself less to humor than federal air safety regulations do. When I flew as a kid, the laminated safety cards in the seat-back pocket scared the hell out of me, and I would pore over them from boarding until takeoff, absolutely sure that something was going to go wrong and I wasn't going to know where my nearest emergency exit was located. *What if it's behind me?* I think I was right to take the cards seriously; after all, this is life-and-death stuff. The Delta videos are clever, but maybe the airline was so busy asking, "Can we make cabin pressure loss funny?" that they never asked if they *should*.

Delta claimed that its videos were only funny in the interest of safety. "We wanted people to laugh and be engaged, because if they're paying attention and watching for the gags, they're also paying attention and listening to the safety instructions," the airline's marketing communications chief told an interviewer. But the jokes quickly became part of Delta's branding as well. Almost four million people have watched the first "Deltalina" video online—home viewers watching for fun, obviously, not studying life vest procedures. That's a strong incentive for an airline to load up its safety videos with laughs, whether or not there's any evidence that funny videos make passengers safer.

And is there any evidence? The Federal Aviation Administration has said that it never studied the question but still plans to do so. In a 2014 experiment, an Australian aviation safety researcher, Brett Molesworth, showed three different safety videos to a group of sixty undergraduates. One was serious, the second was funny, and the third featured celebrities. The funny video made viewers feel better briefly, but it had little effect on their recall. Humor, Molesworth wrote, "is positive in securing attention, but may disrupt processing of key information." In 2016, Delta ended the comedy one-upmanship by debuting a new, more straightforward series of safety videos with an international theme and no jokes.

But that's not the trend. Laughing makes people feel good and pay attention, and that's a powerful combination for anyone whose job is to make people feel good about something: a product, a place, a point of view, a political candidate. It's a simple process psychologists call "affect transfer": I laughed when I saw the funny ad about Old Spice, and I will spend the rest of my life vainly trying to recapture that flash of happiness, by buying Old Spice. "A brief moment of happiness is pretty good," said Jerry Seinfeld in 2014, speaking to a room full of ad industry folks giving him an honorary Clio award. It was a sardonic joke at the expense of advertising, but he wasn't wrong. Sometimes everything's bad, and it's nice that someone cleverly crafted a hopeful little moment to make you feel good about something. That's what advertisers do; it's what comedians do too.

But let's not forget that the people suffusing every second of your day with comedy aren't in it for humanitarian purposes. Funny spreads like a virus because mass media need content, and content pays. YouTube and late-night TV and essentially every other comedy vector in the media exist so they can sell advertising.* And funny advertising is now a $60 billion business annually. Of all the trends that we've seen powering the new humor boom—technology, youth, secularism—consumerism may be the most potent, simply because it's the best funded.

As I left the creatives at Wieden + Kennedy, I mentioned that I had recently picked up my first stick of Old Spice in decades. A few weeks earlier, in need of deodorant, I faced a full drugstore aisle of bewildering, demoralizing choice. After a few minutes of searching, I still couldn't find the exact size and shape of Speed Stick I was replacing. At a loss, I picked out a brand pretty much at random. It was Old Spice, the one with the funny ads. Affect transfer is for real.

"If your grandfather hadn't worn it, you wouldn't exist!" the back of the package announced. Craig Allen explained that Wieden + Kennedy now writes *everything* for the Old Spice brand, right down to direct mailings and label copy, stuff that would normally be segmented among different agencies. "It's very rare to get to do that."

I wondered to myself if the joke was originally pitched as "If your *father* hadn't worn it," which then got rejected as too edgy. Still, it was a bold gambit, to make the customer imagine his grandparents having sex every time he gets out of the shower. It's not reassuring, but it is funny. Today, that's really all that matters.

Why not? It's not a deodorant anymore, it's an entertainment brand.

---

* Not Twitter comedians. They're just venting, or want you to come to their shows.

FIVE

A LITTLE MORE CONVERSATION

The doughnuts had been hurled gleefully into the crowd at least twenty minutes before their owner came to the stage to confess. "They're secondhand," he explained, loud but quiet in the manner of the unmic'ed. "I wouldn't eat the doughnuts. I found them in a garbage can."

"Wait, which doughnuts, the Voodoo Doughnuts or the Krispy Kremes?" demanded our host, stoner comedian Doug Benson. It was the Krispy Kremes. "These doughnuts? Don't eat those ones, you guys. This guy says they're bad." What was actually wrong with the doughnuts? Were they laced with PCP? Human flesh? No one was sure. Who would put a box of tainted doughnuts on a theater stage for a host with the munchies?

I was a guest at a taping of Benson's long-running podcast *Doug Loves Movies*, in which a rotating panel of his comedy friends gabs about their favorite movies and competes at movie trivia games. I'm not a comedian, but occasionally there's a specialty act like me on the panel as well, like the dog acts of the vaudeville era. For many years, I'd been Benson's regular novelty panelist when his show pulled through Seattle, because, I gather, he likes guests who take the trivia games seriously. Also, I live ten minutes from the theater.

"That was one of the weirder exchanges I've ever been a part of," observed fellow podcaster and *Doug Loves Movies* regular Graham Elwood.

" 'Hey, you know those doughnuts you just threw at people?' " Benson said, imitating the matter-of-fact tone of the stage-rusher. " 'They're full of poison.' "

"Whaaa—?!?"

Poisoned doughnuts were a new wrinkle, but I was accustomed to all kinds of comic anarchy at recordings of *Doug Loves Movies*. Benson used to record the show in a studio, but when he started taping it weekly in front of a live audience, the crowd—a weird nexus of movie nerds, comedy nerds, and potheads—became part of the circus. The live show was a dizzyingly colorful coral reef, semirandomly accreting new layers of trivia and tradition every episode. The fans learned their lines and shouted out ritualized answers like a *Rocky Horror Picture Show* crowd. They would leave votive offerings of baked goods onstage for Benson before the show, and dozens of them would hang out at the stage door to smoke up with Benson afterward. In just a handful of appearances on the show, I'd seen the crowd peppered with Nerf darts on one occasion and doughnut holes from a slingshot on another. I'd seen a drone-copter flown over the crowd and a Darth Vader piñata whacked apart onstage. Maybe none of this business *sounds* like the most natural fit for an audio-only medium like podcasting, but fans don't seem to mind. The show gets downloaded by over a hundred thousand listeners every week.

"People drive as much as eight hours to get to my shows sometimes, and they listen to episodes of my shows in the car!" Benson told me, marveling at his devotees' dedication. "Plus there's the name tag thing. I jokingly said that audience members should bring name tags so I can remember their names, and next thing I knew, elaborate name tags started appearing at all of my shows."

To be clear, *Doug Loves Movies* ticketholders don't bring conventional shirt-lapel name tags. Instead these are more often full-sized movie-parody posters that punnily incorporate the fan's name into the title: *Hot Tub Tim Machine*, *Hannah-merican Werewolf in London*, *Ten Things I Hate About Stu*. Each panelist chooses a fan to play for and brings silly prizes for the winner. In 2016, Benson began letting panelists use their name tag owners as "lifelines" during gameplay, so the audience is now *literally* playing along. The fans are surrogate cohosts and writing staff as well, tweeting Benson ideas for games they'd like to see. They suggest categories for *Doug Loves Movies* standbys like "The Leonard Maltin Game" (a *Name That Tune* variant—how many actor names will you need to

identify a movie from a capsule entry in Leonard Maltin's movie guide?)*
or movie combos for "Build-a-Title" (movie titles chained together: *A
Few Good Men in Black Beauty and the Beastmaster and Commander:
The Far Side of the World According to Garp*). The show developed the
same way a "Build-a-Title" does: everything builds on everything else.

Doug Loves Movies is wildly successful, but it's just one of the approx-
imately one billion comedy podcasts being made today.† Most aren't
as extravagantly embellished or as rigorously structured as *Doug Loves
Movies*. A more common template just has a comedian chatting with a
guest or shooting the breeze with a bunch of comedy friends, and then
uploading the recording with very little editing. It's a medium that plays
to a stand-up comedian's natural strengths, it costs almost nothing to
produce and distribute, and when successful it can be a way to reach over
a million listeners per month. Some podcast comedians, like *Comedy Bang!
Bang!*'s Scott Aukerman, *The Nerdist*'s Chris Hardwick, and *WTF*'s Marc
Maron, have even seen their living room–style gabfests adapted into TV
shows and grown to become the cornerstones of mini–media empires.

Podcasting and social media have redrawn the landscape of what it
means to work in comedy today. But more fundamentally, they've also
changed our sense of what it means to be funny.

Why Lenny Can't Cook

In ancient Rome, they had a name for the worst kind of jokester: he was
a *scurra*. *Scurra* has usually been rendered in English as "buffoon" by
translators, but it's also the source for our word "scurrilous," meaning
"vulgar or abusive." To the Romans, the *scurra* was someone who made
his way in society by telling tiresome, insulting jokes—not just a boor
but, in modern comedy parlance, a hack. One of the worst qualities of
a Roman jokester, according to Cicero, was that he used jokes "brought

---

* Film critic Leonard Maltin has been invited on the podcast many times to play "The Leonard Maltin
Game." He's terrible at it.

† That number is accurate. Every man, woman, and child in the English-speaking world is doing, on average,
three different comedy podcasts at any given moment.

from home" instead of ones made up on the spur of the moment. Obviously prewritten quips, Cicero cautioned his fellow orators, "are generally frigid."

But carefully premeditated comedy has been the dominant mode of being funny for most of recorded history, because humor is just too fragile to leave to chance. Even a legend like Mark Twain, when asked to give an after-dinner speech, would laboriously write his remarks out longhand and then memorize them word for word. We love stories of acerbic off-the-cuff put-downs by Winston Churchill or Oscar Wilde, but part of us knows they're fantasies: impossible to verify, probably too good to be true. They're wit porn.

That all changed with Lenny Bruce. In comedy, everything goes back to St. Lenny. Today Bruce is mostly remembered as a free-speech martyr—threatened by vice squads for telling jokes about the Pope, targeted by the cops so many times that a fellow comedian began following him around on tour as an emergency understudy, arrested fifteen times for using words like "schmuck" and "tuches" in his act, sentenced to four months' hard labor in New York State for obscenity, blacklisted by so many nightclub owners that his career died not long before he did (of a morphine overdose at the age of forty). But listening to Bruce today, you don't immediately hear the rabble-rouser. In part that's because his most scabrous nightclub material never made it to magnetic tape. But it's also because jokes that might have pushed boundaries in the straitlaced fifties don't seem nearly as edgy today. In his famous "Christ and Moses" bit, introduced as police evidence at his 1963 obscenity trial in Chicago, Bruce's premise is that if Jesus were to come back today—get this!—He might be shocked at the glitz and hypocrisy of the modern church. Even if that was a fresh take on religion fifty years ago, it certainly isn't today.

What still feels most contemporary in Lenny Bruce recordings is how informal he is, as if thirty years of tuxedoed club comics had never existed. Prior to Bruce, it was clear why comedians called their jokes a "routine" or an "act." The former emphasized the roteness of recycled stage comedy, the latter its inherent dishonesty. On his records, Bruce started out doing a slightly more political take on what were essentially silly Shelley Berman telephone routines: German talent agents remaking young paperhanger Adolf Hitler into a feared dictator, President Eisenhower skeptically interrogating his embattled aide Sherman Adams. But that wasn't how he saw live comedy—even in his most formal surroundings, like when he played Carnegie Hall in 1961. "I can't be ponderous," he explained to the crowd that night. "People say to me, 'How come you don't do the bits in the records?'" He compares that to hearing a neighbor tell the same anecdote over and over at a party as new people join the conversation. By the fifth time, the joke's not making you laugh anymore. "He's corrupt, man, he's not funny! Why doesn't he stop with that boring story? . . . So that's it! If you dig hearing the same thing, go by your neighbor's, man! But I can't. As soon as it becomes repetitive to me, I can't cook with it anymore."

As a result, Lenny Bruce onstage just *talked*. He thought out loud. On his Carnegie Hall recording, he begins by telling a long, aimless story about his recent travel woes trying to get to Philadelphia during a weather delay, then gets sidetracked yelling at some galoot in the balcony for a full minute. Whole sentences fade out into unintelligible muttering. He'll make a funny observation (a mini-story about a doting mother who has no idea that her perfect son is gay—she's always bragging about how much he loves Halloween, brings servicemen home, etc.) and then move on half a sentence later without even finishing the thought. He'll seem to be building to a point, then wander off on a tangent for three or four minutes, then take up the thread again when it peters out. It's brilliant, but it's more like going out to lunch with a nervous, entertaining friend than it is like any kind of *performance*.

Bruce's stage style is often compared to jazz, and his recordings make that an easy comparison today. He keeps calling people "cats" and money "bread" and the venue "this scene." He says "dig it" as punctuation and compulsively snaps his fingers. He's so Lenny Bruce all the time that it's crazy! But the jazzlike improvisation hasn't aged a day, the sense that anything could happen at any point and it would always be something new. Music, like comedy, had been tightly scripted for centuries. Performers would come to the stage and play exactly what someone else had written, down to the littlest sixteenth note. It was part of Bruce's contrarianism that he refused to play the score, even if he had written it himself. Getting sidetracked into his own thoughts and riding them wherever they went was the whole point.

Audiences have long had to grapple with the fact that Bruce wasn't laugh-out-loud funny in the vein of the comedians he so obviously influenced: George Carlin, Bill Hicks, Richard Pryor. I've heard modern comedians from Patton Oswalt to Bill Maher parrot the modern received wisdom: as comics go, Bruce was important, but not terribly funny. The first half of that sentence is undeniable. Lenny Bruce's name is most often invoked to explain boundary-pushing comedians like Sam Kinison or Sarah Silverman, but an act doesn't need shocking sexual frankness to owe a debt to Bruce; his voice is easy to hear anytime a stand-up goes obviously off script into his own head (like Andy Kindler), or giggles at his own jokes (like Mitch Hedberg), or puts candor ahead of polish (like Maria Bamford). Without Bruce, you wouldn't have the confessional alt-comedians of the 1990s, the Janeane Garofalos and Marc Marons, picking at their scabs onstage. You wouldn't have Todd Barry putting together a 2013 "Crowd Work" tour (and subsequent Netflix special) in which he left his jokes at home and just riffed with audience members for almost two hours every night.

But what about the second contention, that Bruce wasn't particularly funny? It might not have bothered him. "Joke-telling is not my shtick," he told the Carnegie Hall crowd. Later in his career, when he would often spend his time at the microphone just reading his own trial transcripts aloud, he would end his performance by apologizing. "I'm sorry I haven't been very funny, but you see, I'm not a comedian. I'm Lenny Bruce."

Naked Honesty

Today, we are living in Cicero's utopia: spontaneous humor, in the form of podcasts, panel shows, social media, and the like, has finally become ascendant over the canned variety. And Lenny Bruce's apology still applies: it's the rare comedy podcast that's as wall-to-wall funny as a scripted comedy act or show, just as few serious podcasts can match the polish or careful research of a nonfiction book or *Frontline* special. But in podcasting, that doesn't matter so much, because the medium is the message. Intimacy, not careful execution, is the engine that drives the whole enterprise. Forty-two million Americans are now weekly podcast listeners, and the average listener spends five hours and seven minutes a week with their shows. Five hours and seven minutes! Your podcasts accompany you to the gym, drive to work with you, ramble on while you make dinner.* Most often, their voices are right in your ears, talking just to you. You're not in an audience. You're in a relationship.

Seattle musician John Roderick became a full-time raconteur when his band, The Long Winters, went on indefinite hiatus around 2010. The following year, he began recording his lengthy phone calls with tech writer Merlin Mann and releasing them in podcast form: *Roderick on the Line.* "After five years, people think they know me," he told me when I asked about his listeners. "To their credit, they know we're not friends, but they think we're the kind of people they *could* be friends with, if not for whatever. 'If I didn't live in Kansas City.' 'If my college friends hadn't all moved away.'" The alienation of modern life is real and devoted friends are sometimes in short supply. We'll settle for kindred spirits.

Comedy podcasting magically grants us a peer group that is not just faithful but *funny.* As listeners, we become part of the sparkling repartee. Late-night talk shows and sitcoms have always traded on the same appeal, of course. Johnny Carson was a reassuringly avuncular guardian angel who would check in on you every night before you went to bed; NBC's *Friends* was your quirky peer group, upgraded. But podcasts are a way to *mainline* that sweet showbiz immersion. Now the chummy comedy voices aren't telling jokes delivered by a room full of writers. The laughs aren't carefully workshopped, with every beat of the delivery timed down to the millisecond. Instead, the rhythm is unstudied, organic. Some jokes fall flat. Mostly the comics are just telling real-life stories undoctored or trading repartee with funny colleagues. That's the same stuff we civilians imagine ourselves doing at our funniest moments. Comedians: they're just like us!

In podcast culture, we also imagine that we are seeing the comedian as they actually are, warts and all. If nothing else, it seems like it would

---

* My wife even keeps a separate queue of soothing, low-pitched podcasts she can fall asleep to at night.

be exhausting to maintain a funny onstage persona over hundreds of hours in front of a podcast mic. There's more than a little truth to this. Many of the most famous stage personas in comedy history have been about as real as pro wrestling gimmicks. In his act, Jack Benny was famed for his cheapness; in real life, he was one of the most generous philanthropists in Hollywood (and generally overtipped waiters, to make sure word never got around that his stinginess was real). In the 1960s, a young comedian named Jack Roy had no success with his angry, hostile stage persona; after some midlife legal troubles, he came back to comedy with a more self-deprecating line of jokes, changed his stage name to Rodney Dangerfield, and the rest was history.

A carefully groomed image can do half the work for a comedian before he even takes the stage. Jack Benny's most famous joke came on his radio show in 1948, when a stickup man threatened him with the line, "Your money or your life!" Benny paused to consider for ten seconds while the studio laughter built to a roar. "I'm thinking it over!" he finally said. The line is only funny because the audience knows about his cheapskate reputation; with any other comedian, it's not even a joke. Kliph Nesteroff memorably wrote that Jack Benny's comedic persona let him land "punch lines in 1959 that had been set up in 1939," an unparalleled feat. Or a comedian can get laughs by swimming upstream against their established persona. A young Woody Allen regularly got his biggest laughs with nonjokes about his sexual magnetism and prowess.*

Everyone has a soft spot for certain comedians with big, exaggerated stage personas—Andy Kaufman, Pee-wee Herman, Phyllis Diller—but that school of comedy has never seemed less relevant than it does right now. Our most beloved comedy stars still have distinctive personalities, but *we demand they be plausible*! Andrew Clay's misogynistic "Diceman" from the 1980s and Phil Soltanek's quavery man-child "Emo Philips" are cartoon characters, but Larry David's "put-upon misanthrope" and Dave Chappelle's "weed-smoking provocateur" and Maria Bamford's "fragile misfit battling both adulthood and mental illness" just seem like

---

* He stays away from that kind of material today, *for some reason.*

honest (if selective) versions of their real selves. Longtime dues-payers like Amy Schumer and Louis C.K. leapt to mainstream stardom not with increasingly clever shtick, but by baring the darkest corners of their souls.

In August of 2012, Tig Notaro went onstage at Los Angeles's Largo comedy club and on the spur of the moment decided to replace her planned jokes with a brutally candid half-hour monologue about three recent blows: a breakup, her mother's death, and a Stage 2 breast cancer diagnosis. "Good evening, hello, I have cancer," she began her set. That's not an opening joke that a Bob Hope or a Milton Berle would necessarily have recommended, but before long the stunned audience was hanging on every word. Two years later, with her cancer in remission, she would often show off her double-mastectomy scars to comedy crowds. Sometimes she would do the second half of her set topless. Instead of alienating audiences, Notaro's frankness about her personal life turned her from a respected "comic's comic" into a household name overnight.* She sold a memoir to HarperCollins, starred in a Netflix documentary about her life, and had her semiautobiographical comedy series *One Mississippi* picked up by Amazon.

It's My Friend Who Doesn't Know Me

Boston-born writer and comedian Jen Kirkman started her popular *I Seem Fun* podcast in 2013. Subtitled *The Diary of Jen Kirkman*, *I Seem Fun* is confessional by design, generally recorded by Kirkman while she's propped up alone in bed, free-associating about stories from her week or pet peeves or whatever comes to mind. When she posted the first episode, she described it like this: "It's stream of consciousness with a point. It's like this—Jen wants to talk to you so that you know who she is. Then we can go from there. It's an easy and free thing to do for thoughts that are too long to tweet and ideas that aren't quite yet stand-up or other things. It's your friend leaving you a *really long* voice-mail message—hopefully an

---

* Almost literally overnight. Louis C.K., who watched Notaro's set backstage, persuaded her the next day to release a recording of the set as a comedy album on his website. The two later fell out over C.K.'s refusal to address the mounting rumors of his sexual misbehavior.

entertaining one." That's as good a mission statement as any for today's more spontaneous, intimate comedy. *It's your friend.*

Kirkman told me that her podcast has changed her career and fan base. The chunk of the audience she actually talks to, the ones who stay for meet-and-greets, all feel like they know her from her podcast. They're invested. "I got a letter once— okay, an e-mail— from a listener," she said. "She had become a fan of my podcast before knowing my stand-up. She said that she went to see me do stand-up and felt herself rooting for me, looking around the room as I got laughs as if she knew me. She felt proud that this person she 'knew' from a podcast was showing a different side of herself and it was working."

That connection is key. In such a crowded comedy marketplace, stand-ups on tour can't expect to sell out shows to clubgoing casuals who are fine with catching Generic Comedian X. ("As seen on *Conan!*") To make a living, they need to be appointment viewing. "It's easy to just decide to skip seeing a comedy show one night because 'she's so funny but I want to stay in tonight and return e-mails,'" said Kirkman. "But if people feel that they *know* a performer and aren't just looking to laugh but to feel connected—they'll come out and see that comic."

The most famous storytelling moment in the history of comedy is probably the last twenty minutes of Richard Pryor's *Live on the Sunset Strip*, in 1982. Pryor relives the night two years earlier when, after a days-long bender freebasing cocaine, he poured 151-proof rum all over his body and lit himself on fire. It was a dazed suicide attempt, and it came within a hair's breadth of succeeding. Pryor spent six weeks in a hospital, undergoing an agonizing series of skin treatments, sessions in a hyperbaric chamber, and surgeries. At first glance, it's not the most promising material for a stand-up set.

But the fire stuff kills, put over by Pryor's dazzling charisma and some of his best jokes of the night. There's an unbelievable story about Pryor in his hospital room watching a news report saying he died five minutes ago ("You find God quick when they find your ass dead!") and an even better one about a hospital orderly who wants Pryor's last autograph. But the highlight is a long chunk about what it's like to get a sponge bath when your body is covered in third-degree burns. Pryor mimes the excruciating pain, begging so convincingly that tears come to his eyes. "Don't wash no more! Not even my little finger!" Huge waves of laughter wash over the stage, but the laughs are different now. This isn't the funny side of his ordeal. This is a show of support; the crowd is responding because they love him and are glad he's okay.

There's something transcendent that happens between a comedian and an audience that I've never seen in any other kind of art or performance. A theater actor barely sees the audience through thousands of watts of stage lighting. Painters and authors work alone for hypothetical eyeballs from the future. Popular music is less of a one-way street: a rock band or hip-hop artist can feed on the energy of the crowd, to the delight of their fans. But that give-and-take feels even closer at a comedy show, because of the total absence of mystique.* The venue is usually smaller, the material more confessional and spontaneous, the performer more relatable. "It's that feeling you get when you're proud of the human race for being able to do something wondrous," comedy writer George Meyer told me, reminiscing about the alt-comedy shows he used to see at LA's UnCabaret in the 1990s. "You just felt all these boundaries falling away like icicles. It doesn't happen enough, but it's probably the best feeling on earth."

Richard Pryor didn't have a podcast, but he understood the personal bond that turns well-crafted comedy into something greater. He introduces the fire story by telling a crowd of three thousand people—not to mention the millions who later bought the album or saw the concert film—that they're all his confidants now. "I'm gonna tell y'all the truth tonight," he says. "You gotta promise not to tell nobody."

The 24/7 Comedian

The risk is oversharing, as Jen Kirkman is no doubt well aware. As a woman in comedy, her day-to-day reality is random creepy guys annoying her online. They feel they know her from her podcast and stand-up work,

---

* You could probably produce a list of comedians with mystique, but I don't know if everyone could agree on who should be on it, at least not after "1. Eddie Murphy."

and whether that's true or not, they haven't made the mental leap to realize that she doesn't know them. And a single off-the-cuff podcast comment can snowball into a *thing*—as it did in 2015, when Kirkman mentioned on *I Seem Fun* that she felt uncomfortable touring with a certain A-list comedian who had made advances to her and had a pervy reputation with women comics in general. Many listeners assumed (correctly, it turned out) that Kirkman was talking about then-beloved comedy star Louis C.K., and suddenly she was getting more media attention for her candor than for her comedy. She quickly pulled the episode.

It can be stressful; a comedian with a podcast or Twitter following is never really offstage. Paul F. Tompkins might be the most prolific podcast comedian of his time, having hosted three podcasts of his own, been a regular cast member on two more, and guested on *hundreds* of others (including at least two hundred *Comedy Bang! Bang!*s). Having fans who think they're actually your friends can lead to entitled nitpicking ("What are entertainers doing here if they don't want feedback?" a critical online follower of his once demanded), but on balance, he told me, the new arena has been a blessing for working comedians. The fragmentation of comedy might mean fewer people are getting fabulous seven-figure sitcom deals, but it's created more avenues to make a good living without being a superstar. "If you've found your people, they will support you," he said.

But the pace never lets up. A new special every year or two isn't going to cut it now; comedy fans expect new laughs *today*. Bo Burnham told the *New York Times* in 2016 that fans will ask him, "Are you dead?" on Twitter if their "IV drip of entertainment" slows down even briefly. "If you're not on [Comedy Central's] *@midnight* every month," he said, "you're Thomas Pynchon."

Tompkins agreed. "It's the pressure of the immediacy of everything now. Just as a consumer of social media, you see how quickly everything moves. So there's a fear of getting lost in the onslaught, a feeling that you have to keep piping up or people will forget you exist. I have definitely had the thought, on more than one occasion, 'I have to tweet *something*.'"

Back in the day, someone like Joey Bishop could put together half an hour of decent material and coast on it for decades, doing the exact same bits the exact same way every night. Today's comedians, by comparison, face an exhausting, never-ending scramble for new jokes—daily, if possible. The boom of friendly, time-filling banter hasn't just been a matter of taste. It's a matter of necessity.

The World Behind the Curtain

Honesty and spontaneity have never been more valued in stand-up than they are right now, but podcasts are still the best delivery vehicle for the new authenticity. They're completely unmediated by *material*, unencumbered by the weird dynamic of an orator addressing a room of strangers. No comedian ever *accidentally* reveals anything real they don't want to in, say, an HBO special, but on podcasts and social media, who knows where the conversation is going to go? Many comedy podcasts have meta moments where the hosts step outside the show to talk about how they think the interview might go, or how it went. WNYC's *2 Dope Queens* might swap notes about their celebrity crushes; Marc Maron might update listeners on his cats or his depression. In effect, we go backstage with them.

Lorne Michaels famously hates it when *Saturday Night Live* cast members "break"—crack up or break character—during a sketch, but in the last few decades it's become a common occurrence on the show. Audiences always go nuts for it. The appeal of seeing Rachel Dratch or Horatio Sanz lose it on live television was hard to articulate. It wasn't just the tingle of superiority, like when you spot a continuity goof or a sloppy special effect in a movie. It was something deeper, more delightful—like it was a mitzvah to be allowed to be a brief, vicarious part of such unplanned merriment!

Old-timey comedy is sometimes a tough sell for my kids, but they both love "The 2,000-Year-Old Man," the Mel Brooks–Carl Reiner recordings in which an interviewer asks an extremely old man about his remarkable life, from prehistoric times down to the present day.

REINER: Did you have a national anthem?
BROOKS: Each cave had a national anthem.

REINER: Do you remember what yours was?
BROOKS: I certainly do. You don't forget a national anthem. [*singing*]
"Let 'em all go to hell, except Cave Seventy-Six!"

What's infectious about the "2,000-Year-Old Man" routine isn't the jokes so much as the sense that the performers are having just as much fun as the listener. Brooks and Reiner began the skit as a gag at cocktail parties, and only went onstage with it when famous friends like George Burns and Steve Allen encouraged them to make a record. The routine's ad-libbed roots are everywhere on the recordings: Brooks trying not to crack up in advance when he knows he has a great joke lined up, Reiner asking questions he genuinely suspects might stump his kvetching partner, both barely stifling laughter sometimes after a surprising exchange. It doesn't hurt that we know the pair were real-life friends for more than sixty-five years, who into their nineties were still meeting up to watch *Jeopardy!* together every weeknight.

Podcasting is a never-ending supercut of "*SNL* cast members goofing" moments, but without the bother of the actual sketch. We're enjoying what we take to be the actual relationship between the comedians involved. The whole *Broadway Danny Rose* thing of comedians hanging out together in Manhattan delis like Lindy's was always real,* but, selfishly, the comics never used to invite us along. Civilians could only get a glimpse into that world by watching televised Friars Club roasts on NBC variety shows, where legends like Groucho Marx and Bob Hope would say terrible things about each other to the merriment of all.† Modern viewers may have only seen celebrity roasts in their twenty-first-century Comedy Central incarnation, in which celebs who are already Internet punch lines (Justin Bieber, Charlie Sheen, Donald Trump) try to win

---

* The popular-circa-1960 joke about a fly in a bowl of soup ("The backstroke, I think") is believed to have its roots in an exchange between a comedian at Lindy's and one of the deli's notoriously snarky waiters.

† The first celebrity roast in recorded history, I believe, took place in 423 BC at the Dionysia festival in Athens. In the comedy competition that year, Aristophanes had submitted his play *The Clouds*, which lampooned the philosopher Socrates. During the performance, confused out-of-towners in the audience kept whispering, "Who is Socrates?" to one another, so Socrates himself cheerfully stood up in the crowd to take the ribbing.

good-sport points by grinning through a series of staffed-out jokes delivered by an odd mix of respected comedians and random outsiders (Jewel, Shaquille O'Neal, Martha Stewart). The format is now in at least its third decade of self-parody, and the only really noteworthy sets in recent years have come from comedians trolling the whole ritual. Norm Macdonald, for example, "roasted" Bob Saget by reading insults from an old joke book that he'd copied onto index cards. "Bob has a beautiful face, like a flower. Yeah, a cauliflower!" Andy Samberg went even further afield in 2013 when he came up to the lectern to roast James Franco and then said incredibly *nice* things about him instead: "*Oz the Great and Powerful?* More like, a movie that transported me to a magical wonderland!" Today's overprogrammed Kabuki roasts give only a faint hint of the drunken, authentic bonhomie that prevailed in Dean Martin's day, when it was clear that everyone was there to have a good time with pals and not because an agent or publicist recommended it.* Milton Berle explained the insult comedy of roasts this way: "It's just a crazy way of telling people you love them."

But the Friars Club ethos of affectionate ribbing is now mainstream. There was always something a little bit combative about stand-up comedy, because in many respects it's a zero-sum game. You have to be a little funnier than the comedian before you and the comedian after you if you ever want to get ahead. The dawn of sketch comedy and especially improv changed that dynamic: they were art forms that put the funny people on the same side, made them into tight-knit little teams. The chilled-out yuk-trading of podcasting and Twitter continues the cooperative tradition. The only way to be funny is to make everyone else look funny as well.

Sure, there are still rough edges, because comedians can be a fragile and irritable lot. It's not always easy to tell when they're really getting along: Are Doug Benson and Bert Kreischer really fighting on this podcast, or just screwing around? Do Marc Maron and Michael Ian Black really hate

---

* It was a total sausage-fest, though. The Friars didn't allow women in their little clubhouse until *1988*. In 1983, when Phyllis Diller wanted to see Sid Caesar roasted, she had to sneak in wearing a man's suit, wig, and fake mustache.

each other today on Twitter, or is this a bit? Sometimes the comedians themselves might not even know for sure; passive-aggressive kibitzing is a tricky medium. In general, though, the modern mood of comedy isn't jealous, bitter neurotics setting each other off, a dynamic that might have boiled a lot closer to the surface in times past. Now it's buddies cracking each other up. A little neutered, maybe, but companionable.

Most importantly, the funny people have let us eavesdrop on their shenanigans. This confers insider status on us as well! To the modern comedy fan, who would collect comedian trading cards if that were a thing, this is nirvana. Lenny Bruce, once again ahead of the curve, spent almost ten minutes of his Carnegie Hall show educating the audience about what it's like to do stand-up in different kinds of clubs. In 1961, that was pretty inside-baseball. But fifty-odd years later, there were so many sitcoms about the life of a stand-up comic that Maria Bamford and Patton Oswalt could rip on the convention in the first episode of her show *Lady Dynamite*. In the age of peak funny, every laugh is a knowing laugh.

Building a Society on the Sweetness of Folly

The drift toward a looser, chattier comedy isn't a shocking innovation. It's just a bigger stage for the way pretty much all people use humor all the time. Our tendency to think of laughter as the result of a joke is in many ways deeply mistaken. Sure, responding to a joke is one thing human beings use laughter for. We also use small amounts of salt in chocolate chip cookies, but cookie-baking isn't really what salt is *for*.

Neuroscientist Robert Provine has spent his thirty-year career studying the psychology of laughter, recording untold hours of conversation in order to quantify how and why people laugh. He and his grad students sat in shopping centers, parks, office cubicles, and food courts, eavesdropping on strangers and creepily noting in thousands of notebook pages the laughter that dotted the conversations around them, like Amazon explorers recording birdsong. His discovery, in short, was this: everything we think we know about laughter is wrong. Most real-life laughs, for instance, didn't follow comments that were funny at all. Even the 10 percent that were provoked by mildly funny remarks weren't linked to *real* jokes, nothing so quotable you'd want to retell it to a friend later. Speakers, surprisingly, laughed 46 percent more than their audiences. And laughter may feel like a freeing paroxysm in the moment, a near-complete loss of control and composure, but Provine found that it actually followed strict mechanics: no laughs that interrupt speech, a reliable 210-millisecond gap between "ha"s, and striking temporal symmetry. (In other words, if you play a laugh backward, you don't get subliminal satanic messages. You still get a human-sounding laugh.)

Provine also found that "LOL" is a lie. We laugh thirty times more frequently with others than when we're alone. (For someone who's alone, "laughing out loud!" is in reality almost always "a small smile," but "ASS" is problematic as a texting acronym.) This isn't the most counterintuitive of his findings, but it might be the most important. Laughter, Henri Bergson wrote a century before Provine, "must have a social signification." This can't be overstated: all jokes require a collaboration. You have to decide to try to make me laugh, and I have to be willing. Failing that second ingredient, even the world's funniest bon mot, unveiled with exquisite delivery and timing, will result in stony nonlaughter. The tacit agreement has to hold on two levels: we both have to share the sense that this is an appropriate situation for joking, and then within the joke itself, we both have to be on board with its style and premise. This is true of all shared merriment. Charles Darwin once noted that even tickling will only produce laughter when "the mind [is] in a pleasurable condition." Otherwise, all you get is a pissed-off ticklee.

Laughter, in other words, may feel deeply personal and involuntary, but in fact it's nearly always helping to order a social web that binds people together. In 2004, two Stony Brook psychologists studying the effects of humor found that jokes told in a first encounter will bond two people faster than shared values. Faster than shared values! Cognitive scientists theorizing about the origins of humor must grapple with the fact that laughter may have evolved not as a side effect of the brain's "amusement" response, but in parallel with it, as a way for early hominids to signal playfulness, relaxation, and intimacy—when tickling each other, when wrestling with other juveniles. In an amazingly prescient evolutionary stroke, laughter may have even predated funniness. We know that many of the great apes make laughterlike sounds when at play, putting the lie to Arthur Koestler's famous assertion that only our species is *Homo ridens*, "the man who laughs."

In 1975, psychologist Antony Chapman recorded children listening to funny audio clips through headphones. The children laughed more when they were tested in groups—even if they weren't listening to the same material. Even more remarkably, the children rated the same recordings as funnier when they were listening with a companion or two in the room. As paradoxical as it sounds, being amused by something can sometimes be the result of laughter, rather than the other way around. I accidentally discovered the same effect while watching old episodes of *M*A*S*H* on DVD. Finally, after twenty years, I had the chance to experience the show the way its creator Larry Gelbart intended: without canned laughter spooned over the top of everything.* But to my surprise, when I chose the laughter-free audio track and settled in to watch, the show felt cold and mirthless, with awkward silences peppering the repartee. Over the decades, I'd become accustomed to a version of *M*A*S*H* that prodded me into laughing not just with the zany antics of Hawkeye and the gang, but through the magic of peer pressure as well. "Our sense of humor," Max Eastman once observed, "is subject to stampede."

Another popular theory about the origins of humor and laughter is that it's all one big mating ritual gone awry. There's some compelling evidence here: a sense of humor could have been valuable in sexual selection for our hominid ancestors, because then as now, it was a hard-to-fake indicator of intelligence, confidence, and other measures of reproductive fitness. On a first date, a bit of quick repartee with the waiter is a more convincing show of brains than telling your date, "Just so you know, *I'm very smart.*" On modern surveys, both men and women consistently rank "a good sense of humor" near the top of the list of traits they look for in a match. (This isn't as symmetric as it might appear at first blush,

---

* CBS insisted on a laugh track, not wanting to risk upending forty years of comedy tradition; Gelbart was anti–laugh tracks in general ("They're a lie!") but especially given the show's wartime setting and subject matter. In the end, he at least extracted a small compromise from the network: no canned laughter would be heard in operating room scenes.

though. When researchers present funny remarks in connection to photos of women, male subjects don't rank the women any higher. It turns out that when men say "a good sense of humor," they mean "someone who will laugh at good jokes, e.g., mine.")

The Renaissance thinker Erasmus is best known today for his satirical 1509 essay "The Praise of Folly." The essay is narrated by Folly herself, the goddess of all things silly and lighthearted, and she claims that no marriage will last long without her gift of good humor. "A wife [does not long tolerate] her husband," she claims, "except as they mutually or by turns are mistaken, on occasion flatter, on occasion wisely wink, and otherwise soothe themselves with the sweetness of folly." In fact, Erasmus goes further than that: Folly claims that this is also true of any relationship, whether in government, business, academics, or friendship. "In sum, no society, no union in life could be either pleasant or lasting without me."

As Erasmus tells it, society would break down entirely without our ability to laugh with each other in daily life. And maybe this is why organic, "caught in the wild" moments of levity go over better today with comedy audiences than canned jokes. They're closer to the value we see in the joking around of daily life, and most likely closer to what humor originally evolved to do. Our intuition that the funnier life is better tends to be borne out by research: funny people are perceived by others to be happier, more agreeable, and more attractive. People with a highly developed sense of humor (affiliative and not aggressive, self-enhancing rather than self-defeating) are indeed better than average at emotional IQ skills like striking up conversations and "reading" other people. Today's dominant comic sensibility in podcasts and the like is the easygoing, collaborative one that powers improv exercises, and it's not a huge stretch of the imagination to think that getting better as an improv partner isn't too different from getting better *at being a person:* open to new ideas and change, not judgmental of others' contributions, willing to take risks, valuing listening above all.

But just because so much good comedy today is communal, let's not start singing "Kumbaya" just yet. Not every joke told in a social context is necessarily going to make the world a better place. Spend a few minutes hanging out on comedy Twitter or listening to old *Opie and Anthony* shows. Joking around with friends can smooth social interactions, defuse stressful situations, and cheer up the lonely—but only if they're the right kind of jokes. Jokes can also be wielded to ridicule, scold, or punish others, or trivialize their concerns. In-jokes can create a powerful connection between people, but even they only work if someone's on the outside of them looking in.

Fugitives from the Grouch Patrol

One thing that long puzzled me about the slow ooze of jokes into every corner of life: what about the workplace? You may not remember the fad for corporate "humor consultants," but they once covered the plains like the buffalo. They wore Groucho glasses or red clown noses and gave presentations with titles like "Getting More Smile-age Out of Your Workday." Where did they come from? Where did they go?

The 1980s were a perfect storm for the creation of the corporate humor industry. Organizations were embracing less hierarchical management models, and the new-model executives were quirky, approachable personalities like ice cream wunderkinds Ben and Jerry or Southwest Airlines founder Herb Kelleher, who came to office Halloween parties dressed as "the High Priest of Ha-Ha" and challenged rival CEOs to arm-wrestling matches. Companies were eager for ways to boost employee creativity and solidarity while reducing conflict and stress, and humor training seemed to check every box. In the world outside the office, club comedy was booming, and some of those enterprising stand-ups discovered they could make more money telling jokes at a single "team-building seminar" than they could in a week of nightclub gigs. Second City held special sessions of its improv training boot camp for business teams. Even John Cleese had a lucrative second career with Video Arts, a company he founded to make droll corporate training videos with titles like *The Balance Sheet Barrier* and *Meetings, Bloody Meetings.*

Once humor consulting became a buzzword, the ranks of moonlighting comedians were joined by hundreds of business speakers with no comedy background chasing the latest management fad. Joel Goodman was a writer from Saratoga Springs, New York, who'd done business presentations on everything from organizational development to stress management. One morning in 1977, he'd had a road-to-Damascus moment on a Houston hospital shuttle, when a jovial driver had needed just four minutes of easygoing jokes to defuse all the family tension around Goodman's father's looming heart surgery. After his dad recovered, Goodman founded a utopian new initiative called the Humor Project that would, as he described it to me, try to replicate his moment of grace in Houston, teaching people and organizations to "'make sense of humor' and serve it to ourselves and coworkers and families and loved ones when we needed it." By 1997, he was receiving twenty requests *a day* for his troupe of humor consultants, who crisscrossed the country educating managers on "the relationship between the funny line and the bottom line."

And so, if you worked at Eastman Kodak during the funny era, you had a gaily colored "humor room" at your HQ, well stocked with Erma Bombeck books, *Candid Camera* videos, costumes, novelty chattering teeth, and a Saddam Hussein punching bag. The room was available anytime an employee needed a brief chuckle or a moment of stress relief. If you worked at Ben and Jerry's, the office "Joy Gang" would periodically surprise you with guerrilla celebrations: an Elvis impersonation contest, Dress Like Your Favorite Freezer Worker Day, Barry Manilow Day. At Apple, employees were instructed to blow on kazoos rather than applaud at quarterly meetings. At Digital Equipment, a roving "Grouch Patrol" wandered the halls looking for sour faces. Anytime they saw a frown that needed turning upside down, their protocol was to reply with the "bat face": tugging the nostrils upward with one hand while flicking the tongue in and out and making a high-pitched bat squeal. Who wouldn't crack up at that?

As anyone who's ever had a job could probably have warned us, humor didn't benefit by putting the word "corporate" in front of it. Teaching managers to say things like "That concludes the musical portion of the program!" after a squeal of microphone feedback, or to carry in their briefcase a "humor first aid kit" consisting of a Batman mask, colorful suspenders, and "whatever else can make you or your co-workers laugh," is unfunny-but-harmless advice. But PowerPoint suggestions like "Staple Kleenex to potentially stressful memos" point out the weird dynamic behind the humor boom: corporations were essentially co-opting fun, forcing it on their employees.* In many cases, humor didn't actually relax the old top-down management structure; it just became a new tool for keeping the employee cogs turning without squeaking. "Copays are doubling on our dental and vision plans, LOL! Here's a Kleenex!" "Lots of unpaid overtime is coming up this quarter, but we're also having an ugly shoes contest!" It doesn't help that all the enforced-fun committees from the era, the Joy Gangs and Grouch Patrols, had names you'd expect to see used by brigades of armed, unsmiling children in totalitarian dictatorships.

John Morreall is the rare humor consultant who was actually a respected humor studies academic before he got into the business. He finally hung out his Humorworks consulting shingle in 1989 at the height of the boom, unable to resist the siren song of the lucrative sideline. Though recently retired from William and Mary when I spoke to him, Morreall was still academia's leading expert on humor in the workplace, and he was surprisingly candid about his fellow humor speakers. "There are a number of people who do this business consulting who have no— how can I put it kindly? They don't have academic credentials and they don't have any special insights."

"Also, shouldn't professional humor consultants be . . . funnier?" I ventured.

"I don't know how to describe it," he sighed. "It's *Reader's Digest* funny. It's funny maybe for my parents' generation. I don't know what to say about the people who like that stuff, but it isn't my stuff."

I found one website for a Seattle-based humor speaker, a woman named Patt Schwab, and she was willing to meet with me to talk about her career. "So you will recognize me, I'll have a rubber chicken head peeking out of my purse," she wrote in her e-mail. Sure enough, when I

---

* This has become a universal enough comic trope that it powered versions of *The Office* in nine different countries, but the definitive comedy treatment of "funny" early-nineties office culture is the "Grass Valley Greg" sketch from the eighth episode of *Mr. Show*. "Work is play, Tofutti break today!"

got to Starbucks, hers was the only purse with a rubber chicken. Schwab had recently taken the chicken with her on a trip to Cuba; in each photo she showed me, the chicken was wearing a different costume: a kimono, a feather dress, a little tuxedo. The outfits, Schwab explained, were actually those novelty covers people buy for wine bottles. A trick of the corporate humor trade.

Like many of her peers, Schwab fell into the humor business accidentally. She was a college administrator when professional contacts started asking her if she could add a workshop on humor to her repertoire. Before long, she was a full-time evangelist of her own LAF management system (*limber* up, *anticipate* change, *foster* fun!) and traveled the country cracking up hotel meeting rooms full of middle managers with lines like, "Ever since I ate my first Oreo, I've realized that good things are in the middle!"

But the high life didn't last. "I was riding a wave and I didn't know it," she said wistfully. In the 1990s, all she had to do was call a presentation something like "Laugh and Everyone Wins!" and clients lined up. But when the humor fad started to fade, she had to find new, more serious-sounding names for all her material. Out went the LAF system, in came "Making Work Work for You."

Most of the humor speakers "went back to their day jobs" when the boom ended, Joel Goodman told me. John Morreall blames the end of the corporate jokester industry on economic downturns and the easy availability of online resources. Bosses looking to fun up the office don't need to pay five thousand dollars to fly in a speaker, if they ever did. Patt Schwab was more frank about those online resources: "One of the killers is that you can't steal jokes anymore," she said. The borrowed puns and cartoons that powered her industry just don't cut it anymore in an age of more relaxed, spontaneous joking around.

Joel Goodman ended the Humor Project's annual conferences in 2012. "There has been some ebb and flow" to the humor business, he conceded, but he seemed reluctant to say that his day has passed. "Humor has gotten woven into the fabric of the culture," he insisted.

I can't agree that Goodman's brand of prefab jollity really represents the comic mood of modern culture. Quite the opposite: comedy as a corporate trend seems to have run its course largely because it was so often glaringly artificial and unfunny in a world that was getting hip to a more genuine comic sensibility. But Goodman is certainly correct in one sense: it's harder to think of laughter as some undervalued, elusive commodity now that it's everywhere. And organized levity is now an expected part of professional life, especially in sectors like tech. A friend of mine briefly worked for a massive Internet search company that will remain nameless. He told me that the buzzy new time-waster at work was trying to handle as much internal communication as possible not with e-mail or instant messaging, but with funny memes. A whole platform was designed from scratch to facilitate this dubious-but-"fun" goal. If the boss from *Office Space* pops up on your screen saying "That'd be great," that's a Level Three problem. But if Rambo pops up, uh-oh. That's a Level Five. You might be working late tonight. "*Considerable* time and effort has gone into developing this tool," my friend said, smiling ruefully.

Humanity's Funniest Home Videos

Such is the allure of today's looser, more improvisatory comic sensibility that even scripted comedy now chases it. The dazzling virtuosity of TV in the baroque *30 Rock* vein can overshadow the parallel strain of comedy vérité that took over streaming television in its wake. *Curb Your Enthusiasm*–descended slice-of-life shows like Aziz Ansari's *Master of None* and Rob Delaney and Sharon Horgan's *Catastrophe* weren't always interested in the artier aspirations of *Transparent* or *Girls*, but they aimed to show funny people as they are, not as they might be if they had a roomful of people sharpening their zingers. You can always tell one of these shows immediately: in violation of decades of sitcom tradition, the characters will often laugh at each other's jokes. You don't realize until it happens how much you were missing it. What could feel less organic than a world where everyone is constantly quipping at each other but no one ever laughs?

The lazy pinnacle of this trend has come in late night: James Corden singing karaoke with celebrities or Jimmy Fallon challenging them to a game of Pictionary, pretending all the while that this qualifies as comedy somehow. "People are having fun, this must be funny!" There was a time when late-night hosts were our sharpest and most experimental comic minds, but in the end our need for breezy social comedy trumped everything else. Leno got the *Tonight Show* instead of Letterman, and Jimmy Fallon held on to it when Conan couldn't. On the other hand, all the genial Fallon-style gimmicks and lip-syncs will probably age better than scripted Letterman monologue jokes or weird Conan O'Brien sketches like "Horny Manatee." Kliph Nesteroff pointed out to me that our modern image of midcentury comedians is largely from clips of them palling around on Jack Paar or *What's My Line?* "That tends to hold up better than their act does," he said. If that's true as a rule, our grandchildren might still be charmed in fifty years by late-night clips of Tina Fey telling vacation stories to Seth Meyers, even while they find the travails of Liz Lemon to feel stylized and dated—"very 2010s."

Spontaneous, conversational humor is now so endemic that we've even had to change the meaning of words. Now that a "joke" is essentially any funny exchange between pals, comedy writers have had to invent a new term for the more classical structured quips and anecdotes of yesteryear; those are "jokey jokes." "Jokey joke" is what's called a retronym—a new term created when old technology gets outpaced or outmoded, like "acoustic guitar" or "silent film." As we've seen, the canned joke has a history going back millennia, so I don't expect jokey jokes to go the obsolete way of silent film anytime soon. But they might become the equivalent of acoustic guitars: a slightly quaint alternative to the hip thing. Good for kids. Easier for beginners to whip out at parties.

In the past, the limits on spontaneous humor were mostly logistical ones: there were books and books of reliable canned jokes, but how often did something truly, memorably funny happen to you in real life? I made a list once, and could only think of half a dozen really anecdote-worthy experiences in my lifetime:

1. Trying to hug the dentist
2. Rooftop animal noises during the blackout
3. The smuggled apple

4. Jerremy the unhelpful waiter
5. Duct tape/pubic hair misunderstanding
6. Sex ed with P. J. Carlesimo

In a world where everyone had only a handful of real-life funny stories, scripted comedy was a lifeline. But today, thanks to Internet sharing, we can see that "jokey" jokes are a drop in the ocean compared to the real-life kind—not just in podcasts, but in all the "found comedy" highlights of random earthlings going through daily life. Maybe a dog in Australia will just *barely* fail to clear a fence and will plunge end-over-end to the sandy beach below in hilarious fashion. Only three people got to see it in person, but if the owner had a camera phone out, that number can become three million by the next morning. A random toddler doing weird stuff to Kanye's "Father Stretch My Hands Pt. 1" will make me laugh ten times harder than any classic Oscar Wilde aphorism or Marx Brothers routine. In the *America's Funniest Home Videos* era, it was possible to treat real-life moments like these as anomalies, an embarrassing "guilty pleasure." But now that we're surrounded by them, we know different. All the podcasts and tweets and YouTube videos are really the same thing: real life with the unfunny parts removed.

Real life was as funny as canned jokes all along, but it was hard to see in close-up. We used to get the funny highlight reel of just one lifetime, but now we get to see millions.

SIX

EVERYONE'S A COMEDIAN

On the evening of Thanksgiving Day 1988, most residents of Minnesota's Twin Cities were probably watching football, if they had their televisions on at all. But any viewers accidentally venturing into the upper reaches of their dial during the fourth quarter of the Cowboys game might have wondered if they were hallucinating in their turkey comas. For reasons not immediately clear, channel 23 was airing episodes of *Stingray*, a 1960s British undersea sci-fi series for children, repackaged into a feature-length movie. In the lower right corner of the screen, a boyish host and two robot puppets were watching the bizarre adventures of the World Aquanaut Security Patrol and occasionally interrupting the movie with a bemused quip. It was the debut of one of the most enduring comedy phenomena of our time, and fewer than four thousand people saw it.

KTMA-TV 23 was the most remote outpost of the UHF wasteland in Minneapolis, filling its prime-time hours with *Hawaii Five-O* reruns and regional pro wrestling. The station's production manager had approached Joel Hodgson, a Wisconsin-born prop comic recently returned from Los Angeles, and asked if he had any ideas for local programming. Hodgson pitched him a twist on the local TV movie hosts he'd grown up with: what if the mad scientist or the vampire lady didn't just appear at commercial breaks, but actually watched the movie along with the home audience? He sketched some silhouetted heads watching B-movies from theater seats*

---

* Hodgson's visual inspiration here was a similar drawing from the album sleeve of Elton John's *Goodbye, Yellow Brick Road*, used to illustrate the lyrics of the ballad "I've Seen That Movie Too."

and gave his pitch the campy sci-fi title *Mystery Science Theater*, later adding the number "3000" to further baffle viewers.

"It was kind of a big misunderstanding, basically, that it even got on TV," Hodgson told me. "As time goes on, I see more and more that it's outside any kind of norm for a TV show and defies a lot of the way TV was done."

Every element of the show's premise stemmed from those first sketches. How to distinguish between a group of cohosts joking in a darkened theater? Make a couple of them robots with distinctive silhouettes. If the movies were so terrible, why wouldn't the hosts just leave? Well, they must be trapped. Where are they trapped, then? Okay, they're in space—on an orbiting satellite, forced by an evil scientist to watch lousy movies against their will. On the strength of a hurriedly shot pilot (a cheesy Japanese alien flick from 1968 called *The Green Slime*), KTMA agreed to air *Mystery Science Theater 3000* weekly, every Sunday night. The budget was $250 an episode, so Hodgson and his collaborators built a flimsy satellite set out of Masonite, insulating foam, and toys from a local Goodwill. The night before the pilot was shot, Hodgson jury-rigged together his robot cohosts.

Suddenly, the station where you could watch *The Andy Griffith Show* reruns while making dinner had an underground hit. The show's answering machine filled up every time Hodgson put the phone number on-screen. Some messages were from testy viewers who preferred their monster movies without smart-alecky jokes ("It was like being in a theater with a bunch of rude junior high teenagers!" one scolded), but most were hooked. Hundreds of letters poured in; by spring, there were a thousand members of the show's official fan club. Less than a year later, HBO bought thirteen episodes of *Mystery Science Theater 3000* for its new twenty-four-hour comedy channel, cleverly named the Comedy Channel (and shortly thereafter renamed Comedy Central).*

---

* More precisely, the Comedy Channel merged with its more catchily named rival Ha! to form CTV. Two months later, CTV became Comedy Central.

A Shoestring Budget and "Minnesota Nice"

But even as it gained a cult following nationwide, airing on basic cable for over a decade, *MST3K*, as fans called it, retained its stubbornly lo-fi sensibility, what Hodgson called its "miniature golf aesthetic." In the age of *Terminator 2* and then *The Matrix*, the robots were still obviously the product of a prop comedian's junk drawer. "Tom Servo" was a gumball machine with doll arms. "Crow" was a Tupperware set topped with cheap sporting goods: a hockey mask, a plastic-bowling-pin nose, and two Ping-Pong ball eyes. After seven seasons, the Comedy Central–era set was still the same one originally built for $200, and up until the bitter end, the show always taped in a makeshift studio in an industrial park for medical equipment companies in suburban Eden Prairie, Minnesota.

For Hodgson, staying in Minneapolis was the secret to the show's success. "They really wanted us to go to New York, and we just knew that would not be good," he said. "Here's the thing about comedy: it doesn't hold up when it's scrutinized. It doesn't hold up when people ask you questions about it. It just sort of evaporates. So you have to avoid being in situations where people ask a lot of questions and challenge you and go, 'Is what you're doing funny?' Because if you're in that situation, it's over, and you can't defend it. So that was really what I was going by. Just leave us alone and let us do this."

There was no mistaking the show's origins. Despite the vogue at the time for edgy shock comics like Sam Kinison and Andrew Dice Clay—and much to Comedy Central's chagrin, at times—*Mystery Science Theater 3000* was more prone to gentle in-jokes about crappie fishing, "hot-dish" casseroles, and the Wisconsin Dells. It's not hard to imagine a version of *MST3K* that skewers its terrible monster movies with the most caustic put-downs imaginable, but the show's Midwestern writers and performers preferred good-natured ribbing. "The idea was, you're watching a movie with companions," Hodgson agreed when I asked him about the show's essential sweetness. "And so if you're an asshole, it's not sustainable. People don't *want* to spend time with you for eighty minutes."

Mystery Science Theater 3000 was a word-of-mouth phenomenon—"Keep Circulating the Tapes," the show reminded us at the end of every episode, blithely encouraging viewer piracy—and every fan (or "MSTie") probably remembers their first exposure. Mine came in high school, while I was channel-surfing at the rural Oregon home of my grandparents, who had just bought a twelve-foot satellite dish. Satellite TV in the early 1990s was a welter of raw news feeds, televangelists, scrambled soft-core, and weird Spanish-language game shows, but the UHF era of the cheesy rainy-afternoon movie was ending. So I couldn't have been more surprised, that Saturday, to flip past a dubbed Japanese *Planet of the Apes* rip-off being gleefully snarked at by robots. "A whole planet of Ron Perlmans," remarked one puppet, marveling at the simian baddies with the unconvincing rubber masks. "A flea-collar concession would really clean up here," said the other puppet. It lasted another hour, and then I immediately looked to see what time it would start on the West Coast feed, so I could watch it again. *What on earth was this thing?*

The low-production-value host skits on *MST3K* were funny, but the core of the show was the three buddies talking back to the movie— the riffing, to use the borrowed jazz term. In any given five-minute chunk of the show, Joel and the 'Bots might name-drop *Waiting for Godot*, the Harlem Globetrotters, the *Beverly Hillbillies* supporting cast, jazz trumpeter Maynard Ferguson, and the Warren Commission. This was "reference humor" as dense and as arcane as anything *Family Guy* or *Community* would try decades later, but—and here's the thing—it felt *accessible*. I had no idea how the jokes on my other favorite TV shows got written, but it seemed hard as hell. *Mystery Science Theater 3000* made me laugh just as loudly as *The Simpsons* or *Seinfeld*, but at heart it was still just three friends joking around about bad movies—something we've all done from our couches, if not as elegantly. Decades before the podcast era, Joel Hodgson and his robot friends weren't just riffing. They were also teaching millions of viewers to do the same. With its homemade sets, low-key joke format, and a cast that seemed largely plucked from community theater, *Mystery Science Theater 3000* was the forerunner of something completely new in comedy: the DIY era.

The Gifted Amateur

There has always been a vast gulf separating the truly, professionally funny from the rest of us: the class clowns, the cubicle jokers, the funny-once-you-get-to-know-us, the funny-after-a-few-drinks, the funny-but-not-haha-funny. And there have always been hopefuls trying to figure out a way to cross that gulf. In 1926, Will Rogers wrote, "I have been interviewed in every Town in the United States, by serious-looking young College Boys with horn-rimmed glasses and no hat, on the subject, 'How would you advise a beginner to be funny.'" Rogers was always happy to offer suggestions. "Recovery from a Mule kick is one way that's used a lot. Being dropped head downward on a pavement in youth has been responsible for quite a few. And discharge from an Asylum for mental cases is almost sure fire."

Today's more conversational comedy vibe, and especially the illusion of intimacy fostered by podcasts and the like, has made comedy feel more accessible, but becoming a *practitioner* can still seem daunting. In the absence of a handy mule, how does an earnest young funny person make the leap? Keegan-Michael Key told Judd Apatow that, as a child, he saw a TV special about John Belushi and realized he wanted to be a comedian, "but it felt like there was no way to get there, you know? There was no conduit." But that was changing as early as 1972. In April of that year, the Comedy Store opened its doors in West Hollywood, giving Los Angeles its first comedy club, and then just a few weeks later, Johnny Carson moved *The Tonight Show* from New York to Burbank. Soon the Comedy Store became *the* place to be seen by television bookers, and maybe land a spot on *Tonight* or another variety show. When Johnny began announcing that his comedian guests were "playing this weekend at the Comedy Store," viewers took note. No longer would funny people just emerge fully formed from a confusing demimonde of bohemian coffeehouses and mobbed-up casinos: there was a Comedy Store now, and hundreds more such "stores" on the way. Suddenly, this was a career path. America knew how to try this.

Today, in the words of the old lament, literally *everyone* is a comedian.

There used to be just one day a year when regular people tried to be funny: it was April 1, and it sucked. Now it's a yearlong pursuit. Twelve thousand people sign up for comedy classes with the Upright Citizens Brigade troupe every year, and UCB is just one of hundreds of groups teaching improv and sketch comedy nationwide. Alternately, you can become a comedian without even having to brave a single open-mic night, because now we have the Internet.

Twitter: Jokes for Dummies

There are people trying to be funny in thousands of ways online, but "riffing" in particular—not on Japanese monster movies but on the events of the day—is the lingua franca of Twitter. When I first signed on to Twitter, I eagerly followed the accounts of people I knew would be funny: Albert Brooks, Sarah Silverman, Conan O'Brien. And they were funny! But to my surprise, literally thousands of oddball Twitter civilians were funnier.

> **Mary Charlene** @IamEnidColeslaw
> do people who run know that we're not food anymore

> **chuuch** @ch000ch
> hi, grandma? can u come pick me up from my rap battle? it's over. no, i lost. he saw u drop me off & did a pretty devastating rhyme about it

> **Fred Delicious** @Fred_Delicious
> science defines a baby as "a small smooth poopy man, no taller than a lamp"

> **jon hendren** @fart
> i saw an ad on craigslist once that said "free firewood, u collect it" so i wrote the guy and said "bud you just wrote an ad for the woods"

stefan heck @boring_as_heck

Next, on TLC's Lunchbox Wanters

RON: Back off, Jim. That box is mine.

[CUT TO INTERVIEW]

RON: No way was I letting Jim get that lunchbox.

If you're a Twitter veteran, you already know this. There are legendary stand-ups and Pulitzer-winning satirists and top-shelf comedy writers who use the site, and yet on any given day, the funniest tweet might very well be from a college dropout in Oregon or a bored computer programmer in Atlanta. His or her name is likely a pseudonym; the avatar photo might be a raccoon or an African dictator or an eighteenth-century woodcut. The joke might be a hot-off-the-presses political zinger, or a silly personal anecdote, or a Mitch Hedberg–style head-scratcher, or a little one-act play. Even with the impassable character-limit moat around each joke, Twitter comedy is surprisingly versatile.

"I think that it feels like a video game," Megan Amram told me about her Twitter habit. Amram moved out to Los Angeles in 2009 in hopes of breaking into TV, and got hooked on Twitter as a way of polishing her joke-writing skills. "There is some tweet out there that no one has written yet that completely sums up the human experience in a hundred forty characters, and every day I wake up and hope that I figure it out. And it's a weird, almost masochistic game: can I think of the thing that resonates with the most people today?"

For generations, comedy writers and performers have grappled with this question: are the professionals, the big-name stand-ups and showrunners, truly the world's funniest people? When asked about this in 1983, Jerry Seinfeld came down unequivocally on the side of the professionals, because stand-up is so difficult. "If everyone in the country decided to be a comedian," he said, "there would still be only six terrific ones, like there are now." A decade later, the overheated expansion of the comedy circuit made Seinfeld look prophetic. Suddenly there were hundreds of hacky white guys in sports jackets standing in front of brick walls at clubs and even on our TVs, all doing the same Nicholson impressions and telling the same jokes about airline snacks and shopping carts with one stubborn wheel. Sure enough, even most of the people who *thought* they could do this couldn't really do this.

But let's leave out the stagecraft. Presence, timing, crowd work, all the hard stuff that takes decades of apprenticeship. What about raw funniness? Many comedians are on record saying that, just as not all the world's best-looking people are models, not all the funniest people go into comedy. Megan Amram always cites her twin brother as the *real* funny person in the family. He's an ophthalmologist. Another TV writer told me about Matt, a college friend "who just seemed like the funniest, cleverest guy in the world. He was so much funnier than me that it sort of unnerved me."

Did Matt go into comedy? "He didn't—he's a social worker somewhere in Canada now. I tried shooting him a message a few years ago through Facebook, and his response was embittered and unfunny. So it goes."

Twitter gave the rising generation of aspiring jokesters an outlet, but more importantly, it gave them a community, a place to play together. There's a reason why comedy is often collaborative—why comics enjoy telling jokes to each other, why TV shows have writers' rooms. Ideas spark, jokes cross-pollinate, sensibilities evolve. Twitter is a global writers' room, and it's making everyone a little sharper.

I recently ran across an old tweet of mine, and I did what you're not supposed to do: scroll down to read the replies. I was pleasantly surprised: people were riffing!

Ken Jennings @KenJennings
It's actually illegal to wear your sunglasses on the back of your head unless you have ID proving you're an assistant Little League coach.

- "GOOD EYE THERE, BLUE!"
- I've got a warrant for one "Guy Fieri"
- sales reps for Yeti coolers are legally allowed to wear these as well

- that seems really unfair to lifeguards.
- Professional Bass Fishermen are grandfathered in
- I think it counts if you have a Coors Light in one hand and a
  motorboat steering wheel in the other

I didn't know who left these replies—I'm going to go with "random millennials"—but they are perfectly serviceable sunglasses-on-back-of-head jokes, my friends. You'll see the same thing anywhere on the Internet. Sure, the top comments on your local newspaper's website (average commenter age: 110) are going to be a cesspool. But the top exchanges on the same story on Reddit or some other younger-leaning forum are almost always jokes, and most are good for a slight smile, or even the elusive brief chuckle. The only downside is that you'll have to spend time on Reddit.

Scratching Away in the Chinese Room

The Twitter joke boom strongly suggests that a sense of humor can be learned—at least to some degree. Cicero didn't think so, writing in *De Oratore*, "This talent cannot possibly be imparted by teaching." I asked humor researcher Peter McGraw if that was really true. Surely science has advanced in the two thousand years since Cicero.

No dice. "No one has done that work," McGraw said. "There's absolutely zero research that tries to make people funnier. None at all." There are interventions on countless other positive traits: ways to make people more grateful, forgiving, and so forth. "But nothing on comedy."

I'll volunteer as a case study here. My time cracking wise on Twitter seems to have made me funnier—or at least better at Twitter. Looking back on my old tweets, I see lots of jokes that were confusing, or pointless, or "edgy" in a cheap way, or contrived, or overexplained, or any number of other offenses. But over time, I got a little smoother. You can't spend all day watching hundreds of bored, funny people trade jokes and not start to pick up some tricks.

But is that really the same as getting funnier? In artificial intelligence research, there's a thought experiment called the "Chinese room," first presented by philosopher John Searle in 1980. We're asked to imagine a computer programmed to communicate with human users by exchanging snippets of text in Chinese. This computer can pass the famed Turing test—that is, users actually think they're interacting with a human Chinese speaker. Now imagine a human being in a room who speaks no Chinese but has a hard copy of the same computer program handy. As a result, when given a set of Chinese characters as input through a slot in the door, he can laboriously trace through the program and produce the same output symbols that the computer can. It would *seem* like he was speaking Chinese. But we know he can't, right? He's just mindlessly stepping through a printout. Therefore the computer doesn't understand what it's doing either, and artificial intelligence is bunk. QED.

I think about the Chinese room a lot when I'm on Twitter—and not just because I'm usually sitting in a small room trading garbled messages with a bunch of strangers. What if I'm like the English speaker in the room, learning a trivial set of basic manipulations that cleverly *simulate* humor but never really getting to the soul of what makes things funny? The more time you spend on Joke Twitter, the more you see that this is surprisingly plausible. A lot of the funny stuff that gets tweeted relies heavily on joke formats. These canned templates cycle in and out of fashion, but when one is at its peak, literally hundreds of people will be trying their hand, and even the funniest people won't be immune.

Some popular Twitter formats are more or less writing prompts, like the "Damn girl!" pickup lines that were the flavor of the month in early 2013.

demi adejuyigbe @electrolemon
damn girl, are you the wife of a convict serving a long term in a federal penitentiary, because you left before i even finished my sentence

Tony Logan @tnylgn
Damn girl are you a pizza at a Chinese buffet because I'm not feeling it right now but I see you over there doing you and I respect that.

Eireann Dolan @EireannDolan

Daaaamn girl is your name Katrina because my lower 9th just flooded

Yes, I know. The all-time champion "Damn girl" tweet is actually a 9/11 joke of jaw-droppingly poor taste, and is not appearing in this book because I'm not an idiot.*

Other Twitter formats are such rigid templates that they require about as much comic invention as doing Mad Libs. Put the word "Sext:" before a decidedly unsexy clause,† or add "and chill" to the end of one. End an unpopular or ridiculous idea with ". . . said no one ever!" The most useful formats survive because they provide a satisfying sense of "joke-ness" to what would otherwise be an only mildly amusing observation. They're like the stock ending of a Restoration comedy, the happy wedding that wraps everything up with a little bow and gets everyone offstage. Take these variants of the old sitcom "pull-back/reveal" joke:

OhNoSheTwitnt @OhNoSheTwitnt

Since Ariel was 16 when she became human do you think she got her period immediately?

Boss: I meant any questions about the presentation.

Jason Miller @longwall26

If it facilitates the consumption of liquids, can it really be called a "crazy straw"?

Lawyer: I think we'll pass on this juror, your honor

---

* In my memory, I had avoided the "damn girl" craze entirely. But a quick search revealed that I succumbed to temptation exactly once, on March 10, 2013. "Damn girl, are you the second season of *Friday Night Lights* because you are playing an awful lot of Wilco." Now *there's* a joke that will stand the test of time.

† The "Sext:" format was only funny in the hands of its inventor, poet Patricia Lockwood, who used it for oddball tweets like "I am a living male turtleneck. You are an art teacher in winter. You put your whole head through me."

These get a lot funnier when someone figures out a darker way to tweak the format.

Dollars Horton @crushingbort
me: Carly Rae Jepsen's new album attains an 80s pop authenticity
Taylor Swift could only dream of

ISIS captor: hold on its not recording yet

Knock Knook. Who's There? Joke Fads.

Joke formats predate Twitter by centuries, but that can be hard to remember sometimes because each hot new thing comes and goes so quickly. Who remembers Wellerisms, popularized by Charles Dickens in his first novel *The Pickwick Papers*? (A Wellerism is a familiar cliché or proverb given some colorful twist by a clever attribution—"'Every little bit helps,' as the old woman said when she pissed in the sea.") Who remembers the wind-up doll jokes of the early 1960s ("The Fidel Castro doll: wind it up and watch it turn red!") or Rich Hall's invented "Sniglet" words of the early 1980s ("flopcorn: the unpopped kernels at the bottom of the cooker")? In hindsight they seem like a form of mass hypnosis. How were templates like these ever the hottest thing in jokes?

Folklorists love joke fads because they're the closest thing we still have to the oral traditions of preindustrial societies. *Seinfeld* quotes and "You might be a redneck" lists are our epic poems and fireside tales. Honest-to-God academic journal articles have been written about how Helen Keller jokes were a reaction to the mainstreaming of children with disabilities in American schools, and how elephant jokes were a cleverly coded way for whites in the 1960s to worry about the real "elephant in the room": the civil rights movement. But the real explanation is much simpler and more universal than that: joke fads catch on because they make the mystery of humor seem *attainable*, for everyone. Each one is a little lesson in how to be funny, or at least "funny." They're puzzles. Can you spot the pattern here? If so, you too can crack a joke.

For many years, the vectors of joke-telling didn't require even that limited creative process. Joke-tellers were mimics, like parrots. If you could repeat the latest naughty yarn about a traveling salesman in 1958, or could say "Yeah, baby!" in an Austin Powers voice in 1998, you could be the good-time office cutup. That kind of thing still exists today, of course, in the form of pass-along social media ephemera: today's new meme or Photoshop or cat GIF. It's still easy to make all your friends laugh without actually thinking up something funny. But Twitter is something different: not just an audience to repeat jokes to, but a place where you can use the comic sensibilities of others as training wheels to develop your own.

Funniness starts to seem less and less elusive the more time you spend around funny people. It's the peek behind the curtain Moshe Kasher and Chelsea Peretti described, like seeing the same magic trick night after night. The first few times you'll be wowed, but soon you might start to see the strings—especially if you're shown variations on the same trick. The patterns you learn aren't strict joke formats; they're more general comic devices. Reversal is a common one: just take a common situation and turn it exactly on its head. In its most basic form, this is the syntactic flip behind a Yakov Smirnoff–style joke: "In Soviet Russia, TV watches you!" But semantic flips can produce more sophisticated results as well, everything from Rodney Dangerfield one-liners ("I played hide and seek, and they wouldn't even look for me") to an elaborate piece of comedy like Dave Chappelle's "black white supremacist" sketch. Or try applying a situation unexpectedly to itself. Recursion is the transformation behind reflexive jokes as dumb as a "Dyslexics of the World Untie!" T-shirt or as complex as the "Pre-Taped Call-in Show" sketch from *Mr. Show* that I watched several hundred times in college. Once you see the strings, it's remarkable how many jokes are constructed on equally simple mechanisms: combining pieces of two disparate situations, for example, or asking "But what if . . . ?" about a common assumption.

Artificial Japes, Stand-up, and Wisecracks

But that doesn't mean joke production is as easy as memorizing a cheat sheet of five simple rules. If humor really were purely algorithmic, machines could do it, and that's not happening. My own experience with computer intelligence is limited to Watson, the IBM program that destroyed me at *Jeopardy!* in 2011, and believe me, there was nothing funny about it. Endless factual recall was trivial for a computer with sixteen terabytes of RAM, enough to store every word in the Library of Congress. But the ability to get a joke—something a four-year-old human can do—was well beyond its abilities. *Jeopardy!* clues with any kind of conceptual or playful element—anything approaching creativity or humor, in other words—were like kryptonite to Watson.

That's because humor is one of the hardest problems in artificial intelligence research today. Researchers have written countless joke-telling programs—JAPE, STANDUP, WISCRAIC—but their output is generally as unfunny as their acronymic names.* The jokes they produce are limited to a very narrow domain—mostly punny riddles. (There's a reason why those were the first kinds of jokes you could master in kindergarten.) WISCRAIC's best output was a series of homonym puns along the lines of "The performing lumberjack took a bough." JAPE's highlight reel includes "What do you call a depressed train? A low-comotive." These algorithms are also completely clueless as to which of the output they've generated actually qualifies as funny, though to be fair that's true of many carbon-based comedians as well. I've tossed off plenty of dumb Twitter jokes that, to my shock, circled the world within seconds of my hitting "Send." Conversely, I've tweeted plenty of things that cracked me up in my head but amused literally no one else. On Twitter, when a joke doesn't land, there aren't even glasses clinking and a single dry cough from the back of the room. There's just the void.

But there's a very logical reason why computers can't evaluate their own humor: no one has ever taught them, in a language they can process, what makes jokes work. A Purdue linguistics professor named Victor Raskin has been studying this problem for years, developing a formal language called OST (Ontological Semantic Technology) that

---

* JAPE is the Joke Analysis and Production Engine. STANDUP is the System to Augment Nonspeakers' Dialogue Using Puns. WISCRAIC is Witty Idiomatic Sentence Creation Revealing Ambiguity In Context. URRGH (Unfunny Researchers Rarely Get Humor).

will theoretically help computers "understand" the interplay between meaning and ambiguity that makes things funny. His goal is to be able to convert any joke into a labyrinthine "text-meaning representation," or TMR—essentially a computer program for humor. OST is so complex that a simple two-sentence quip can break down into a text-meaning representation that's pages and pages long. Here's a vastly simplified TMR for the seven-word joke "A man walks into a bar. Ouch!":

> TMR1: walk (agent (person (gender(male)) (age (adult)))) (location (bar))

> TMR2: collide (agent (person (gender (male)) (age (adult)))) (theme (pole)) (instrument (leg))

See? See how funny it is now?

My favorite joke algorithm, DEviaNT, was developed at my old school, the University of Washington, in 2011. DEviaNT had it all, from a bad acronymic name—"Double Entendres via Noun Transfer"—to an incredibly limited humor domain. All it was programmed to do was to read a sentence and then determine whether or not it would be funny to follow that sentence with "That's what she said," in the manner of Michael Scott, Steve Carell's character from *The Office*. But DEviaNT, it turned out, was no Michael Scott. It could only identify 8 percent of the possible "That's what she said" opportunities, and it notched so many false positives that its jokes were only successful 71 percent of the time.

Just 8 percent! Keep in mind that this program didn't even have to invent or understand jokes. It had exactly one job: to learn how to use a single canned sentence, the purposely unfunny catchphrase of a TV character. That's not hard at all* and it still couldn't quite nail it.[†]

If DEviaNT is the state of the art, we don't need to worry about funny supercomputers writing our sitcoms anytime soon. Robots will be

---

* That's what she said.

[†] That's what she said. Hey, this is that recursive-joke thing from two pages back.

killing us with lasers long before they start killing with their stand-up.* It's tempting to think that the rise of humor in discourse today is because we all sense this on some level: the ability to crack a joke is one of the most essentially human traits we have left. A good nine-to-five assembly-line job used to be a prestigious career, before machines could do those jobs faster and better than we could. It isn't just that wages dropped; the whole enterprise started to seem less admirable to us somehow once a robot rendered humans obsolete. Even the knowing of facts, my only marketable skill, seems quaint and silly in the age of Watson and Google. But jokes! The machines aren't coming for our jokes yet, and so we cling to the small things that can't be automated away.

Incidentally, the most common rebuttal to the "Chinese room" problem in artificial intelligence circles is "the systems reply." This argument holds that, even though the person in the room doesn't speak Chinese, the entire system taken as a whole—the beleaguered occupant plus the program and all the room's pencils and scratch paper and whatnot—does, effectively, speak Chinese. The *room* (and, therefore, the computer) knows what it's doing, even if the individual doesn't. So computer scientists would say that I *am* getting funnier—because my system now includes all the mechanisms I learned and joke-sparking connections I made online. In other words, my brain is just one node of Twitter now. Maybe a social media network will be the first artificial brain to achieve joke-telling sentience.

The Big Leagues

Megan Amram @meganamram
At the intermission of musicals there should be a very short football game

---

* In 1999, two psychologists at the University of California San Diego decided to test whether or not machines could make humans laugh another way: by tickling us. After all, it's impossible to tickle yourself, right? There has to be a tickler and a ticklee. But does the tickler have to be human? The study found that subjects laughed just as hard when they believed their tickler to be mechanical. (But I'm skeptical about the findings for one reason: the robotic tickling hand in the experiment was just a prop, and the blindfolded subjects were actually being tickled by a hidden human.)

Bryan Donaldson @TheNardvark
If Natalie Portman dated Jacques Cousteau they would win celebrity couple nicknaming forever with "Portmanteau."

If you want proof that Twitter really does work as a comedy laboratory, you don't have to keep staring into the microscope at individual tweets. At some point, you should be able to see the clinical trials working on your test subjects.

When Megan Amram joined Twitter, she thought it would be a good comedy writing exercise, a way of collecting jokes for the TV pilot script she hoped to write. Many funny tweeters seize first upon the transitory nature of Twitter, and their output is loose and goofy, like texts to a friend. Instead, Amram focused on the medium's brevity. She took the 140-character limit as a challenge: "Can I think of a bon mot that stands by itself? Can I write a perfect little puzzle?" Her jokes were tiny gems that sparkled in the river of Twitter silt. They felt like discoveries. "There's literally no way to know how many chameleons are in your house." "WHY was Mario Kart not called 'Mario Speedwagon?'" Even her "damn girl" joke put on a clinic: "girl are u my neighbor's wifi? cuz u have a stupid name and im having trouble connecting."

A friend of a friend saw her tweets, then met up with her at a comedy show. He wanted her help with a TV job he was writing for. On the strength of her Twitter feed, Amram had just been hired for her first gig, and it was the 83rd Academy Awards. About one hundred million people worldwide heard her first televised jokes.

Bryan Donaldson also hopped on Twitter in 2010, to kill time at his IT job for a central Illinois insurance company. Hoping to stay anonymous, he called himself "the Nardvark." If you were writing his story as fiction, you would never include the fact that he lived in Peoria, the proverbial backwater opposite of the coastal entertainment capitals. Seems a little on-the-nose.

I followed Donaldson's feed in 2011 and immediately saw that he had a hits-to-misses ratio as high as anyone on Twitter. Tweeting is so easy—too easy, sometimes. As in many sports, it's all about the shots you don't take. But Donaldson, like Amram, was irritatingly disciplined and consistent. He only tweeted when he had a great idea. I liked his dry observational tweets, largely of the long-suffering-Midwestern-dad variety ("When my wife gets a little upset, sometimes a simple 'calm down' in a soothing voice is all it takes to get her a lot upset" or "Relaxing family vacation. Pick two") but he also had a knack for political zingers.

It was the topical jokes that brought him to the attention of writer-producer Alex Baze, who in 2013 was hiring writers for Seth Meyers's new late-night show. He sent Donaldson a Twitter message asking if he wanted to submit a packet. "What's a packet?" Donaldson wondered.

"I didn't know the first thing about writing comedy or how it worked," Donaldson told me. "'Oh geez, this guy thinks I'm a comedy writer and not an IT guy.'" But he flew to New York for a fifteen-minute interview, and was offered the job. He didn't have an agent, a manager, or any comedy experience. His entire résumé was, as he put it, "dick jokes written while sitting on the toilet."

At the age of forty, Donaldson moved his family from East Peoria to the New York suburbs. The banner on his Twitter page is now a shot of the Manhattan skyline from the roof of Rockefeller Center, the building where he works every day on the *Late Night* monologue. It's just like an amped-up day of Twitter: setups will arise from the day's headlines (now collected for him by a team of writers' assistants) and Donaldson is on the hook for forty to sixty punch lines. But today, when he nails a joke, he doesn't just get a few hundred ego-stroking "likes" on his phone. He gets to hear it read by Seth Meyers.

"Twitter is way easier to use to get *fired* rather than hired," Donaldson observed to me, but in fact his and Amram's stories are starting to feel less like one-offs and more like the start of a trend. At *Parks and Recreation*, Amram worked with Joe Mande and Jen Statsky, both stand-up comedians hired on the strength of their Twitter quips. The original *Late Night with Seth Meyers* writing staff included Alison Agosti and Michelle Wolf, writers who, like Bryan Donaldson, had been spotted by Alex Baze on Twitter. "Twitter has democratized the process," Seth Meyers said.

Outsider Art, Without Going Outside

And today Twitter is just one of many ways to become a comedy megastar without even having to leave your bedroom. In 2009 and 2010, UCB improv vets Abbi Jacobson and Ilana Glazer self-produced thirty-three episodes of their web series *Broad City*, about their own lives as two slacker best friends at play in the Big Apple. Most of the zero-budget episodes were just two or three minutes long, some even shot as video chats. The web series never really went viral, but Amy Poehler was a fan and helped shepherd the show into development at Comedy Central, where it quickly inherited the mantle of *Girls* as TV's foremost millennial voice. And Bo Burnham was just a high school junior in Essex County, Massachusetts, when he started uploading his home videos onto the Internet. He would sit in his bedroom with an acoustic guitar or digital piano and sing satirical self-written tunes like "My Whole Family (Thinks I'm Gay)." Within a few years, he was selling out theaters on both sides of the Atlantic and was the youngest stand-up ever to have to his own hour-long Comedy Central special.

In 1982, veteran comedy writer Gene Perret wrote, "There's a myth around that hidden somewhere in the United States are people much more talented than the big names. . . . The guy in the next office writes better than Neil Simon, but no one has discovered him yet." But the Internet has now proved Perret's "myth" to be shockingly close to the truth. Just as the vogue for singing-contest shows brought us legitimate stars like Carrie Underwood and Jennifer Hudson, we now know that the world is full of comedy Susan Boyles, secretly hilarious sleeper agents toiling (or, more likely, smoking weed and playing video games) in obscurity. Maybe Twitter's best amateur joke writers aren't Neil Simon, but without any of the advantages of the established LA or New York comedy scene, some of them are already ready for prime time. The ones who make it are the ones who hustle, of course, and it takes time to develop raw talent into real greatness. But it's a start, and everyone has to start somewhere. Steve Martin used to make balloon animals at Disneyland. Bob Newhart was an accountant for a drywall company.

Even in ancient Athens, a playwright needed a wealthy backer called a *choragus* to get his comedy produced by paying for costumes, rehearsals, extras, and so forth. So today is the first time in about 2,500 years when it's possible for funny people to make an end run around the gatekeepers and find a mass audience directly. This is great news for diversity in comedy, since it's an alternative to the old-boy network that can dominate hiring: which smart-alecky young white guys did they write with at their last job, who did they go to Harvard with. It also empowered everyone—beginners like the *Broad City* duo and old hands like Louis C.K. alike—to try out the *Mystery Science Theater* DIY model. They could build an audience on their own and cut deals that kept control of their work far away from network executives, even if that meant taking smaller paychecks. Before its star's 2017 comeuppance, *Louie* wasn't filmed in a suburban Minneapolis industrial campus, but it might as well have been for how little FX, the cable channel where it aired, tampered with its riskier material. This was a series that ended its pilot—its *pilot!*—with its star telling a three-minute story about the day they put down his childhood dog. Ratings gold!

The Funniest Kids in the World

For comedians who spent decades in depressing clubs paying their dues, the explosion of amateur Internet comedy is a sobering development. "We had a monopoly before," one stand-up told me. There's certainly a potential economic impact: why would you pay a $15 cover charge (plus two-drink minimum) to hear jokes from a professional when hundreds more will be scrolling by on your phone for free? If everyone's a comedian, no one is.

But I worry more about what it's doing to the rest of us. When my daughter was in fourth grade, she brought home a book from the school library called *How to Be the Funniest Kid in the Whole Wide World (or Just in Your Class)*. On the back cover was a photo of its author, Jay Leno, clad in all the denim in creation. She had no idea who he was. Most of the jokes inside were typical elementary school riddle-book material: "What kind of math can you teach to cows? Cow-culus." They could have been written by Bazooka Joe or JAPE or WISCRAIC. Other jokes had confusingly old-timey references to *Funny Girl*, Seabiscuit, Wurlitzer organs . . . you know, all the stuff that fourth-graders love. School Library Jay Leno actually made *Tonight Show* Jay Leno seem funny by comparison. But I'd never seen Katie more excited by a new book! She holed up with it for days, eager to become, as promised, the funniest kid in her class. Somehow she had gotten the message: this is how you navigate the world now.*

Look, I like jokes as much as anybody, but they shouldn't be *compulsory*. We don't need Jay Leno–run reeducation camps, constantly making sure the unfunny are giving it their best in a national game of *Last Comic Standing*. My personal problem is social media, with its constant pull to *always* tell another joke and be validated for it, whether I feel like it or not, whether I have anything funny to say or not. Megan Amram, even as a successful TV writer, said that she still wakes up every single morning thinking, "Okay, what am I going to tweet today?" The gamification has worked, the Twitter blessing and curse of knowing, with great precision, how numerically funny everything you said was. "You have other things you've done, you have other accomplishments, but the feeling of having a tweet go viral is this immediate thing that's still amazing." A writer friend of mine adamantly refuses to join Twitter because that instant gratification might be a little *too* amazing. She thinks it rewires you so that, eventually, you're unable to produce anything without it.

And most of us produce nothing at all! The constant cavalcade of jokes contributes to our modern culture of "content," where we're all just consumers, all the time. We have tastes instead of hobbies, we race to respond to new ideas with "takes" instead of actually engaging with them. We've mastered the language of comedy, but what are we using it for? The riffing on *Mystery Science Theater* wasn't a license to make idle snark a default response to all culture. "It's kind of like being a vampire," Joel Hodgson told me. "You have to be invited. We're not riffing against your will. That's heckling."

---

* A few months later, she also told me she wanted to take improv classes, which she had learned about on some PBS show. "Do you even know what improv is?" I asked. "Making up a play and adding on to what someone else is saying. If someone says, 'My cat got out,' the second person says, 'Okay, let's go look for it.' They don't say, 'Who cares? Look, here's a pretty seashell.'" In the 1970s, children's television taught me to read. Today, it teaches kids to "yes, and."

The Not-So-Distant Future

Mystery Science Theater 3000 ran for seven seasons on Comedy Central and then another three on the Sci-Fi Channel, revived by a fan letter-writing campaign. The entire cast had turned over by the time it razzed its final movie (*Danger: Diabolik*) in 1999. Even Joel Hodgson had left five years in after feuding with his co–executive producer, but he was seamlessly replaced as host by the show's head writer, Michael J. Nelson. When the show ended, the cast and writers went their separate ways, but over the following decade, they gradually returned to the business of terrible movies. It was a diaspora, not a reunion; the cult success of *MST3K* had created a whole new cottage industry. Joel Hodgson and his original cast, along with some later additions, toured as Cinematic Titanic, performing live riffs of the usual B-movies and monster fare. When Cinematic Titanic called it a day, Trace Beaulieu and Frank Conniff, the mad scientist baddies of the show's Comedy Central era, carried on as the Mads. The core of the Mike Nelson–era cast formed RiffTrax, recording standalone commentaries that customers could sync up and stream as they watched movies at home. True to the show's DIY spirit, RiffTrax even allowed fans to record and trade their own "iRiffs."

Mystery Science Theater 3000 was never a ratings bonanza, but its cult and its critical reputation grew steadily, even after multiple cancellations. In 1993, the show won a prestigious Peabody Award. "With references to everything from Proust to *Gilligan's Island*," the citation read, "*Mystery Science Theater 3000* fuses superb, clever writing with wonderfully terrible B-grade movies." In the new millennium, *Time*, *Entertainment Weekly*, and *Rolling Stone* all put *MST3K* on their lists of the one hundred best TV shows of all time. Joel Hodgson, who had begun working to regain the rights to the series and revive it, noticed that he was being treated with a new respect in industry meetings. "Suddenly you're an elder statesman, or a guru," I said. "That must be very gratifying."

"Yeah," he agreed. "It's awesome."

In 2015, Hodgson launched a Kickstarter with the aim of crowd-funding a *Mystery Science Theater* revival, which he would produce but not host. The initial $2 million goal would have funded three episodes. On board was an entire generation of writers and entertainers who had been influenced by the show: Patton Oswalt, Jack Black, Joel McHale, Bill Hader, Neil Patrick Harris, *The Book of Mormon* composer Robert Lopez, *Community* and *Rick and Morty* creator Dan Harmon, *Adventure Time* creator Pendleton Ward. The Internet went bonkers, raising $6.3 million in just over a month, enough to produce a full fourteen-episode season 11 (which Netflix later picked up). It was the most successful video crowdfunding project in history.

Conspicuously absent from Hodgson's monthlong tsunami of hype was any guarantee of the show's original cast and writers returning, and this was no accident. A series of terse denials from his former satellite-mates made it clear that they were quickly distancing themselves from the reboot. They didn't share Hodgson's ownership interest in the show, after all, and many now had successful bad-movie-ribbing enterprises of their own that even made them semi-competitors. The riff rift took some of the air out of the MSTie enthusiasm balloon. After a fifteen-year absence, their favorite show was, against all odds, returning from exile— but with none of their old favorites aboard.

That's why there was such a collective sigh of relief a few months later when RiffTrax announced that its tenth-anniversary celebration would be a full-fledged *Mystery Science Theater 3000* reunion, with riffing from essentially all of the show's original cast, the Hodgson synod as well as the Nelson. The sold-out show, from the State Theatre in (where else?) Minneapolis, would be simulcast in movie theaters across the country.

I bought tickets for me and my son, who was already a die-hard *MST3K* fan at thirteen, just a year younger than I was when I saw *Time of the Apes* in 1989. The series had never been on TV during his lifetime, but he didn't care. When I told Hodgson about Dylan's abiding love for his creation, he wasn't surprised. "Kids like the show—and they don't have a problem with references they don't understand, because their life is like that. They're constantly being confronted with things they don't understand, but they start to find meaning in the words and the tone in which they're delivered. The way we move into the world is the same way. You kind of learn things by proxy."

On the night of the show, our multiplex was full of MSTies some-where between my age and Dylan's, all enjoying the preshow trivia. As we squeezed into two of the last available seats, the happy geek couple in front of us was singing along to "The Greatest Frank of All," from a sketch in episode 523, *Village of the Giants*. They knew every word.

The anniversary show was a series of bizarre midcentury short films—a genre beloved by the fans—razzed by just about every possible permu-tation of the show's cast over the years. It had been a long time since I'd seen a movie riffed in a theater, and I'd forgotten what a rich communal experience it is: there's the movie, and the first audience watching it carefully, weaving in and out of dialogue, finding their spots and their rhythm, and then the *second* audience watching both the movie and the first audience. We are the communicants, and the comedians on the screen intercede for us with the B-movie gods, making their wrath bearable. We're all in on the jokes—and probably mentally pitching our own—and we're all audience members as well, even the professional riffers. The bright line between performer and amateur faded away when the lights went down. This is increasingly how comedy works now.

The liturgy on this occasion included educational and industrial shorts with titles like *More Dates for Kay*, *Shake Hands with Danger*, and *At Your Fingertips: Grasses*, each more ridiculous than the last. My son and I laughed until our cheek muscles literally hurt. For the final three shorts, the cast was joined by Hodgson and comedian Jonah Ray, who had been named the host of the new rebooted *MST3K*. It was his public movie-riffing debut. "Can I just thank you guys for making *Mystery Science Theater 3000?*" an obviously moved Ray asked his castmates. "It made me who I am." He could have been speaking for any of us.

SEVEN

BON JOVI, COME HOME

I was late getting my son to a friend's birthday party, and we didn't have a gift, so we ran into a drugstore for a gift card. "Get a birthday card too," I told Dylan. "That makes it a little less tacky."

Five minutes later, we were still late and he was still mesmerized by the massive wall of greeting cards at the front of the store. Specifically, he was trapped at the "Birthday Cards—Funny" shelf, which dwarfed all the other birthday card sections put together. A placard over one side of the shelf had the logo for a brand called Shoebox, with a laughing face replacing the first letter *o*. Shoebox, a subtitle assured us, was "Hallmark Approved. Sorta."

"Let's get this one," Dylan decided, grabbing a card and envelope. A bottle of red wine was cartooned on the front. "I know you would love a bottle of wine!" it announced in kicky, hot-pink cursive. I opened it up. "But here's a card instead!"

"Hey, Dylan, this is what moms get for, like, their friend at the office. It's not really a card for a fourteen-year-old boy."

"That's why it's perfect. Ben will think it's funny. It's a birthday card, but it's ironic."

If you still associate greeting cards with old-school sentiment— sparkly hearts and flowers to or from Grandma—get with the times. Edgy, winking humor has increasingly become the dominant voice in a shrinking market under siege from free new competitors: e-cards and Facebook birthday wishes. "With texting now the primary form of communication, it has changed the nature of how we talk to each other," Sarah Tobaben told me. She's the creative director for Shoebox, the quirky "alternative" card line Hallmark launched in 1986. "People are much more quick, casual and less formal. And of all the genres of greeting cards, humor cards are the most quick, casual and least formal."

A few weeks later I was driving Dylan and a friend home from a thing* and it turned out they hadn't eaten, so we stopped to grab tacos. The two of them were talking about *Bee Movie*, Jerry Seinfeld's animated 2007 nonhit. I looked up from my phone.

"Dylan, you've never even seen *Bee Movie*."

His friend was shocked. "You *haven't?*"

"Dad!" I didn't realize I wasn't supposed to out him.

"Jasper, why are you guys talking about *Bee Movie* anyway? It came out ten years ago and it's not any good."

"We like it ironically," explained Jasper.

"It's in memes, Dad."

I remembered the birthday card. "Okay, here's a game. I'm going to name some weird, old-timey thing you guys are into, and you have to tell me if you like it sincerely or ironically."

"Okay."

"Rubik's Cubes."

"Sincerely," they said immediately.

"Those Jack Chick religious tracts."

"Ironically," they agreed. Some church had been giving them out on the corner in front of their middle school and now Dylan had a shelf full of mini-comics where Satan welcomes Catholics, Jews, heavy metal listeners, and Dungeons & Dragons players down to hell. "HAW, HAW, HAW!" he always laughs.

"Bob Ross, *The Joy of Painting.*"

Long pause. "Sincerely," said Dylan.

"*Really?* You wear Bob Ross socks. That's not a pose in any way?"

"I think his paintings are really good. I looked online if I could buy one but they sell for like ten thousand dollars now."

---

* When you have a thirteen-to-fifteen-year-old you are never not driving them to or from a thing and you don't even remember or care what it is. It's all the same thing, one long thing, and it doesn't end until they learn to drive.

What else? "When you call chicken tenders 'tendies.'"

Dylan said "Ironically" at the exact same time Jasper said "Sincerely." Split decision.

In the car on the way home, "Africa" by Toto was playing and somehow both kids knew all the words, though it was a hit twenty years before either had been born. "How about this song? Ironically or sincerely?"

"I really like it," said Dylan.

"Have you seen the video?" asked Jasper. "We like the song for real but the video ironically."

The Man in the *Eiron* Mask

When I was my son's age, English teachers would tell us in class that "irony" meant "the opposite of what you would expect." I was skeptical. By this bizarre definition, the smirky one-liners of David Letterman were not ironic (in that they were exactly what I expected every weeknight), while any sports upset—take Super Bowl XXII, in which the Washington Redskins trounced the favored Denver Broncos—was the height of irony. I wasn't sure what irony was, but I knew what it wasn't, and it wasn't just a subpar outing at quarterback from John Elway. Once in ninth grade, when I tried to question a teacher on this point, he reassured me that yes, this was exactly how irony was defined—on Friday's quiz, so let's move on. From then on, when irony came up in class, I still didn't understand it, but I kept my head down and worked on the elaborate ballpoint doodlescapes on my Trapper Keeper folders.

If a working definition of irony seems hard to pin down today, that's in large part because it's been a moving target for thousands of years. Our word "irony" comes from the *eiron*, one of the most important stock character types of the Old Comedy period of ancient Greece. Greek comedies were often built around the conflict between the *alazon*, a swaggering, hypocritical braggart, and the *eiron*, a clever everyman who would deflate the *alazon*'s ego with wry self-deprecation. Today, we can find traces of the *eiron-alazon* act in the DNA of many sitcom pairings: Norm and Cliff on *Cheers*, Jerry and George on *Seinfeld*, Marshall and

Barney on *How I Met Your Mother*, Donna and Tom on *Parks and Recreation.**

Here's a sample *alazon* takedown from Aristophanes' oldest surviving comedy, *The Acharnians*. The crafty protagonist is Dicaeopolis, a farmer fed up with the Peloponnesian War currently raging between Athens and Sparta. Halfway through the play, the fiery general Lamachus bursts onto the stage in full battle armor, holding a shield with the image of a Gorgon's head on it and wearing a helmet flamboyantly crested with ostrich plumes. The chorus immediately rats Dicaeopolis out, telling Lamachus that the lowly citizen has been grousing about the Athenian war effort.

"How dare you, you wretch of a beggar?" he booms.

Dicaeopolis immediately backpedals, in full *eiron* mode. "Oh, General Lamachus, my hero, do pardon me. Even a beggar has the right to speak his mind."

"What did you say about me? Out with it!"

"Um, I don't remember. It's your armor, it's making me nervous. Can you cover up that hideous face?"

Lamachus covers his shield. "Is that better?"

"Now turn it facedown on the ground."

"There you go."

"And can I have a feather or two from your helmet?"

Lamachus hands him a plume. "Here's one."

Dicaeopolis makes to gag himself with the ostrich feather. "All right, hold my head while I puke, your helmet crest makes me sick."

You can imagine the beefy Gaston type in his ridiculous battle dress turning red with rage. This may read like a silly "slow burn" routine straight out of Laurel and Hardy, but there's actually a much sharper edge: Aristophanes wrote *The Acharnians* in the sixth year of the long and bloody Peloponnesian War, and Lamachus was a real (and famously bombastic) Athenian general. Dicaeopolis goes on to undermine Lama-

---

* Falstaff is an *alazon;* so is Ralph Kramden. Ferris Bueller is an *alazon* with a sweet car. Lightning McQueen is an *alazon* who *is* a sweet car. The *eiron* type was so influential that it pretty much defined comedy for millennia, from the scheming slaves of Plautus's Roman comedies to Figaro and other clever servants of the Renaissance. The archetype continued through P. G. Wodehouse's Jeeves and even survived the end of the servant class in Europe. Today's clever comic underdogs are wage slaves instead.

chus' case for making war and convinces the chorus that his clever solution—negotiating a private peace treaty between himself and Sparta—is the better way to go.

To Aristophanes, the important thing about the dissembling of the *eiron* was that it relied on restraint rather than boasting, making it closer to the device we call litotes today. Litotes is a kind of comic understatement using reversal, like a man opening a door onto a blizzard and observing, "It's not exactly a nice day out."* Today this kind of thing still seems ironic, but it's gentle irony, Hugh Grant irony, *dad* irony. A more advanced practitioner of *eironeia* was Socrates, who according to Plato would feign ignorance on a topic or even pretend to be convinced by an opponent as a ploy to draw out the weaknesses in the other's argument. This question-asking tactic is still part of the modern Socratic method, so ingrained that we don't even call it "irony" anymore. We call it "law school."†

But Socratic irony quickly blossomed into a broader device, the ability to say something and mean the exact opposite—and still be understood, as long as one used the right markers. Verbal irony is often seen as synonymous with sarcasm, but in fact the overlap isn't perfect. "Sarcasm" comes from the Greek word for "flesh" (just like "sarcoma" and "sarcophagus") and refers to any witty put-down so caustic that it metaphorically "strips the flesh" off another. Remarking, "Ah, I love my commute!" while stuck in a traffic jam is irony, but it isn't designed to wound anyone, so it isn't sarcasm, strictly speaking. Conversely, when a member of Parliament said to Churchill in 1946, "Winston, you are drunk," and he famously replied, "Bessie, my dear, you are disgustingly ugly. But tomorrow I will be sober and you will still be disgustingly ugly," that was sarcasm but not irony—he meant every word.‡

---

* Whereas to the Greeks, *litotes* just meant plainness or asceticism of lifestyle. Couldn't those guys get anything right? Unlike irony, "litotes" was precisely and correctly defined by my ninth-grade English teacher, though he pronounced it wrong.

† From 1971 to 1978, it was also the premise of the TV series *Columbo*.

‡ Churchill's bodyguard Ronald Golding insisted that, of all the great apocryphal withering-Churchill-put-down stories, this one actually happened, and he himself heard it firsthand. If that's true, though, Churchill borrowed the line from W. C. Fields, because a very similar riposte can be found in the 1934 movie *It's a Gift*.

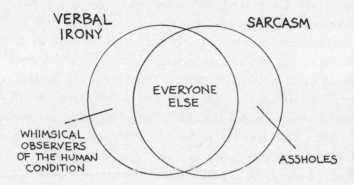

You Oughta Know

In drama, the canonical example of irony is a character being unaware of something the audience already knows. Just as with verbal irony, the literal words of the text conceal a metamessage of precisely opposite meaning to the careful listener. Dramatic irony dates back to Greek tragedies like Sophocles' *Oedipus the King*, in which Oedipus spends the first scenes of the play in pursuit of the man who murdered King Laius and thus cursed the city of Thebes. The audience knows that Oedipus himself is the unwitting killer (and has married his own mother to boot!), which gives us a little thrill of superiority during all of his tirades. We're a step ahead. Shakespeare used the device so often you'd think he was getting paid by the dramatic irony: Othello praising the loyalty of Iago, Duncan praising the integrity of Macbeth. (Spoilers: both are bad hiring decisions.) In those cases, dramatic irony emphasizes the contrast between well-meaning men and the tragic doom that awaits them. But sometimes it's nothing more than a smart way for an author to put readers through the wringer, as when Romeo plans to kill himself with poison alongside Juliet's body in her tomb, though the audience knows she's not dead, merely asleep. Hitchcock told François Truffaut that this was the difference between surprise and suspense: if a bomb is planted under a table where two people are talking, a director might be tempted to withhold that information until the last moment, but in fact it's best to show the bomb to the audience as soon as possible. "In these conditions," he explained, "the same innocuous conversation becomes fascinating because the public is participating in the scene. The audience is longing to warn the characters on the screen: 'You shouldn't be talking about such trivial matters. There is a bomb beneath you and it is about to explode!'" This is why, in his film *Vertigo*, one of the all-time-great twist endings in movie history is revealed to viewers via flashback almost an hour before the end of the film.

If we move dramatic irony into real life—that is, we assume all the world's a stage, with an enthralled audience out somewhere in the darkness and a puckish Hitchcockian god pulling the strings—we get cosmic irony. Adolph Coors III was allergic to beer. Fitness guru Jim Fixx died of a heart attack while out for a jog. In our more enlightened age, when we assume quirks of fate like these to be part of the naturally occurring order of the universe, we prefer the less grandiose term "situational irony." Instead of Oedipus wailing to the gods about the plague of Thebes, it's a man complaining to coworkers about the smell in the break room fridge, only to find that his own forgotten sandwich is to blame. At long last, we're getting close to what my ninth-grade teacher meant when he said irony was "the opposite of what you expect." What he didn't explain was that not every unexpected occurrence is ironic, because the crucial thing—the crucial *irony*—about situational irony is that the outcome, though unexpected, must somehow seem entirely fitting at the same time. Often, a situation is neatly reflected back on itself in some way: a marriage counselor files for divorce, a school marquee offers "Congradulations" to a spelling bee champ, the firehouse burns down, the meteorologists' picnic gets rained out.

But what about rain on your wedding day? In her hit 1995 song "Ironic," Alanis Morissette cataloged what she considered to be some of life's everyday ironies, and was immediately taken to task by scolds everywhere, in newspaper columns and stand-up comedy routines. Dying after winning the lottery or getting ten thousand spoons when all you need is a knife is merely an unfortunate *coincidence*, was the smugly in-the-know thing to say about the song. Coincidences aren't ironies.

Even lexicographer Bryan A. Garner, writing about the word "irony" in his *Garner's Modern English Usage*, takes a full paragraph to opine that Morissette "crossed the line" in the song. "All [these situations] amount to tough luck, but they are hardly ironic," he notes sternly. In a 1,056-page reference work, "Ironic" is the only alternative rock song of the 1990s so strongly condemned. Hootie & the Blowfish are* not mentioned once.

But if a situational irony is at its heart just an occurrence that's "the opposite of what you expect," then Garner's distinction isn't clear at all, because *so is a weird coincidence.* If we're going to distinguish so disapprovingly between the two, a lot must be riding on just how unlikely the coincidence is, or how strikingly apropos the twist. Granted, if you're getting married in Seattle in April, then rain on your wedding day is merely unfortunate, not ironic. But what if you've planned an outdoor ceremony in Palm Springs during an otherwise bone-dry July, and the rainclouds gather just as the service begins and part just as abruptly during the recessional? In other words, *just how many spoons* need to come out of the knife dispenser before a simple run of bad luck with flatware takes on an ironic tinge? (More than ten thousand, says Mr. Bryan A. Garner.)

One objection to this broadening of the definition of irony might be that the twist ending is merely an escalation, not a reversal, of the expected outcome. Take Alanis Morissette's story of "Mr. Play It Safe," who finally goes on vacation after being grounded by a lifelong fear of flying—only to die in a plane crash. To an irony purist, the problem here is that the man *was* expecting to die, so the crash is the opposite of irony. An ironic version of the story would have to end with him heroically taking over for the pilot, or sleeping through a terrifying near miss, or dying in a car accident on the way to the airport, or something. No one has articulated this viewpoint more elegantly than word nerd George Carlin, who wrote, "If a diabetic, on his way to buy insulin, is killed by a runaway truck, he is the victim of an accident. If the truck was delivering sugar, he is the victim of an oddly poetic coincidence. But if the truck was delivering insulin, ah! Then he is the victim of an irony."

* Is? Mr. Garner?

I'm as big a usage stickler as anyone, not to mention a huge Carlin fan, but I'll say it: this seems like splitting hairs to me. A news story about a diabetic run over by a sugar truck tickles the funny bone in *exactly the same mordant way* as one about an insulin truck. (And if we're nitpicking, I'm skeptical that an "insulin truck" is actually a thing.) Neither accident has some immediately perceptible aura of ironic perfection that the other does not. And in any case, English doesn't really *have* a word for "coincidental in a dark and oddly poetic way," so in the post-Alanis era, its close cousin "ironic" might have to do.

A Perpetual Knowing Wink

Twenty years later, it's hard to believe grammarians ever had their panties in a bunch over the iffy situational ironies of Alanis Morissette, because the irony umbrella has stretched further still. What was once an occasional rhetorical tool has metastasized into a way of life. Today, you can have ironically baroque facial hair and a closet full of ironic hats and varsity jackets. Your walls can be covered in bad garage-sale landscape paintings with UFOs or Bigfoots added in by later hands, your DVR full of the reality shows you hate-watch. Ride your ironic brakeless bike to get together with your kickball league or Boggle bros or some other "Can you believe we're doing this?!?" ironic pastime, which was announced on the Evite in Comic Sans. More serious apostles of irony might even scour Craigslist for an ironic car (2003 PT Cruiser?) in an ironic color (Pastel Yellow? Deep Cranberry Pearl?) and then slap an ironic Hello Kitty sticker on the bumper before hitting the road. What's next, the ironic college degree? The ironic relationship? The ironic career? "Check this out—I just spent twenty-seven years selling processing systems for a bulk material handling company. Oh, it was *hilarious.*"

The stereotype of the contemporary hipster is rooted in what might be called post-irony. For thousands of years, the drifting definitions of irony all had one thing in common: a gap between the signifier and signified whereby something could be represented by its exact opposite. "Smooth move!" meant "Unsmooth move!" "Water, water, everywhere" meant "Nor any drop to drink." But an ironic pizza tattoo does *not* mean

"I hate pizza," or even "This tattoo is bad." Instead, an ironic, self-aware pose bestows plausible deniability, the ultimate concession to our modern cult of cool. If you think my T-shirt of an astronaut Smurf captioned with the words "SPACED OUT!" is good, "I know, right?" But if you think it's dumb, "I know, right?"* Maybe I'm not sure myself, or maybe it's both at the same time. Schrödinger's kickball league.

Nostalgia looms large in modern irony, as my middle school Toto fans apparently figured out early. To me, it's one of hipster irony's potentially redeeming qualities: the refusal to let go of childhood completely, the insistence on room for play. The first lifestyle ironists were the early adopters of "camp" in the 1950s, putting the aesthetic of the previous generation in quotation marks for their own affectionate amusement. Susan Sontag enumerated their colorful canon for the straights and squares: art nouveau posters, *King Kong*, flapper dresses, ballet, *Flash Gordon* Sunday comics, Bellini operas, Tiffany lamps. But to camp tastes, a Tiffany table lamp wasn't just a lamp. It was a "lamp," a comment on lamps, a prop in the grand theater of life. As camp irony aged, its referents moved forward with it on a sliding scale from Mae West and Carmen Miranda into the television age, and you wound up with eighties yuppies ironically glued to the Nick at Nite reruns of their boomer childhood. But since the timeline of nostalgia icons passed 1966—the debut of *Batman* on TV, the enshrinement of camp into the mainstream—our millennial ironic signifiers have increasingly become things that were self-aware to begin with: the Spice Girls, *Goosebumps*, SpongeBob, Tarantino, *Scream*. Camp has eaten itself.

As a result, the potential for charm and whimsy in ironic nostalgia has been tainted. There's nothing pure or childlike about having to like something "ironically." What does that even mean, that you don't really like it but everyone is talking about it? Or, even worse, that you actually like something that doesn't match your sophisticated persona, so it has to be a "guilty pleasure"? God forbid any actual enjoyment should overwhelm our studied pose of world-weary nonchalance.

---

* For the record, I really do own this shirt, which was $1.50 at Goodwill, so even my millennial-scolding here is winking and self-aware, and therefore okay.

The Comedy of Deconstruction

Postmodern irony became the default voice in comedy in the mid-1970s, so I'm happy to blame the Vietnam-and-Watergate cocktail of disillusionment that ruined everything else. *Saturday Night Live* was a much more knowing affair than the typical comedy-variety sketch show of its era, which it explicitly indicated by dubbing its cast the Not Ready for Prime Time Players. *SNL* was a television show about television, just as its early mascots Albert Brooks and Steve Martin were becoming stars by performing stand-up comedy about stand-up comedy. By 1977, Steve Martin was selling out stadiums and seeing albums go platinum on the strength of a routine with almost no jokes at all. I'm serious; try listening to a record like *Let's Get Small* today. Martin brings out a banjo but never gets around to singing a real song, just nonsense syllables. He discusses material he's not going to do. He pretends to yell at the backstage crew. He gets applause for his catchphrases ("Well, excuuuse me!") but frames them explicitly as lame catchphrases. It's funny, but you find yourself waiting for the actual routine to begin. The whole thing is delivered in an affectedly zany voice more on the level of Pee-wee Herman or Bobcat Goldthwait than the gentle ironist you'd expect from his later film persona. In short, he's performing stand-up and deconstructing it at the same time. "Yes, *this is comedy!*" he yells at one point.

But the standard-bearer for Generation X irony was David Letterman. I can still remember the first time, as a kid, that I saw Letterman do the thing where he would repeat something funny until it became unfunny (or vice versa!) and then just kept going until it looped back around again. It seemed like he was defying all laws of comedy, or even logic, but there it was. The detached superiority of a Steve Martin would have been too much to take every weeknight, but Letterman's ironic remove was balanced by a genuinely amused glee—that wide grin, that cocked eyebrow, the best laugh on television.* He was in on the joke, but he wanted us to know that he was enjoying it as much as we were.

---

* I don't know if I remember what Steve Martin's laugh sounds like. Have I ever heard him genuinely laugh? Would any of us really be that surprised if his real laugh sounds just like a fake laugh?

That didn't keep the show's pioneering anticomedy from bemusing audiences, though. The first decade of *Late Night with David Letterman* was, largely thanks to cocreator and head writer Merrill Markoe, a never-ending parade of completely gonzo comedy ideas delivered in the most deadpan fashion possible: a humidifier locked in battle with a dehumidifier, chatty check-in phone calls to a random book publicist visible in an office across the street, "Shoe Removal Races" between a podiatrist and a shoe salesman, a full 360-degree rotation of the televised image during the course of one show, a rerun episode dubbed by a cartoon voice-over cast. (Those last two stunts resulted in hundreds of phone calls from confused viewers.) Even the show's signature bit, the Top Ten List, began life as a joke-free take-off of magazine polls, with Letterman straight-facedly listing ten "Words that Almost Rhyme with 'Peas.'"* On that historic September 1985 show, Letterman treated the list like the ironic throwaway it was, hurrying through the ten items so fast that bandleader Paul Shaffer didn't even have time to strike up a drum roll until number seven. There was almost no audible laughter for the odd conceptual gag, exactly as the show intended.

But there's a difference between a comedian who doesn't care if the audience always laughs and one who almost prefers that they don't. One is the genially weird Letterman, begetting ironically self-aware talk shows through the decades down to *Space Ghost Coast to Coast*, *Comedy Bang! Bang!*, and Tom Scharpling's *The Best Show*. The other is Letterman's frequent early guest Andy Kaufman, genuinely *hoping* that audiences are annoyed and bewildered when he wrestles women or reads page after page of *The Great Gatsby* in his live act. Without that kind of perverse commitment, you don't get the middle-finger-to-the-audience of *Tim and Eric* and the whole Adult Swim ethos, so many levels of irony deep that it recedes to infinity like two mirrors reflecting each other.

In twenty-two minutes of absurd TV or Internet comedy, that kind of nihilism can be bracing. But as a lifestyle? At best, it's just a way to avoid getting pinned down to a principle or a preference at all. Take

---

* For the record: "heats," "rice," "moss," "ties," "needs," "lens," "ice," "nurse," "leaks," and "meats."

that too far and you wind up with a society so cynical that caring about *anything* seems a little suspect. What's up with these goody-goody environmentalists, so sincere about everything all the time? And devout religious people, what sick secret guilt are they overcompensating for? At this point, when I see a young urbanite wearing a trucker hat, I'd rather the subtext be "I am wearing this ironically, in that I think trucker hats look bad and all rural Americans are shitheads," which is dumb but at least is an opinion, rather than "I am wearing this ironically, in that I think trucker hats are funny and cool . . . *or do I?!?*"

Take the Skinheads LOLing

At worst, that kind of pointless irony can be the last refuge of scoundrels. It's a way to deflect criticism from viewpoints that might be not just uncool but actively evil. In recent years, white supremacists have had considerable success joining online havens for Internet trolls like 4chan—places where anonymous, lonely young men gather to say outrageous things about women and minorities just for the "lulz"—and then recruiting them as actual neo-Nazis. As Andrew Anglin boasted on his neo-Nazi website the Daily Stormer, "The sentiments behind the jokes slowly became serious, as people realized they were based on fact. . . . The rehabilitation of Adolf Hitler and the NSDAP [the Nazi party] largely took place on 4chan." Anglin called this new tactic "non-ironic Nazism masquerading as ironic Nazism."

. And it wasn't just some underground, deep-web phenomenon. In 2016, a new late-night series called *Million Dollar Extreme Presents: World Peace*, from the titular Rhode Island–based sketch group, debuted on Adult Swim and became an instant hit among the "alt-right." Long threads on online white nationalist forums dissected each episode of the bizarre fifteen-minute sketch show, which posters were convinced espoused their far-right ideology. You didn't have to watch the show for long to see what they were seeing: three minutes of cast member Sam Hyde in blackface screaming at a woman in exaggerated vernacular; a kids' TV parody called *Jews Rock;* a non sequitur blaming the water crisis in

Flint, Michigan, on gay sodomy; a man calling a woman fat and stupid, knocking her through a glass tabletop, and then charging her two thousand dollars to replace his bloody carpet; a black reality show contestant bragging that she gets "over forty grand" a year in disability payments. An Adult Swim source told Buzzfeed that the network had repeatedly found and removed "coded racist messages" in the show, including swastikas. Hyde himself moderated one of the show's most enthusiastic online forums and used his Twitter account to troll progressive celebs, calling Lena Dunham a "fat pig" and accusing Patton Oswalt of killing his own wife. Most disturbingly, a video began to make the rounds of a 2013 stand-up set by Hyde at a comedy club in Brooklyn, in which his act consisted of reading fifteen minutes of antigay pseudoscience and homophobic rants about the "faggot brain." He finished the set by blaming pro-gay propaganda on the Zionist "media machine" and then left the club to argue with some of the "hipster faggot" audience who had walked out.

Throughout all this, *Million Dollar Extreme* on Adult Swim was drawing over a million viewers per episode. In any other field, there would have been an immediate outcry, but in our postmodern age of edgy, ironic comedy, Sam Hyde and his collaborators had some cover. This seemed like racism, anti-Semitism, and misogyny, but surely it was some kind of *comment* on racism, anti-Semitism, and misogyny, right? What if they weren't Nazis, just extremely committed surrealist "hoaxsters" and "provocateurs"? And, hey, isn't the best comedy uncomfortable sometimes? After six months of mostly-behind-the-scenes controversy, two popular Adult Swim writer-performers, Brett Gelman and Tim Heidecker, publicly criticized the network for airing *Million Dollar Extreme*, and the show was canceled three weeks later. When the *Hollywood Reporter* spoke to Hyde to get his reaction, he was still doing his metacomedy performance-art shtick, beginning the interview by telling the reporter, "Thanks for giving a racist like me a platform to spew my hate. I'm kidding. I'm just messing with you." Stand down, everyone! The racist guy is reassuring us that his racism wasn't really racist. Or . . . (smiling impishly with pinky finger raised to mouth) *was it?!?*

I Was a Teenage Spy

If David Letterman was my gateway drug to ironic remove, *Spy* magazine was the hard stuff. The legendary satire monthly was founded
in 1986 by journalists Kurt Andersen and Graydon Carter, and barely
lasted into the next decade before its original editors moved on and
the magazine's genius sputtered out. But during that short time span,
New York's rich and powerful lived in fear of its roving eye. Some of
the names among *Spy*'s frequent targets—Mayor Ed Koch, John Gotti,
Al Sharpton, *especially* Donald Trump*—were ones I knew. But I was
just as excited to read about the hijinks of media moguls and Nouvelle
Society fixtures I had never heard of: Laurence Tisch, Nan Kempner,
"Punch" Sulzberger, Gloria von Thurn und Taxis. Each issue I pulled
off the newsstand was like an entrée into a bigger, livelier world where
everyone who mattered was *in the know*.

Everything about *Spy* was clever, from the endlessly inventive lists and
charts and squibs littering its "Naked City" section ("Separated at Birth"
celebrity lookalikes, mutually fellating pairs of book blurbs, horoscopes
of public figures on the day they were fired/assassinated/disgraced) to the
incredibly research-intensive megaprojects in six-point type that no other
magazine would even attempt (Mike Ovitz's top secret Hollywood client
list, a complete index to *The Andy Warhol Diaries* for readers looking up
famous names, "1,000 Reasons Not to Vote for George Bush"); from the
brainy cover packages nailing down elusive but pernicious social trends
of the 1980s (postmodernism, yuppie lifestyle porn, organizer fetishism)
to puckish celebrity pranks (which infamous tycoons will cash a $0.13
check?); from its arch house style (everything in *Spy* was "*faux-*" or "*über-*"
something, often "preternaturally" so) to its dense, elegant design.† The

* *Spy* is probably best remembered today for its feud with Trump, who was always referred to as a "short-
fingered vulgarian" in its pages. For decades, editor Graydon Carter has said, Trump would send him an
occasional envelope of magazine photos, in which Trump would circle his hands with gold Sharpie and
write, "See, not so short." Trump wasn't the only prescient name on *Spy*'s enemies list. I also remember
eyebrow-raising profiles on then-beloved family men Bill Cosby and Arnold Schwarzenegger.

† Within five years, pretty much every lifestyle and entertainment magazine on the newsstand was aping
Spy's playful "charticles" and layouts and sidebars.

magazine was often laugh-out-loud funny as well, but "clever" was what really spoke to seventeen-year-old me, precocious and irritating and desperate to seem grown-up.

When my high school newspaper, the *Spirit*, retired its advice columnist character "Dr. Blunt" at the start of my senior year, I was asked to fill in with an anonymous school gossip column, titled, in a burst of originality, "The *Spirit* Spy." I assembled twenty-four column inches of cafeteria and teachers' lounge rumors and wrote them up in my best approximation of acid-tipped *Spy* prose. I even laid out the first column at home on our Atari ST's primitive desktop publisher, in an attempt to duplicate *Spy*'s fiddly, serifed typography—and to ensure that no one else touched the text. Nobody was very happy when the issue came out. What was this scathing, bitchy gossip column doing in a student paper right next to the bake sale rundowns and JV volleyball scores? "The *Spirit* Spy"'s anonymity lasted for about five minutes, and then I was called into the principal's office for a very serious conversation about respect and journalistic responsibility. The next day, my editors and I agreed that "The *Spirit* Spy" should be retired. I'd used up all my ideas in the first column anyway.

Leaving the principal's office, I was ecstatic with my newfound status as a parochial school Lenny Bruce, a Martyr for Satire. But when I dug "The *Spirit* Spy"'s short-lived oeuvre out of my garage for a reread decades later, I immediately saw that my high school principal had had a point. The same gleeful spite and withering disdain that *Spy* brought to bear on political hypocrites and vulgarian billionaires wasn't a good look when turned on the computer club, senior lock-in, or student production of *You're a Good Man, Charlie Brown*.* I had read *Spy* and thought, "These people are smart and talented, and are sometimes dicks in print. Therefore, if I am a dick in print, I must be smart and talented." (To be fair, *Spy*'s founders were probably thinking the same thing, only their reference point was H. L. Mencken.) Without a cause or a deserving victim, my work wasn't satire. It was satire's eyeball-rolling teenage nephew, snark.

---

* Even if, as I still maintain today, it was a little lackluster. *Lackluster!*

Snide Effects

Though *Spy* was capable of masterful satire and hard-hitting investigative journalism, much of its own output stayed well within the snark infield as well. It could be argued, looking back, that its snarky editorial voice was, for better or for worse, the magazine's greatest legacy to the cultural landscape. What is snark? Snark is irreverent kibitzing as a way of life—the curled lip, the bored sneer. Snark is too detached and superior to really function as criticism, since it looks to put down *everything*, but it hates sincerity and sentiment above all. Satire denounces; snark merely dismisses. The word is onomatopoetic, from the ironic snorting sound often associated with a snide put-down, and originated with the German *snarken*. It was, in fact, a German stock character who brought snark to the modern urban scene: Eckensteher Nante, a familiar figure on the Berlin stage and in comic pamphlets from the 1830s on. "*Eckensteher*" means, roughly, "corner-loitering," and Nante was the archetypal Berlin day laborer who preferred to spend most of his time loafing on the city's sidewalks, clutching a bottle of schnapps and aiming droll, mouthy remarks at passersby. In one typical story, a Berliner tries to hire Nante to haul a heavy chest of drawers for him, but the man is so miserly that they can't agree on a price. "Just leave it here on the street and wait until nightfall," retorts Nante, who couldn't care less. "Then someone will carry it off for nothing!"

About the same time, the snarky wisecrack was catching on across the Atlantic as well. Mark Twain's friend and collaborator Charles Dudley Warner explained how the emerging American sense of humor was largely a response to the goopy sentimentalism then fashionable in poetry and essays. "I need not say how suddenly and completely this affectation was laughed out of sight by the coming of the 'humorous' writer, whose existence is justified by the excellent service performed in clearing the tearful atmosphere. His keen and mocking method . . . puts its foot on every bud of sentiment, holds few things sacred, and refuses to regard anything in life seriously." Josh Billings agreed, using spelling that a frontier version of *Spy* certainly would have called *faux-naif*: "Amerikans love caustick things; they would prefer turpentine tew colone-water, if they had tew drink either. So with their relish of humor; they must hav it on the half-shell with cayenne."

But the "caustick" burn of cayenne is no longer just a condiment for us, an occasional sprinkle of comic pizzazz. In the media today, and particularly online, empty snark is now the entire cuisine. Consider: The central joke of *Seinfeld* was always that the four main characters were *terrible* people. They smugly dissected the faults of everyone they knew, they treated any actual striving or suffering by another human being as fodder for observational comedy, they would cynically push a senior citizen aside to make a cowardly exit from a kitchen fire or to grab a loaf of marble rye. Even the collapse of an entire publishing firm or the death of a fiancée *at their own hands* left them completely unmoved. It was a good joke, but we didn't get it. We wanted to be their friends.*

I enjoyed *Seinfeld*'s celebrated "No hugging, no learning" credo, but I don't think we had to engineer an entire culture from it, like *Star Trek* aliens remaking their whole planet in the image of a single book about gangsters or Nazis or something. If George Costanza and his single-camera sitcom descendants aren't going to feel bad about, say, poisoning a woman with cheap wedding invitation envelopes, then what life situations *do* require real sentiment anymore? If even Hallmark cards are offering best wishes ironically, what's left?† I once walked by a "LOST CAT" poster tacked to a telephone pole in my neighborhood that read as follows.

> Wanted! [Preferably not] dead or alive!
> My beloved Bon Jovi got out and is living on a prayer . . .
> I know he just wants to live while he's alive, but we really miss him!
> While he might be walking the streets with a loaded 6-string on his
> back, we can't help but feel like we've been shot through the heart.

---

* The show's final episode, in which writer Larry David foregrounded the characters' near-sociopathic narcissism for the first time, was widely regarded by viewers and reviewers as a tone-deaf misstep.

† A comedy writer once told me that her brother and his fiancée had decided to send out ironic (but non-poisonous) wedding invitations. Their names are Alec and Eliana, and the front of the save-the-date was the A&E network logo. "I guess I have to give you credit for making a joke out of literally everything in your life," she told him.

All we have left are pictures hung in shadows . . .
Come home, Bon Jovi. It's been raining since you left me.

I understand the impulse of the funny person to want to be funny
wherever possible, and I *certainly* understand the impulse of the rock fan
to quote the haunting desert poetry of Jon Bon Jovi wherever applicable.
But why did a missing-pet bulletin need to be "punched up" with jokes
at all? Can't we even advertise the loss of a beloved cat without resorting
to ironic nostalgia?

Maybe, I told myself, Bon Jovi's owner is mourning and this kind
of detachment was exactly what he or she needed in a moment of grief.
Certainly it's true that a little ironic distancing can work wonders as a
coping device. At Groucho Marx's separation from his first wife, Ruth,
for example, he told a joke. After many unhappy years, they had agreed
to a divorce, and so she packed up the car and was leaving the house
for the last time. Groucho put out his hand and said, "Well, it was nice
knowing you . . . and if you're ever in the neighborhood again, drop in."
Ruth laughed, and the tension was broken. It was the unprecedented
and awkward seriousness of the moment that led to the ironic farewell,
Groucho explained to his son. "I didn't know quite what to say."

But when things *really* go wrong, we seem to know almost instinctively
that irony is the wrong note. One week after September 11, 2001, no less
an authority than *Spy* cofounder Graydon Carter decreed that the terror
attacks spelled "the end of the age of irony." The statement is mostly
resurrected today to show how ridiculous it was, since the brave new
irony-free era lasted only a month or two before everything went back to
normal, but with more wars. Less often remembered is how obvious and
right Carter's decree felt at the time. Lorne Michaels's earnest "Can we be
funny?" appeal to Rudy Giuliani on *Saturday Night Live* notwithstanding,
nobody was in the mood for wisecracks that autumn. The *Onion* had just
completed its historic move from Madison, Wisconsin, to Manhattan,
and on the eve of September 11 was celebrating its first New York issue,
scheduled to go to press the very next day. Instead, the staff spent the next
two weeks trying to figure out how to treat a gaping national wound as
a joke premise. The resulting issue is widely considered a comedy classic,

and even an act of bravery and ingenuity in the face of evil. Some of the articles do hold up well, especially Carol Kolb's heartbreaking "Not Knowing What Else to Do, Woman Bakes American-Flag Cake." But at the time, I couldn't bring myself to laugh much at the issue. Clever takes like "American Life Turns into Bad Jerry Bruckheimer Movie" and "Rest of Country Temporarily Feels Deep Affection for New York" felt trivial; morally outraged ones like "God Angrily Clarifies 'Don't Kill' Rule" and "Hijackers Surprised to Find Selves in Hell" just felt ponderous. If this was the smartest comedy that could be wrung out of the deaths of three thousand people, then maybe comedy didn't have much comfort to offer in the face of the deaths of three thousand people.

In comedy's defense, nothing much else did either.

The Importance of Being Earnest

But wounds heal, and irony always comes back. Occasionally trend pieces will trumpet a "New Sincerity" movement set to storm irony's ramparts at any moment, hopefully citing as evidence any new sign of earnestness or sentiment in the culture: Dave Eggers books, Korean soap operas, heartfelt emo music, cosplay. Yes, those fads are driven in part by a yearning to peel back the ironic reserve of modern life. Ironic reserve can be exhausting and lonely! But it's never going to happen, as 9/11 demonstrated. Once the genie is out of the bottle, an irony culture is never going to go back to being a sincerity culture, because the roots go too deep. Authenticity is often uncomfortable and revealing; ambiguous snark never is. Who wants to be the only vulnerable poet soul in a world of irony-clad scoffers?*

The overflow of the comic outlook into every corner of public life has largely come in the form of lifestyle irony. But look: the fact that irony has changed shape so many times over the millennia, morphing from rhetorical tool to literary device to comedy sensibility to way of life, means that we have more than two options in how we think about irony today. We don't have to choose between all and nothing, snark

---

* Unless you are in your early twenties and in the throes of a serious crush. Those folks should go right ahead. That kind of heedless, intoxicating sensitivity is invulnerable in its own way.

and Fall Out Boy. In particular, irony doesn't have to be cynical. It's just been a vehicle for cynicism so long that we forgot that.

The canonical literary example of irony is Jonathan Swift's "A Modest Proposal." In that anonymous 1729 pamphlet, Swift drew attention to the problem of rural poverty and overpopulation in Ireland, and then suggested a novel solution: have parents sell their spare children as food for the wealthy! "A young healthy child well nursed, is, at a year old, a most delicious nourishing and wholesome food, whether stewed, roasted, baked, or boiled," he argued, "and I make no doubt that it will equally serve in a fricassee, or a ragout." He went on to do some back-of-the-envelope calculations on how the logistics for his scheme would work out, sketched the wide-ranging social benefits of a world where plump and delicious toddlers are farmed like veal, and even suggested recipes.* In modern comedic parlance, Swift *commits to the bit.* In well over three thousand words, he never drops the ironic pretense, never once winks to let us know that, hey, he's not *really* a weirdo with a cupboard full of Irish baby jerky at home.

As Swift's original readers would have noticed immediately, his essay was a pitch-perfect parody of the popular do-gooder pamphlets of the day. "A Modest Proposal" took aim at two targets at once: both the deplorable indifference to poverty plaguing society at large, and the callous social engineers hyping their own silly fixes. I can find no evidence that any clueless contemporaries actually fell for the gag and wrote outraged letters to the editor. In fact, Swift's friend Lord Bathurst wrote to him joking that, in lieu of repaying a two-hundred-pound debt, Bathurst should just send Swift four or five of his own children, all of whom were "very fit for table." Good old Lord Bathurst, always "yes, and"–ing!

"A Modest Proposal" is an extended irony, but not a snarky one that leaves the author's true feelings a carefully layered enigma. The ironic device doesn't hide Swift's righteous fury; if anything, it sharpens it. This kind of irony, *principled* irony, comes with advantages going back to Socrates. By pretending to espouse an opposing argument, an author can highlight its flaws and let an audience feel they've come around to the "right" conclusion as a discovery of their own.

---

* He does *not* propose a "Soylent Green"–like trade name for his new Irish food staple, but I suggest "Tater Tots."

It's also a convenient way to fight for a cause while staying one step ahead of oppression. In 1987, Poland's Communist government geared up for a big celebration of the seventieth anniversary of the Russian Revolution. In response, Lech Walesa's Solidarity trade union sent around brochures imitating the bombastic language of government propaganda. "It is time to break the passivity of the popular masses!" began the leaflet, which invited supporters to wear red at a massive October rally. Everyone knew it was a put-on, but what could the government do? Strictly speaking, an enthusiastic embrace of Communist symbology *was* the party line. Sure enough, crowds showed up in laughably over-the-top garb: red coats, red scarves, red lipstick. Police were forced to stand by and watch helplessly as an *ironically pro-Soviet* demonstration took over the streets. Finally, some onlookers who wanted to get in on the fun began flocking to a nearby food stall for ketchup-dipped breadsticks to wave aloft. *Then* fed-up police finally moved, shutting down the stall and arresting one would-be ketchup purchaser. Solidarity's ploy had worked: everyone had a good time, and the authorities looked like idiots. It was the beginning of the end. The following September, the government agreed to talks with the opposition, and within two years multiparty elections were scheduled.

Authoritarianism still has no idea what to do about irony. In 2016, sources in North Korea reported that the Kim Jong-un regime, having survived *The Interview*, had now banned sarcasm altogether, because it feared that apparent statements of patriotism were being used to criticize the government. In particular, the ironic use of "This is all America's fault!" as a response to any hardship of North Korean life was condemned by authorities. Apparently, "This is all America's fault!" is the "Thanks, Obama!" of North Korea.* And lest you think that irony is only a valuable survival tool in a totalitarian rogue state, the U.S. Secret Service

---

* "Thanks, Obama" was a rare political slogan that became widespread on three different irony levels. A supporter, jazzed about health care reform or same-sex marriage, might offer a sincere "Thanks, Obama," while an opponent might give an ironic "Thanks, Obama" on the subject of, say, the Iran deal. But the meme *really* caught on when used faux-ironically by supporters to blame any random mishap or inconvenience in life on the president. "Christmas is on a Sunday this year? *Thanks, Obama.*" In a 2015 video, the president himself was seen sitting in the White House library, unsuccessfully trying to dunk a too-large cookie into a glass of milk. "Thanks, Obama," he mutters.

announced in 2014 that it was looking for a reliable "sarcasm detector" algorithm, one that could distinguish between sincere and insincere professions of loyalty and disloyalty online. Good luck! I'm a human being who can pass the Turing test with flying colors and *I* have no idea how many irony levels deep we are in half the Twitter conversations I read.

It's ironic (or, if we're using Strict Alanis standards, it's *unfortunate*) that snark became the lingua franca of the Internet, which is the worst possible medium for it. Nuances of tone are notoriously hard to convey online. In a 2005 study, e-mail senders were asked to predict how often recipients would pick up on their sarcasm, and they optimistically put the number at 78 percent.* Fully 90 percent of e-mail recipients were confident they could do so. But when researchers tested them, their sarcasm detection rate in practice was only 53 percent. (Even in spoken conversation, the study's authors found it hovering around 73 percent.) This is an ongoing problem, but it could have been trivially solved if we as a society had adopted one of the irony punctuation marks that various typographic visionaries have been trying to get going for centuries. The movement dates back to the 1580s, when English printer Henry Denham first proposed the percontation point, a backward question mark (⸮) to signpost verbal irony—specifically, rhetorical questions. Can you imagine how many clueless Facebook and Twitter replies we could avoid with this thing⸮

Outgrowing Snark

Irony as a literary device, as something to *observe*, is fine. But as a way to live your life? Cloaking every thought, word, action with the implication that you might not mean any of it? That's a pathology. Unless ironic distance is the only way to keep government authorities off your back, it shouldn't be the only pitch in your repertoire. The occasional curveball is only effective if you can throw a fastball and a changeup as well. "A Modest Proposal" is funny and effective, but let's not pretend

---

* Which in itself is crazy! Why, in important business and personal communication, do we routinely write things that we assume will be badly misinterpreted 22 percent of the time?

it accomplishes all the same things that a heartfelt plea for starving children would. You don't always get to the same place by taking the opposite route.

In an age of irony, it will always be a temptation to use it as a cop-out, because it's easier to smirk at things than solve them. Maybe the real *Spy* magazine took on worthier targets than my high school knockoff did, but whether its tone was playful or mean-spirited, it was always so unrelentingly *negative.* "The moment has come to grow up, get serious, address the issues of the day carefully, thoughtfully, straightforwardly," wrote Kurt Andersen in one of the tour de force "Great Expectations" essays that opened every issue of *Spy.* "Enough jokes, enough merry-making. It's high time that we told the world not just what repels and astounds us, but what we are *for.* [Pause.] We're thinking."*

An air of detached superiority is one of the easiest facsimiles of adulthood to mimic, which is why teenagers grab on to it so eagerly. And even when irony is used to make a worthy point, it's still the clever way to make that point, the contrarian way. Cleverness and contrarianism are hallmarks of adolescence, but it's not too late to decide what we're for and say so. It's not too late to grow up.

I mean, would it kill us?

---

* Let the record show that, this being designed-within-an-inch-of-its-life *Spy*, the pause was actually a little red glyph of an umbrella.

EIGHT

MIRTH CONTROL

The comedy boom of our era is the story of a decline as well: the declining influence of the forces of anticomedy. In the usual comedic parlance, "anticomedy" is a self-aware performance that mines laughs from its utter lack of conventional punch lines. It's Norm Macdonald telling a meandering shaggy-dog joke to a talk show host, or Eric Andre shouting belligerently at a stunned guest. But I mean a different, more literal kind of anticomedy. I'm thinking of forces devoted to stomping out comedy in all of its forms, the way antiaircraft guns shoot at aircraft or antimatter cancels out matter. Jokes have long felt threatening to many, many people, and as a result, as far back as we have a record of laughter, we also have evidence of grim, self-serious folks devoted to stifling it. But the influence of the buzzkills and the critics is waning.

The Dour and the Glory

Plato and Aristotle, as we've seen, were deeply skeptical of jokes and worried at length about the effect they could have on impressionable youth—one of the earliest examples of "Won't somebody *please* think of the children?!?" in the history of moral panic. But by the Middle Ages, with the great comedies of antiquity largely forgotten, the most powerful force arrayed against comedy was religion.

John Chrysostom, the fourth-century archbishop of Constantinople, was the first church father to condemn jokes, noting that "to speak jocosely does not seem an acknowledged sin," but it nevertheless often *leads* to sins, like ridicule and scorn. Saint Basil wrote that "unrestrained and immoderate laughter is a sign of intemperance, . . . of failure to repress the soul's frivolity by a stern use of reason." What seems to have worried the early bishops most about laughter was the loss of control it brings, the embrace of a pleasurable feeling. Laughter feels good in the moment, just like lots of sins do. Therefore, they reasoned, laughter must be sinful, or at least highly suspect. In particular, the carnal relationship between humor and sex seemed obvious to them. Both are, after all, a tickling of our pleasure centers that can lead to a noisy bodily eruption. On more than one occasion, Saint Jerome advised young women not to encourage flatterers by indulging in any "buffoonery" or laughing at men's jokes. (If pickup lines in the third century were as funny as they are today, this was probably pretty easy advice to follow.) John Chrysostom went one step further: for virgins, with their chastity teetering above a gulf of sin at every moment, even the slightest *smile* was a bad idea.

There was also a scriptural basis for restraining laughter, the early church fathers reminded their flocks. In the Bible, as in Homer, laughter is almost always a cruel act of mockery, whether at the expense of man or God. In Ephesians, Paul specifically condemns *eutrapelia*, Greek for "wittiness."* Sure, the Book of Proverbs recommends a "merry heart" and a "cheerful countenance," but the church took pains to clarify that passages like that refer to a deeply spiritual kind of joy, nothing so coarse as *laughter*. When theologians from Saint Augustine down to Bernard of Clairvaux denounced laughter, their trump card was a scripture that *didn't* exist: in the four Gospels, the church fathers repeatedly pointed out, Jesus doesn't laugh once, and therefore we shouldn't either.† It doesn't

---

* English Bible translations usually render the word as "coarse jesting" or "vulgar talk." Ironically, a few centuries earlier, *eutrapelia* had been the word Aristotle used for the refined kind of joking that he could personally put up with, neither too pointed nor too silly.

† There are similar debates in other religious traditions, but with stronger evidence on the "funny" side. Buddhist texts often refer to the master's "faint smile," for example. And some of the oral hadith describing the deeds of Muhammad portray the Prophet as a bit of a jokester. In one story, he's eating dates with some followers and keeps pushing all his seeds onto his cousin Ali's plate, to make it look like Ali's been hogging the dates. Ali looks at Muhammad's empty plate and replies, "Who's the hog? You're the one who eats his dates whole, even the seeds!" Owned.

seem to have bothered anyone that, by this justification, Christians also shouldn't cough, clip their nails, or go to the bathroom.

Today, there's lively debate among scholars as to which Bible stories, if any, can be read comedically. Could Jesus's parables have been delivered as jokes? ("Did you hear the one about the sower?") Is God being sarcastic when he asks rhetorical questions to Moses and Job? Is Jonah best understood as a bumbling comic loser, Larry David as prophet of doom? Kurt Vonnegut once gave a sermon in which he explained Christ's puzzling observation to Judas Iscariot from John 12:8—"You will always have the poor among you, but you will not always have me"—as a mordant joke. In Vonnegut's mind, Jesus was smiling wryly as he told his most disappointing apostle, "Judas, don't worry about it. There will still be *plenty* of poor people left long after I'm gone."

But these readings are largely modern inventions. For centuries, the dour and monastic strain of Christianity dominated Europe. We even have records of religious scholars tut-tutting about specific medieval joke fads. In the fourteenth century, the most popular funny folktale was the story of the *Veilchenschwank*, or "violet trick." The joke concerns a sensitive court poet named Neidhart who's overjoyed to discover the first violet of spring and places his cap over the flower to mark the spot. While he's gone, some passing prankster lifts up the cap, picks the flower, and squats down to leave his own souvenir in its place. Neidhart returns with the entire court, does a celebratory dance around the cap, and then removes it with great ceremony and aplomb . . . revealing a fresh, steaming pile of human shit. This was the funniest thing anybody in medieval Germany had ever heard, and variations on the story were recycled in song, dance, prose, drama, and art *for decades*. For a time, it was even fashionable for people to replace the portraits of the saints in their homes with paintings of the violet trick, as we know from a sermon in which the Augustinian monk Gottschalk Hollen gloomily lamented the joke fad's popularity. He's the patron saint of every conservative scold writing editorials about the tasteless depths to which Garbage Pail Kids or *Beavis and Butt-Head* have sunk modern comedy, every grown-up who wouldn't let you watch *South Park* or buy *Mad* magazine.

The subtext of all the clerical hand-wringing over jokes is clear: life shouldn't be too fun. The thought of heaven—the thing that keeps us on the straight and narrow—only appeals if our mortal life seems gray and miserable by comparison. So when the early Christian ascetic Origen read about "a time to weep and a time to laugh" in Ecclesiastes, he decreed that the time to weep was now; the time to laugh was in the next life. Anybody laughing now was Doing It Wrong, and forfeiting Jesus's promise that "blessed are ye that weep now, for ye shall laugh" in heaven. And so "No jokes!" became the standard of Christian conduct for hundreds of years. The medieval *Rule of Saint Benedict* decreed that monks could be booted from their orders for laughing aloud—or even making someone else laugh.

A typical moral fable from this climate is the popular seventeenth-century Dutch chapbook *Duyfken and Willemynken*, in which the two title sisters go to a town fair. Willemynken ("I Pursue My Will") can't get enough of the puppet show, maypole dance, singing contest, and other entertainments. "I have to laugh every now and then!" she insists to her sister Duyfken ("Little Dove"), who objects primly to these time-wasters. At every turn, the laughing girl gets her comeuppance: she gets lice from the puppets, is splashed with goat manure at the dance, and is awarded rotten fruit for winning the singing contest. In the end, Willemynken is literally lured down to hell. But her pious sister has wisely postponed her joy—saved her virtue, even—for heaven.

Words You Can't Say

Duyfken and Willemynken was reprinted more than twenty times across the Netherlands and loved by generations of enthusiastic young girls. But ironically enough, most readers probably enjoyed the comic antics of Willemynken more than her sister's dull sermonizing. I hope none of them laughed out loud while reading—or if they did, I hope they were immediately splashed with goat poop.

Even the strictest of priests couldn't keep Europe a comedy-free zone for centuries, just as puritan attitudes toward sex didn't prevent plenty of illegitimate children and venereal diseases. Although many orders of monks were theoretically bound by vows of soberness, we know that much of the medieval humor that survives was preserved by clerics, since they were the largest educated class. Monasteries were popular stops for traveling troupes of performers, and monks circulated their own joke books on the down-low. A thirteenth-century monk named Radulphus created the enormously popular mock sermon "Saint Nobody," which he gave as a present to the future Pope Boniface VIII. Its central joke is still kind of funny today: compiling all the Bible verses that use the word "nobody" and conjoining them into one confusing hagiography. ("Nobody conquers God"? "Nobody can serve two masters"? Who *is* this guy?)

The Renaissance and the birth of humanism largely ended the broad religious stigma against comedy—in Christianity, anyway. In the Muslim world, the last decade has seen a sharp rise in blasphemy trials, many targeting satirists and other public quipsters. But in the West, the last gasp of religious control over humor came in the form of twentieth-century obscenity crusades against comics like Mae West, Lenny Bruce, and George Carlin. West's travails aren't as well remembered as Bruce's or Carlin's, but she was banned from national radio for over a decade after a 1937 broadcast in which she talked dirty to, of all people, Edgar Bergen and Charlie McCarthy. She praised the ventriloquist's dummy as her perfect man—"all wood and a yard long"—and provided America with a truly disturbing mental image when she confided that she still had splinters from their last rendezvous.* In 1930, West even served a ten-day jail sentence when her Broadway debut, *Sex*, was found to be indecent. She could have paid a fine but thought the jail time was better publicity. "I believe in censorship. I made a fortune out of it," she later laughed.

To a layperson, it may seem as if the most obvious change to modern comedy is the new freedom with sex and scatology. It was once a notable and controversial move for a comedian to "work blue"—comedy slang for using off-color material, which derived from the blue envelopes that vaudeville bosses used to notify performers when they deemed a

---

* She also told McCarthy, "Come home with me now, honey, I'll let you play in my woodpile," which to my mind seems to be mixing up the metaphor a bit.

particular joke too saucy to stay in the act. But today, it's a surprising novelty when a comedian, a Brian Regan or a Jim Gaffigan, makes it their brand to work clean. Being a parent turned me overnight into the worst kind of comedy crank, a sputtering Steve Allen constantly annoyed that there were so few comedians I could watch with my young kids without wincing a little bit. I wasn't against R-rated comedy. I just wished there were more options.*

Freud wasn't wrong about how it's easier to laugh at things we normally repress. Dirty words aren't funny by themselves, but their aura of mild taboo makes them effective joke punctuation. In fact, they're so effective at propping up punch lines that comedy now seems strangely anemic when it has to go without. Jerry Seinfeld has argued against profanity for that very reason—it's a crutch, it makes it too easy to get flat material over. He stopped swearing in his act around 1980, when he noticed that his critique of the George Reeves *Superman* TV show—"The *Daily Planet*, supposedly the largest-circulation newspaper in the entire city, they got three reporters. And each week two of them are stuck in a cave!"—only got laughs when it was "Two of them are stuck in a f—king cave!" Personally, I never bought into the comedy principle behind this objection. There are *lots* of phrasing changes you could make to a punch line to help put it across. Why is this particular kind a cheat?

On a larger scale, though, the frankness of modern comedy isn't a new development at all. That's an illusion, harbored only by two or three generations who happened to come of age during the relatively short period when jokes had to pass through a heavy-handed media establishment to reach the marketplace. The movie industry's Production Code, for example, was a strict comedy gatekeeper but lasted for less than forty years. During that era, the corner tavern was still full of dirty jokes, but Hollywood made sure it only told neutered versions of them to an audience that, for the most part, knew very well what was going on. When Bob Hope shocked Paulette Goddard by telling her, "I'd

---

* This only goes for stand-up, interestingly. The post-Pixar world is an unprecedented golden age of family-friendly TV and movie comedy that's also hip and funny. In my day, comedy for children was almost uniformly terrible. We had nothing but *Herbie Goes Bananas* and cheap-ass Hanna-Barbera shorts and syndicated *Brady Bunch* reruns, and we liked it! We couldn't get enough of it!

like to kiss you 'til your ears fly off," most viewers could probably hear the actual word that "kiss" was replacing. Our word "obscene" literally means "out of the scene," which was how the ancients described all the delightfully indecent things an audience has to imagine going on offstage.

Settings like Victorian England and Eisenhower's America, when mass entertainment couldn't work blue, are the exceptions in human history. For the most part, comedy has *always* been dirty. In the Old Comedy of Ancient Greece, male characters clomped around the stage with big red leather phalluses jutting from their hips, and playwrights got laughs by having their characters repeatedly soil themselves with chronic diarrhea. The surviving comedies of Aristophanes and his peers contain, according to the count of one scholar, 106 different words for male genitalia, 92 for female genitalia, and 178 vulgar names for various sex acts. I can't think of any modern writer or comic who could compete with that. Petronius, Chaucer, Rabelais—all the big names in comedy wrote about all kinds of degeneracy in perfectly filthy fashion. Even a good Catholic boy like Dante put fart jokes in canto XXI of his *Inferno*, when he watches the demon Malacoda rally the armies of hell not with a trumpet, but with "his bugle of an ass-hole." "I have seen scouts ride . . . to the accompaniment of every known device," Dante deadpans, "but I never saw cavalry or infantry . . . signaled to set off by such strange bugling!"

So the coarseness of modern comedy isn't a sign of moral decline; it's a return to normalcy after a few decades of artificially enforced inoffensiveness. In fact, you could say the same thing about comedy's modern ascendancy in general: it's happening in fields that were long allowed to be funny, before a small group of prigs in the academy insisted on seriousness as the new rule. This is true of the comedy resurgence in three diverse genres in particular: pop music, poetry, and award-bait Hollywood film.

I'm Not Crazy, I Perform This Way

Readers of a certain age: you might be picturing "Weird Al" Yankovic incorrectly. The sui generis accordionist and novelty song legend has dialed down the "weird" somewhat since his 1980s heyday of "Eat It" and

"Like a Surgeon." A couple decades ago, he revamped his iconic white-and-nerdy image: he got LASIK surgery, shaved the goofy mustache, and retired most of the Hawaiian shirts. Now a teetotal vegetarian with his wavy hair parted sleekly down the middle, he looked ageless and serene when I met him, more yoga instructor than RadioShack employee.

His chairs, however, were still weird. "Do you want to try these out?" he asked. We were at his home in the Hollywood Hills, in a downstairs den mid-remodel, surrounded by unhung art and gold records and other "Weird Al"–abilia. I briefly settled into one of the odd, red, spinning chairs, furniture straight out of a Jacques Tati movie, but it was like perching in an egg cup. We moved to the boring couch.

I had been listening to Yankovic for well over thirty years and knew his origin story well. He was a pioneer of the DIY comedy ethos that also produced *Mystery Science Theater 3000* in the 1980s. A high school valedictorian from the Los Angeles suburbs, Yankovic was already getting home-taped versions of his comedy songs played on *The Dr. Demento Show* by the time he started college at the precocious age of sixteen. Nobody was making novelty records in 1976; Barry "Dr. Demento" Hansen was filling his show with a lot of old Stan Freberg and Tom Lehrer songs before Yankovic began sending in his accordion originals. "I filled a vacuum," he told me.

Like his *MST3K* contemporaries, "Weird Al" is an unfailingly affectionate parodist, not skewering pop songs so much as riffing on them. He favors genial jokes about the most universal slices of everyday life: food, TV, riding the bus. Most Internet song parodies "go for the jugular," Yankovic said, making "mean-spirited points about the original artist and the original song. It's a valid way to do parody, but it's not my personal taste." In most "Weird Al" songs, the source is irrelevant, except for the shadow cast by the original lyrics. The backing track conditions you for street poetry about gang-banging in Compton, and instead you get silly jokes about Amish barn-raising. The comedy is in the negative space.

As an aside, Merv Griffin credited the success of Yankovic's 1984 song "I Lost on Jeopardy" with helping return the venerable 1960s quiz show to the airwaves later that year. If this is true, I owe more than a few polka-fueled laughs to "Weird Al" Yankovic. I owe him my entire career.

When I spoke to him, Yankovic was at home between two sprawling megatours supporting his recent album, *Mandatory Fun*. The album had won him a fourth Grammy and spawned a Top 40 single in his fourth consecutive decade ("Word Crimes," a substantially more grammar-focused version of Robin Thicke's "Blurred Lines"). But most impressively, the record had debuted atop the *Billboard* album chart. No comedy record had been at number one since the era of Allan Sherman and "Hello Muddah, Hello Fadduh!" fifty years before. In prerecorded podcasts Yankovic had joked with interviewers that the new record was a number one smash. "That was the most crazy thing I could think of to say at the time," he explained. By the time the interviews aired, the tongue-in-cheek prediction had come true and no one could understand what he was laughing about.

The thirty-five-year "Weird Al" success story says something about niche geekery becoming mainstream American culture in the Internet age, and also something about the decline of music retail sales to the point where an artist like Yankovic, one with a dedicated, multigenerational fan base, could outsell new records by established rock artists like Jason Mraz and Rise Against. But when a comedy record tops the pop charts, it's something more than that. It's a moment of reckoning.

That's because rock, the dominant mode of popular music for decades, is avidly, studiously unfunny. "I once had a girl—or should I say, she once had me" is a pretty good joke. So is "God said to Abraham, 'Kill me a son.' Abe said, 'Man, you must be puttin' me on.'" But the puckish John Lennon/Bob Dylan school of rock made little progress against a tide of soulful authenticity. "As we got into the sixties and seventies, pop—and rock in particular—started to take itself very seriously," Yankovic told me. "There became a general feeling that if you were funny with your music, you were of lesser value. You were not an artist, you were not to be taken seriously. You were a clown. So for a long time, people were pretty guarded about their senses of humor." The ponderousness of rock was a stake to the heart of novelty music.

I understand the problem: the lower-brain-stem groove of a lot of rock and pop music is a bad match for cleverness of any kind. Henri Bergson believed that "laughter is incompatible with emotion." He probably wasn't thinking about the brooding intensity of Eddie Vedder, but he was absolutely right: the amusement reflex doesn't layer neatly on top of *real* emotions. You have to ALT+TAB away from anger or sadness or passion to focus on humor. You can't dance to it; you can't air-guitar to it. When we're lost in a driving rock song or a plaintive ballad, that can feel like an experience too primal for something as delicate as laughter.

But consider: other genres of music have no problem with humor. The seventeenth-century inventors of opera tried unsuccessfully to banish comic opera from the genre, but it was just too popular with audiences; now it's a respected part of the canon. Show tunes are funny. Rap has its origins in the playful insult-trading of "the dozens," and its popularity still relies heavily on quick wit and verbal dexterity. Country music is so comedy-friendly that in Nashville, iconic songs regularly get written around good title jokes, like Loretta Lynn's "You're the Reason Our Kids Are Ugly" and Jerry Reed's "She Got the Goldmine (I Got the Shaft)." Johnny Cash, Waylon Jennings, and Faron Young all had hits with songs by comic poet Shel Silverstein, most notably Cash's "A Boy Named Sue." Dolly Parton's "Single Women" was originally written by Michael O'Donoghue for a 1981 *Saturday Night Live* sketch. *New York* magazine, in its regular literary competitions, often asked readers to submit ideas for over-the-top country song titles. I recently discovered that, thanks to a list of past winners that circulated widely on the Internet, two of those joke titles have since inspired real songs: "Ain't No Trash Been in My Trailer Since the Night I Threw You Out" (Colt Ford) and "She Chews Tobacco but She Won't Choose Me" (Dierks Bentley).

In other words, the hegemony of earnestness in popular music—now being challenged on all sides by hip-hop virtuosity, self-aware country corn, sassy pop stars, whimsical indie rockers, and old-school musical comedians like Yankovic—was a temporary embargo enforced by a small cabal of moody rock critics and front men. Rock could have been funny all along.

Freed Verse

The world of poetry has also been stuck in a similar state of affairs, poet Billy Collins told me. For centuries, the poetic canon accepted comedy at its highest levels: the dick jokes of Chaucer, the sitcom misunderstandings of Shakespeare, the wordplay of the Metaphysical poets, the satire of Pope and Dryden. "But then you get to the Romantic poetry, into Wordsworth and Coleridge and Shelley, and then humor dies. What I imagine is that those three poets go into some kind of back room and lock the door and pull down the blinds and they make this deal. And the deal is that they're going to remove from poetry sex and humor, and substitute in landscape—which is a crappy deal, I think."

Collins credited twentieth-century trailblazers like Philip Larkin and Charles Simic with reassuring him that poets could be funny. "I didn't think humor was allowed in poetry—and my thinking was quite correct there. It wasn't allowed, really. If you were humorous in poetry, you risked being demoted to this condition of light verse." That's the poetry equivalent of "Weird Al" Yankovic's novelty ghetto, and Collins has certainly wandered right up to the edge. He writes colloquial, "hospitable"* verse that mines humor out of fanciful images (the Buddha shoveling snow, an annoying barking dog joining the percussion section of an orchestra, Smokey the Bear finally snapping and burning down a forest) or observations that escalate into funny exaggerations, the way a comedian builds a bit. "The Lanyard" trades on the lame insufficiency of summer camp gifts for parents; "Litany" bites the hand that feeds by making fun of loopy poetic metaphors. Thanks largely to the element of comedy, his verse read aloud to audiences like a dream, and Collins's success on the lecture circuit and public radio soon made him the best-selling poet in America. He received a six-figure advance, unprecedented in the poetry world, when he moved to Random House in 1999. Two years later, he became poet laureate of the United States.

---

* Collins's work has been referred to so often as "accessible" that he now chafes at the word, calling it a "light burden." But there's no getting around it: his work *is* reader-friendly, even if critics might disagree on whether its simplicity is a virtue.

Collins took pride in the 2010 publication of *Seriously Funny*, an anthology of funny contemporary verse, which includes four of his poems. "Humor has recovered its place in poetry, but it's still anathema to people who take things quite seriously."

"I guess I can see the immediacy of humor not working well with many poems—like dense, elliptical Wallace Stevens things," I said. "You only get a laugh when something's *not* opaque, when everyone understands it instantly."

"But there's something very authentic about humor, because anyone can pretend to be serious," Collins replied. "Anyone who has had a job or sat in a classroom knows how to pretend to be serious. You just put on the serious look and maybe put your hand under your chin and wrinkle your brow. But you can't pretend to be funny. It's either funny or it isn't, so there's something kind of authentic about that. It can't be faked."

Collins's ultimate nod to reader "hospitality" might be his boyish first name—"more like a third baseman" than a poet's name, he says— which he adopted as a young poet to avoid confusion with the very serious eighteenth-century English lyric poet William Collins. Today, the two are listed back to back in the index of *The Norton Anthology of Poetry*.

The Not Ready for Subprime Time Players

In popular music and poetry, funny work was ghettoized because the critical establishment didn't think it was worth their time. In part, this is the dead frog problem: What is there to say about a joke? What analysis improves it? The rigid barrier between *real* work and funny counterfeits was enforced with implacable semantics: This song is pop or rock, because it isn't funny. This other one in the very same musical style has jokes, so it goes into the trash heap of "novelty songs."

The presumption that drama is inherently superior to comedy can be traced back to Aristotle, who held that "tragedy is a representation of men better than ourselves," but "comedy . . . is a representation of inferior people," "a species of the base and ugly." The simplicity of comedy works against it here—its one goal is to make us laugh. A YouTube video of a teen magician running into a door frame and falling down can make me laugh so hard that I can't breathe, but it's hard to argue that, as art forms go, this seven-second video is the equal of *Paradise Lost* or the Sistine Chapel. As a result, high schoolers reading Shakespeare are inevitably assigned *Romeo and Juliet* or *Hamlet* instead of *Twelfth Night* or *A Midsummer Night's Dream*, either of which might be an easier sell. And when comedy does get a little respect, it's often reserved for a very particular kind of comedy. Evelyn Waugh always maintained that the only two great artists in Hollywood were funny ones, Walt Disney and Charlie Chaplin—but note that he chose those two men over, say, their contemporaries Tex Avery and Buster Keaton. Disney and Chaplin were the comedians who larded their work with plenty of mawkish sentiment on top of the laughs, to make sure the critics could see that they weren't doing *mere* comedy.

You might not immediately think of the Academy Awards as a joke-hostile colossus along the lines of the medieval Christian church, but the most influential gatekeeper of film "prestige" has never been too impressed by funny movies. Comedy is the most successful box office genre of the modern era, but niche categories like war movies and biopics have each won more Best Picture Oscars than comedies have. In fact, the last capital-*C* Comedy to win the Best Picture Oscar was *Annie Hall* in 1978.* But that's changing. In 2016, many handicappers believed that Adam McKay, of all people—the longtime writing partner of Will Ferrell—came within a whisker of defeating the Very Serious Issue Movie *Spotlight* with his Best Picture nominee *The Big Short*.

The Big Short was also an issue movie, an adaptation of Michael Lewis's deadly serious 2010 book about the recent U.S. housing bubble collapse, in which ten million Americans lost their homes and the world economy plowed into a severe recession. It's never easy to adapt a dense nonfiction book to the screen, but *The Big Short* faced a particularly steep uphill climb: to convey the full weight of the crisis, it needed a lay

---

* Several more recent winners have been dramas with comedy *elements*. There's *Terms of Endearment, Rain Man, Driving Miss Daisy, Forrest Gump, Shakespeare in Love*, and *The Artist*.

audience not only to understand the mechanics of hedge funds, subprime mortgage trading, credit default swaps, and tranches of collateralized debt obligation, but *to see the inherent drama in them.*

Other directors might have approached this task very differently, but McKay, the director of goofy screen comedies from *Anchorman* to *The Other Guys*, decided to dive in using the full postmodern comedy tool kit, like he was making a very long Funny or Die video. There were onscreen cartoon doodles, funny cutaways à la *The Simpsons*, even scenes that ended in the middle of a line of dialogue, like Tim & Eric do on Adult Swim. When the macroeconomic exposition got particularly dense or technical, McKay would deploy a celebrity to break the fourth wall and explain the action directly to the audience. Anybody will listen to a short lecture on global finance as long as it's coming from Margot Robbie in a bubble bath.

During the third such cutaway cameo (Selena Gomez at a blackjack table!), it was hard not to feel a little guilty. Are we children? Is this what we need to understand current events now, comedy blanketing everything like the cloying grape flavor in pediatric cough syrup? Take your medicine, America, it's okay. *There will be a joke every few minutes.*

But *The Big Short* actually does something much cannier with its comedy. The story of the housing bubble and the dopey people who made it happen is full of ludicrously over-the-top moments, the kind that you'd never believe in a dramatic Hollywood screenplay. But in a comedy, McKay can have his characters literally testify to the movie's accuracy. "If it seems almost too perfect," Ryan Gosling's character tells the audience at one point, "trust me, this happened." In many ways, the housing crash was a comedy of errors, if a pitch-black one. Getting an audience to laugh at those errors—and then feel weird about laughing—is a perfect way to tell that story. I walked out of the theater convinced that *The Big Short* would be its generation's *Dr. Strangelove.* In the same way that today we remember and understand the tense absurdities of mutually assured Cold War destruction largely through the lens of satire, someday *The Big Short*, not any actual econ textbook or news coverage, will be the way people remember the 2007 financial crisis.

If Thou Canst Not Beat Them, Joinest Thou Them

It's now been more than half a century since the holy Church, once the world's biggest name in joke-squelching, elected its first funny pope. Beginning in 1962, the historic Second Vatican Council spent three years reinventing Catholicism for the modern world. Out went papal infallibility, anti-Semitism, and the Latin Mass; in came ecumenism, expanded liturgy, and an embrace of human rights. We shouldn't be surprised that the man behind these changes—Pope John XXIII, who convened the council—also broke with tradition by displaying a keen sense of humor in office. After hearing complaints that the Vatican had raised staff salaries to a point where ushers were making as much as cardinals, Pope John is said to have replied, "That usher has ten children. I hope the cardinal doesn't." In his most repeated quip, Pope John was asked by a reporter how many people worked at the Vatican. "About half of them," His Holiness grinned. Most stories about John XXIII's impossible wit have the distinct air of apocrypha to them, but that's missing the point. What was new was the world's Catholics taking pride in their funny pope and inventing tall tales about his good-humored wisecracks. Similar stories were told about John's most iconic successors, John Paul II and Francis. For the foreseeable future, it looks as though the papacy will have to be centered on that same common touch, that twinkle in the eye. Upon this rock will I build My church.

The befunnying of modern religion is, at least in part, a calculated act of self-preservation. The churches are watching their pews empty in an increasingly secular society; as a result, homilies and sermons now have to be entertaining, in order to compete with the wash of jokes everywhere else. The free advertising on the church signboard out front can't be merely a Bible verse anymore. Instead, short, clever jokes are the industry standard.

LOOKING FOR A LIFEGUARD? OURS WALKS ON WATER.

ETERNITY: SMOKING OR NONSMOKING?

LET'S MEET AT MY HOUSE SUNDAY BEFORE THE GAME.
—GOD

CH__CH. WHAT'S MISSING? U R.

They're dad jokes, but from a heavenly father rather than an earthly one. And the desperation to seem current is almost palpable in these little aphorisms. E-mail is often compared—unfavorably! —to "knee mail." Workout buffs are urged to be "cross-fit." In 2014, with the Seahawks headed to the Super Bowl and Seattle awash in "12th Man" fever, a church near my house even opted for the unfortunate observation "JESUS HAD 12 MEN TOO."

The jokes may be corny, but like the sex ed classes and "funny" paintings we saw earlier, they benefit immeasurably from their staid context. It doesn't take much to seem hip or slightly irreverent by the standards of organized religion. Books of marquee ideas circulate in Protestant circles; these one-liners have become churches' "number-one outreach tool," a Methodist minister told the *Washington Post*. A Sunday sermon about Jesus will last half an hour and reach the same one hundred people—preaching to the choir, in some cases literally. But a little signboard pun about how brightly "the Son shines" is visible 24/7, and can reach thousands.

I graduated from Brigham Young University in Provo, Utah, a Mormon monoculture that takes its annual "Most Sober School" rating from the Princeton Review very seriously. BYU's strict honor code prohibits alcohol, sex, drugs, beards, "revealing" clothing, coed housing and post-curfew socializing, and pretty much every other reason most people go to college. It was, as you'd expect, not a hotbed for comedy. But in 2014, a video from *Studio C*, a mild, wholesome sketch show that aired on the campus television network, went viral on YouTube. "Top Soccer Shootout with Scott Sterling" was a simple slapstick idea in which the titular goalie keeps inadvertently blocking penalty kicks with his face, but it unexpectedly racked up ten million views in just over a week. Suddenly BYUtv, of all places, had a hot comedy property on its hands, and saw an opportunity to promote its family-friendly brand to a vast new fan base. The *Studio C* troupe was dispatched to conventions and podcasts and even showed up on Conan O'Brien's show, after Conan learned that his kids were fans. In the age of peak funny, even Provo—where caffeinated sodas were always banned in campus vending machines and Rodin's *The Kiss* was once pulled from an art museum for being too naughty—is a comedy factory.*

Forced Laughter

At the end of the movie *Mary Poppins*, the crusty bank manager Mr. Dawes (played by a heavily made-up Dick Van Dyke, doing double duty) summons Jane and Michael Banks's buttoned-down father to the bank after hours and fires him for bringing anarchy to the world of finance, just as his new nanny Mary Poppins has brought anarchy to the Banks home. Seeing his carefully constructed world toppling around him, Banks begins to laugh hysterically, and feels moved to tell the bank directors his kids' favorite joke:

"I know a man with a wooden leg named Smith."

"What's the name of his other leg?"

After Banks skips merrily out of the meeting, the old bank president puzzles over the joke. "A wooden leg named Smith? A wooden leg . . . named Smith." Finally he gets it, and begins to laugh so uproariously that his effervescent good humor carries him magically out of his chair and up to the ceiling.†

* The oddities of BYU notwithstanding, I should not imply that Mormons are gloomy puritans. In fact, they see themselves as happy and fun-loving. After the Mormon pioneers arrived in the Salt Lake Valley, the very first building they built was a shaded bowery, which was soon used for music and theater. When Brigham Young dedicated a more permanent playhouse in 1862, he asked that only comedy be performed in it. His people had known "enough of tragedy in everyday life," he said, "and we ought to have amusement when we come here." But before 2014 and Scott Sterling, the Mormons' idea of fun had never aligned with American comedy norms. *Donny & Marie*, our previous high-water mark, debuted on ABC in 1976, when *Saturday Night Live* had already made prime-time variety shows effectively obsolete.

† In a bizarre twist, we learn in the movie's final scene that his violent laughing fit killed him. Do you think he sank back to the floor gradually as the life ebbed out of him, or did he plummet immediately the second his heart stopped?

This is a common fictional archetype: the old curmudgeon whose heart is softened by the purity of a child's laughter. Does it ever happen in real life? Even if people do sometimes embrace humor overnight by finally "getting the joke"—and I'm skeptical!—institutions do not. Institutions, whether rock or poetry or religion, are more like Ebenezer Scrooge: they have to be dragged kicking and screaming by the ghosts of their worst nightmares to arrive at their comic epiphany.

The establishment, in other words, came around to humor for purely self-serving reasons, not out of the goodness of its heart. Much as post-Enlightenment religion has been forced to grapple seriously with science instead of sneering at it or locking it in dungeons, it now has to accept laughter and comedy as facts of life. Being comedy-skeptical just isn't an option anymore in a post-serious world. It makes institutions look oblivious and out of touch—not to mention intolerably dull. In the last decade, the Catholic Church briefly tried out a throwback, unfunny pope; he lasted only eight years before stepping aside for a jollier, more quotable model.

The decline of anticomedy has been a liberation: everyone in society now has implicit permission to be funny, whatever they're doing. On Twitter, on cocktail menus, or in the workplace, that can sometimes be oppressive, but in fields once kept joke-free only by critical fiat, the new possibilities can be a godsend. Think of the generations of funny Christians, musicians, and poets forced to drop out or keep their sense of humor deeply closeted. If the gatekeepers to humor had never given up their posts, we would never have had *The Big Short*, or a Billy Collins, or a "Weird Al." Those last two creators would probably be working dull nine-to-fives somewhere; the jokes are so central to their art that it's hard to imagine them doing purely serious work. There's probably no parallel universe in which "Normal Al" Yankovic is noodling on guitar with his jam band, or William J. Collins is undertaking a ten-year terza rima translation of Dante instead of writing poems about his dog.

It's now a world without censors—which must be dispiriting for Mae West types who thrive on the martyrdom, and the publicity, of being persecuted truth-tellers. This is no doubt why many comedians bristle today at even the most innocuous pleas for civility. There's no angry Legion of Decency or vice squads to contend with nowadays, so slightly-over-the-hill comics are reduced to complaining about how they can't say things are "gay" or "retarded" anymore. That's not censorship in any meaningful sense, but it's all they have now.

In Western liberal democracies, that is. The end of enforced serious-ness has created one strident new strain of humor foe: angry religious extremists more than willing to start shooting people when they don't like a cartoon. But when I think about how religious power in the West devolved from severe monks to punster youth pastors, I wonder if this is a problem that will solve itself in Islam as well. Surely it's only a matter of time before radical Islamist terrorists borrow a playbook from Madi-son Avenue advertisers and neo-Nazi trolls and political candidates and Christian churches. Don't oppress humor; co-opt it. Make it work for you. Get a little wordplay going on those madrassa marquees, drop some wholesome sketch comedy about soccer into your propaganda videos. Let's get those ironic sharia memes out there.

NINE

A BLURRY, AMORPHOUS THUD

Abraham Lincoln gathered his cabinet to the White House early on the morning of September 22, 1862. His overworked secretary of war, Edwin Stanton, arrived late and was annoyed to find the president reading aloud excerpts from the first book by Artemus Ward, the country-fried humorist who would export American comedy to London with his comic lectures in 1866. The president was already a big fan.

He was reading a sketch called "High-Handed Outrage at Utica," about a traveling salesman trying to impress upstate New Yorkers with his wares: wax figurines of the twelve apostles. A local ruffian ruins his trip by pounding his Judas Iscariot statue all to hell in a fit of religious fervor. Lincoln was laughing loudly by the time he got to the end—"without a single member of the Cabinet joining in," Stanton observed icily. Undeterred, the president proceeded to read *a second chapter.* Stanton was about to walk out when Lincoln finally decided to end the open-mic night and get to the business at hand. Pulling a piece of paper from his trademark hat, he read to them from a document he had just finished revising and had decided to issue: the Emancipation Proclamation, freeing every slave in the Confederacy.

That Lincoln was telling jokes minutes before abolishing slavery wouldn't have surprised anyone who knew him well. From youth, his ravenous reading habits included a ribald British jokebook called *Quinn's Jests,* and he grew to adulthood on the frontier, swapping yarns with groups of men around fireplaces and woodstoves. Like so many other funny people before and since, Lincoln battled clinical depression as an adult, and jokes kept him going in his darkest moments. During the

Civil War, humor collections starring Lincoln with titles like *Old Abe's Jokes* and *Wit at the White House* were big sellers in the North. Abraham Lincoln isn't just the nation's secular saint. Before Mark Twain, he was also the first name in folksy, irreverent American humor.

But curiously, Lincoln's famous sense of humor was much more restrained in public. Editing a 1910 collection of Lincoln's addresses, Daniel Kilham Dodge noted that Lincoln only gave one "purely humorous" speech in his political career, delivered to Congress in 1848 on the subject of then–presidential candidate Zachary Taylor. "As a rule, he confined his story-telling to conversations," Dodge wrote, observing that even in his rough-and-tumble debates with Stephen Douglas, Lincoln steered clear of the homespun anecdotes he was forever tossing off in daily life. "The occasion is too serious, the issues are too grave," Lincoln explained to friends who wanted him to be funnier on the stump. "I do not seek applause, or to amuse the people, but to convince them." Much of our modern conception of Lincoln as a public jokester comes from his enemies in the press, who had political incentives to portray him as a backwoods figure of fun. And Lincoln's biographer Carl Sandburg, perusing the fad Lincoln joke books, found that, rather than collecting actual quips from Honest Abe, they mostly recycled stale old jokes, using Lincoln "as a handy peg on which to hang them."

There have been a handful of truly funny world leaders down through history. In the Middle Ages, monarchs like England's Henry II, France's Louis IX, and Spain's Jaume I inspired the Renaissance ideal of the *rex facetus*, the "jesting king," who ruled with shrewd wit and brightened life for all his subjects with his laughter.* During the Stuart period, Robert Harley, the first Earl of Oxford, was Queen Anne's prime minister by day and a member of the famed Scriblerus Club by night, dining and trading wisecracks with all-time A-list satirists like Alexander Pope and Jonathan Swift. But for the most part, Western civilization has chosen to maintain a careful line between government and comic entertainment.

---

* Louis IX, however, abstained from laughter on Fridays out of religious piety, as he was an incredibly devout Catholic. He was canonized after his 1270 death in the Crusades, and the city of St. Louis, Missouri, is one of many places still named for him.

Look at the marble statues in London and Paris and Washington—they're none of them grinning. Not even Lincoln.

Repealing Corwin's Law

In the United States, this bright line even has a name: Corwin's Law. Nineteenth-century politician Thomas Corwin advised future president James Garfield, "Never make people laugh. If you would succeed in life, you must be solemn, solemn as an ass. All the great monuments of earth have been built over solemn asses." Corwin had been governor of Ohio, a United States senator, secretary of the treasury, and minister to Mexico, and is best remembered for the (appropriately unfunny) Corwin Amendment, an abortive attempt to permanently enshrine slavery in the Constitution. Though biographers agree that Corwin was privately a man of "infinite humor," his gambit appears to have worked. In his legacy of photographs and portraits, he unfailingly has the bland, unamused look of a Victorian butler.*

Corwin's Law held sway over American politics for over a century—and, remarkably, comedy largely returned the favor, keeping its nose out of government. Granted, there have always been political jokes. The classics of Athenian Old Comedy were loaded with so many then-topical references that they would have felt like episodes of *South Park* to an ancient Greek audience. And a candidate for the oldest recorded joke in human history is a political zinger, appearing in hieratic script on a four-thousand-year-old sheet of Egyptian papyrus. "How do you entertain a bored pharaoh? You sail a boatload of young women dressed only in fishing nets down the Nile and urge the pharaoh to go catch a fish." I'm sure that in the Fourth Dynasty, this was a pretty sick burn on the carnal foibles of pharaoh Sneferu, but I find it a little confusing today. He's supposed to go fishing for women . . . but they're already in the nets? They're the fish and they've

---

* In Corwin's defense, portrait photography was seen as a formal occasion in his day, so almost *everyone* chose a look of stern disapproval when being immortalized. That tradition, together with the long, smile-unfriendly exposures of the daguerreotype period, has contributed to our modern misconception of the past as a miserable and humorless place, when it was merely a miserable one.

caught themselves? Is he going to have sex with the "fish"? This could use some work in my opinion.

But in our age of bottomless topical satire, it's hard for us to imagine how toothless most "political" humor used to be. Gilded Age cartoonists were pretty good at riling up urbanites against corrupt political machines, but with the dawn of the twentieth century, comedy began to take pains not to alienate either side of the aisle. Even a moral conscience and voice of reform like Will Rogers carefully aimed his wisecracks at out-of-touch politicians in general, giving birth to a century of hacky-but-nonpartisan quips about "those clowns in Congress." Before Mort Sahl, no one ever got up on a nightclub stage and spun topical jokes out of the day's headlines—and Sahl's fellow comedians warned him he'd never make it if he didn't trade his V-neck sweater in for a tuxedo and get back to one-liners about mothers-in-law, like a real comedian. When Sahl poked fun at the Kennedy administration, Joe Kennedy tried to get him blackballed from clubs, because joking about the presidency in 1962 Just Wasn't Done. Even a good-natured comedy record like *The First Family*, with impersonator Vaughn Meader parodying life in the Kennedy White House, was turned down by four different record labels before a small outfit called Cadence Records agreed to release it. One label executive, former Eisenhower press secretary James Hagerty, warned that the album, with its gentle jokes about touch football and rocking chairs, would be "degrading to the presidency" and a Christmas present to "every Communist country in the world." Hagerty was proved wrong: *The First Family* was not a hit in Russia or Cuba,* but it did immediately became the fastest-selling record in U.S. history.†

In the early 1960s, just as it was about to revolutionize pop music as well, Britain changed the comedy rules. The same year that U.S. radio stations were pussyfooting around *The First Family*, the BBC debuted *That Was the Week That Was*, a groundbreaking Saturday-night satire program

---

* "Kyoo-ber."

† Meader's meteoric rise to fame ended abruptly on November 22, 1963. On his way to a gig in Wisconsin that night, a cabbie asked him, "Did you hear about Kennedy in Dallas?" "No," Meader replied, "how does it go?" A few days later, Lenny Bruce took the stage for his first show after the assassination and paced back and forth for what seemed like an eternity before unleashing his opening joke: "Whew, Vaughn Meader is screwed!"

hosted by David Frost. In defiance of polite comic tradition, *That Was the Week That Was* took off the gloves and gleefully named names, savaging hypocrisy and corruption everywhere it could find it, from business to religion to royalty—but particularly in the government of Prime Minister Harold Macmillan. *TW3*'s weekly meat-grinding of Home Secretary Henry Brooke, including accusations at one point that he was essentially complicit in murder, helped hasten the end of Brooke's political career. This was the beginning of Britain's great satire boom of the 1960s, and you can draw a straight line directly to the Smothers Brothers and *Laugh-In* and *Saturday Night Live* and *The Daily Show* and all the American shows that soon began to blur the once-abandoned DMZ between comedy and politics.

The first high-profile violation of Corwin's Law appeared on *Laugh-In*, in fact. In 1968, on the second-season premiere of the fast-paced sketch show, a close-up of presidential candidate Richard Nixon abruptly appeared onscreen, like a mad genius commandeering the airwaves in a movie. The election was just two months away. "Sock it to *me?!?*" he asked incredulously. The cameo lasted just four seconds, and then the awkward, jowly specter was gone, replaced with more conventional candy-colored sixties shtick. Audiences might have wondered if they had just imagined it. "Was . . . was that Nixon?"

The clip is even more bewildering now, out of context. "Sock it to me" was one of the most popular *Laugh-In* catchphrases, from a bizarre running gag in which sweet young British actress Judy Carne would stand on an empty stage in a minidress and say, "Sock it to me!" after which she would be abused in humiliating ways (sprayed with water, pounded by a caveman club, dress ripped off) while the laugh track roared. This was very funny at the time, because she was a woman. The unexpected substitution of Nixon was the curveball, and was a last-minute Plan C when the candidate refused to try other *Laugh-In* catchphrases like "What's a bippy?" and "Good night, Dick." The four-word segment took six takes, because Nixon's line reading kept coming off as "too angry." But how did the least funny president in recent memory* wind up on a comedy show anyway?

---

* It's a clear sign of the waning influence of Corwin's Law that each political party's last big presidential flameout—Richard Nixon and Jimmy Carter, respectively—was also its last unfunny president.

It wasn't just a comic whim. Though audiences at the time didn't know it, *Laugh-In* head writer Paul Keyes was a longtime Nixon speechwriter who was still on the campaign payroll. Keyes told Nixon that a *Laugh-In* cameo, by appealing to young voters, could be a game-changer in a tight election. Nixon believed Keyes because he had been right before. In 1963, Keyes had urged Jack Paar to invite Nixon onto *The Tonight Show*, at a time when Nixon was still in political exile after losing the 1960 presidential election to the slicker, more TV-friendly John F. Kennedy. Paar and Keyes had softened Nixon's image by bringing on a grand piano and having him play a concerto of his own composition. Describing the appearance in 1964's *Understanding Media*, Marshall McLuhan didn't miss its import. "A few timely touches like this would have quite altered the result of the Kennedy-Nixon campaign," he noted ominously. Five years later, McLuhan was proved right: Keyes's *Laugh-In* gambit paid off. The press pool was amazed to see college kids start showing up at Nixon rallies with "Sock it to me, Dick, baby" signs. In November, Nixon narrowly won the popular vote over a split Democratic Party, and forever credited *Laugh-In* with the win.*

Once politicians saw that Corwin's Law no longer applied in the mass media era, there was no stopping them. The appeal of watching government bigwigs loosen their ties and goof around is obvious: it's the same voyeuristic impulse behind *Us Weekly*'s feature "Stars—They're Just Like Us!" *plus* the added geopolitical frisson of somehow peeking behind the curtain, getting a forbidden look at what really happens in the corridors of power when the photo op is over. But the candor is all a charade—as Nixon proved, no actual comedy chops are even necessary. In 1984, Margaret Thatcher, one of the least funny people of the twentieth century, wrote her own sketch based on the BBC's hit comedy *Yes, Prime Minister*,† privately rehearsed it twenty-three times with staff, and persuaded the show's stars to act it out with her on an awards show. Why was the most powerful woman in the world going to all this trouble? "She

---

* In the interest of equal time, the show invited Nixon's opponent, Vice President Hubert Humphrey, to appear the following week. Humphrey said no, to his eternal regret.

† Or so she claimed. In fact, her press secretary, Bernard Ingham, wrote the sketch.

was losing popularity," explained *Yes, Prime Minister* cocreator Jonathan Lynn, "and, though not very amusing herself, she knew the power of humor. She was co-opting the show to make people like her more."*

The Comeback Kid

The dam broke in 1992. I was a college freshman, and eager not merely to vote for the first time but to "Rock the Vote," as MTV was then insisting. The recording industry organization of that name was nominally nonpartisan (and had actually been founded in 1990 to oppose Tipper Gore's music censorship efforts) but the Left began to see youth turnout as a possible way to end their twelve years in the wilderness following the Reagan Revolution. And this election in particular felt like a generational shift: for the first time, a baby boomer, raised on television with his mother's milk, was running for president.

Bill Clinton's career had already been saved once by TV comedy. In 1988, as governor of Arkansas and a rising star in the Democratic Party, he'd been given a plum role at the party's Atlanta convention: a prime-time speech officially nominating Michael Dukakis for the presidency. But Clinton's speech was an unqualified disaster. He lost the crowd early and rambled on for twice his allotted time. The networks cut away, and delegates began to yell, "Wrap it up!" Thirty-three minutes in, when he began a sentence with "In closing," cheers finally rang through the hall.

Linda Bloodworth-Thomason, the producer of the hit sitcom *Designing Women* and a close friend of the Clintons, had watched the speech and knew Clinton's political future was on the line. In the middle of the night, she woke up her husband, Harry, with an idea straight from her wheelhouse: television comedy. "Look," she said, "he's got to go on the Carson show to make this right." The next day, *The Tonight Show*'s producers told the Thomasons that it wasn't going to happen; Johnny never had politicians on as guests. But Harry had a brainstorm: what if

---

* This may explain why Thatcher's friend Ronald Reagan, despite his famous screen charisma and media connections, never descended to comic TV appearances: people already liked him. Or it may be that to a big-screen star of the studio era, entertainment television seemed too disposable and lightweight a medium for the president of the United States.

Clinton went on and played saxophone with the band? The producers finally agreed to the appearance, and Clinton's rueful self-deprecation charmed the socks off Johnny, ending his bad media cycle within a week. The media called it the fastest turnaround in political history, and everyone took note.

So it was no surprise four years later when Clinton made the Thomasons' playbook central to his own presidential campaign. He spent as much time talking to Larry King and Phil Donahue as he did with the reporters of *Meet the Press*. He dusted off his saxophone to wail away on "Heartbreak Hotel" with Arsenio Hall's house band and spent an hour nodding empathetically with college kids at an MTV town hall two weeks later. It's a measure of just how starchy American politics was in 1992 that flannel-wearing Gen X slackers immediately seized on Clinton as the "cool" candidate even though he was a middle-aged southern man playing thirty-five-year-old Elvis tunes in *Risky Business* sunglasses.

This was one of those rare moments in culture where everything changed permanently and everyone knew it at once. Barbara Walters protested that Clinton's TV offensive was "undignified"; conservative bloviator George Will began a decade of screeds about how the "vulgarian" Clintons were coarsening American culture. *New York Times* columnist Tom Wicker worried about "the association with jazz music and dark shades and *The Arsenio Hall Show*," a take that even for 1992 seems to be going out of its way to sound racist. In the same vein, when Clinton's opponent George H. W. Bush insisted that he would never appear on shows like *Larry King Live* or *Donahue* "because I'm the president," his press secretary clarified that he would actually accept "just about any invitation"—except one from Arsenio Hall. But the ferocity of the old-media pushback just showed how abruptly and irrevocably the ship had sailed. Clinton won the presidency decisively, with young people voting in record numbers.* "The separation between theater and

---

* Within two years, he was back on MTV telling a college student that he mostly wore briefs, not boxers, and millions of Clinton voters were surprised to find themselves suddenly thinking that maybe George Will had a point.

state broke down," comedian Robert Klein observed, "and show biz and politics came crashing together with a blurry, amorphous thud."

Working the Media in a Post-Corwin World

By the time of the 2008 election, late-night TV had become the front line of political messaging in America, with elected officials selling policy right alongside actors selling a new sitcom or pop stars selling a new record. Political candidates appeared on *The Tonight Show* twenty-two times, and twenty-one times on *The Daily Show*. Today the idea of a powerful politician avoiding funny chitchat with TV hosts seems quaint at best, and suspiciously undemocratic at worst. Of *course* we need to see senators and cabinet members maintaining rictus grins as they play along with "desk bits" by Leno and Letterman and their successors. Of *course* political candidates should have an array of one-line zingers at the ready during debates, like insult comics. Of *course* the president, in addition to his mastery of legislative, regulatory, economic, military, and diplomatic issues, should be forced to do a tight fifteen minutes of stand-up at the White House Correspondents' Dinner every April. (That once-obscure event snowballed into such a national media circus in the age of politics-as-showbiz that in Washington it's now nicknamed "Nerd Prom.")

The 2008 election produced an even smoother, funnier, more media-friendly president than Clinton, one who thrived in this new arena. Barack Obama looked comfortable "slow-jamming the news" with Jimmy Fallon, sparring with Charles Barkley about the relative merits of Jordan vs. LeBron at the NBA All-Star Game, or joking about reality TV with the hosts of *The View*. A fan of cool comedians from Richard Pryor to Louis C.K., Obama had a calm, slightly detached comic persona that turned out to be a perfect match for the *Daily Show* era. At the 2013 Correspondents' Dinner, he had no fear about trying an acidly blunt antijoke like this one, about the Republican senate majority leader:

> Some folks still don't think I spend enough time with Congress. "Why don't you get a drink with Mitch McConnell?" they ask. Really? Why don't *you* get a drink with Mitch McConnell?

On the page, it doesn't even read as a joke, but Obama's pause after "Really?" and the slight exasperation in the punch line earned him his biggest laugh of the night. There was no Reaganesque twinkle in his deadpan; he was skating closer to the edge.* "I was very impressed with that," Andy Kindler told me. "You have to have a very good sense of humor to sign off on that joke, and good delivery to sell it. He's got—well, I'd like to say a refined sense of humor, but I hear he liked *Entourage.*" Nobody's perfect.

The decline of traditional news and balkanization of media led Obama far afield to reach millennial voters, and comedy outlets—particularly new digital ones—were among the most surprising beneficiaries. Even in 2015, it was still eye-opening to have a sitting president discussing race relations in Marc Maron's garage—the first episode of *WTF* ever where Maron didn't spell out for listeners what the podcast's title stood for—or pondering his political legacy while tooling around the South Lawn in a 1963 Corvette Stingray for Jerry Seinfeld's web series *Comedians in Cars Getting Coffee.* The title made it official: The president of the United States wasn't just a guy that comedians sometimes nervously joked with, which was the novelty of the Clinton and Bush years. He was now the comedian in chief.

Policy with Punch Lines

The most surprising presidential drop-in took place in March 2014, when, without any fanfare or warning, the comedy website Funny or Die posted a new installment of its periodic web series *Between Two Ferns with Zach Galifianakis. Between Two Ferns* was a mock public-access show, in which an A-list celebrity of the "good sport" variety (Jennifer Lawrence, Jon Hamm) sat opposite the *Hangover* star in front of a black backdrop and parried or squirmed through three minutes of inept interview. Galifianakis told Brad Pitt he looked "like Hitler's dream,"

---

* Conservative commentators and Republican critics like Rand Paul complained that the gag was everything wrong with Obama's administration: nakedly partisan, more than a little patronizing. In response to the joke, McConnell tweeted out a goofy photo of himself at a bar gesturing to the empty stool next to him. McConnell has a beer, like a real American; he's ordered a glass of red wine for the president.

requested a donation of his sperm, and played him the *Friends* theme song; Natalie Portman was asked point-blank for her phone number and then about pubic hair grooming. Much of the comedy is created in the editing, as the pair is often allowed to sit in uncomfortable silence while the audience cringes at Galifianakis's latest mumbled question. Barack Obama was the last person anyone expected to see on the show, but there he was, gritting his teeth through stupid questions like "What should we do about North Ikea?" for three minutes before pivoting the conversation toward his new health care bill. "Okay, let's get this out of the way," sighed Galifianakis, obviously annoyed. "What did you come here to plug?"

Galifianakis and Scott Aukerman, the *Comedy Bang! Bang!* host who cocreated *Between Two Ferns* with him, had been trying unsuccessfully to get Obama on the show for six years. But by the time of the Obamacare rollout, when the administration actually started warming up to the idea, they'd pretty much given up. "We just wanted it to be good," Aukerman told me. "We didn't care whether it happened or not. Also, we did *not* think it was going to happen." At the time of the video's release, the White House had warned him not to discuss its filming, not even how long it took to shoot. But when I spoke to him, almost two years had passed and Aukerman didn't mind talking about it. We were at a Thai restaurant in upper Hollywood, and political primary coverage was playing on the TV over the bar. It was a week before Christmas, and Obama was entering his last year in office.

"We were pushing for doing it exactly as we'd always done it," Aukerman said. On a typical *Between Two Ferns*, the guest is told to show up with no publicist or entourage, and then just sits on a makeshift stage for an hour or two with Galifianakis, their responses fully unscripted. "Charlize Theron just drove up herself, did the show, left. That's really the way to do it." The White House, unsurprisingly, didn't think the president could just drive himself to a basement or shed for a couple hours of improv. Aukerman was reluctant to compromise, and it wasn't just because he was worried about losing the show's improvised feel.

"We thought the minute that they saw the jokes they were going to cancel the whole thing," he said. "So we were doing everything we could to make sure they never saw the jokes." Finally, Funny or Die agreed to show an outline to its White House contact, a speechwriter. "Oh my God, this is so funny!" he said, reading through it. Then he started going through the outline joke by joke and explaining why they wouldn't be able to use any of their material. Aukerman realized he'd been right, this was never going to happen. He was ready to pull out. In today's world, the White House auditions for comedy writers, not the other way around.

But suddenly the staffer changed his mind. "You know what?" he said. "In my job, I'm always the guy who's being asked to pull back on stuff. You shouldn't have to do that. You guys should be able to do these jokes." The speechwriter didn't like Obama taking a second jab at Galifianakis's weight ("We don't want to make it seem like it's a go-to joke for him") but for the most part, the script ended up in the teleprompter untouched. Galifianakis realized he was actually going to have to ask Obama, "What's it like to be the last black president?"*

"With any Hollywood star, half of the jokes would have been killed before we started the interview," marveled Aukerman. "But there was something about the White House where they weren't from Hollywood, and they weren't used to dealing with asshole Hollywood publicists who like to kill everything—maybe they didn't know they could kill jokes. They let us do stuff that I never in a million years thought they would let us do."

On the day of the shoot, the Funny or Die crew set up in the Diplomatic Room, a reception room on the ground floor of the White House. Their greenroom was the adjacent Map Room, its walls covered with marked-up maps from historic military campaigns. They were told they would only have the president for fifty minutes, so the crew prepped everything they could, then waited. And waited. They grabbed lunch with White House staffers and even bowled a few frames in the Truman Bowling Alley. The president was running late. Galifianakis kept sitting

---

* "Zach is always embarrassed to do the rude jokes," said Aukerman, who always ended up playing bad cop from behind the camera. When he reassured Galifianakis that the White House had already vetted the "last black president" joke, the host still resisted. "Um, but he'll be mad!"

on antique chairs in the Map Room and getting scolded by a guard—"but then he would never give us chairs," Aukerman remembered.

Finally Obama appeared, and everyone, staffers and video crew alike, snapped noticeably to attention. He greeted Galifianakis and they started chatting about actor Bradley Cooper, the mutual acquaintance who had helped Funny or Die get their foot in the door with the administration. But by now time was even more limited. "The president is a one-and-done guy," an aide told Aukerman. "He's only going to do one take."

"What if I'd like him to do another?"

"Why would you want him to do another take?" replied the aide, genuinely confused and a little unnerved by the idea of a comedian giving direction to the most powerful man on earth.

"Oh, if I just want a different read or something."

"Why would he need to read something differently?"

Aukerman realized he wasn't speaking the right language. "What if he gets a fact wrong?"

This finally got through. "Oh, something like that, okay. Tell you what: the president looks to me to get him out of situations. If you need to do another take, look to me, give me a sign, and I'll give the nod to the president to let him know it's okay. If you *really*, really feel like you need one."

Two minutes into the first take, the crew was told they only had fifteen minutes left, much less than the hour they were promised. "I could see the video, the chances of it being good, disappearing before our very eyes," Aukerman said. The first take wasn't going well, largely due to Galifianakis's evident nervousness at having to repeatedly insult and annoy the president of the United States just a few hundred feet from the Oval Office. But about halfway through something changed. The interview started clicking. Galifianakis and Obama had loosened up and were trading jokes, improvising around the outline. Aukerman began wondering if there was any way to save the unfunny first half in the editing room, and when the cameras cut, he immediately looked for the aide who was supposed to be his advocate with the president.

But before he could make eye contact, Obama turned to Aukerman. "Well, what do you think?"

Despite strict warnings not to do precisely this, Aukerman screwed up his courage. "Well, Mr. President, to be honest, halfway through it got so good and really loosened up. I wish we could do the first half with that kind of fun and energy, but I'm told that you have to go."

"Let's do it again," Obama told the room.

"Instinctively, I think he knew when it got good," Aukerman remembered. "He stopped [the second take]. He went, 'That was it, right?' and I said, 'Yeah, actually that was the moment when it got really good.'" The president went around the room thanking everyone—"even the twenty-two-year-old weird bearded cameraman from Funny or Die"— and that was a wrap.

Aukerman and Galifianakis couldn't believe what they'd gotten away with. That night at an after-party, a staffer congratulated them on how well the sketch had gone, but added, "Well, we're going to want to cut it down so the Obamacare stuff is the majority of it." That sent them into another panicky tailspin, but a few weeks later when Aukerman sent his edit to the White House, complete with all the testy sparring and awkward silences and side-eye of a regular episode of *Between Two Ferns*, it was a big hit. The administration's only request: add one cutaway to Obama smiling, so it's clear he's in on the joke and having fun. Except for that, the only question was, "When do we put it out?"

The video went live on Funny or Die just two weeks later. It was viewed twelve million times on its first day, and became the number one referrer to the Obamacare website. Health secretary Kathleen Sebelius called it "the Galifianakis bump." But to Aukerman, the real point of pride had nothing to do with the uninsured. It was that the video had turned out funny—and not "funny" like you usually get from Washington, warmed-over Bob Hope stuff, but the real deal. Comedians were calling and texting him nonstop congratulating him on the coup. He couldn't figure out why the White House had trusted them, but he knew the video wouldn't have moved the needle for Obamacare otherwise. "I don't know what it was, but it was absolutely the only way to do that kind of thing. Because people can smell when something is inauthentic and when someone is just trying to curry favor with young people."

One of the interminable string of Republican primary debates had begun on the TV in the corner while Aukerman was telling me the story. Rand Paul and Ted Cruz were sniping at the long-shot candidate, Donald Trump, in broken closed-captioning.

"Look," I said. "You're framing this as a subversive thing that you guys got away with, but in five years, if President Rubio wanted to do *Between Two Ferns* promoting, like, a tax cut for the rich, or tightening immigration, you wouldn't be like, 'Okay, let's do a funny video about deportation,' right? As a comedian, are you worried that the powers that be have figured out that they need to have comedy working for them?"

"We've been asked to do—well, for instance, say Dick Cheney wanted to do *Between Two Ferns*. Our idea if Dick Cheney were to do it was to just drop all jokes and start grilling him on why he's a war criminal. That would have been funny to us."

"How hypothetical is this Cheney example?"

A long pause. "I don't know. Can't say."

Trump was speaking silently now in close-up, the captioning barely able to keep up with his run-on sentences. "I do think that you could do something with Trump," Aukerman mused. "Trump is a magnetic dude. You could do a viral video with Trump and have it be funny."

I was absolutely certain that no viral video could get Donald Trump, of all people, elected president, and said so. But Aukerman had had this conversation before. Back in 1999, he said, his *Mr. Show* castmates Bob Odenkirk and David Cross were both convinced that George W. Bush would never be president and laughed at Aukerman's theory that nowadays, name recognition and celebrity were enough to put someone in the White House. "But that's what happened. He was *famous* enough.

"The best advertisement for Trump's campaign is *Celebrity Apprentice*, where he's never talking about politics. Today any reality star could make a go of it."

Trump and Jeb Bush were in split-screen now, talking over the top of each other. They were the two candidates most likely to get a head start from name recognition, but onscreen their demeanors couldn't have been more different. Bush was staring blankly ahead with his shoulders slumped and his mouth a hard little hyphen, as if he'd rather have been anywhere else. Trump, by contrast, was a cartoon character, grinning and mugging and gesturing with his arms so widely that his half of the screen couldn't even hold him. He seemed like a force of pure television energy too big, too intense, to be contained.

President Wrestlemania

There are hundreds of narratives to explain Donald Trump's shocking rise to the presidency in 2016, and because voting blocs are not monolithic, most of them are true in one way or another. Automation and outsourcing had been catastrophic for working-class Americans, who were largely left behind by the Obama-era recovery. The Democratic Party had passed up their chance to become the champions of economic equality and fell back again on the centrist strategies of the Clinton era. If that wasn't enough to depress turnout, Republican efforts to make voting more difficult had succeeded in many states following a Supreme Court decision weakening the Voting Rights Act of 1965. Hillary Clinton ran against unfavorability numbers unmatched for any presidential candidate in history aside from her opponent, and her campaign mistakenly believed they could win in a landslide by playing defense. Russians hacked the Democratic National Committee, and the director of the FBI announced new evidence in the recently closed investigation of Clinton's e-mails just two weeks before the election, contributing to an unprecedentedly late swing in the polls. The Electoral College neutered millions of Democratic voters in safe coastal states and placed the presidency in the hands of, as it turned out, eighty thousand Rust Belt voters. The rise of the Internet and the declining influence of the media establishment made it easy for voters to find stories that matched their political convictions, whether they were true or not. And it turned out that, deep down, a depressingly large number of white voters were looking for a forceful figure to tell them exactly what to do, that they weren't powerless, that there was someone else they could blame for many of their problems.

It's all true. But it's also a fact that none of that would have been sufficient for most outsider candidates. (George Wallace, the previous high-water mark for this sort of thing, managed 13.5 percent of the popular vote in 1968.) The secret to Donald Trump's success—and no one likes to say this about a blustering racist demagogue—is that he was so entertaining. He was, to his audience, funny.

By some accounts, Donald Trump's serious presidential ambitions were born out of a comedy routine. At the 2011 White House Correspondents' Dinner, President Obama began his after-dinner speech with a solid four and a half minutes of jokes about "birther" conspiracy theories questioning his citizenship, of which Donald Trump had been a loud and recalcitrant champion. Then, after a run of jokes on other media and political subjects, Obama returned to his muse. "Donald Trump is here tonight!" he announced, to delighted whoops from the crowd, and dove into another two minutes of jokes about *Celebrity Apprentice*, each one twisting the knife a little more as he painted Trump as a buffoon and a lightweight, whose reality TV decisions—like whether he should "fire" Meat Loaf or Gary Busey—had nothing in common with the rigors of the presidency. (Those rigors were not hypothetical for Obama that night. He had given the order to raid Osama bin Laden's Pakistan compound the day before, though no one would know about the operation until the following night.) These jokes were too pointed to be mere potshots at a target-rich environment. Trump's embrace of the racism at the core of the birther movement had clearly irked Obama.

Adam Gopnik of the *New Yorker*, sitting a few tables away from Trump, watched his reaction closely. "Trump's humiliation was as absolute, and as visible, as any I have ever seen: his head set in place, like a man in a pillory, he barely moved or altered his expression as wave after wave of laughter struck him." Instead of displaying "that thick-skinned cheerfulness that almost all American public people learn, however painfully, to cultivate," Trump "sat perfectly still, chin tight, in locked, unmovable rage." Could that rage have fueled him for the next five years? Gopnik wondered in hindsight.

Working crowds on the campaign trail, Trump's style couldn't have been further from Obama's bone-dry alt-comedy sensibility at a Washington black-tie dinner. But there was no mistaking the showmanship: Trump would bluster like a pro wrestler, free-associate insults about his opponents as the crowd whooped him on, punctuate his speeches with cartoonishly broad sneers and scowls and snorts of disbelief. Other Republican candidates figuratively wrapped themselves in the flag; Trump would do it *literally*, always getting big laughs and cheers when he'd come to the side of the stage to lovingly cradle Old Glory in his arms, like a drunken boss sneaking off to give his secretary a squeeze at an office Christmas party. The *New York Times* noted that crowds leaving Trump rallies would often praise their candidate in the language of comedy fans who'd just seen a favorite rage comedian do a blistering hour-long set. Their man wasn't "politically correct"—he said what we're all thinking. He wasn't afraid to "go there."

And as much as he drew on his supporters' energy, leaning hard on big applause lines—Build that wall! Drain the swamp! Hillary has to go to jail!—he clearly wasn't just in it to win their love. Trump's inner comedian would sometimes push back against the crowd, unable to resist a good punch line. In August 2016, at a rally in Virginia, Trump heard a baby crying in the audience. "I love babies. I hear that baby cry, I like it," he gushed to the crowd with his trademark logorrhea. "What a baby. What a beautiful baby. Don't worry, don't worry. The mom's running around—like, don't worry about it, you know? It's young and beautiful and healthy and that's what we want." But just a minute or two later, as Trump was inveighing against China, the baby started crying again. "Actually I was only kidding, you can get the baby out of here," Trump said. "I think she really believed me that I love having a baby crying while I'm speaking. That's okay. People don't understand. That's okay." Banning babies on the campaign trail rather than kissing them was a new move in American politics, and the media reported it as another in a series of Trump's bizarre and erratic "gaffes." Virginia governor Tim Kaine, Hillary Clinton's running mate, even defended the baby on Twitter. But any comedian watching the video would see it immediately: Trump didn't really care that much about the crying baby. What he liked was the abrupt sitcom turn of unexpectedly zinging the crying baby. He was doing a bit, seeing how far the crowd would go with him.

Softening the Blowhard

Was Hitler funny in front of a crowd? You sure don't get that impression from newsreel clips, where he always looks so stiff and angry (although Heinrich Mann called him "the Austrian comedian" and the British fascist Diana Mitford, when asked what she remembered about Hitler, once replied, "The laughs," so who knows?). But Trump's charisma was different. The clowning and on-camera ease were the great levelers that, against all odds, convinced millions of people that a Manhattan landlord billionaire was one of them, a champion of the working family.

Let me be clear: the xenophobia and the racism were also part of Trump's appeal to big swaths of his base. But Trump's over-the-top comic persona seems to have helped him there as well. In a 2008 experiment, political scientists assigned one group of college students to watch clips from *The Colbert Report*, Stephen Colbert's mock-conservative comedy talk show, while another group watched commentary on the same subject from *actual* cable blowhard Bill O'Reilly, the target of much of Colbert's satire. Surprisingly, the group that had watched Colbert's sly left-leaning satire—even knowing it was satire—afterward reported *more* support for President Bush, congressional Republicans, and Republican policies on the economy and terrorism than the group that had watched O'Reilly! And, despite the fact that these were fairly politically savvy undergraduates, the ones who watched the *Colbert Report* clips said that they felt less confidence in their ability to understand issues. The extra level of distancing in Colbert's satire had been more confusing, perhaps, than intended. In other words, the study's authors concluded, political messaging (in this case, conservative messaging) is more convincing when couched in humor than otherwise. In Trump's case, the extra level of distancing was perfect for undecided voters who *wanted* to believe in the candidate. It enabled them to claim, as I once heard a Trump supporter say in a radio interview, "He doesn't mean half the things people think he means." Anything indefensible he said about the (choose one: wall with Mexico, Muslim ban, legality of torture, Chinese global-warming hoax, prosecutions for journalists, and so on ad infinitum) could be met with a dismissive "Oh, that's just Trump being Trump!"

At the same time, Trump's goofy showmanship also kept his opponents from taking his campaign seriously until it was too late. The media narrative could always be, "Can you believe how crazy this is? No, really, Donald Trump!" instead of truly grappling with the ugly looming possibility of an actual Trump presidency, even after he won the Republican nomination and was running competitively in swing-state polls. To some voters, especially young ones disillusioned by Bernie Sanders's hard-fought primary loss, the idea of President Donald J. Trump seemed like a fitting capstone for our age of irony, the perfect middle-finger punch line, rather than a real threat. In the days following the election, an MSNBC clip making the rounds online showed reporter Chris Jansing on Election Day at a polling precinct in Cleveland, in a county Obama had won by forty points. A young black voter at a table behind her turns around to peek at the camera, then slyly lifts up his hoodie to show off a red "Make America Great Again" cap, which he points at, grinning. It's a telling clip: the kind of voter Democrats largely took for granted, enjoying the transgressive comic thrill of voting for—can you believe it?—Donald Trump from *The Apprentice!*

Send in the Clowns

"Everything is changing in America," Will Rogers prophesied almost a century ago. "People are taking their comedians seriously and the politicians as a joke." And it literally came true: a third of Americans—and 46 percent of young voters—report that their vote is informed by what they learn on comedy shows like *Saturday Night Live* or *The Daily Show.* On the other side of the age and ideology gap are twenty-four-hour cable news and talk radio, which may not have as sharp a comic voice but are still fundamentally news-as-entertainment. We created a culture where politics and political commentary are expected to be funny, sometimes above all else. We can't pretend to be surprised when that system produces winners who are entertaining but otherwise completely unqualified to govern.

It's not comedy's fault, but there's no getting around it: comedians are among those who taught us that saying anything we're thinking is an absolute good, as long as it gets a laugh. Audience reaction is the only measure of success. (Think about it: a drama can move or affect you in a hundred different ways, but comedy only has to make you laugh.)* Trump was the clickbait candidate, the one who learned first that attention and celebrity weren't just a plus in an election, they were enough by themselves to assure a win. It didn't matter if the headline matched the story. It didn't matter if the facts were accurate, or even internally consistent. You just needed the reaction, more laughs than the other candidate, more eyeballs than the other candidate. It was painful to watch his political rivals come to the same realization: Marco Rubio stumbling through jokes about Trump's "spray tan" and small penis,† Hillary Clinton tweeting out memes and dabbing with Ellen DeGeneres. But it was too late.

"Part of it is that our election cycle is so long," comedy writer Rob Kutner told me. He wrote for *The Daily Show* for most of the Bush era, winning five Emmys. "It's so boring. We've been stuck with these people for months and months, so we just go with the guy who's the most entertaining." Trump was certainly catnip for the news media, which couldn't help but cover the hell out of a candidate who was saying something novel and outrageous literally every day. In the last months of the campaign, network news spent 64 percent more time on Trump than it did on Clinton.‡ But TV comedy is an especially big part of our reductive, short-attention-span political lens. Comedy privileges brevity, one-liners, an idea that can be tightly distilled and immediately understood by an audience, or else it fails. That's fine for jokes about celebrities and sports teams, but when it comes to politics, it ceded the

---

* Yes, it *can* do more. But when someone asks about a comedy or a comedian, they're not asking, "How incisive is the social commentary?" or "Is there a level of bittersweet yearning underlying the jokes?" They just want to know, "Will I laugh?"

† Rubio was visibly uncomfortable adding the insult routine to his stump speech, telling the crowd almost apologetically, "I like debates about ideas . . . but you cannot have a policy debate with someone who has no policies." Once one candidate breaks the glass on Corwin's Law, it's an arms race.

‡ The coverage was largely negative, focusing on his scandals, but for a candidate like Trump, that turned out to be irrelevant.

field to someone like Trump by abandoning policy entirely in favor of punch lines.

Over the last two decades, political jokes in late-night monologues have generally boiled down to a litany of repeated and near-identical premises about candidates. Bill Clinton is horny, George W. Bush is dumb, Bob Dole/John McCain is old, Al Gore is stiff, John Kerry is wishy-washy, Mitt Romney is square.* (Obama was death to late night; there was no nonracist four-word pitch a studio audience could grab on to.) When *Saturday Night Live* asked Donald Trump to host their show in the middle of primary season, or when Jimmy Fallon goofed around good-naturedly with Trump's comb-over, with no troubling mention of anything like mass deportations or serial harassment of women, there was a clear subtext. How could this be the most dangerous presidential candidate in over a century? the shows seemed to protest. He's just a fun old white guy who's a little bit wacky. You know, like Christopher Walken!

Rob Kutner called this the "Faustian bargain" of topical comedy: anytime you get someone to laugh about something, you might also be unwittingly making light of it, normalizing it. Lampooning the media, which has for many years been *The Daily Show*'s bread and butter, "blurs the line between news and entertainment, so news starts trying to be more entertaining." Even hard-hitting, substantive jokes about government mostly serve to reinforce cynicism about politics, and that can both discourage participation in the democratic process and boost candidates with outsider cred, the kind who say they want to go after all those bozos in Washington.† All these tendencies played right into Donald Trump's hands.

* In 1996, this got so bad that David Letterman switched to metajokes *about* "Bob Dole is old" jokes. He would wander down to a special "Bob Dole Is Old" joke storeroom in the basement of the Ed Sullivan Theater to pick up a new batch, or have Paul Shaffer play a special fanfare for the show's ten thousandth "Bob Dole is old" joke.

† Jody Baumgartner and Jonathan S. Morris, the same political scientists who published the work on the counterintuitive effects of *Colbert Report* viewing, confirmed Kutner's intuition in a 2006 article titled "The *Daily Show* Effect." Jon Stewart's viewers were significantly more cynical about politics on both sides of the aisle than non–*Daily Show* fans.

And it's not as if late-night hosts don't benefit when the more out-rageous candidate, the better joke target, wins an election. As a silver lining, they're getting four more years of great material. "That's always the double-sided coin," said Kutner, who was writing for *The Daily Show* when Bush beat Kerry in 2004. "Both things exist in contradictory fashion. Good for business . . ."

"Bad for the real world," I finished.

"The Man" Who Laughs

Americans have always loved to see politicians let their hair down and tell self-deprecating jokes about themselves, thinking we were seeing their most human side. One hundred and fifty years ago, Lincoln was famous for making light of his rustic background and rough-hewn features. (Sample joke, when accused of being two-faced: "I leave it to my audience. If I had two faces, would I be wearing this one?") But it's remarkable how quickly politicians realized they could benefit by poking fun not at harmless foibles, but at their most serious and controversial Achilles' heels. John F. Kennedy would make fun of his wealthy family's reputation for political corruption, quoting his father as telling him, "Don't buy a single vote more than necessary. I'll be damned if I'm going to pay for a landslide." Four years later, when Barry Goldwater's political views were being painted as hopelessly old-fashioned and reac-tionary, he got out in front of the joke, telling crowds that if he lost the election, he could at least go write for *The Flintstones* or "18th Century Fox." Election fraud and slashing Social Security aren't funny topics to many voters—but that's precisely why those candidates went there. It's the same reason I told jokes at my own expense in fourth grade. In doing so, they inoculated themselves against criticism to some degree by preadministering the antibody of self-deprecation. Could this issue *really* be such a political liability, they were saying, if I'm willing to openly joke about it? In ancient Rome, Cicero recommended humor to the clever orator, because it very often "dispels extremely ugly matters that will not bear to be cleared up by proofs." Sure enough, much political humor today is a calculated tool used to parry and deflect.

And when humanizing self-deprecation drifts to the CIA starting a "funny" Twitter account to soften its image (which debuted in June 2014 with the line "We can neither confirm nor deny that this is our first tweet"—it's funny because they're so secretive!), it's yet another reminder that everything subversive eventually gets subverted. Satire used to be *our* weapon against powerful institutions with little accountability. But if the CIA now has as many Twitter followers as John Oliver's show, what do we have left? If you were fine with Obama joking about drone strikes at the White House Correspondents' Dinner in 2010 because you think he's a likable guy, ask yourself what you might think about Donald Trump or some successor using the same bully pulpit to get big laughs about invading Iran.

The Funniest of Times, the Unfunniest of Times

Aaron Sorkin has called Donald Trump "the end of political satire," and though I don't think the writer of *The Newsroom* is the best judge of what quality topical humor looks like today, I understand the sentiment. There's a point at which you have to wonder how modernity supports comedy, because what are you even trying to expose anymore? Where's the surprise? Donald Trump wasn't your typical two-faced political hack. Sixty million people knew exactly who he was, mostly because he bragged endlessly about it, and they voted for him anyway. No sly *SNL* sketch or "epic" John Oliver takedown is going to change that. But take note that people have been writing satire's obituary for at least half a century. In Tom Lehrer's opinion, "political satire became obsolete when Henry Kissinger was awarded the Nobel Peace Prize." Conan O'Brien said essentially the same thing about the Monica Lewinsky scandal of the 1990s: "Clinton was wildly generous to the comedic mind. . . . He made our job so easy it was a challenge not to feel irrelevant."* But somehow political humor soldiered on even when Vietnam took all the

---

* According to the databases of the Center for Media and Public Affairs, Bill Clinton was one of the three most-joked-about political figures on television for *fifteen* years running, from 1992 to 2006, an unprecedented achievement in American politics.

most absurd, horrifying exaggerations of pitch-black wartime satire and put them on the nightly news in living color, or when the lurid details of *The Starr Report* outshone a century of rumored political sex scandals, on page 1 above the fold.

Today, it's possible for comedians to do more by doing less. In 2008, Seth Meyers and Tina Fey wrote a *Saturday Night Live* sketch lampooning a disastrous interview Sarah Palin had done with Katie Couric, one of the best gags was Fey-as-Palin giving a stumbling, incoherent answer to a question about bank bailouts. Most of the line was taken directly from the *CBS Evening News* transcript of Palin's answers, and it still killed. And Jon Stewart's *Daily Show* essentially invented a new kind of comedy where the satirist is the straight man, often doing no more than rolling a clip of an outrageous sound bite or media take and then turning to the camera in wide-eyed silence. As any boardwalk cartoonist will tell you, only attractive people are *really* hard to caricature. The funnier the face, the less work there is for the artist to do.

But for many funny people, professional and amateur alike, the more pressing and unprecedented problem was that Trump's election put a pall on comedy altogether. Joking about his inadequacies had clearly failed, and had possibly even normalized him to the public. Joking about any other subject felt like rearranging deck chairs on the *Titanic*. (In this analogy, the captain of the *Titanic* is a shallow narcissist with no nautical training who doesn't believe in icebergs.)

"How can there be mirth when the world is on fire?" the Buddha once asked his disciples. If he or they had an answer, history doesn't relate it. In repealing Corwin's Law, we created a culture where everyone is expected to be entertained by politics all the time, and after we finally did it, when we finally voted in the showman whose candidacy had seemed the funniest, no one felt much like laughing at all.

TEN

WE SHALL OVERCOMB

O n the evening of December 3, 2014, crowds gathered in lower Man-
hattan's Foley Square to protest the death of Eric Garner, an asthmatic
African American man killed in police custody. Earlier that day, a Staten
Island grand jury had declined to indict Daniel Pantaleo, the officer who
had placed Garner in a fatal chokehold, in violation of NYPD policy. "I
Can't Breathe," read many of the signs at the rally, a slogan taken from
Garner's own last words in the infamous cell phone video of his arrest.

One young woman held a sign with a longer message about not
being able to breathe. "Telling me that I'm obsessed with talking about
racism in America is like telling me I'm obsessed with swimming when
I'm drowning," it read. The quote, which had circulated widely online,
came from *Waiting for 2042*, by a former Seattle immigration rights
activist named Hari Kondabolu. The title of *Waiting for 2042* refers to the
year when the United States is projected to become a majority-minority
country, and it's been assigned as a text in curricula from high school
to grad school for its insights on immigration and race. But *Waiting for
2042* wasn't a book of essays or a documentary or a TED talk. It was a
live comedy record.

Kondabolu, a Queens-born American of Indian descent, drifted
from activism into stand-up in his twenties. His debut album didn't feel
like a political treatise—it had long chunks about Weezer, *Back to the
Future*, and Matthew McConaughey. But in just fifty-six minutes, it also
managed to touch on topics like global warming, the public option for
health insurance, interracial adoption, Guantánamo, model-minority
stereotypes, Hillary Clinton, the English-only movement, religious

homophobia, white privilege, straight privilege, and, yes, police brutality.*
It's unfailingly funny, but these aren't funny topics.

When I asked him about the record, Kondabolu resisted the notion
that his new day job in comedy is a continuation of his activism. "If you
start viewing it as activist work, it's not going to be good. The goals are
different. The goal of the activist is to create a change that they want to
see. For the comedian, if you have that activism lens, you lose the ability
to communicate to a broader group of people." The subtext was clear:
Please, for the love of God, don't make me sound like a guy with a cause
and a clipboard. That doesn't seem funny at all! Even on the album,
after he delivers the "obsessed with swimming" line, he undercuts it.
"And that was the slam poetry section of the show," he says, apparently
uncomfortable with ending the bit on a note of such earnestness and
anger. Throughout, he's careful to structure jokes to avoid what Seth
Meyers called "clapter": the applause that can follow a lame nonjoke
that an audience happens to agree with politically.

Protest signs have not, historically, been a real hotbed of comedy.
The civil rights marchers of the 1960s traded in the kind of quiet dignity
needed to persuade a skeptical America of the righteousness of their
movement. "All Men Are Created Equal." "We Shall Not Be Moved."
"We Shall Overcome." The Vietnam protests were angrier and aimed to
shock. "Hell No We Won't Go." "LBJ Is a War Criminal!" "Heil Nixon!"
But something was different about the protest signs of the Trump era.
Despite the protesters' conviction that this was every bit as critical and
turbulent a time as the 1960s, the signs were now *funny*. The slogans
weren't all borrowed from stand-up routines, but they felt like lines that
had been workshopped by a room of comedy writers, not scrawled by
dorm rooms full of rabble-rousers.

- Trump Eats Pizza with a Fork
- Orange Will Never Be the New Black

---

* Full disclosure: the *Back to the Future* bit turns into a bit about what people of color would do with time
travel, and the Matthew McConaughey chunk is entirely about the star's clueless attempt at an LGBT-friendly
interview with the *Advocate*. But the Weezer stuff is about nothing but Weezer!

- Build a Wall Around Trump, I'll Pay for It
- Not Usually a Sign Guy but Geez
- I've Seen Better Cabinets at Ikea
- We Gave You Hummus, Have Some Respect
- I Know Signs, I Make the Best Signs. They're Terrific. Everyone Agrees.
- Free Melania

Yes, these were in part the fruit of social media. College kids and annoyed urbanites making signs could now consult hundreds of online photos of other protests and cherry-pick the best slogans—an option not available in 1968. The Internet was also a powerful incentive to be creative in your march prep. If your sign was funny enough and your six-year-old was cute enough, you might just go viral!*

But they were also a symptom of how fast the culture was changing. Social protest was borrowing the language of comedy, because comedy was quickly absorbing the concerns of social protest.

The Heirs of Will Rogers

Satire is not a modern invention, of course. As we've seen, comedy has been speaking truth to power since Aristophanes lampooned the Peloponnesian War. And satire became the dominant voice of modern culture sometime in the middle years of the twentieth century. Consider: the two great, abiding antiwar novels about World War I are *All Quiet on the Western Front* and *A Farewell to Arms*. They are devastating, sincere, pull-no-punches tragedies. The two great antiwar novels about World War II, on the other hand, are *Catch-22* and *Slaughterhouse-Five*. In the space of thirty years, pitch-black comedy had become the preferred way to understand and to protest modern warfare.

But the weapons of satire are ridicule and disdain; satire is against something. This is very different from modern social movements, which

---

* This effect also lined the margins of protests with trolls holding antisigns they hoped would make the news. "I Made a Sign!" "I Like Turtles!" "Bring Back Crystal Pepsi!"

are usually framed as being *for* something: for peace, for the environment, for equality. Fighting *against* social ills (a war on poverty, on cancer, on drugs) is generally how governments, not activists, frame policy. I suppose you could argue that all satirical comedy is an implicit plea for the opposite of the thing being satirized: *Dr. Strangelove* is for nuclear disarmament, *Huckleberry Finn* is for abolition. *Veep* is for, uh, having fewer sad, terrible people in politics, I guess? But I'm not buying that. *Dr. Strangelove* never mentions nuclear disarmament. *Huckleberry Finn* never beats the drum for abolition. That's not a coincidence; it's inherently easier to use comedy to criticize a viewpoint than to praise one. Historically, comedians who have become crusaders have found that passion wasn't always compatible with their act. Lenny Bruce was funnier before legal troubles forced him into becoming a full-time First Amendment advocate. Bill Hicks's political material was sharper when he wasn't going down onstage rabbit holes into Waco and JFK conspiracy theories. The great Dick Gregory had perhaps the most sensible solution of all. When he found himself becoming a full-time human rights activist (and health food faddist!) in the early 1970s, he retired from comedy almost completely, not really returning to stand-up until the 1995 premiere of his one-man Broadway show.

Will Rogers was different. An early vaudeville and movie star, Rogers became the most beloved American of his era on the strength of the political commentary delivered in his weekly radio broadcasts and *daily* newspaper columns. Today we probably imagine Rogers's act as a series of bland, folksy aphorisms ("Every time Congress makes a joke it's a law. And every time they make a law it's a joke!") but, in fact, the "cowboy philosopher" was a surprisingly well-informed and incisive—if studiously bipartisan—political commentator. During the high times of the 1920s, he repeatedly warned of a coming crash, and once the Depression hit, his columns were full of specific policy recommendations on populist issues like agricultural tariffs, financial regulation, and government aid. His weekly newspaper audience was forty million Americans, fully one-third of the nation. In 1932, he spoke at both the Republican and Democratic National Conventions, receiving twenty-two second-ballot votes for the presidential nomination at the latter.

Rogers was also an activist. In 1931, with crops dying of drought and farms going under in the Dust Bowl, the Red Cross launched a massive disaster-relief campaign and fund-raising drive. Rogers personally visited President Hoover at the White House but was unable to convince the fiscal conservative to approve federal loans. The following week, Rogers flew to Texas and Arkansas to do a series of live shows and radio benefits for the marching sharecroppers. "Well folks, sure glad to be here with you," he told a crowd in Fort Smith, Arkansas. "Glad you are starving, otherwise I would never have met you." Rogers's aw-shucks common-man persona was no put-on, according to Jennings family lore. My great-grandfather, the late Gardner Othneil Jennings,* always drew crowds to his little general store in Muleshoe, Texas,† in early July. Those were the days when Will Rogers, visiting friends on a ranch nearby, liked to stop by the store and trade stories with townsfolk around the cracker barrel.

Will Rogers was the forerunner of today's alternative to political satire: comedy that doesn't merely mock a deserving target but advances a clearly articulated alternative as well. That path, of course, runs squarely through Jon Stewart's *Daily Show*. From 2005 until 2014, while Stephen Colbert held down his half of Comedy Central's evening programming block with traditional straight-faced satire of institutional buffoonery, Stewart's show was increasingly a pulpit for his earnest brand of skepticism and outrage. In retirement, as Stewart became an advocate for the most vulnerable victims of government bureaucracy—veterans' groups, 9/11 first responders—it was even easier to see the parallels with Will Rogers out marching with the Arkansas farmers.

Stewart's onetime guest host and spiritual successor John Oliver took the comedy of conviction to its inevitable end. His *Last Week Tonight* series on HBO is weekly, freeing him and his writers from the frenetic pace of the other two hundred late-night topical comedy shows, and it's ad-free, allowing him to slow the pace down for viewers. The combination

---

* I know, right?

† I know, right?

allowed for longer-form deep dives into surprisingly wonky issues never heretofore touched by monologue: civil asset forfeiture, digital encryption law, Tibetan sovereignty, payday loans, voting rights in Guam. Along with the bubbly comedy, audiences were getting a high-level overview of some important but under-the-radar policy debates, but they were getting the program's strong editorial viewpoint as well.

The success of the Jon Stewart/John Oliver school of issue-based comedy, along with hard-hitting sketch shows from Dave Chappelle and his spiritual successors, opened up new vistas of possibility for all kinds of comedy. It wasn't surprising when a niche prestige comedy like *Transparent* tackled a different gender issue every episode, but soon mainstream family comedies were foregrounding social issues of the moment in a way not seen in America since the heyday of Norman Lear: immigration (*Fresh Off the Boat, Superstore*), addiction (*Mom*), race (*Black-ish, The Carmichael Show*). On the woke sitcom, every episode was a "very special episode," and many of them ended up providing the definitive comic take on hot-button subjects of the day, from Black Lives Matter to the election of Donald Trump. On movie screens, a low-budget horror-comedy like Jordan Peele's *Get Out* could make over $250 million by moving its social metaphor from subtext to—what's more obvious than text? Supertext? And Hari Kondabolu could build a comedy album around observations like "I don't think you can be environmentally friendly in a capitalist society" and "Race is a social construct! It's a way to divide us!" That's not really mere satire anymore.

Ethnic Stereotypes: Measuring the Canyon

The use of comedy to talk frankly about race was particularly striking, because comedy's past record on race and ethnicity might be worse than that of any other art form. More racist than opera? Yes. Westerns? Yes. Aryan black metal? It might be a close call. Minstrel shows, with their grotesque caricatures of African Americans, were the most popular form of entertainment in America for almost half a century. *Captain Billy's Whiz Bang* was the leading humor magazine of the 1920s, selling (according to its publisher, anyway) over a million copies every month. It traded heavily in jokes about every minority under the sun: Jews, blacks, Italians, Irish, Asians. Five-dollar prizes were offered to readers who submitted the "Best Hebrew Joke" or "Best Colored Joke." Even America's patron-saint humorists, champions of the little guy like Mark Twain and Will Rogers, weren't immune to the prejudices of their day. Rogers joked about passing through black communities that were "so dark you couldn't make your way around without a light!" Twain's famous essay "How to Tell a Story," about the importance of comic timing, ends with his describing the "Negro ghost story" he would act out as the big finish to his stage show. For five minutes he would shuffle and shiver around the stage, bugging his eyes out and saying thing like "My lan', what dat?" in exaggerated African American dialect. It brought the house down every night.

Abe Lincoln loved minstrel shows.

But without people of color, modern comedy as we know it wouldn't even exist. In her influential 1931 book *American Humor*, Constance Rourke included the "Negro minstrel" alongside the frontier backwoodsman and the Yankee peddler as one of the three archetypes that birthed the brash, mischievous American sense of humor. To her, they all represent the same thing: comic triumph, resilience in the face of adversity. Today, that seems to conveniently elide the fact that minstrel "darky" stereotypes were constructed by outsiders and oppressors in a way that the frontiersman and the Yankee "sharp" were not, but it's true that at least *some* of the music and culture preserved by the minstrel genre was authentic, and in later years a surprising number of troupes were actually made up of African American performers. (Many, confusingly, still wore blackface.) Minstrel shows, with their simple comedy sketches delivered by two actors called "end men" and a longer stand-up routine called a "stump speech," begat musical revues and vaudeville, which begat pretty much every modern comedy form. Then in 1955, Redd Foxx single-handedly invented the modern comedy album by recording his nightclub act for a tiny black label called Dooto Records. His "party records" broke with tradition by including no novelty songs, just a half hour of jokes told to a live audience. They were a smash hit. Foxx sold over ten million albums in all, and opened doors for his fellow comedians of the segregated "Chitlin' Circuit," like Pigmeat Markham and Moms Mabley, to get their routines on vinyl as well. Within a few years, Bob Newhart, Nichols and May, and Bill Cosby were using the new medium to become household names.

The abundance of unpleasant racial and ethnic jokes in comedy history has less to do with the specific social views of funny people than with the inherent immediacy that humor requires. Understanding a joke usually involves a mental leap from the setup to the laugh. Jerry Seinfeld has compared this to a daredevil's leap across a canyon: Make the jump too far, and you won't get across. You'll lose the audience. Make it too short, and you'll bore them; the step across will seem trivial. There's a happy medium where the twist is surprising but not *too* surprising. And this is where stereotypes come in handy. Observe:

> Did you hear the one about the stupid guy whose library burned down? He lost both his books, and he hadn't even finished coloring the second one.

It's not great, because the canyon's too narrow. The setup tells us he's stupid and then explains that he did a stupid thing. What's surprising about that?

> Did you hear the one about the Spanish king Charles II, whose library burned down? He lost both his books, and he hadn't even finished coloring the second one.

Now the canyon's too wide. What, you didn't know Charles II of Spain (1661–1700) was famously an inbred imbecile?

> Did you hear the one about the Polack whose library burned down? He lost both his books, and he hadn't even finished coloring the second one.

There we go.

Let's be clear: the result is offensive to Polish people. But it's important to note that antipathy to Poles is not what fuels the joke—it's the fact that we've chosen a subject that makes the leap across the canyon the right length. The coloring-book owner doesn't have to be Polish; he or she just has to be a member of some group that we, the joke-sharing community, mutually understand to be a little slow. Ethnic-joke scholar Christie Davies has pointed out that "Polack jokes" boomed in the United States in the late 1970s, when Polish Americans were no longer a suspicious, marginalized ethnicity. His implication: the target of disparagement humor can sometimes be almost arbitrary. It just has to be a convenient stereotype. Any real malice or racism might make the joke less funny, by introducing a second variable—potentially a controversial and distracting one—into the equation.

In fact, there's no reason why the out-group in a joke like this has to be an ethnic one at all. *Blasons populaires*—"popular emblems," the term folklorists use for historical stereotypes—can encompass anything from professions (lawyers are crooks!) to hobbies (gamers are virgins!) to hair color (blondes are dumb!). But the original medieval *blasons* were tales told about neighboring villages: these guys up north are cocky, those guys out west are rural and backward, those other guys across the river are stingy as hell. By far the most common local stereotype was a "fooltown," a city of purported dunces used to tell ancient and medieval versions of our Irish jokes and blonde jokes and drummer jokes. In ancient Rome, the target was Abdera, a city in remote Thrace.

> A man from Abdera saw a eunuch talking to a woman, and asked if it was his wife. The man replied that eunuchs can't have wives. "My mistake!" said the man from Abdera. "She must be your daughter."

England alone had forty-five different regional fooltowns over the centuries, most prominently Gotham in Nottinghamshire. When Washington Irving nicknamed New York City "Gotham" in 1807, it wasn't really a compliment.

But when national identities began to replace regional ones, most of the stereotypes became ethnic as well.* The English tell jokes about the Irish, the Russians tell jokes about the Ukrainians, the Iranians tell jokes about the Armenians, the Danes tell jokes about the Norwegians, the Tajiks tell jokes about the Uzbeks. The most common joke is how stupid or rural the out-group is, and a surprising number of slurs revolve around their food. The French are "frogs," the English "limeys," the Germans "krauts," the Mexicans "beaners." Davies believes the implication is that these poor, backward people have to eat weird food—not like us! we eat meat!—but I wonder if what's really to blame is the failure of imagination typical to racism. "Ha ha, look at these Germans. Always, uh . . . eating sauerkraut. You know what, I'm gonna call them 'krauts'!"

In an interesting twist, many cultures make jokes not just about their dumb neighbors, but also about their cannier opposite numbers, a culture that's, if anything, a little *too* clever. In England, the dumb Irish are offset by the sly Scots; elsewhere, the targets are often East Asian immigrants or Jews. The jokes can be just as mean, often revolving around the targets' supposed conniving or miserly character. One such joke, about Scottish tightwads, is among the shortest jokes I've ever seen.

Scotland Yard: 2'11".

Get it? They're so cheap that they shortchanged our yard by an inch. The joke isn't really *funny* in any meaningful way, but it shows the powerful economy that comes by trading in stereotypes. A punch line in a funny story is often the collision between two "scripts"—two different ways of understanding some event. Stereotypes allow jokesters to tell the full joke while only having to spell out one of the two stories. The second script ("The Scots are cheap!") is already out there in the ether.

And there's the rub: ethnic jokes are generally powered by a wide-

---

* Local stereotypes still exist today, of course. They're just not universal enough to power much pop culture. When I was young, Seattle had a local sketch comedy show called *Almost Live!* that would air before *Saturday Night Live.* (Joel McHale and Bill Nye both got their starts as cast members.) *Almost Live!* was, as you'd expect, full of Seattle in-jokes about local neighborhoods: Renton was white trash, Mercer Island was snobbish old money, Ballard was full of elderly Scandinavians. Comedy Central briefly aired reruns of the show in the 1990s, puzzling America with incomprehensible Ballard jokes.

spread attitude of, at best, superiority, if not suspicion or outright dislike. According to Davies, the existence of both "canny" and "foolish" stereotypes in many cultures suggests that their purpose is self-congratulatory for the joke-tellers: *we* are neither too clever nor too dumb, *we* are just right. The joke reveals more about the teller than about the target. As a result, Davies doesn't think we should fret excessively about the connection between ethnic jokes and bigotry. In a world with a history of *actual* horrific genocides against Jews, for example, mere jokes don't strike him as the greatest danger. "To treat [Jewish] jokes as if they were merely and inevitably covert anti-Semitic utterances," he writes, "is crass and simplistic and ignores the crucial distinction between that which is intrinsically anti-Semitic and that which might be exploited by anti-Semites."

Personally, I'm not sure how crucial that distinction is anymore. Today, more people are conscious of the possibility that racism doesn't have to be of the cartoonish, men-in-hoods variety to be pernicious. It can be a subtler, institutional thing, largely invisible but still advanced in thousands of tiny ways by generally well-meaning people. What effects could racially edgy jokes have on a playing field like that one? And what role could they play as the old-school kind of racism—cops beating on people of color, swastikas sprayed on synagogues—starts to come back?

The Glass Ceiling

Of all the stereotypes that fuel racial and ethnic jokes, humorlessness isn't generally one of them. Generally, minorities have the opposite problem. Their portrayal as fun-loving clowns can be used as evidence of their lower intelligence or to belie the seriousness of their plight. Women in comedy face a very different battle: a widespread assumption that they're not as funny as their male counterparts. That's because comedy has, through most of recorded history, been seen as a male endeavor. In ancient Greek comedies, just as with the Elizabethans, female performers weren't allowed onstage. It's not clear that women were even allowed in the audience when female-friendly comedies like Aristophanes' *Lysistrata* were first performed.

Human cultures have, pretty uniformly, assumed that men were much, much funnier than women. In mythology, the trickster figure is almost always a male god—Loki, Anansi, Puck, Old Man Coyote—and that's no coincidence; the point is often driven home by giving him a big old phallus. The messenger god Hermes was honored on Greek roadsides with herms, square pillars usually decorated with just two features: Hermes's head, and his erect genitalia. The Winnebago trickster Wakdjunkaga was even better endowed: his penis was so long that he had to wrap it around him when he walked and carry it on his back in a box.

And men, of course, wrote the history books. We remember Mark Twain as the great superstar of nineteenth-century American humor, but his contemporary Marietta Holley is almost forgotten. Holley, believe it or not, was every bit as popular as Twain in their day, selling millions of copies of her novels about a no-nonsense farmwife named Samantha Allen. Her *Samantha at Saratoga* was the nation's top-selling book in 1887, and by 1893, she commanded a then-unheard-of $14,000 advance for *Samantha at the World's Fair*. Women loved her books, but they weren't marketed solely as chick lit. Clubs sprang up around the country to do dramatic amateur readings of her work, and were attended by men and women alike (including, in one case, prominent clergymen and a U.S. senator). Many readers assumed that, because the Samantha Allen books were so funny, Holley had to be a man writing under a pseudonym. Even after she added a photo to her book jackets in 1883, one stubborn reader insisted, "That book was written by a man!" "I have always supposed it was a compliment," Holley would say.

She and Twain shared the same publisher, the same illustrator, and largely the same readership, but today, more than a century after his death, Twain is still a household name, while none of Marietta Holley's books remain in print. As the aggressively self-promoting Twain traveled the world winking and harrumphing on the lecture circuit, Holley stayed at home in the quiet Victorian country house she had built in upstate New York. Susan B. Anthony and Elizabeth Cady Stanton urged her to attend women's suffrage events—incognito, if necessary!—but Holley demurred. And no one in the literary establishment pushed for Holley's addition to the canon, though she mixed sharp regional humor with progressive issues like race and social reform just as Twain did.

Holley's contemporary Sara Willis was the highest-paid newspaper columnist in America, but she had to use the pseudonym "Fanny Fern," because her family had been so appalled to see their little girl go into the humor business. When she was just starting out, she sent writing samples to her brother Nathaniel, a successful magazine editor. He replied with a cold rejection letter, telling her that he'd be ashamed if his sister's "vulgarity" and "indecency" ever came to light.* It suited and flattered men to keep comedy a male clubhouse, and then to use that status quo as evidence for the inherent unfunniness of the female mind. Author Kate Sanborn noted in 1885, "There is a reason for our apparent lack of humor, which it may seem ungracious to mention. Women do not find it politic to cultivate or express their wit. No man likes to have his story capped by a better and fresher from a lady's lips. What woman does not risk being called sarcastic and hateful if she throws back the merry dart, or indulges in a little sharp-shooting? No, no, it's dangerous—if not fatal. 'Though you're bright, and though you're pretty, / They'll not love you if you're witty.'"

It would be nice to think that those ideas were entirely uprooted by a century of feminism, but change has been slow in coming. Even as women like Lucille Ball, Joan Rivers, and Phyllis Diller began to challenge the male stranglehold on comedy, that generation of "comediennes," no matter how glamorous offstage, had to deal in frazzled or frumpy comedy personas and tell self-deprecating jokes about how they were too gross to get a man. The laughs had to be at their own expense. Decades of humor-studies research seemed to prop up the idea that men were funnier than women, during a time when men were designing most of the studies. For example, it was long held that women didn't laugh at sexual humor the way men did; more nuanced research has since found that women are mostly turned off by sexual humor *when women are the*

---

* He insulted and refused his own sister's work even though she was living in abject poverty at the time, cut off by her whole family for leaving an abusive husband. What a guy.

butt of the jokes. Studies on humor production—getting men and women to write funny captions for cartoon panels, for example—long favored men, but a 2011 study found that the biggest difference was confidence. The men who took those tests were writing more *un*funny captions as well. They were getting more laughs for the same reason that NBA star Allen Iverson always made a lot of baskets: because they were taking more shots. Studies of conversational humor have found that men are more prone to witty teasing, the kind of thing that's easily quantifiable as a joke, but that women tell more funny anecdotes and jokes that build solidarity between people.

Circling the Wagons for Rape Jokes

The success of above-the-title funny women like Amy Schumer and Tina Fey may give the impression that comedy's gender gap is gone completely, but working comics know that's not true. Many gatekeepers in comedy still hold to the rule of thumb used by legendary *Saturday Night Live* writer Michael O'Donoghue: "It does help when writing humor to have a big hunk of meat between the legs. . . . Mr. Ding Dong, I think, has a lot of comedy genes in there." Writing for *Vice* in 2015, LA stand-up Megan Beth Koester described the world of regional club comedy as one of "outright hostility to women," a time-machine world where outrageously misogynistic material goes unchallenged and clubs and festivals routinely offer slates that are all male, or nearly so, without a second thought.

"When I started writing at Jezebel, it was totally accepted that women are less funny than men," Lindy West told me, and I immediately pictured diagrams comparing men and women's skulls, something out of the self-published phrenology or eugenics book of a turn-of-the-century crackpot. West started out covering local comedy and writing funny movie reviews in the *Stranger*, Seattle's alt-weekly. In 2012, she was hired to blog for Jezebel, and almost immediately saw her career take an unexpected turn. That summer, Daniel Tosh, the edgy—just ask him!—host of Comedy Central's *Tosh.0*, lost his cool during a set at the Laugh Factory, when a woman in the audience heckled a rape joke in his act. "Wouldn't it be funny if that girl got raped by, like, five guys right now?" he asked the crowd. "Like right now? What if a bunch of guys just raped her?" The woman's account of the exchange went viral on social media, and it took the conversation about misogyny in comedy into the mainstream media. Many prominent (male) comics lined up to defend Tosh on Voltairean grounds—isn't it great that comedians can say anything, even offensive things? It wasn't so clear to West that comedians musing aloud about uppity women getting gang-raped was an ultimate social good, and she wrote a piece for Jezebel proposing that, at a bare minimum, jokes about rape should target rapists, not their victims. Suddenly, she was the face of comedy censorship and PC thuggery, invited on cable news to explain Rape Culture for Dummies and then harassed endlessly—and I mean for years—by the Internet's angry anonymous every time she wrote about issues of feminism or social justice. One particularly vicious troll pelted her with insults using the identity of her late father, an experience that West described in a memorable episode of *This American Life*.

"Being in a fight with all of comedy really sucks," West said. Her 2016 memoir *Shrill* might as well be called *The Passion of the Lindy*: her battles with comedy professionals and fans turn her life into a demoralizing gauntlet of abuse. She had grown up as an obsessive comedy geek, feeling at home among the outsiders there. Then, without warning, she found herself Public Enemy Number One in that world just for taking the art form seriously, for saying that comedians should be responsible for their jokes. Even comics skeptical that comedy had a misogyny problem, like Patton Oswalt, eventually changed their tune after reading through online responses to West, which she patiently screencapped for the benefit of skeptical readers.

no need for you to worry about rape uggo

What a f—king c—t. Kill yourself, dumb bitch.

Jesus Christ this woman is about as fun as dry rape. Lighten up Lindy!

"Did that take a big psychic toll?" I asked her.

"I don't go to see stand-up anymore. I don't watch stand-up specials. I don't want to go to comedy clubs. I feel like I was rejected by that community, and they were shitty to me, so *fine*. Good luck."

Can You Have Your Racism Cake and Eat It Too?

It's a stretch to call Daniel Tosh's hypothetical rape threat a joke in any real sense, but that's how he explained it away in his Twitter apology a few days later. "The point I was making before I was heckled is there are awful things in the world but you can still make jokes about them," he said. Dissection of comedy is now a regular sidelight in our culture. Was this joke in last night's monologue on the right side of the issue? Was the comedian in that cell phone video out of line? In defense of comedians, this is in part a side effect of technology. Phone recordings and social media posts can skewer joke-tellers for tasteless one-off remarks never meant for mass consumption. In the past, Tosh might have seen a week-night Laugh Factory set as a chance to workshop new material, testing the limits on sensitive subjects *before* tackling them in the public eye.

But the real reason for all the Monday-morning quarterbacking of comedy is that *we* changed. We know now how powerful jokes can be: they can raise or lower a politician's poll numbers, transform public opinion on an issue, boost product sales by hundreds of millions of dollars. With stakes like that, the traditional "But I was just *joking!*" that Tosh trotted out no longer works as a blanket hall pass. Of course you were joking. But that just *begins* the conversation about what you were trying to say, or what its effects were. It doesn't end it.

Comedy is often lauded for taking risks with subject matter and view-point, but let's not mince words: it's possible to tell potentially offensive jokes for noble reasons—to make an audience listen to hard truths, for example—but it's easier to do it for hacky reasons. Carlin's adage about "suppressed laughter" being the easiest kind to get is important here. Funny people figure out pretty early that even jokes that aren't particularly insightful or well constructed can get big laughs, if the audience thinks the subject matter is sufficiently edgy. Shock value covers a multitude of sins.

Punch lines that are overtly racist or misogynistic or homophobic just won't cut it anymore—there's also such a thing as being *too* transgressive. Today, Eddie Murphy couldn't open two straight million-selling comedy records by telling the crowd at length about his fear of "faggots." Woody Allen used to do a queasy joke about running into his ex-wife on the street and not even recognizing her "with her wrists closed." And people forget that Andrew Dice Clay, the biggest fad comedian of the early 1990s, wasn't just a ludicrously over-the-top chauvinist onstage, but also filled his act with so many anti-immigrant jokes that the *New York Times* compared one of his shows to a "Nazi rally." Times have changed, but comedians are still eager for the sweet seductive thrill of shock. So one thing you see a lot is self-consciously offensive material foregrounded, but couched in irony. In his comedy film *Hilarious*, Louis C.K. repeatedly tells jokes that want to have it both ways. He claims that he'd have sex with a dead child—but then tells the audience he only did the joke to enjoy their offended response. He does a singsongy throwback "Ching chong ching!" impression of an Asian lady—but insists that the butt of the joke is his own dumb self. He shocks the crowd with a joke where he calls a woman with a "big nose" and "frizzy hair" a Jew, but then softens it into an observational bit about using the word "Jew" as a slur. I'm not convinced that the ironic distance excuses these jokes at all. They worked! He got the laugh twice—once for telling us racism was funny and once when he told us that, just kidding, it wasn't.

Lots of funny people do this, and the winking subtext is always the same: "It's okay when *I* do this, because my heart is pure. I'm one of the good ones." The problem is that this defense is meaningless; literally every human on earth believes they're one of the good ones. It is the one awful thing in life, as Jean Renoir once said: "Everyone has his reasons." I become newly skeptical of this comedic device every time I resee an old tweet of mine where I tried the faux-naïve thing of sounding dumb or regressive on some issue of the day—but ironically! Without the benefit of being back in my own head, experiencing all my good intentions firsthand, the tweet doesn't read as faux-dumb. It just seems dumb. I sound bad and dumb.

Why is it so much easier to tell a sarcastic joke that pretends to espouse the opposite of what we believe, as opposed to a sincere, constructive one that accurately reflects our viewpoint? There's something nuclear about humor, in that it can be so easily used to blow things up and scorch the earth. You *could* harness that same power to produce heat and light, but it requires so many safeguards and careful calculations. The risk of meltdown is always going to be there. Is it really worth all the effort? When you could use the same material to make a dirty bomb in five minutes?

In Praise of the Killjoys

More and more, we hear about comedians who care enough about their act to idiot-proof it. Eschewing ironic offensiveness isn't enough: you shouldn't dabble in jokes that could even be *accidentally* taken literally. Chris Rock became the biggest comedian in America with his 1996 "N———s vs. Black People" routine, but he never did it again after that tour, because he thought it was giving white audiences too much license with the n-word.* In 2005, Dave Chappelle walked away from his hit sketch show and a $50 million contract offer at least in part because of one incident when a white crew member laughed a little too hard at a blackface sketch. "I want to make sure I'm dancing and not shuffling," he told *Time*. Sarah Silverman calls those unintended responses "mouthfull-of-blood laughs." "They're the laughs you don't want."

Hearing Dave Chappelle tell Oprah that story was hugely validating for Hari Kondabolu. "There's a lot of us that were like, 'That's what we've been saying!' They're not just jokes. They're ideas. They can influence and have impact with people."

Kondabolu and his friend and podcast cohost W. Kamau Bell are often the panel that white comedians run racially iffy jokes by. "Is this okay to say?" What they want is permission, a Get Out of Jail Free card from a certified person of color. Instead of offering a verdict, Kondabolu

---

* Speaking for clueless white people, I would like to validate Rock's fear here. I had two different college friends who thought the popular routine entitled them to tough truth-talking about how they had nothing against black people, just against—well, you know.

tries to start a dialogue: What is the comic trying to accomplish with the joke? What compromises or unintended side effects would he be okay with? "It's weird being a killjoy in comedy," he said. "It's not something I thought comedy was going to be for me."

But the research backs up the killjoys. It's now well established in humor studies that disparagement humor comes with actual costs. Hearing one racist or sexist or homophobic joke might not "convert" every listener, but it can be persuasive to members of the audience already predisposed against the target. The experiments are often structured like this: Groups of participants are exposed to different materials. One group reads or watches disparaging jokes; the others might get neutral jokes or disparaging material that's not comedic. Then the groups are asked to plan some task relating to the jokes' target, like making a donation to a women's organization or divvying up a college budget between different student groups. Demeaning jokes do more to change participants' decisions than neutral jokes or, interestingly, demeaning nonjokes. The effect may be akin to the "confused" Stephen Colbert viewers in the previous chapter. The layer of irony in a Louis C.K. bit that traffics in race might be enough to sneak past our careful social conscience in a way that more overt material cannot.

Sadly, the effects of disparagement humor aren't limited to the lab. The controversy over President Truman's integration of the United States military in 1948 largely surrounded the notion, embedded in the chains of command, that African Americans were unfit for duty due to cowardice. This stereotype dates back to the Civil War and explains why black Union soldiers were largely kept out of active combat, and were paid less and equipped poorly compared to their white counterparts. The irony is that the antebellum image of the quivering black scaredy-cat, as employed by Mark Twain and others, was a self-serving one created to protect white interests! A population of four million passive and superstitious black people, whites imagined, could be subjugated into slavery. Four million fighters, bloodied but unbowed, would be another matter entirely. Once embedded in the culture and spread through minstrel humor, those stereotypes kept on influencing military policy, and reinforcing racism in the armed services, for decades.

For a more recent example, ask any Asian American who grew up in the John Hughes era about "Long Duk Dong" and look for the shiver of response. When I watched *Sixteen Candles* as a kid, the character of the clueless foreign exchange student, played by Gedde Watanabe, seemed goofy but harmless. I laughed when the "Donger" tried to use a fork and spoon like chopsticks or tried ineptly to put the moves on yet another pretty white girl. But in many American schoolyards, Long Duk Dong was the only Asian face in popular culture, and his inept brand of comic relief became implicit permission to tease the Asian kid in the class. "Jeer pressure" is a real and scary phenomenon: watching someone else be teased makes bystanders more likely to pile on. It is no exaggeration to say that, for the sake of a few cheap laughs,* John Hughes made the childhood of hundreds of thousands of people a little harder, a little more cruel. I know he didn't mean to. But jokes have real-life consequences.

If this can happen even in the case of a writer like John Hughes, whose reputation rests largely on his sympathetic, sensitive ear to kids and teens, just think what disparagement humor can do in the hands of every other idiot in the world. In 1993, the *Tucson Citizen* reported on the case of a fifth-grade teacher in rural Arizona who got fed up with John Henderson, a big kid in the class who often fell behind due to numerous learning disabilities and delayed motor skills. At the year-end class awards ceremony, Henderson was publicly presented with three "funny" distinctions: the Procrastinator's Award, the Pigsty Award, and the World's Worst Athlete Award. The boy was devastated and tried to hide the certificates from his parents. When they finally found out, they were furious. Their son had an "emotional breakdown," they told the newspaper, and it took years of therapy and a change of schools to get him back on track.† All because of one teacher who didn't understand how humor works.

What's most interesting to me, when it comes to mean or insensitive jokes, is that it's not always the most outrageous offenses that are the

---

* And that sweet gong crash every time the Donger appears on-screen! Hilarious!

† They sued the school district, which apologized and agreed to a $25,000 annuity to help pay for Henderson's college.

most dangerous. In 1993, Ted Danson emceed at a comedy roast for his then-girlfriend Whoopi Goldberg, and appeared in blackface. He launched into a long, raunchy routine about his interracial sexual relationship with Goldberg, ate watermelon onstage, and used the n-word no less than twelve times. Ted Danson! If you didn't live through this, you probably think I'm making it up, but it happened, and it was a huge deal. A thousand thousand thinkpieces agreed, quite correctly, that a line had been not merely crossed, but plowed three feet into the dirt.* But here's the thing: *l'affaire* Danson didn't lead to a racist epidemic of celebrity or civilian blackface speeches. It was so clearly over the top that everyone just shook their heads in bemusement and moved on. It's the small offenses, closer to defensibility, that can actually affect the way we treat other people. The "c'mon, surely that's harmless" ones. The white comic who affects a caricatured "black" voice in his act but then jokes about it afterward. The *SNL* sketch that uses two guys kissing as an outrageous topper. The Long Duk Dongs.

The Price

The opposing view is often framed this way: sure, prejudice is bad in all its forms, but what do we lose if we become so hypersensitive to boundary cases that we steer away from jokes about tricky subjects altogether? Often, professional funny people are the ones sounding this alarm. They see themselves as sentinels on the walls watching the barbarians amass, the canaries in the coal mine while the growing climate of "political correctness," as they will say, becomes suffocating. First, they came for the hacky club comics, and I did not speak out, because I was not a hacky club comic.

I get it. No one likes to be told how to do their job. In particular, it must be galling to be a professionally funny person and still face perpetual criticism from less funny people with a long list of complaints. I'm not a comedian, but I waste a lot of time on Twitter, and Twitter is the single best invention in human history for telling jokes to thousands of people who

---

* The only actual humor to result from the routine came a week later, when Carl Rowan closed his column on the controversy this way: "I offer no 'cheers' to Mr. Danson."

don't like or understand jokes. If you have a sufficiently large following, you will get helpfully corrected just about every time you say anything. It's the kind of place where a joke about bees will be met within minutes by a reply from a beekeeper saying that kind of levity isn't helpful to his field.* I once tweeted a lousy pun my son had made and asked readers if I should have him put up for adoption or killed. "Good joke, but next time skip the implication that adoption is a punishment," one reader instructed. (The murder threat was apparently okay.) *That very night* I was in a taco place that had photos of Mexican actors Cantinflas and Katy Jurado on the respective restroom doors, and I posted a photo with the note that, luckily, I identify sexually as a Cantinflas. One reply told me I was hurting the cause of trans people by making light of gendered restrooms.

Responses like that make a common enough mistake: confusing a joke *about* a subject with one *targeting* the subject. A joke that mentions adoption does not necessarily stigmatize adoption, just as a photo of funny themed labels on restaurant restrooms isn't there to disparage trans people. A joke about rape can target rape culture instead of rape victims. But I understand that these aren't my go-to issues, and others for whom they loom larger will experience them differently. Their reluctance to laugh about a subject that hits close to home isn't something I need to correct or rebut. Let's be honest, their priorities (be inclusive toward adopted people and trans people) are nobler than mine (make dumb jokes on social media out of a bottomless need to feel validated by strangers).

That's just part of the social contract of joking. If I think something is funny, I can try out a joke about it, and if someone doesn't think it's funny, they're free to leave, or explain why. (Twitter isn't a nightclub, where joke critiques ruin the "show" for others.) My right to free speech isn't being constrained in any way. "The 'thought police' aren't a real police," Hari Kondabolu pointed out. "There's no jurisdiction that has the thought police. So you can say what you want to say, but you have to face the consequences of what you say. That's not a novel idea!"

If, as a comedy fan, you feel you must side with a comedian who publicly complains about something he (or she, but come on, usually he)

---

* I wish this example were hypothetical.

"can't joke about anymore," ask yourself a few questions. First, do these objections ever age well? Is there ever a kind of insensitive joke that came back into style once everyone realized we were overreacting? Generally, that doesn't happen. Mean jokes go out of style because civilization moves on. There's a transcript of a White House press briefing from the early days of the AIDS epidemic in which Reagan's spokesperson and the press corps share a hearty laugh at the idea of a "gay plague" and kid each other that—uh-oh!—what if one of them had it?!? It's funny, because that would mean they were homosexuals! I'm sure all of these people would have scoffed at the idea that their little joke, and the attitudes behind it, did any harm. But looking back, it's clear who was on the right side of history during that era, and it wasn't all the people doing easy AIDS jokes.

Second, what real harm has been done by the pushback to jokes? Is our culture suffering from not enough quippy people being able to speak their minds? Is that really what's causing most of our problems right now—everyone's too kind and sensitive, and so marginalized people have it too easy? A 2016 analysis of survey data from the American National Election Study found a gaping divide on the question of "political correctness": respondents who said they've never been the victims of discrimination overwhelmingly agreed that "people are too easily offended" these days. Having experienced discrimination made people more than twice as likely to support more inclusive language. In other words, the complaints about "thought police" are coming almost entirely from people who have the luxury of not having to worry much about the issue either way. Firsthand experience might change their mind.

Many comedy people now take the more enlightened line that if a controversial joke "offends," it just means it wasn't funny enough. The audience has spoken; write a better joke. That's true as far as it goes, but to me it misses the point. In a world of omnipresent comedy, getting a laugh isn't all that rare, or difficult. It's certainly not an absolute defense. Reagan press secretary Larry Speakes got laughs with his "gay plague" joke at that briefing, but that doesn't make him right. And it's not like "tell sharper AIDS jokes" would have been the best advice for him; as it turns out, what we really should have done in 1982 is take the epidemic more seriously early on.

It's been said that "political correctness is just good manners," and of course that's not an absolute defense either. There are thousands of things more important than manners. But it's an illuminating comparison, because I think most people *would* like to live in a society where good manners are the rule, and where they're only dispensed with when there's a higher good at stake, an urgent need. "I just thought of a little joke" doesn't always qualify. Historically, we've tended to except comedy from the requirements of manners, because these people are special: they're our truth-tellers, our impudent court jesters. But in a time where everyone's a comedian, when there are literally millions of truth-telling court jesters, that carve-out seems less necessary than ever. Today comedy *is* mainstream discourse, not just a quick break from it.

"Are comedians right that there's a price to monitoring their jokes more carefully?" I asked Lindy West. "What would happen?"

"All of these institutions would unfurl and make themselves available to all the people who have felt unwelcome and unwanted in that community." She thought we were already starting to see it. "The comedy landscape feels different to me today, the way women are given much more default respect. All of those women who are starting out right now, who are geniuses, might never have started if the climate hadn't opened up a little bit. That's the 'price'! It's that you actually get to know and hear the stories of all these other people who had previously been excluded or discouraged."

Sure, the change may have involved external pressure, West concedes. But just as it didn't really matter how many alt-right provocateurs were dabbling in Nazism *ironically*, someday it won't matter how many shock comedians just toned it down so feminists would stop yelling at them. "Even if that's the reason, that's fine! Because the generation behind them won't know that was the reason."

Changing the World with Ping-Pong Balls

Comedy can make backward social views seem more palatable and even harmless. But for the same reasons, jokes have also become a uniquely powerful way to argue for positive change.

For starters, they can be the spoonful of sugar that helps the medicine go down. "People let their guards down when they hear comedy," Hari Kondabolu told me. Even a skeptical audience member, he said, might think, "I'm willing to listen because I paid for the ticket, I still think this is funny, and he's going to reward me at the end with a laugh." Recently, journalists have noted the "John Oliver effect," in which the long-form desk pieces delivered by Oliver on *Last Week Tonight* have changed the status quo where years of op-eds and direct-mail appeals have not. Oliver's little lectures are dotted with plenty of snarky asides and cringily millennial-friendly pop culture similes (the United States uncovering FIFA soccer corruption was "like finding out that Ke$ha arrested a group of bankers involved in commodities fraud!"), but they get results. When Oliver explained the issues surrounding net neutrality, viewers submitted forty-seven thousand new comments to the FCC, enough to crash its website. He did a segment on how badly large poultry companies treat their suppliers, and the next appropriations bill to pass the House of Representatives strengthened legal protections for chicken farmers. A month after Oliver complained about the bail bond system in America, New York mayor Bill de Blasio announced reforms to the city's bail procedures. None of these issues were drifting anywhere close to the top of the public mind before *Last Week Tonight*'s writers dressed them up in jokes.

Humorists also have rhetorical tricks at their disposal that reporters do not. "Straight journalism can't use hyperbole," Lindy West observed. "What satire does is it just makes something truer than the truth. You spin it out to its ultimate conclusion and then you can really look at how absurd or dangerous or cruel or petty this thing is." That can lead to real-world change—most famously, in the case of William Tweed, the corrupt boss of the Democratic political machine in Gilded Age New York. In the early 1870s, the *New York Times* was documenting "Boss" Tweed's shady world of kickbacks and extortion in a series of exposés, but what really stuck in the popular imagination were the caricatures of Tweed that cartoonist Thomas Nast published in *Harper's Weekly*, which depicted him variously as a vulture, Napoleon, a corpulent titan with a money bag for a head, and a giant thumb crushing Manhattan. "Stop them damn pictures!" Tweed fumed to his Tammany Hall underlings. The Tweed Ring offered Nast half a million dollars to "go study art in Europe," but Nast refused. In the end, it was Tweed who fled to Europe to avoid trial—only to be arrested by Spanish officials, who recognized him from one of Nast's drawings! The cartoon they had seen showed Tweed in prison stripes, hauling two street kids around by the collar, and the *guardia* thought they had tracked down a dastardly child kidnapper. The power of hyperbole!

Finally, humor has the distinct advantage of overcoming power asymmetries: if protesters can drag a debate into the level of the ridiculous, the powers that be have much more to lose than they do. In his book *Blueprint for Revolution*, Serbian activist Srdja Popovic lists examples of what he calls "laughtivism": deflating authority in ways that are hard to retaliate against, because they provoke laughter instead of anger or violence:

- Opposition leaders in Serbia painted dictator Slobodan Milosevic onto barrels, then placed them around Belgrade along with baseball bats. "Smash his face for just a dinar," read the sign. Delighted citizens lined up for a turn. When police showed up, there were no organizers to arrest—so they arrested the barrels.
- Syrian protesters wrote antigovernment slogans on Ping-Pong balls and dumped them out in public places. Soon cops were being deployed to chase little bouncing Ping-Pong balls, something that no one in history has ever looked cool or scary doing. The demonstrators also rigged up tiny USB speakers to say things like "Assad is a pig!" on a loop, and left them in garbage cans and manure piles, for the authorities to dig around in.
- Russians in one Siberian city were denied permits to protest against Putin, so they placed little plastic toys in the streets to march in their place. The trend for toy demonstrations began to spread, so the government was forced to ban assemblies of Lego mini-figures and the little plastic toys from Kinder eggs.

As the Italian situationists warned oppressive governments, "a laugh will bury you!" This line of protest seemed especially promising when it came to the thin-skinned Donald Trump. The marchers with funny signs may not have wounded him, but TV and Internet jokers realized that the president's massive ego, his own deluded mystique of mastery, was his greatest weakness. Jokes about the unimpressive crowds at his inauguration immediately produced defiant tweets and defensive press conferences. Jokes referring to White House aide Steve Bannon as "President Bannon" led to Bannon's swift demotion from the National Security Council, the *New York Times* reported. The leader of the free world could be manipulated into changing policy by pointing and laughing at him; this was either hopeful or horrifying, depending on your point of view.

Thermometers and Thermostats

There is abundant precedent for world leaders who, like Trump and Kim Jong-un, took jokes about their government seriously. The Nazis made joking about the Reich a capital crime in 1935, and Joseph Goebbels banned all political humor in 1939.* Thousands were sentenced to death under the law. Under the czars as well as under Stalin, Russians could be sentenced to ten years of forced labor for telling jokes about the government or the party. Given the condition of czarist prisons and Siberian gulags, that was usually a death sentence as well.

But satire and comedy haven't had a great track record against totalitarianism. Popovic's student movement in Serbia did actually help to topple the government of Slobodan Milošević, who ended up dead in a Dutch prison cell while on trial for war crimes. But there's not a long list of powerful people brought low by jokes. Putin and Assad have so far managed to survive the Ping-Pong balls and Lego sets strewn on sidewalks by their unhappier citizens. "There are those who thought that we could laugh Hitler and Mussolini out of court," remembered theologian Reinhold Niebuhr, "but laughter alone never destroys a great seat of power and authority in history."

---

* Goebbels called anti-Nazi jokes "feces of the soul," but he didn't want to give people the crazy idea that Germans were humorless. So when the Reich banned cabaret humor, it set up newspaper joke contests with hundred-mark prizes for the winners. One contest in Hamburg was won by a story that turned out to have been plagiarized from a famous Jewish author.

This raises the possibility that subversive jokes might actually be counterproductive. What if they're just a convenient escape valve, a way for unhappy people to let off steam and feel better about their lot without actually fighting back against oppression? Medieval kings and churchmen, even at the height of Christianity's distaste for comedy, long tolerated yearly spring carnivals and "feasts of fools" at which social rules were suspended and topsy-turvy merriment reigned: a peasant boy was dressed as a bishop, pigs were put on mock trials, processioners cross-dressed and danced the night away. The powers that be didn't mind a little mockery, because the peasants would generally work all the harder for the rest of the season. "Wine barrels burst from time to time if we do not open them and let in some air," the Paris School of Theology wrote in defense of the festivities. Some later revolutionaries avoided humor for the same reason: it seemed to undermine the seriousness of their struggle. Hungarian humorist George Mikes claimed that, in Eastern Europe during the Cold War, the secret police would actually invent and spread their own antiregime jokes, so they'd have more control over the level of discontent in the comedy climate.

It's easy to find evidence that today's topical comedy, no matter how sharp it feels, can be more of an opiate than a cattle prod. Late-night monologues are on before bedtime. We don't watch someone make fun of the bad men and then feel empowered to call our senator or volunteer for a nonprofit. We hear the jokes and drop off to sleep. In 2011, an eighty-year longevity study announced the counterintuitive finding that cheerful people actually die younger, which goes against everything we thought we knew from *Patch Adams* about the healing power of laughter. Coauthor Leslie Martin speculated that in some cases, people with a cheery, optimistic outlook might actually take their health too blithely or find themselves emotionally unequipped to deal with setbacks.

A Lithuanian émigré named Alexander Shtromas was the only political scientist to predict the end of the Soviet Union as early as the late 1970s, when the Soviet Union seemed to be thriving to other onlookers. How was Shtromas so sure? Because of the jokes. Officially, there was no dissident movement in the USSR, and yet Shtromas was collecting hundreds of whispered jokes, from an informal news apparatus that Russians jokingly called the OBS (Odna Baba Skazala, "an old woman said").

A woman is walking down the street with a bag full of rolls of toilet paper. A passerby sees her and asks, "Hey, mother, where did you buy them?" "Buy? Are you crazy? Where could I buy them nowadays? They're five years old. I'm taking them back from the cleaners."

A man called KGB headquarters on business and was told, "We can't help you today, the KGB has just burned down." Five minutes later he called back and was again told that the KGB has burned. When he called a third time, the operator recognized his voice and asked, "Why do you keep calling back? I just told you, the KGB has burned down!" "I know," the man replied. "I just like to hear it."

But it's important to note that Shtromas described these jokes as the result, not the cause, of Russian dissatisfaction. They didn't bring down the party. In the words of Christie Davies, "jokes are thermometers, not thermostats."

The makers of *The Daily Show* know that better than anyone. When I asked former staff writer Rob Kutner about the influence the show had on the real world, he laughed. "Mostly you'd find the opposite: *not* having an effect," he said. In the run-up to the 2004 election, the writers' room felt pretty good about their nightly lampooning of the war on terror: mission accomplished. "We all thought that we had exposed Bush's follies and there would be some kind of reckoning. We didn't think he'd get reelected." When the *New York Times* asked Jon Stewart the same question at a panel shortly after the 2016 election, he was even more damning. "Controlling a culture is not the same as power," he said. "While we were all passing around really remarkable, eviscerating videos of the Tea Party—that we had all made great fun of—[they were] sitting off a highway at a Friendly's taking over a local school board." Organizing is *always* a thermostat.

But comedy is no longer just snarking from the sidelines, and maybe that will change the rules. Our modern sense of humor seems more concerned than ever with the real-world effects of our jokes, and less prone to misanthropic shock value. Maybe a more idealistic, less cynical sense of humor will be able to do what many satirists of the past have not: get people to take problems more seriously, not less. When a funny person dabbles in real issues, there will always be someone to criticize them for "getting political"—and that only ever means "poking fun at *my* political viewpoint." But in fact, all comedy is political. When hate crimes are on the rise, jokes that still traffic in the old iffy stereotypes about race and gender and sexual identity are a political statement. Even to keep on telling nothing but the same old determinedly apolitical observational jokes in that climate would be a political statement.

Today one ironclad rule of joke ethics is often given as "don't punch down"—that is, make sure the targets of your jokes are more powerful than you, not less. This is revolutionary; "punching down" was once the only acceptable form of humor. "As for jest, there be certain things which ought to be privileged from it," wrote Francis Bacon in 1597, and went on to list "religion," "matters of state," "great persons," and "any man's present business of importance." Cicero and Castiglione agreed: it's bad form to make fun of the rich and powerful. The elite jokesters of the past saw that rule as a way of staying apolitical, above the fray, but leaving the status quo unchallenged has effects as well.

In a comedy-saturated world, the challenge for socially conscious humorists will lie in choosing the jokes that they tell and not relying on joking alone to fix all injustices. In Mark Twain's unfinished final novel, *The Mysterious Stranger*, the title character is the devil himself. "You have a mongrel perception of humor," Satan tells the narrator at one point. "This multitude see the comic side of a thousand low-grade and trivial things. . . . Your race, in its poverty, has unquestionably one really effective weapon—laughter. . . . Against the assault of laughter nothing can stand." The devil's desperate hope is that mankind never wises up, never learns to tell the *right* jokes. Because those could change the world.

ELEVEN

NEW TIRYNTHA

When Mark Twain had Satan hype the lofty possibilities of comedy in *The Mysterious Stranger*, the Lord of Darkness was clearly speaking for the author. "Humor is the great thing, the saving thing," Twain had written in an 1895 essay. "The minute it crops up, all our irritations and resentments slip away and a sunny spirit takes their place." I always picture Martin Starr as the nerdy Bill Haverchuck in the next-to-last episode of *Freaks and Geeks*, coming home to an empty house after yet another bleak day of getting pushed around at high school. He fixes himself a snack and sits down to watch TV— Garry Shandling doing stand-up on Dinah Shore's talk show. Bill starts laughing so hard that he's literally flailing on the couch. Grilled cheese is stuck to his teeth; brownie crumbs fly out of his mouth. It's a wordless scene that says everything about what comedy can mean to people going through a bad time. For one brief moment in Bill's life, everything is okay.

But much has changed since Bill Haverchuck's latchkey 1980 childhood. Comedy was once a hard-won respite from the drudgeries of life. Today a surprise appearance by a favorite comedian wouldn't be an unexpected treat, because Bill would come home every day to an essentially unlimited supply of dazzlingly high-quality jokes on his TV or phone. Can comedy still be "the saving thing" in a world where it's gone from the exception to the rule?

Nothing Succeeds Like Excess

When I asked comedy guru George Meyer about the new joke saturation, he remembered something a professor once told him: "Throughout history, man has screwed up good things by concentrating them." When people were drinking beer, that didn't lead to a lot of problems, but once we figured out how to distill beer into liquor, drinking alcohol became a harsher experience. Incan coca tea begat powdered cocaine, which begat freebasing. We bred stronger and stronger strains of marijuana until eventually people just started inhaling dabs of pure THC. "At some point," Meyer observed, "you're on the catastrophic side of the hill."

The comparison between drugs and laughs isn't just hypothetical. Movie directors today can use digital editing and recorded test screenings to precisely shape comedy for audiences. They're timing jokes down to the exact twenty-fourth of a second to maximally jolt the brain, the way Chuck Jones used to do in animation. Comedy, in other words, isn't just a minor relaxant now. We've engineered it into a designer drug: ever faster, smarter, stranger, crueler, more ironic. We may be pushing the envelope of just how refined it can get.

It's not a coincidence that our bizarre and rarefied comic sensibility, so "advanced" that much of it isn't even recognizable as jokes to those not in the know, developed in a time of new abundance. Our sense of humor has evolved—or mutated, given the pace of change—to suit the fact that comedy is now the dominant voice of our culture. When taste and technology allow you to hear hundreds of jokes a day, novelty becomes more important, and that's what pushes speed and absurdity to new heights. It also makes topicality essential. Can you imagine a late-night staff trying to write dozens of joke candidates every day without twenty-four hours of new headlines to prime the pump? I don't think they could handle the volume. The conversation is now moving too fast for many kinds of joke-tellers to keep up with demand, so a chattier voice has replaced the glib, prepared "routines" of the past. And faster, smaller, more reactive jokes can squeeze their way into ever more corners of modern life, so even more jokes get told. It's a feedback loop of nonstop hilarity!

In the end, the twenty-first-century ubiquity of jokes and the escalation of everything about those jokes aren't two different things. They're the same savage *more*-ness. They're driven by the same insatiable appetite.

The stakes are higher now that comedy has been weaponized by its newest establishment practitioners: corporations, political parties, governments. Billions of dollars and the shape of the future are now at stake when organizations crack jokes. It's easy to imagine a world where the co-opting of jokes by the Man defanged them, reduced them for the lowest common denominator to an inoffensive mush. But in our world, with powerful voices deploying jokes on all sides, it started an arms race. No one's going to remember the slightly silly ad when there's a *very* silly one coming up right behind it. No one's going to laugh at the prepared zingers of an affable political candidate when there's an unpredictable force of sheer id on the debate stage. And as long as these jokes are told with a sufficiently ironic wink, the agendas behind them are harder to criticize. Not everyone crafting and telling these jokes is a gifted comedian, of course, but that's almost beside the point. There's so much comedy in our culture now that everyone's internalized its tone and tropes. Anyone can *sound* like they're being funny, whether they've genuinely made a real joke or not.

We've caught on to the influence of jokes enough to police them more carefully in ourselves. We indulge in long debates over what targets are appropriate for jokes, and which jokes are on the right side of the issue. But as carefully as we're now monitoring the ethics of comedy, we haven't really turned that same careful eye on the most powerful joke-tellers. No one is asking if presidential debates should be funny, if the CIA should be funny, if a huge demographic should be getting most of its news from comedy shows. It all changed so gradually we didn't really notice it.

Are powerful organizations getting quippier today because we are, or are we getting quippier because of them?

Mandatory Fun

The modern comedy glut has, paradoxically, made life harder in many ways for people who tell jokes for a living. Most obviously, they're now competing in a more crowded market. Who will pay for their jokes when there's no shortage of others to choose from? Since 1986, a "humor consultant" named Malcolm Kushner has published the annual Cost of Laughing Index, tracking the effects of inflation on expenses like whoopee cushions, *Mad* magazine, and novelty singing gorilla telegrams. "Are we paying more bucks for less yucks?" he asks.* But his calculations are a relic from a strange and ancient culture that lived very differently. Today, essentially unlimited access to thousands of hours of comedy, more than you could ever possibly watch, can be yours for less than ten dollars, via a monthly subscription to a streaming video service. Access to the avalanche of daily jokes on social media is free.

And what happens to the sense of newness and discovery that draws young people into comedy? "Everything's been done," writer-comedian Stephen Merchant has said. "You're just doing variations on a theme." We've seen it all. I played a board game once that said, "Fun for kids from 5 to 105!" and made a joke on Twitter about how hurtful that must be to 106-year-olds. The first reaction was a disapproving reply from a reader who considered this to be a "hacky" subject for a joke. Ah yes, board game age recommendations. That old comedy saw.

It can be joyless to have to keep on constantly producing more and more jokes in a world that clearly already has plenty of them. What good is enforced merriment? Don Marquis, the American writer who created Archy and Mehitabel,† came to see his humor column for the *New York Herald Tribune* as "a grave, twenty-three inches long, into which I buried myself every day." I think about Marquis's words every time I open Twitter and see that empty white rectangle with the "What's happening?" prompt. The rectangle just wants more and more jokes. It's never satisfied.

For the comedy audience, the problem is the acceleration of the hedonic treadmill. We have come to see our daily mega-calorie dose

---

* Shouldn't it be "fewer yucks"? I'm intrigued by Kushner's grammatical position that "yucks" is an uncountable noun.

† Archy and Mehitabel are a cockroach and an alley cat, respectively, and they're best friends. If you're not yet familiar with Marquis's light verse, you're in for a treat.

of jokes as the new normal and take it for granted. "The audience becomes inured to it, and jaded, and un-entertainable," said George Meyer. "I think about people watching a dozen *Curb Your Enthusiasm*s in a row. The bingeing seems almost manic and pathological to me. At the end of it, are you really going to enjoy the twelfth one you watched as much as the first one?" The old Anglo-Saxon custom was to literally roll around on the floor when amused. Today, that's diminished down to a knowing nod: "Yes, this joke meets with my approval."*

And the same audience is getting more and more savvy; it can't be surprised anymore. That can be fatal to jokes; so much of laughter is defamiliarization, seeing something about life in a new and unexpected way. Preparing their 2006 book on humor *Only Joking*, writer Lucy Greeves and comedian Jimmy Carr sorted through over twenty thousand jokes, looking for the best ones. Greeves wrote that she "went temporarily 'joke-blind'—an affliction that renders the sufferer incapable of distinguishing a funny joke from a hopeless one." Carr, interestingly, "was completely unaffected" by this immunity to humor. As a professional comic, he was in many ways *already there*.

The most common defense of comedy is to describe it as a self-evident good because it feels good. It provides a moment of comfort and distraction in a dark world. "If I laugh at any mortal thing / 'Tis that I may not weep," as Byron wrote. And that feels truer than ever today: the stress and alienation of modern life is indeed the commonality that underlies consumerism and secularism and prolonged adolescence and all the other drivers of the West's growing appetite for comedy. Humor is a coping mechanism deeply wired in the human brain; we can see that every time we recall a once-painful experience and realize it's somehow funny now. But that impulse can lead to some dangerous places. Unless comedy is used very carefully, it's a reaction to modern problems that

---

* Or, even more annoyingly, the opposite. One of Twitter's great gifts to comedy is the chance for audience members to send disappointed replies like "Do better" or "A rare miss" every time they're let down by a joke. Oh no, a rare miss! I'm so sorry this free eight-word joke wasn't up to your usual lofty standards, m'lord!

does nothing to remedy them. There are many accounts of Holocaust Jews maintaining their sense of humor in the ghettos and camps, usually told to demonstrate defiance and pluck in the face of suffering and oppression. "I have more faith in Hitler than in anyone else," a prisoner says sardonically to Elie Wiesel in *Night*. "He alone has kept his promises, all his promises, to the Jewish people." Journalist Steve Lipman has called these mordant jokes in the midst of a collapsing world "the currency of hope."

But I can't read about gallows humor in the face of tragedy without being overwhelmed by the sense of how heartbreakingly inadequate it all was. Viktor Frankl wrote that a popular running gag in the camps was to joke about how strange the episode would all seem once everyone was free *and life was back to normal*. A man might ask his hostess at a fancy dinner party to stir up the soup from the bottom—the least watery part of the meal, back in Dachau—and everyone would laugh. Frankl survived the Holocaust with his humanity intact, and maybe a sense of humor helped, I don't know. But the fact remains that millions of people did not survive. In hindsight, we hear their jokes about returning to their old lives, and we know that never happened. It all seems so small and ineffectual in the face of systematic murder.

The endpoint of laughter as a survival strategy can be glimpsed in Colin Turnbull's book *The Mountain People*, about the eighteen months he spent living with the Ik people of northeast Uganda. The Ik were subsistence farmers being slowly winnowed into extinction by drought and famine, and their lives were an endless parade of the worst hardships imaginable. All ideals of family and compassion were utterly lost to them. But Turnbull marveled at one thing: how, amid their hopelessness, they laughed constantly. They laughed with unfailing amusement, but without joy. Mothers laughed as babies crawled into the hot coals of a fire; young people laughed as they pulled morsels of food from the mouths of their own weakened grandparents.

The fact that gallows humor is all that survives in the face of dehumanizing catastrophe isn't an argument for gallows humor. It's an argument against dehumanizing catastrophe.

Predicting the Hot New Dystopia

The Greek philosopher Theophrastus related the strange story of Tiryntha, or Tiryns, the Peloponnesian city where Heracles once lived. The Tirynthians, said Theophrastus, were addicted to laughter. They were amused by everything, and it was ruining their lives and endangering the city. They sent to the oracle at Delphi to see what could be done, and were instructed to sacrifice a bull to Poseidon and throw it into the sea without laughing. The Tirynthians, determined to follow the oracle's pronouncement to the letter, barred children from the ritual to ensure that no one cracked up. But one boy stole into the crowd to watch the sacrifice, and when he piped up to ask what was going on, he made an accidental pun* that sent the whole crowd into gales of laughter. The sacrifice was spoiled. "They perceived," wrote Athenaeus centuries later, "that the god meant to show them by a fact that an inveterate custom cannot be remedied."

Over the past century, and particularly in the last twenty years, we have seen an accelerating crescendo of humor in our culture. Like the Tirynthians, we seem to be unable to navigate life or conduct business without it, but it's hard to imagine what comes next. It's easy to say that comedy booms, like all fads, are cyclical, and that this one will peter out just like the club boom of the 1980s did. But that underestimates the ways in which our current age has embedded jokes deep in our corporate cultures, politics, journalism, technology, and other institutions in ways that are unprecedented and completely unrelated to the comedy industry. It also ignores the fact that our postwar comedy crescendo has survived generational upheavals, unspeakable tragedies, and existential crises while barely skipping a beat. Kliph Nesteroff tells a story about the *Saturday Night Live* crew backstage on September 29, 2001, as the show prepared to display a stiff upper lip by going back on the air less than three weeks after thousands of people had been killed by terrorists just a short cab ride away. The mood was not upbeat. "I'm not ready to watch this," said one unenthusiastic prop guy.

---

* He meant to say, "Are you afraid I'll upset the sacrificial bowl?" but confused the very similar Greek words for "bowl" and "victim," and asked if they thought he would knock over the *bull*. I guess you had to be there.

But the show went on. The show always went on. The 9/11 attacks sidelined *The Daily Show* for a whopping nine days.* Donald Trump was supposed to be the end of satire, but that was only true if by "the end of satire" you meant "an incredible proliferation of satire."† Comedy now seems to be an independent variable, self-sustaining and unmoored to any actual trend in the public mood.

If it's hard to imagine comedy saturation slowly declining due to burnout, then what happens instead? We may discover whether or not there are hardwired physical limits on human amusement. How fast can jokes get, for example? The speed of sitcom jokes has doubled in the last fifty years; surely that pace can't continue. Can their complexity, irony, or absurdity escalate indefinitely, or is there a point at which the brain will be unable to process them as humor?

Here's an easier prediction: I can guarantee you that jokes will continue to squeeze into more and more places where they were once, either explicitly or informally, completely verboten. Ironic eulogies and funny headstones are coming. Funnier appliance manuals, funnier judges giving funnier decisions. Jokes on traffic signs. Jokes in legislation. Jokes in scientific and medical research. "Neutral" and *especially* "serious" won't be good enough anymore. Funny is going to colonize every level of human expression and interaction, and that will become the new baseline. I can't name one area of life where "playful humor" ever became the dominant mode of discourse but then we changed our mind and walked it back. Even the seeming exceptions (the decline of corporate humor consultants, say, or the traditional three-camera sitcom) prove the rule; they were the victims of their own success. Comedy became so endemic to their landscapes that their little specialized niche became unnecessary—or worse, started to seem "corny." "Corny" is the enemy. We need more, we need new.

---

* The BBC's plan for Queen Elizabeth's eventual death will pull comedy from the airwaves, but only until her funeral. Things will be back to normal in less than two weeks.

† David Letterman and Jimmy Fallon, two fairly apolitical late-night hosts, were replaced in quick succession by, respectively, Stephen Colbert and Seth Meyers, two men who had made their reputation doing fake news behind a fake anchor desk. After brief and fairly unsuccessful attempts at broadening their acts, both reinvented their shows in the Trump era by tacking hard toward political material.

Movies have predicted many different futures for media and the public sphere: sterile and dull (*2001*), fascist (*V for Vendetta*), annoying (*Minority Report*), sexy and Asian (*Blade Runner*). It's odd that no one has predicted a "funny" future, with every corner of the planet crammed to within an inch of its life with attempts at humor.* It's almost certainly coming.

There's an unpleasant third option: could something so terrible happen to our culture that it would shock us straight, reboot our institutions in a more sober vein? It would have to be worse than Watergate and Vietnam, worse than 9/11, worse than Donald Trump. When I asked *David Letterman* and *The Simpsons* writer Tim Long about the modern abundance of comedy, he had had enough. "You kind of just have to throw your hands up and tell the world, 'Stop being hilarious!'" he said. "If there is a third world war, one of the great benefits will be, maybe, a ten-year palate cleansing. The upside of nuclear devastation is no one will be joking around for ten years. And then we can start anew."†

It's at least *possible*, I guess, that our comedy decadence is a fore-warning of a civilization-wide collapse to come. Under this theory, all the jokes are part of a bigger problem: we're learning to laugh at problems instead of solving them, or self-medicating with jokes so we don't have to face ominous facts. The Tirynthians' addiction to laughter, history tells us, was less permanent than they believed. In the fifth century BC, their city was conquered by nearby Argos. The lower city was overrun and the acropolis abandoned as surviving residents fled to other nearby towns. Today the citadel is still just a deserted hillside surrounded by olive orchards. For twenty-five hundred years, Tiryntha has been laughter-free.

---

* Mike Judge's *Idiocracy* is probably the closest, but the movie is very clear that the goofy America it envisions is just an effect, not a cause, of a dumbed-down populace.

† Maybe. One of many horrifying things about the story of the Ik people is the implication that unfunny, joyless comedy could, like cockroaches, even survive a nuclear war.

A Momentary Anesthesia of the Heart

My kids are growing up in this world, and they are not unspoiled. My ten-year-old daughter, Katie, inspired by her Jay Leno library book, recently started taking improv classes at a little theater up the street. My son, Dylan, and his friends communicate largely in Internet memes; he seems annoyed and impressed when I know them all too. I don't know where children first hear of comedy as a language, as a career; it scarcely seems to matter. My little nephew spent a year or two saying, "Waka waka waka!" every time he made a joke, because that's what the Muppets' Fozzie Bear always does. He assumed it was a necessary part of the formula.

We were visiting my wife's parents not long ago, and I wound up comparing notes with my brother-in-law on what it's like to have your oldest son suddenly be a teenager. Dylan wasn't hulking and surly yet, but he was suddenly *mouthy*, as my mom used to say, with an unsolicited opinion or flippant comeback to everything.

"Ah, he's sarcastic, like you," said my brother-in-law knowingly.

He didn't mean anything by it, but it stung me to the quick. Sarcastic, *like me?* Telling jokes has been a big part of my identity as far back as I can remember, but being reduced bluntly to the Sarcastic One was devastating. I don't like the Sarcastic One. I'm not sure if anyone does. It's hard to get to know people who constantly deflect conversation with quippy asides—which is probably why they started doing it, as a way to talk without revealing anything, risking anything. Even if it's just a tic, even if there's more to someone than the sarcasm, it's tiresome as a first response. But here we are: to much of the outside world, I'm—above all else, maybe—the person who can be counted on for a flip, sarcastic take on everything.

Later, when I told my wife about the conversation, Mindy nodded understandingly. "Right," she said. "You don't want to be Chandler." Talk about twisting the knife! Some people worry about turning into their mother or their father. I'm turning into Chandler from *Friends*. Could that *be* any more unflattering?

It stung because I knew there was truth to it. If you have children, you already know this: watching them use habits and mannerisms they picked up from you is taking a long, unpleasant look at the man in the mirror. With Dylan, the snarky, reflexive jokes are a constant barrage.

ME: Set the table, Mom's going to be home soon.
DYLAN: Your face is going to be home soon.

Repeat ten to twenty times a day.

It's performative; he knows it's silly. But he's just mimicking things he's heard grown-ups like me say and do. The same stupid jokes I made without thinking are boomeranging back on me. I'm the latest person who knows me—but probably not the last!—to become incredibly annoyed by my sense of humor.

For all that gets written about the therapeutic power of good humor and its imagined ability to cure pretty much every ill, I have been forced to confront a difficult truth: being funny is not making me a better person.

It seems like a generous impulse, to always be looking for openings to make others laugh, but most joke-tellers are interested in the validation, the approval. The laugh doesn't mean "I'm happy" to them; it just means "You're good" or "You're smart." They're not overly concerned with the broader effects of humor—as they often learn when a joke cuts a little closer than intended, or isn't recognized as a joke, or has an unintended victim. Then the Sarcastic One isn't merely off-putting; he or she might be actively making people feel bad. As science fiction author John Scalzi once wrote, in response to the default snarky tone of Internet conversation, "the failure mode of clever is 'asshole.'"

Why does nothing ever come out sounding *nicer* than we meant it? Why only meaner? I am weary, deeply weary, of people who always have something quick and clever to say. I find great solace in the company of people who are quiet and filled with a great light and generosity of spirit, like tall trees in a sunny glade, though I know I am not one of them, and perhaps never will be.

It's easier to tell a negative joke than a positive one, and so the undercurrent of a lot of humor is ridicule and scorn. In the process of writing this very book I find my unguarded tone slipping sometimes into the withering condescension of the critic—even on subjects I don't particularly dislike, even on subjects I don't particularly care about! The superiority is a coping strategy, the same insecure self-protection mechanism that made me a class clown as a kid. Have a funny take, get people laughing at something else, anything else, as long as it's not you. It takes effort and energy to fight the pull. In *Pride and Prejudice*, when Mr. Darcy grumps about people "whose first object in life is a joke," Elizabeth Bennet stops short. "I hope I never ridicule what is wise or good," she replies. That sentence should be in the text entry box of every comments section on the Internet.

I love those moments in comedy when the audience rallies around a performer baring his or her soul: Richard Pryor at the Palladium, Tig Notaro at Largo. But those sets were notable because they're so rare; they require a gifted performer and a tuned-in *congregation*, like in a revivalist's tent. The modern sense of humor, as we see it in daily life, is not often a voice of warmth and fellow feeling. Generally, we laugh *instead* of feeling empathy. Bergson was so sure that laughter was incomparible with emotion that he claimed that comedy demands "something like a momentary anesthesia of the heart." Clinical studies agree: people who enjoy cutting or macabre humor are less emotionally responsive to the situations of others. I tend to take pride in the fact that I'm not easily offended by jokes, but that's nothing to brag about if it blinds me to the sensitivities of others, because I wrongly assume they're as impervious as I am.

I recently clicked through to a web video of a car accident that had happened in my neighborhood. It was nighttime surveillance footage from a service station, looking down on two deserted lanes of gas pumps. Suddenly, after a few long seconds of stillness, an SUV careered into the frame, not down one of the lanes, but plowing across them all at a ridiculous speed. It collided with the gas pumps at the right edge of the frame, producing a massive fireball. Just like when the hawk swooped down on Kermit the baby bunny, my first reaction was a quick bark of laughter—even though I already knew from the headline that the accident took place just a few miles from my house and had, in fact, been fatal for a bystander. It's hard to imagine a scenario less fertile, on paper, for comedy. But the unexpected ending of the video, straight out of a violent cartoon, anesthetized my emotional response and replaced it for a fraction of a second with a comedy response. I laughed, and then I felt terrible about it.

The great satirist Tom Lehrer once wrote in his liner notes, "If, after hearing my songs, just one human being is inspired to say something nasty to a friend, or perhaps to strike a loved one, it will all have been worth the while." He was being sardonic, but he wasn't wrong. The effects of the jokes we tell aren't just limited to ourselves. Comedy can make us callous, and that callousness can radiate outward if we make "getting a laugh" our highest goal in life. We might be making other people meaner as well.

Inveterate jokers can also find themselves unable to escape their reputation: like the boy who cried wolf, no one takes them seriously when they're *not* trying to get laughs. Allen Funt, the host of *Candid Camera*, was flying with his family to Miami in 1969 when hijackers took over the plane, put a knife to the neck of a flight attendant, and demanded to be flown to Cuba. Everyone was terrified—until one woman recognized Funt. "It's a *Candid Camera* stunt!" she said. The whole plane started laughing and ignoring the hijackers. Some passengers even sent airsickness bags up to Funt's seat to be autographed. The merriment ended when the plane actually landed in Havana and the Cuban military boarded the plane. All the passengers filed by Funt one at a time, angry at him for "tricking" them. "Smile, my ass," said the last man as he passed.* I've never told so many jokes that I was blamed for terrorism, but I've certainly had the unpleasant experience of saying something into a mic, getting a laugh, and then having to insist that, hold on, that wasn't really the funny part. "When a man once puts on the cap and bells," wrote Josh Billings, "the world will insist upon hiz wearing them."

---

* In rare cases, Comedy Cassandra Syndrome can be fatal. Redd Foxx suffered a heart attack on a TV soundstage in 1991, while cast and crew laughed instead of immediately calling for medical help. They were convinced he was doing his famous "I'm coming, Elizabeth!" routine from *Sanford and Son*.

Surely You Can't Be Serious

There's an old joke about a man who's walking down the street and runs into a friend he hasn't seen in years. He immediately notices his friend has a big, round, bright orange head.

"Wow, what happened to you?" he asked.

"Oh, that," the friend says. "It's a long story. A few years ago I found an old lamp, and when I rubbed it, a genie came out and granted me three wishes. For my first wish, I asked for a hundred million dollars, which is how I got all my money. For my second wish, I asked to have the most beautiful woman in the world fall in love with me. And that's how I met my wonderful wife.

"For my third wish—and this is where I think I may have gone horribly, horribly wrong—I asked to have a big, round, bright orange head."

It's important to remember that the reason for our comedy-choked world is that *we wished it this way*. It feels undeniably good to laugh; that's how our brains evolved. And there's nothing wrong with that! In writing this book, I come to praise comedy, not to bury it. You could tell the story of my life in the things that have made me laugh, and even spool it up like the supercut of kisses at the end of *Cinema Paradiso*. Buster Keaton battling a windstorm, Groucho dancing with Margaret Dumont, the *SNL* "men's synchronized swimming" sketch, that old *Batman* comic from 1951 where the Joker keeps saying "boners," Patrice O'Neal sparring with the chicken fingers lady, Holly Hunter crying in *Raising Arizona*, any sentence in any Charles Portis novel, the bathroom nosebleed scene in *Veep*, David Letterman tugging on his jacket lapels so his striped tie would dance, that web video where the dog gets his head stuck under the couch, any web video where a skateboarder wipes out, Jack Soo eating the hash brownies on *Barney Miller*, Joel and the 'Bots roasting *Attack of the Eye Creatures*, General Ripper's "precious bodily fluids," the game show episode of *BoJack Horseman*, Eddie Murphy calling his stepfather at the end of *Raw*, the megaphone crooners from *Mr. Show*, "Marriage" by Gregory Corso, Bart Simpson tricking Milhouse into thinking he never had a goldfish, the *Onion* piece about the fun toy banned thanks to "three stupid dead kids," the credits of *The Palm Beach Story*, Amy Sedaris flirting as Jerri Blank, the way Owen Wilson says "Look at these assholes" in *The Darjeeling Limited*, Lucy Ricardo with her head stuck in a trophy, the incomprehensible tweets of Senator Chuck Grassley (R-IA), that home run that bounced off Jose Canseco's head, "Business Time" by Flight of the Conchords, Jackie Chan with or on a ladder, Artie heckling Hank Kingsley in the mermaid costume, Bugs Bunny and Yosemite Sam on the high-dive platform. It could go on for days.

But what I'm saying is this: Comedy already had comedy. Did it also need news and politics and advertising and all the rest? Our wish for an endlessly amusing world came true, but my fear is that we didn't consider the risks. What if it all went horribly wrong?

Maybe it's too late for me, or society at large, to change our smart-alecky ways. The Tirynthians may very well have been right that "an inveterate custom cannot be remedied." But it might do us good to try. If I were to make a Jonathan Swift–style modest proposal, it wouldn't be that we cook and eat comedians, or even their babies. It would be as simple as this: let's keep some part of the public sphere laughter-optional, so that serious engagement and earnest emotion don't become completely taboo.

We can do this in small ways. We can advocate for things we believe sometimes, instead of satirically adopting the opposing view. We can supplement our diet of comedy news shows with actual journalism. We can ensure that our decisions—as both consumers and citizens—are based on the merits of the products or issues or candidates involved, not just on the funny messaging. We can take breaks from social media, so our brains don't settle on hundreds of jokes an hour as the new normal. We can spend time in nature, which hasn't gotten notably funnier since the platypus evolved twenty million years ago.

We can look for chances to talk about things we enjoy, not just ridicule the things we don't. We can ask ourselves what others need to hear, not what we could amuse ourselves by saying. We can genuinely listen to them, rather than look for openings to crack jokes. We can acknowledge compliments instead of deflecting them with nervous quips. We can skip the affectionate jabs and roasts sometimes and just tell the people we love how much they mean to us.

None of this sounds funny at all, I know. But it'll just be for a second, and you'll feel good, and then I promise you can take a breath and get back to the jokes.

NOTES

ONE: OUR FUNNY CENTURY

4 88 percent of millennials: Bill Carter, "In the Tastes of Young Men, Humor Is Most Prized, a Survey Finds," *New York Times*, February 19, 2012.

5 consult Frinkiac: http://www.frinkiac.com. They have the Internet on computers now!

5 "Nothing disturbing happens": "Kazakhstan in the 21st Century: Looking Outward," *New York Times* advertising supplement, September 27, 2006

5 Hingle McCringleberry: Scott Rafferty, "Key and Peele Paid Von Miller's Fine for Imitating 'Three-Pump,'" *Rolling Stone*, August 11, 2017, http://www.rollingstone.com /sports/news/key-explains-why-he-and-peele-paid-von-millers-2015-fine-w497247.

5 interview the Dalai Lama: "The Dalai Lama Walks into a Pizza Shop . . . ," *Today* television clip, June 9, 2011, https://www.youtube.com/watch?v=x1Irl80og8c.

5 interview with Benito Mussolini: Robert Benchley, "Mr. Benchley Interviews Benito Mussolini," *Life*, April 8, 1926.

5 Bugs Bunny terrorized Hitler: The Führer appeared in no fewer than thirteen Looney Tunes cartoons. He and Goering were Bugs's targets in 1945's "Herr Meets Hare," also the first short in which Bugs ever notes that he should have taken that "left turn at Albuquerque."

6 Hitler ever even saw it: Chaplin told friends that, according to a Nazi émigré, Hitler had privately screened the film twice, but this is impossible to verify. Henry Gonshak, *Hollywood and the Holocaust* (London: Rowman & Littlefield, 2015), p. 25. After the war, Albert Speer told American journalists that the Reich had indeed obtained a print of *The Great Dictator* via neutral Portugal, but Hitler himself had never watched it. Niels Kadritzke, "Führer befiehl, wir lachen!" *Süddeutsche Zeitung*, January 12, 2007.

6 "the most blatant act": Abby Phillip, "North Korea Threatens 'Merciless' Retaliation over James Franco and Seth Rogen Assassination Comedy," *Washington Post*, June 25, 2014.

6 rewriting the ending: Meg James, Daniel Miller, and Josh Rottenberg, "Sony Pictures Execs Debated Risk of *The Interview* Before Cyberattack," *Los Angeles Times*, December 9, 2014.

6 "Some kind of humanitarian disaster": Melissa Maroff, "*The Interview:* An 'Act of War,'" *Creative Screenwriting*, December 18, 2014.

7 Bowen made headlines: "Dead Parrot sketch ancestor found," BBC News, November 13, 2008, http://news.bbc.co.uk/2/hi/entertainment/7725079.stm.

8 *SeinLanguage:* Bill Cosby's bestseller *Fatherhood* and its 1980s follow-ups predated *Sein-Language*, but Seinfeld's book was the one that kick-started a trend, selling so many copies that publishers were throwing briefcases full of money at every sitcom comedian in America: Tim Allen, Paul Reiser, Ellen DeGeneres. (By 1996, even Sinbad had a book deal.) Also, unlike Cosby, Seinfeld didn't use a ghostwriter.

8 Gloria Steinem and Amy Schumer: Steinem can be seen with the squad on Schumer's Instagram at https://www.instagram.com/p/BCmUODwKUJ5.

9 overstated in the press: Ethan Epstein, "The Myth of Jon Stewart's 'Millennial' Following," *Weekly Standard*, February 11, 2015.

9 the same reach as *USA Today:* Amy Mitchell, Jeffrey Gottfried, Jocelyn Kiley, and Katerina Eva Matsa, *Political Polarization & Media Habits*, Pew Research Center, October 21, 2014.

9 repeatedly neutered: The travails of the Smothers Brothers are the first of the four case studies in David S. Silverman, *You Can't Air That: Four Cases of Controversy and Censorship in American Television Programming* (Syracuse: Syracuse University Press, 2007).

10 highest-paid performer: Stephen Battaglio and Michael Schneider, "TV's Highest Paid Stars: What They Earn," *TV Guide*, August 20, 2013.

10 secretly summoned Stewart: Chris Smith, *The Daily Show (The Book): An Oral History* (New York: Grand Central, 2016), p. 359.

11 "O, laugh, laughers!": This translation drawn from *From the Ends to the Beginning: A Bilingual Anthology of Russian Verse*, an online archive translated by Tatiana Tulchinsky, Andrew Wachtel, and Gwenan Wilbur, http://max.mmlc.northwestern.edu/mdenner/Demo/texts/invocation_laugh.html.

11 "laws of time": Raymond Cooke, *Velimir Khlebnikov: A Critical Study* (Cambridge: Cambridge University Press, 1987), p. 148.

14 a lavatory urinal: Sophie Howarth and Jennifer Mundy, "*Fountain*," Tate Modern, http://www.tate.org.uk/art/artworks/duchamp-fountain-t07573.

15 "is a machine for living in": Le Corbusier, *Towards a New Architecture* (Mineola, N.Y.: Dover, 1986), p. 95.

15 "For a building, is it funny?": Bruce Handy, "A *Spy* Guide to Postmodern Everything," *Spy*, April 1988.

15 young Cassius Clay: David Remnick, *King of the World: Muhammad Ali and the Rise of an American Hero* (New York: Vintage, 1999), p. 120.

16 to a man, not funny: Babe Ruth was a sleepy-eyed white man with a beer belly, but he was also a quotable, larger-than-life megacelebrity, making him the most prominent exception here.

17 "What a revoltin' development!": Lee himself always credited Durante. The Thing first borrows the radio catchphrase in Stan Lee and Jack Kirby, "Calamity on the Campus," *The Fantastic Four* 35, February 1965.

17 "Well it's not Dr. Kildare": Stan Lee and Steve Ditko, "Nothing Can Stop . . . the Sandman!," *The Amazing Spider-Man* 4, September 1963.

17 "I sure ain't Albert Schweitzer": Stan Lee and Steve Ditko, "The Strangest Foe of All Time . . . Doctor Octopus," *The Amazing Spider-Man* 3, July 1963.

18 "Like costume heroes?": Stan Lee and Steve Ditko, "Spider-Man!," *Amazing Fantasy* 15, August 1962.

19 chic novelties: These sound like made-up dishes, but they're real. The mango ravioli and black-olive Oreos were mainstays at elBulli before it closed in 2011. The edible fob watch and mandarin orange "meat fruit" are Heston Blumenthal's, from the Fat Duck and Dinner, respectively.

21 "There were more jokes": Joe Randazzo, *Funny on Purpose: The Definitive Guide to an Unpredictable Career in Comedy* (San Francisco: Chronicle, 2015), p. 43.

21 The headline in the print edition: Kate Murphy, "Killing a Patient to Save His Life," *New York Times*, June 9, 2014.

21 a YouTube-famous band: The musicians are Scott Bradlee and Postmodern Jukebox, and the recording can be viewed on UberConference's corporate blog at http://blog .uberconference.com/2014/05/im-on-hold-with-scott-bradlee-postmodern-jukebox.

21 "the best buns": Jena McGregor, "Even on This, America Is Divided: Was Cinnabon's Carrie Fisher Tweet Offensive?" *Washington Post*, December 28, 2016.

23 popularity is predicted: Lawrence W. Sherman, "Humor and Social Distance in Elementary School Children," *Humor: The International Journal of Humor Research* 1, no. 4 (1988), pp. 389–404.

24 "Comedy is controlling": *WTF with Marc Maron*, episode 578, February 19, 2015.

25 "An Orwellian world": Neil Postman, *Amusing Ourselves to Death: Public Discourse in the Age of Show Business* (New York: Viking, 1985), p. 156.

25 "junk entertainment": Ibid., p. 159.

26 the "Weekend Update" desk: Al Franken and Lorne Michaels agree that this is why Franken left *SNL* in James Andrew Miller and Tom Shales, *Live from New York: The Complete, Uncensored History of "Saturday Night Live"* (New York: Little, Brown, 2014), p. 410.

TWO: FUNNY FOR NO REASON

28 "Whenever we go out": *Premium Blend*, season 2, episode 1, Comedy Central, May 23, 1998.

29 "That comes with": *John Mulaney: New in Town*, Comedy Central, January 28, 2012.

33 "Analyzing Humor": The actual quote is substantially less pithy than the version usually quoted today: "Humor can be dissected, as a frog can, but the thing dies in the process and the innards are discouraging to any but the pure scientific mind." Is this how White sounded when he wasn't being edited by Harold Ross? E. B. White and Katharine S. White, eds., *A Subtreasury of American Humor* (New York: Coward-McCann, 1941), p. xvii.

33 "a man with any tincture": Cicero, *De Oratore* 2.54.

33 "In order to laugh": Robert Benchley, "Why We Laugh—or Do We?" *New Yorker*, January 2, 1937.

34 cringe-y story: Peter McGraw and Joel Warner, *The Humor Code: A Global Search for What Makes Things Funny* (New York: Simon & Schuster, 2014), p. 18.

36 "The passion of laughter": Thomas Hobbes, *The Elements of Law, Natural and Politic*, ed. J. C. A. Gaskin (1640; Oxford: Oxford University Press, 1994), p. 54.

36 "intensely melancholy": George Henry Lewes, *The History of Philosophy from Thales to Comte*, 3rd ed., vol. 1, *Ancient Philosophy* (London: Longmans, Green, 1867), p. 203.

36 "was never seen to laugh": Or so said Heraclides of Lembos, according to Diogenes Laertius. Alice Swift Riginos, *Platonica: The Anecdotes Concerning the Life and Writings of Plato* (Leiden, Neth: E. J. Brill, 1976), p. 151.

36 "As sad as Plato": Lewes, *History of Philosophy*, p. 204.

36 "Most people delight": Aristotle, *The Nicomachean Ethics*, ed. Lesley Brown, trans. David Ross (Oxford: Oxford University Press, 2009), p. 78.

37 a David Mitchell bit: American readers may not be familiar with Mitchell, who is a major TV star in his native Britain. Please consult the Internet for Mitchell's most essential

panel show appearances and highlights from his several series done with sketch partner Robert Webb. That's Numberwang!

37 "Nervous excitation": Herbert Spencer, "The Physiology of Laughter," in *Essays: Scientific, Political and Speculative* (London: Routledge/Thoemmes, 1996), 1:453.

38 our mothers' nipples: "So far as I know, the grimace characteristic of smiling, which twists up the corners of the mouth, appears first in an infant at the breast when it is satisfied and satiated and lets go of the breast as it falls asleep." Sigmund Freud, *Jokes and Their Relation to the Unconscious*, trans. and ed. James Strachey (New York: W. W. Norton, 1960), p. 179.

38 Shurcliff conducted: Arthur Shurcliff, "Judged Humor, Arousal, and the Relief Theory," *Journal of Personality and Social Psychology* 8, no. 4 (April 1968), pp. 360–63.

38 "Laughter is an affection": Immanuel Kant, *Critique of Judgment*, trans. and ed. J. H. Bernard (London: Macmillan, 1892), p. 223.

39 a famous 1970 experiment: Göran Nerhardt, "Humor and Inclination to Laugh: Emotional Reactions to Stimuli of Different Divergence from a Range of Expectancy," *Scandinavian Journal of Psychology* 11, no. 3 (September 1970), pp. 185–95.

40 a web video: "Bunnies Can Fly . . . Proof," September 25, 2013, https://www.youtube .com/watch?v=IxFfxTZA6ao.

41 "The correct explanation": Max Eastman, *Enjoyment of Laughter* (New York: Halcyon, 1939), p. 41.

41 genesis of the joke: "Such a Clean Old Man," *A Hard Day's Night* DVD supplement, Miramax, 2002.

42 six thousand nonsense words: Chris Westbury et al., "Telling the World's Least Funny Jokes: On the Quantification of Humor as Entropy," *Journal of Memory and Language* 86 (January 2016), pp. 141–56.

42 except in two areas: Willibald Ruch and Sigrid Rath, "The Nature of Humor Appreciation: Toward an Integration of Perception of Stimulus Properties and Affective Experience," *Humor: The International Journal of Humor Research* 6, no. 4 (1993), pp. 363–84.

43 Charles Addams drew: "The Skier," *New Yorker*, January 13, 1940. Addams was paid $45 for the cartoon that, to his surprise, made him world-famous. Linda H. Davis, *Charles Addams: A Cartoonist's Life* (New York: Random House, 2006), p. 62.

43 "the lunacy is no longer incipient": Wolcott Gibbs, introduction to *Addams and Evil* (New York: Random House, 1947), p. iii.

43 Hammer was bewildered: "The Press: Puzzle," *Time*, October 7, 1946.

43 the word "Zamboni": Schulz's 1970s-era conviction that ice sports were terribly funny is one of *Peanuts*'s odder legacies, and probably owes much to the Santa Rosa, California, ice rink that Schulz opened in 1969.

44 "sweaty" comedy: Mike Sacks, *And Here's the Kicker: Conversations with 21 Top Humor Writers About Their Craft* (Cincinnati: Writer's Digest, 2017), p. 208.

44 "*ready-to-sting bees*": *The Simpsons*, season 11, episode 22, "Behind the Laughter," Fox, May 21, 2000.

45 "Election Night Special": *Monty Python's Flying Circus*, series 2, episode 6, "It's a Living (or: School Prizes)," BBC, November 3, 1970.

45 "We know the degree": George Meredith, "On the Idea of Comedy and of the Uses of the Comic Spirit," in *The Works of George Meredith*, vol. 23 (New York: Scribner, 1910), p. 49.

46 "Nothing odd will do": James Boswell, *The Life of Samuel Johnson* (London: John Sharpe, 1830), p. 304.

46 "The highest part of this mountain": These excerpts from Ward's stage lectures, as well as the review that ends this paragraph, from "Artemus Ward," *Spectator*, November 24, 1866.

46 "that true Transatlantic type": Ward's conquest of England is considered in Eastman, *Enjoyment of Laughter*, p. 173.

46 "He conkerd the world": Melville D. Landon, "Traveling with Artemus Ward," *Galaxy*, September 1871. "Eli Perkins" was the pseudonym of Melville Landon, just as "Artemus Ward" was a creation of Charles Farrar Browne and "Josh Billings" was Henry Wheeler Shaw.

46 "Essa on the Muel": David B. Kesterson, "The Literary Comedians and the Language of Humor," *Studies in American Humor* 1, no. 1 (June 1982), pp. 44–51.

47 gelotophyllis: Mary Beard, *Laughter in Ancient Rome: On Joking, Tickling, and Cracking Up* (Berkeley: University of California Press, 2014), p. 25.

48 "I went into a place": Steven Wright, *I Have a Pony*, WEA International, 1985

48 "If you ever drop": Jack Handey, *Deeper Thoughts* (New York: Hyperion, 1993), p. 3.

48 "I protest that I do": Max Beerbohm, *And Even Now* (New York: E. P. Dutton, 1921), p. 306.

48 a 2006 experiment: Jennifer Uekermann, Shelley Channon, and Irene Daum, "Humor Processing, Mentalizing, and Executive Function in Normal Aging," *Journal of the International Neuropsychological Society* 12, no. 2 (March 2006), pp. 184–91.

50 *Simon & Simon* opening credits: This was, believe it or not, a real thing. *The Greatest Event in Television History* aired on Adult Swim on October 12, 2012. Subsequent installments reenacted the credits of *Hart to Hart*, *Too Close for Comfort*, and *Bosom Buddies*.

50 a 2015 episode: *Rick and Morty*, season 2, episode 10, "The Wedding Squanchers," Cartoon Network, October 4, 2015.

50 "Why are cobs so terrifying?": "A *Rick and Morty* Opera: The Terrible Cobs," September 14, 2016, https://www.youtube.com/watch?v=j2cCwEP1SiA.

51 "There are few good": Gene Perret, *Comedy Writing Step by Step* (Hollywood: Samuel French, 1990), p. 49.

52 making of a sketch show: *W/ Bob & David*, episode 5, "Behind the Making of the Scenes," Netflix, November 13, 2015.

53 "won't stand much blowing up": White, *Subtreasury of American Humor*, p. xviii.

53 "Life is a tragedy": The quote was attributed to Chaplin by Richard Roud, cofounder of the New York Film Festival, in 1972. Carol Kramer, " 'Little Tramp' Triumphs: Chaplin Savors His Renaissance," *Chicago Tribune*, April 6, 1972.

53 "It seemed to me that": Hugh Kenner, *Chuck Jones: A Flurry of Drawing* (Berkeley: University of California Press, 1994), p. 47.

53 a *Simpsons* episode: The episode was the Lego-centric "Brick Like Me," which eventually aired on May 4, 2014.

54 "Antique funnyings": Eastman, *Enjoyment of Laughter*, p. 213.

56 *Hogan's Heroes*: Greg Steinmetz, "In Germany, *Hogan's Heroes*, Loosely Translated, Is a Hit," *Wall Street Journal*, May 31, 1996.

56 back to Cicero: In *De Oratore* 2.59–61, Cicero distinguished between jokes contained in the wording (*de dicto*) and those contained in the thing itself (*de re*); the latter kind of joke, he noted, will "lose its pungency" if the words are changed.

56 "A man narrowly misses": Christie Davies, *Ethnic Humor Around the World: A Comparative Analysis* (Bloomington: Indiana University Press, 1990), p. 221.

58 two comedians golf: This was, believe it or not, a real thing. The two comedians were playing for real, to benefit real charities. *The Adult Swim Golf Classic* aired on Adult Swim on April 8, 2016.

59 "at least it's funny": As Max Eastman put it, "[The mystic] declares that all the failures and imperfections in the bitter current of time's reality are a part of God's eternal perfection, and so he makes himself happy to suffer them. The humorist declares that they are funny, and he accomplishes the same thing." Max Eastman, *The Sense of Humor* (New York: Scribner, 1921), p. 24.

59 "Jokester": *Isaac Asimov: The Complete Stories*, vol. 1 (New York: Broadway, 1990), pp. 123–34.

THREE: THE MARCH OF PROGRESS

61 his second hit comedy album: Woody Allen, *Volume 2*, Colpix, 1965.

62 his 1971 *Tonight Show* debut: *The Tonight Show*, NBC, January 8, 1971.

63 the seat of humor: "This part is also the chief seat of gaiety of mind, a fact which is more particularly proved by the titillation of the arm-holes." "Titillation of the arm-holes"?! Pliny, *Natural History*, trans. and ed. John Bostock and H. T. Riley (London: Henry G. Bohn, 1857), 3:70.

63 London scientists: Vinod Goel and Raymond J. Dolan, "The Functional Anatomy of Humor: Segregating Cognitive and Affective Components," *Nature Neuroscience* 4, no. 3 (March 2001), pp. 237–38.

63 one done at Stanford: Dean Mobbs et al., "Humor Modulates the Mesolimbic Reward Centers," *Neuron* 40 (December 4, 2003), pp. 1041–48.

63 zapping a certain area: Itzhak Fried et al., "Electric Current Stimulates Laughter," *Nature* 391 (February 12, 1998), p. 650.

64 expanded into a book: Matthew M. Hurley, Daniel C. Dennett, and Reginald B. Adams Jr., *Inside Jokes: Using Humor to Reverse-Engineer the Mind* (Cambridge, Mass.: MIT Press, 2011).

64 "benign violation" theory: McGraw and Warner, *Humor Code*, p. 10.

65 modern jokes are cheats: The *Inside Jokes* authors memorably refer to this process—creating artificial incongruities for ourselves that we can quickly debug—as "a sort of mental masturbation, rewarded not with orgasm but with mirth." Hurley et al., *Inside Jokes*, p. 294.

66 the character Gelasimus: Beard, *Laughter in Ancient Rome*, p. 149.

66 "When the garrulous barber": *Philogelos*, trans. and ed. William Berg (London: YUDU, 2008), p. 55, http://publishing.yudu.com/Library/Au7bv/PhilogelosTheLaughAd.

66 politician Enoch Powell: Beard, *Laughter in Ancient Rome*, p. 213. Beard points out that Powell—best known for his race-baiting 1968 "Rivers of Blood" speech, about the evils of immigration—was a classical scholar before entering politics, and may have been very aware of the ancient origins of his joke.

66 Mark Twain was right: Mark Twain, *A Connecticut Yankee in King Arthur's Court* (London: Penguin, 1971), p. 60.

67 a standard baseball routine: Kliph Nesteroff, *The Comedians: Drunks, Thieves, Scoundrels and the History of American Comedy* (New York: Grove, 2015), p. 31.

67 Milton Berle lifted: Ibid., p. 19.

67 "According to my records": Eastman, *Enjoyment of Laughter*, p. 93.

67 unforgettable sixth episode: *Freaks and Geeks*, episode 6, "I'm with the Band," NBC, November 13, 1999.

68 "Advances are made": Mike Sacks, *Poking a Dead Frog: Conversations with Today's Top Comedy Writers* (New York: Penguin, 2014), p. 12.

68 his second one-man show: Mike Birbiglia, *My Girlfriend's Boyfriend*, Comedy Dynamics, 2013.

69 a 1971 *Esquire* article: "Albert Brooks' Famous School for Comedians," *Esquire*, February 1971. The subsequent short film aired later that year on PBS's *The Great American Dream Machine* and was finally released on home video by S'more Entertainment in 2015.

69 interview with Noel Gallagher: David Walliams, "The Gallagher Interview in Full," *Observer Music Monthly*, June 2005. "They're not even English!" his brother Noel patiently explains to him. "One of them is married to Jamie Lee Curtis." "'I'm not f— kin' 'avin' that," Liam replies, and marches right out of the Spinal Tap concert. I laugh *every single time* I read this interview.

70 first comedy record: Hannibal Buress, *My Name Is Hannibal!*, Stand Up! Records, 2010.

70 the audience remembered: In 2014's *I'm Sorry You Feel That Way*, Burr introduces a bit about buying a .22 by saying, "The last time I came through town, I wanted to get a gun." The Atlanta audience immediately laughs, remembering the first line of *You People Are All the Same*—"I wanna buy a gun!"—which Burr recorded in 2012 at the very same theater.

70 a full year: Episodes 30 (March 15, 2015) and 65 (March 20, 2016), respectively, of the HBO hit.

71 "Army Surplus Office Supply": *Arrested Development*, season 2, episode 11, "Out on a Limb," Fox, March 6, 2005.

71 their third thought: Adam McKay interviewed in Sacks, *Poking a Dead Frog*, p. 123.

72 five hundred headlines: Todd Hanson interviewed in Sacks, *And Here's the Kicker*, p. 141.

72 "The current tax code": Dennis Miller, *I Rant, Therefore I Am* (New York: Broadway, 2001), p. 173.

72 "Dennis Miller Ratio": *The Simpsons*, season 10, episode 22, "They Saved Lisa's Brain," Fox, May 9, 1999. (For the record, Professor Frink uses it to describe his "C:\DOS\ RUN" T-shirt.)

72 dropped rhymes: Garfunkel and Oates, "Fadeaway," *Secretions*, No One Buys Records, September 10, 2015.

72 imagined Dan Cortese: *Saturday Night Live*, season 40, episode 3, NBC, October 11, 2014. Mulaney copped to swapping in jokes hoping to get Hader to "break" in Miller and Shales, *Live from New York*, p. 611.

73 Oksana Baiul: *Family Guy*, season 2, episode 20, "Wasted Talent," Fox, July 25, 2000.

73 "Tillie Olsen": Patton Oswalt, *Werewolves and Lollipops*, Sub Pop, 2007.

73 "An Englishman wants": *The Complete Works of Josh Billings* (New York: G. W. Dillingham, 1876), pp. 435–36.

74 "Mark Twain can": Eastman, *Enjoyment of Laughter*, p. 170.

74 "To-day the joke": W. D. Nesbit, "The Humor of To-Day," *Independent*, May 29, 1902.

74 "*The New Yorker* will be": [Harold Ross], "Of All Things," *New Yorker*, February 21, 1925.

74 no New York paper: Nesbit, "The Humor of To-Day."

74 "astonished and alarmed": [Harold Ross?], "Of All Things," *New Yorker*, February 28, 1925.

74 "like their roads": *The Essential Samuel Butler*, ed. G. D. H. Cole (London: Jonathan Cape, 1950), p. 519.

75 "Its essence lies": Stephen Leacock, ed., *The Greatest Pages of American Humor* (Garden City, N.Y.: Sun Dial Press, 1936), p. 271.

75 "The minimum amount": *Talking Funny*, HBO, April 20, 2011.

76 *one more example:* I am indebted here to Art Spiegelman (as related by Scott McCloud), who once noted cartoonist Ernie Bushmiller's economy in always drawing exactly three rocks to convey "some rocks" in his minimalist comic strip *Nancy.* Two rocks would not be "some rocks," you see. Four rocks *would* be "some rocks," *but it would be one rock more than was necessary!*

76 "Today, I was": Steven Wright, *The Tonight Show*, NBC, August 6, 1982.

76 "Tonight's forecast": From his variety show character Al Sleet, the "hippie-dippie weatherman." George Carlin, *FM & AM*, Little David Records, 1972.

76 court stenographer: Nesteroff, *The Comedians*, p. 299.

78 bit cost $12,000: Horace Newcomb, ed., *Encyclopedia of Television*, 2nd ed. (London: Routledge, 2004), p. 814. In today's money, that would be well over $100,000 that Dutch Masters cigars paid to, quite literally, be thrown into a hole. Kovacs left his wife, Edie Adams, deep in debt when he died in a 1962 car accident. He lost control of his car while trying to light one of his trademark cigars.

78 "That's *not* a television show!": Nesteroff, *The Comedians*, p. 200.

80 forty million American adults: The Anxiety and Depression Association of America, https://adaa.org/about-adaa/press-room/facts-statistics.

80 the Good Samaritan: John M. Darley and C. Daniel Batson, "'From Jerusalem to Jericho': A Study of Situational and Dispositional Variables in Helping Behavior," *Journal of Personality and Social Psychology* 27, no. 1 (July 1973), pp. 100–8.

81 "Where am I going to get": Plautus, *Persa* 157–60.

81 "I do this kind of stuff": "Wabbit Twouble," *Merrie Melodies*, Warner Bros., 1941.

81 "Now's the time": *The Road to Bali*, Paramount, 1952.

82 "What an odd remark!": *The Simpsons*, season 4, episode 20, "Whacking Day," Fox, April 29, 1993.

82 "There's got to be": *Arrested Development*, season 2, episode 1, "The One Where Michael Lives," Fox, November 7, 2004.

83 Kindler wrote: Andy Kindler, "The Hack's Handbook: A Starter Kit," *National Lampoon*, February 1991.

83 *New York Times* piece: Jason Zinoman, "Andy Kindler Gives the Funny Business Its Annual Review," *New York Times*, July 22, 2015.

84 every comedy record: Billy Crystal, *700 Sundays* (New York: Warner, 2005), p. 90.

84 "My Favorite Jokes": Judd Apatow, *Sick in the Head: Conversations About Life and Comedy* (New York: Random House, 2015), p. 306.

84 green tape recorder: Ibid., p. xiv.

84 most successful documentaries: *The Aristocrats* earned $6.3 million at the U.S. box office, putting it among the top ten highest-grossing documentaries ever at the time of its release (not allowing for inflation). *Box Office Mojo,* http://www.boxofficemojo.com /genres/chart/?id=documentary.htm.

85 an expensive flop: James L. Neibaur, *The Fall of Buster Keaton: His Films for MGM, Educational Pictures, and Columbia* (Lanham, Md.: Scarecrow, 2010), p. x.

85 Harrison mortgaged: Eric Idle interviewed in *The Pythons: Autobiography by the Pythons* (New York: Thomas Dunne, 2003), p. 285.

85 women's lawn bowling: Stephen Merchant interviewed in Sacks, *And Here's the Kicker*, p. 22.

85 "The most successful": Mitchell Hurwitz interviewed in Sacks, *And Here's the Kicker*, p. 177.

87 "If you want to make": Virginia Hefferman, "Anchor Woman," *New Yorker*, November 3, 2003.

FOUR: NOTES FROM AN EPIDEMIC

89 Gary Gilmore: David Gianatasio, "Nike's 'Just Do It,' the Last Great Advertising Slogan, Turns 25," *Adweek*, July 2, 2013.

91 "Be serious": David Ogilvy, *Confessions of an Advertising Man* (London: Southbank, 2004), p. 166.

91 "To Wake Up GAY": Jim Heimann, ed., *All-American Ads 40s* (Cologne: Taschen, 2001), p. 410.

91 "I don't know what I hate": *Mad Men*, season 1, episode 3, "Marriage of Figaro," AMC, August 2, 2007.

92 "It's either a big bargain": Melvin Helitzer, *Comedy Techniques for Writers and Performers* (Athens, Oh.: Lawhead, 1984), p. 287.

92 "We have agencies": Gerald Nachman, *Seriously Funny: The Rebel Comedians of the 1950s and 1960s* (New York: Pantheon, 2003), p. 193.

92 refused to shill for tobacco: Stan Freberg, *It Only Hurts When I Laugh* (New York: Times, 1988), p. 117.

92 last network comedy show: Ibid., p. 118.

93 "the father of the funny commercial": Douglas Martin, "Stan Freberg, Madcap Adman and Satirist, Dies at 88," *New York Times*, April 7, 2015.

93 twenty-one Clio awards: Ibid.

93 120,000 encyclopedias: "Encyclopedia Britannica Ends 244 Years of Print," Associated Press, March 14, 2012.

94 "Smell Like a Man, Man": "Old Spice | The Man Your Man Could Smell Like," February 4, 2010, https://www.youtube.com/watch?v=owGykVbfgUE.

94 viewed thirteen million times: Andrew Adam Newman, "Old Spice Argues that Real Men Smell Good," *New York Times*, July 15, 2010.

95 Ogilvy famously recanted: David Ogilvy and Joel Raphaelson, "Research on Advertising Techniques That Work—and Don't Work," *Harvard Business Review* 60, no. 4 (July–August 1982), pp. 14–16.

95 buying the gorditas: Greg Hernandez and Greg Johnson, "Taco Bell Replaces Chief, Chihuahua as Sales Fall," *Los Angeles Times*, July 19, 2000.

97 "funny or light-hearted": "Does Humor Make Ads More Effective?" *Millward Brown Perspectives* 6, no. 3 (September 2013), p. 23. Of the most impactful ads, fully 69 percent used humor.

97 just 2.5 percent: Anupreeta Das, "Berkshire Sees Green with Geico," *Wall Street Journal*, August 24, 2014. Over the next decade, Geico's annual advertising expenditure increased sixteen-fold.

98 Sixty-four percent: Gerry Smith, "Some Hits, Misses in Super Bowl Ads," *Boston Globe*, February 2, 2015.

98 left Nationwide: Ashley Rodriguez, "Nationwide CMO Exits in Wake of 'Dead Boy' Super Bowl Ad," *Ad Age*, May 6, 2015.

99   362 paid media ads: Media Dynamics, *America's Media Usage & Ad Exposure: 1945–2014*, September 21, 2014.

99   Beard opined: Fred K. Beard, "Advertisement," in *Encyclopedia of Humor Studies*, ed. Salvatore Attardo (London: SAGE, 2014), p. 4.

99   Williams admitted: Kevin Maney, "Why Twitter Is More CB Radio Than Uber," *Newsweek*, August 8, 2015.

100   DID YOU KNOW!: Ken Jennings (@KenJennings), Twitter, February 15, 2011, https://twitter.com/KenJennings/status/37504161998180352.

101   the brothers Grimm: Jan Bremmer and Herman Roodenburg, eds., *A Cultural History of Humour* (Cambridge, UK: Polity, 1997), p. 8.

101   corn that grew so fast: These colorful examples are drawn from Constance Rourke's monumental work on frontier jokes, *American Humor: A Study of the National Character* (New York: Harcourt, Brace, 1931), pp. 47, 49, 60.

102   "an existence of jumpiness": James Thurber, *My Life and Hard Times* (New York: HarperPerennial, 1999), p. xx.

102   "look so swell": Eastman, *Enjoyment of Laughter*, p. 343.

102   Fourth of July picnic: Wes Gehring, "Oh, Why Couldn't It Have Been Robert?" *Humor: The International Journal of Humor Research* 6, no. 3 (1993), pp. 285–98.

105   YouTube's reputation: Nate Anderson, "Did 'Lazy Sunday' Make YouTube's $1.5 Billion Sale Possible?" Ars Technica, November 23, 2008, https://arstechnica.com/uncategorized/2008/11/did-lazy-sunday-make-youtubes-1-5-billion-sale-possible.

105   This chart: Tim Brooks and Earle Marsh, *The Complete Directory to Prime Time Network and Cable TV Shows, 1946–Present*, 9th ed. (New York: Ballantine, 2007), pp. 1687, 1692.

107   "bits of humor": Daniel Yee, "With a Wag of the Finger, Delta Produces Safety Video," *Pittsburgh Post-Gazette*, April 2, 2008.

109   "Thirty-three percent": Relayed to me by *Conan* writer Rob Kutner.

110   plans to do so: Matt Kempner, "Funny Flight Videos Might Keep Us Alive. Or Not," *Atlanta Journal-Constitution*, August 13, 2015.

110   In a 2014 experiment: Brett R. C. Molesworth, "Examining the Effectiveness of Pre-Flight Cabin Safety Announcements in Commercial Aviation," *International Journal of Aviation Psychology* 24, no. 4 (2014), pp. 300–14.

110   "A brief moment of happiness": Zachary M. Seward, "Jerry Seinfeld Ripped Apart the Advertising Industry on Its Biggest Night," *Quartz*, October 5, 2014, https://qz.com/276396.

FIVE: A LITTLE MORE CONVERSATION

114   a *scurra*: Beard, *Laughter in Ancient Rome*, pp. 152–53.

114   "brought from home": Cicero *Orator* 89.

115   then memorize them: Eastman, *Enjoyment of Laughter*, p. 300.

115   an emergency understudy: Drummer-turned-comic Herkie Styles. Nesteroff, *The Comedians*, p. 226.

115   arrested fifteen times: Paul Krassner, "Remembering Lenny Bruce, 50 Years after His Death," *Los Angeles Times*, July 28, 2016.

115   "Christ and Moses": Lenny Bruce, *The Carnegie Hall Concert*, Blue Note, 1995.

115   Berman telephone routines: Today, we associate this kind of comedy monologue with Bob Newhart, but Newhart got it from Berman. These routines are on *The Sick Humor of Lenny Bruce*, Fantasy, 1959.

117 Netflix special: Todd Barry, *The Crowd Work Tour*, Netflix, 2014.

117 "I'm sorry": Ralph Gleason, "The Trials of Lenny Bruce," *Guardian*, April 27, 1965.

118 Forty-two million Americans: The listenership statistics here are all drawn from *The Podcast Consumer 2017*, Edison Research, April 18, 2017, http://www.edisonresearch .com/wp-content/uploads/2017/04/Podcast-Consumer-2017.pdf.

118 musician John Roderick: About a year after we had this conversation, Roderick and I decided to start up our own podcast, *Omnibus*.

119 overtipped waiters: Charlotte Chandler, *Hello, I Must Be Going: Groucho and His Friends* (New York: Doubleday, 1978), pp. 516–17.

119 Jack Roy had no success: Nesteroff, *The Comedians*, p. 91.

119 "I'm thinking it over!": *The Jack Benny Program*, NBC, March 28, 1948.

119 "punch lines in 1959": Nesteroff, *The Comedians*, p. 33.

120 half-hour monologue: Andrew Marantz, "Good Evening. Hello. I Have Cancer," *New Yorker*, October 5, 2012.

120 double-mastectomy scars: Andrew Marantz, "Tig Notaro's Topless Set," *New Yorker*, November 7, 2014.

120 "It's stream of consciousness": *I Seem Fun: The Diary of Jen Kirkman*, Episode 1, "What's the Hook?" May 16, 2013.

121 famous storytelling moment: *Richard Pryor: Live on the Sunset Strip*, Columbia, 1982.

123 attention for her candor: Lara Zarum, "Jen Kirkman on Election-Night Anxiety, Touring as a Woman, and Dealing with Rumors," *Village Voice*, September 18, 2017.

123 "TV drip of entertainment": Jason Zinoman, "Bo Burnham, Discovered on the Internet, Now Challenges It," *New York Times*, June 3, 2016.

124 Michaels famously hates it: Miller and Shales, *Live from New York*, pp. 479, 613.

124 "Did you have a national anthem": Mel Brooks and Carl Reiner, *2,000 and One Years*, Capitol, 1961.

125 George Burns and Steve Allen: Ari Karpel, "A Shtick with a Thousand Lives," *New York Times*, November 12, 2009.

125 to watch *Jeopardy!* together: *Comedians in Cars Getting Coffee*, season 1, episode 9, "I Want Sandwiches, I Want Chicken," September 20, 2012.

125 "The backstroke, I think": Earl Wilson, "Tales of Lindy's Waiters Revived," *Dallas Morning News*, September 22, 1969.

125 The first celebrity roast: Aristophanes, *Clouds*, ed. K. J. Dover (Oxford: Oxford University Press, 1970), p. xix.

126 "Bob has a beautiful face": *Comedy Central Roast of Bob Saget*, August 17, 2008.

126 "*Oz the Great and Powerful?*": *Comedy Central Roast of James Franco*, September 2, 2013.

126 "It's just a crazy way": "TV Roasts: A Crazy Way of Telling People You Love Them," *TV Guide*, May 11, 1974.

126 she had to sneak in: Anthony Slide, *Eccentrics of Comedy* (Lanham, Md.: Scarecrow, 1998), p. 44.

127 rip on the convention: Oswalt appears as a bike cop who encourages Bamford *not* to put stand-up in her show, because it's now so overdone. *Lady Dynamite*, season 1, episode 1, "Pilot," Netflix, May 20, 2016.

127 His discovery, in short: Robert R. Provine, *Laughter: A Scientific Investigation* (New York: Penguin, 2000), pp. 4, 27, 40.

128 strict mechanics: Ibid., pp. 37, 57, 62. The only asymmetric thing about a typical laugh is loudness. Playing a laugh backward, says Provine, produces a Woody Woodpecker–like crescendo.

128 thirty times more: Ibid., p. 45.

128 "a social signification": Henri Bergson, *Laughter: An Essay on the Meaning of the Comic*, trans. Cloudesley Brereton and Fred Rothwell (New York: Macmillan, 1914), p. 8.

128 "the mind [is] in": Charles Darwin, *The Expression of the Emotions in Man and Animals* (New York: Appleton, 1899), p. 199.

128 bond two people faster: Barbara Fraley and Arthur Aron, "The Effects of a Shared Humorous Experience on Closeness in Initial Encounters," *Personal Relationships* 11, no. 1 (March 2004), pp. 61–78.

129 *Homo ridens*: Arthur Koestler, *The Act of Creation* (New York: Dell, 1964), p. 63.

129 recorded children: Antony J. Chapman, "Humorous Laughter in Children," *Journal of Personality and Social Psychology* 31, no. 1 (January 1975), pp. 42–49.

129 "Our sense of humor": Eastman, *Sense of Humor*, p. 230.

129 hard-to-fake indicator: Hurley et al., *Inside Jokes*, pp. 11–12.

129 "They're a lie!": Deborah Starr Seibel, "Funny Business: TV Laugh Tracks Can Still Cause Frowns, but the Studios Feel a Need to Be Humored," *Chicago Tribune*, April 16, 1992.

130 photos of women: Eric R. Bressler and Sigal Balshine, "The Influence of Humor on Desirability," *Evolution and Human Behavior* 27, no. 1 (January 2006), pp. 29–39.

130 "A wife": Desiderius Erasmus, *The Praise of Folly*, trans. Hoyt Hopewell Hudson (Princeton, N.J.: Princeton University Press, 2015), p. 28.

130 perceived by others: Gil Greengross and Geoffrey Miller, "Dissing Oneself Versus Dissing Rivals: Effects of Status, Personality, and Sex on the Short-Term and Long-Term Attractiveness of Self-Deprecating and Other-Deprecating Humor," *Evolutionary Psychology* 6, no. 3 (2008), pp. 393–408.

130 emotional IQ skills: Jeremy A. Yip and Rod A. Martin, "Sense of Humor, Emotional Intelligence, and Social Competence," *Journal of Research in Personality* 40, no. 6 (December 2006), pp. 1202–8.

131 "the High Priest of Ha-Ha": Terrence E. Deal and Allan A. Kennedy, *The New Corporate Cultures: Revitalizing the Workplace After Downsizing, Mergers, and Reengineering* (New York: Basic, 1999), p. 8.

131 boot camp for business teams: Anthony Effinger, "Improv Training Is Making Management Throw Away the Script," *Bloomberg Business*, September 29, 2015.

132 "humor room": John Morreall, *Humor Works* (Amherst, Mass.: HRD Press, 1997), p. 8.

132 "Joy Gang": Kateri Drexler, *Icons of Business: An Encyclopedia of Mavericks, Movers, and Shakers* (Westport, Conn.: Greenwood, 2007), 1:86.

132 blow on kazoos: Leigh Branham, *Keeping the People Who Keep You in Business: 24 Ways to Hang on to Your Most Valuable Talent* (New York: Amacom, 2001), p. 251.

132 "Grouch Patrol": Morreall, *Humor Works*, p. 18.

132 "That concludes the musical portion": Michael Iapoce, "Giving Trainees the Last Laugh," *Training and Development Journal* 44, no. 8 (August 1990), pp. 13–15.

132 a "humor first aid kit": Geeta Dardick, "Learning to Laugh on the Job," *Principal* 69, no. 5 (May 1990), pp. 32–34.

133 "Staple Kleenex": Branham, *Keeping the People*, p. 251.

133 "Grass Valley Greg": *Mr. Show with Bob and David*, season 2, episode 4, "If You're Going to Write a Comedy Scene, You're Going to Have Some Rat Feces in There," HBO, December 6, 1996.

SIX: EVERYONE'S A COMEDIAN

138 fewer than four thousand people: According to *MST3K* superfan and ephemera collector Tom Noel.

138 drawing from the album sleeve: Brian Raftery, "*Mystery Science Theater 3000:* The Definitive Oral History of a TV Masterpiece," *Wired*, April 22, 2014.

139 The budget was $250: Chris Morgan, *The Comic Galaxy of "Mystery Science Theater 3000": Twelve Classic Episodes and the Movies They Lampoon* (Jefferson, N.C.: McFarland, 2015), p. 12.

139 a flimsy satellite set: Trace Beaulieu, Paul Chaplin, Jim Mallon, Kevin Murphy, Michael J. Nelson, and Mary Jo Pehl, *The "Mystery Science Theater 3000" Amazing Colossal Episode Guide* (New York: Bantam, 1996), p. xxxi.

139 "It was like being in a theater": *Mystery Science Theater 3000*, season 0, episode 4, "*Gamera vs. Barugon*," KTMA, December 4, 1988.

140 in an industrial park: Raftery, "The Definitive Oral History."

141 *Planet of the Apes* rip-off: *Mystery Science Theater 3000*, season 3, episode 6, "*Time of the Apes*," Comedy Central, December 4, 1988.

142 "I have been interviewed": *How to Be Funny, and Other Writings of Will Rogers*, ed. Steven K. Gracent (Stillwater: Oklahoma State University Press, 1983), p. 112.

142 "but it felt like": Apatow, *Sick in the Head*, p. 249.

142 Carson moved *The Tonight Show:* Nesteroff, *The Comedians*, p. 294.

143 twelve thousand people: Jason Zinoman, "Upright Citizens Brigade Raises Prices. Comedy Fans Shouldn't Laugh," *New York Times*, January 30, 2017.

143 do people who run: @IamEnidColeslaw, Twitter, October 20, 2014, https://twitter.com/IamEnidColeslaw/status/524331993819910146.

143 hi grandma?: @ch000ch, Twitter, October 19, 2013, https://twitter.com/ch000ch/status/391611930865303551.

143 science defines a baby: @Fred_Delicious, Twitter, October 17, 2012, https://twitter.com/Fred_Delicious/status/258533115830599680.

143 i saw an ad on craigslist: Jon Hendren (@fart), Twitter, May 25, 2012, https://twitter.com/fart/status/206196131316744104.

144 Next, on TLC's Lunchbox Wanters: Stefan Heck (@boring_as_heck), Twitter, May 29, 2014, https://twitter.com/boring_as_heck/status/472061177498467328.

144 "If everyone in the country": Apatow, *Sick in the Head*, p. 5.

145 It's actually illegal: Ken Jennings (@KenJennings), Twitter, July 18, 2016, https://twitter.com/KenJennings/status/755065977981767680.

146 "This talent cannot": Cicero, *De Oratore* 2.54.

146 the "Chinese Room": John Searle, "Minds, Brains, and Programs," *Behavioral and Brain Sciences* 3, no. 3 (September 1980), pp. 417–57.

147 damn girl, are you the wife of a convict: Demi Adejugigbe (@electrolemon), Twitter, May 1, 2013, https://twitter.com/electrolemon/status/329782507140689920.

147 Damn girl are you a pizza: @tnylgn, Twitter, October 7, 2013, https://twitter.com/tnylgn/status/387350810176147456.

148 Daaaamn girl is your name Katrina: Eireann Dolan (@EireannDolan), Twitter, February 6, 2013, https://twitter.com/EireannDolan/status/299318413821465856.

148 Sext: I am a living: Patricia Lockwood (@TriciaLockwood), Twitter, August 8, 2011, https://twitter.com/TriciaLockwood/status/100808023307587584.

148   Since Ariel was 16: @OhNoSheTwitnt, Twitter, June 22, 2016, https://twitter.com/OhNoSheTwitnt/status/745607683882029056.

148   If it facilitates: Jason Miller (@longwall26), Twitter, July 17, 2016, https://twitter.com/longwall26/status/754657121359106048.

148   Damn girl, are you the second season: Ken Jennings (@KenJennings), Twitter, March 10, 2013, https://twitter.com/KenJennings/status/310802028391718712.

149   me: Carly Rae Jepsens new album: @crushingbort, Twitter, August 22, 2015, https://twitter.com/crushingbort/status/635226763094831104.

149   "'Every little bit helps'": This Wellerism is *not* from Dickens. Nobody pisses in Dickens. I first came across it in Neil Gaiman's *Sandman*, but versions using an ant or bird instead of an old woman date back to the Middle Ages.

149   wind-up doll jokes: This unfunny example and seventy-two others are in Maurice D. Schmaier, "The Doll Joke Pattern in Contemporary American Oral Humor," *Midwest Folklore* 13, no. 4 (Winter 1963–1964), pp. 205–16.

149   "flopcorn": Rich Hall, *Sniglets: Any Word That Doesn't Appear in the Dictionary, but Should* (New York: Macmillan, 1980) p. 33.

149   Helen Keller jokes: Mac E. Barrick, "The Helen Keller Joke Cycle," *Journal of American Folklore* 93, no. 370 (October–December 1980), pp. 441–49.

149   elephant jokes: Roger D. Abrahams and Alan Dundes, "On Elephantasy and Elephanticide," *Psychoanalytic Review* 56, no. 2 (February 1969), pp. 225–41.

150   "In Soviet Russia": Smirnoff's act is often remembered today as a series of "In Soviet Russia . . ." reversal jokes, but in fact he almost never used the format. This particular joke actually dates back at least to the 1958 Oscars, when Bob Hope told it. Mason Wiley and Damien Bona, *Inside Oscar: The Unofficial History of the Academy Awards*, 2nd ed. (New York: Ballantine, 1996), p. 289.

150   "I played hide and seek": Dangerfield says this was the joke that prompted him to introduce his "I don't get no respect" hook. Lawrence Christon, "The Education of Rodney Dangerfield," *Los Angeles Times*, July 1, 1986.

150   "black white supremacist": "*Frontline*: Clayton Bigsby," *Chappelle's Show*, season 1, episode 1, Comedy Central, January 22, 2003.

150   "Pre-Taped Call-in Show": *Mr. Show with Bob and David*, season 3, episode 10, "The Return of the Curse of the Creature's Ghost," HBO, December 5, 1997.

151   mostly punny riddles: Graeme Ritchie, *The Linguistic Analysis of Jokes* (London: Routledge, 2004), pp. 148, 153.

151   a formal language called OST: Victor Raskin, Christian F. Hempelmann, and Julia M. Taylor, "How to Understand and Assess a Theory: The Evolution of the SSTH into the GTVH and Now into the OSTH," *Journal of Literary Theory* 3, no. 2 (December 2009), pp. 285–312. The example here is from Julia M. Taylor, "Do Jokes Have to Be Funny?: Analysis of 50 'Theoretically Jokes,'" *AAAI Artificial Intelligence of Humor Symposium*, Arlington, Va., November 2–4, 2012.

152   DEviaNT, it turned out, was no Michael Scott: Chloé Kiddon and Yuriy Brun, "That's What She Said: Double Entendre Identification," *Proceedings of the 49th Annual Meeting of the Association for Computational Linguistics*, Portland, Ore., June 19–24, 2011.

153   At the intermission: Megan Amram (@meganamram), Twitter, February 5, 2017, https://twitter.com/meganamram/status/B28414875156217856.

153   by tickling us: Christine R. Harris and Nicholas Christenfeld, "Can a Machine Tickle?" *Psychonomic Bulletin & Review* 6, no. 3 (September 1999), pp. 504–10.

154 If Natalie Portman dated: Bryan Donaldson (@The Nardvark), Twitter, October 23, 2014, https://twitter.com/TheNardvark/status/525323195566170115.

154 "There's literally no way": Megan Amram (@meganamram), Twitter, December 2, 2015, https://twitter.com/meganamram/status/672151849278951424.

154 "WHY was Mario Kart": Megan Amram (@meganamram), Twitter, May 11, 2012, https://twittercom/meganamram/status/201142970383212544.

154 "girl are u my neighbor's wifi?": Megan Amram (@megananamram), Twitter, November 13, 2015, https://twitter.com/meganamram/status/665261002791981056.

155 "When my wife gets a little upset": Bryan Donaldson (@The Nardvark), Twitter, September 26, 2011, https://twitter.com/TheNardvark/status/118383154598907905.

155 "Relaxing family vacation": Bryan Donaldson (@The Nardvark), Twitter, June 22, 2014, https://twitter.com/TheNardvark/status/480886627292971010.

155 spotted by Alex Baze on Twitter: Jennifer Rogers and Callie Wright, "How a Middle-Aged IT Guy from Peoria Tweeted His Way into a Writing Job on *Late Night with Seth Meyers*," Vulture, April 6, 2014, http://www.vulture.com/2014/04/guy-tweets -his-way-from-peoria-to-30-rock.html.

156 the youngest stand-up ever: Jason Zinoman, "Evolving Young Satirist Stands Up to Convention," *New York Times*, December 25, 2013.

156 "There's a myth": Perret, *Comedy Writing Step by Step*, p. 217.

157 a three-minute story: *Louie*, season 1, episode 1, "Pilot," FX, June 29, 2010.

157 a book from the school library: *Jay Leno's How to Be the Funniest Kid in the Whole Wide World (or Just in Your Class)* (New York: Aladdin, 2005).

159 "With references to everything": The Peabody Awards, Winter 1993, http://www .peabodyawards.com/award-profile/mystery-science-theater-3000.

160 most successful video crowdfunding: William Hughes, "*MST3K* Breaks Kickstarter Records, Secures 14 New Episodes," AV Club, December 12, 2015, https://news.avclub .com/mst3k-breaks-kickstarter-records-secures-14-new-episod-1798287322.

160 tenth-anniversary celebration: *RiffTrax Live: MST3K Reunion*, RiffTrax, 2016.

SEVEN: BON JOVI, COME HOME

165 a sample *alazon* takedown: Aristophanes, *Lysistrata and Other Plays*, trans. and ed. Alan H. Sommerstein (London: Penguin, 1973), pp. 74–75. I've colloquialized the Sommerstein translation somewhat.

166 according to Plato: In *The Republic*, Thrasymachus laughs at Socrates's putting on a pretense of ignorance "so that [he] may contrive, as he always does, to evade answering himself but may cross-examine the other man and refute his replies." Plato, *Republic* 337e.

166 Ronald Golding insisted: *Winston Churchill, Myth and Reality: What He Actually Did and Said* (Jefferson, N.C.: McFarland, 2017), p. 229.

168 "In these conditions": François Truffaut, *Hitchcock*, rev. ed. (New York: Touchstone, 1983), p. 73.

168 allergic to beer: Mara Bovsun, "The Case of Adolph Coors," *New York Daily News*, September 13, 2009.

168 Jim Fixx died: Jane Gross, "James F. Fixx Dies Jogging; Author on Running Was 52," *New York Times*, July 22, 1984.

168 her hit 1995 song: Alanis Morissette, "Ironic," *Jagged Little Pill*, Maverick, 1995.

169 a full paragraph: Bryan A. Garner, *Garner's Modern English Usage*, 4th ed. (Oxford: Oxford University Press, 2016), p. 529.

169 "If a diabetic": George Carlin, *Brain Droppings* (New York: Hyperion, 1997), p. 116.

171 Sontag enumerated: Susan Sontag, "Notes on 'Camp,'" *Against Interpretation, and Other Essays* (New York: Picador, 2001), p. 277.

171 glued to the Nick at Nite reruns: The eighties camp aesthetic is well described in Paul Rudnick and Kurt Andersen, "The Irony Epidemic," *Spy*, March 1989.

172 its early mascots: It surprises many people to learn that neither Albert Brooks nor Steve Martin, despite their close association with *Saturday Night Live*, was ever a cast member.

172 almost no jokes: Steve Martin, *Let's Get Small*, Warner, 1977.

173 a humidifier locked in battle: *Late Night with David Letterman*, season 2, episode 77, NBC, July 5, 1983.

173 a random book publicist: Meg Parsont of Pocket Books made the first of her thirty-odd appearances on *Late Night* in season 9, episode 12, NBC, February 15, 1990.

173 "Shoe Removal Races": *Late Night*, season 7, episode 66, NBC, October 11, 1988.

173 a full 360-degree rotation: *Late Night*, season 5, episode 140, NBC, December 9, 1986.

173 a cartoon voice-over cast: *Late Night*, season 5, episode 10, NBC, rerun, September 25, 1986.

173 "Words That Almost Rhyme with 'Peas'": *Late Night*, season 4, episode 87, NBC, September 18, 1985.

173 *The Great Gatsby*: *Saturday Night Live*, season 3, episode 13, NBC, March 11, 1978.

174 Anglin boasted: Andrew Anglin, "A Normie's Guide to the Alt-Right," Daily Stormer, August 31, 2016. The site has since been banned by domain registrars.

175 "coded racist messages": Joseph Bernstein, "Adult Swim Talent Want the Network to Cancel Its Alt-Right Comedy Show," BuzzFeed News, November 16, 2016, https://www .buzzfeed.com/josephbernstein/adult-swim-talent-trying-to-cancel-million-dollar-extreme.

175 troll progressive celebs: Seth Abramovitch, "Sam Hyde Speaks: Meet the Man Behind Adult Swim's Canceled 'Alt-Right' Comedy Show," *Hollywood Reporter*, December 8, 2016.

175 a 2013 stand-up set: Still posted on Million Dollar Extreme's official YouTube page. "Privileged White Male Triggers Oppressed Victims, Ban This Video Now and Block Him," June 4, 2013, https://www.youtube.com/watch?v=Tt19Vp9uBiQ.

175 over a million viewers: David Sims, "The Battle over Adult Swim's Alt-Right TV Show," *Atlantic*, November 17, 2016.

175 publicly criticized the network: Bernstein, "Adult Swim Talent."

175 "Thanks for giving a racist": Abramovitch, "Sam Hyde Speaks."

176 a bigger, livelier world: Future *Time* humor columnist Joel Stein describes a similar childhood experience in Kurt Andersen, Graydon Carter, and George Kalogerakis, *Spy: The Funny Years* (New York: Miramax, 2006), p. 61. *Spy* was evidently a gateway irony drug for a *lot* of 1980s kids.

176 Mike Ovitz's top secret Hollywood client list: "Ten Percent of Everything Everybody Makes," *Spy*, September 1988.

176 index to *The Andy Warhol Diaries*: "*Spy*'s Exclusive Unauthorized Index to Andy Warhol's Diaries," August 1989.

176 "1,000 Reasons": Joe Conason et al., "1,000 Reasons Not to Vote for George Bush," July–August 1988. In the story, *Spy* gave the first national coverage to long-standing rumors that Bush was involved in an extramarital affair with assistant Jennifer Fitzgerald.

176 a $0.13 check? Julius Lowenthal, "Every Man Has His Price," July 1990. Arms dealer Adnan Khashoggi and *Spy* favorite Donald Trump were the only two moguls who bothered to deposit the smallest check.

176 "See, not so short": Graydon Carter, "Steel Traps and Short Fingers," *Vanity Fair*, November 2015.

178 Eckensteher Nante: Mary Lee Townsend, *Forbidden Laughter: Popular Humor and the Limits of Repression in Nineteenth-Century Prussia* (Ann Arbor: University of Michigan Press, 1992), p. 119.

178 "I need not say": Charles Dudley Warner, *Washington Irving* (Boston: Houghton Mifflin, 1884), p. 19.

178 "Amerikans love caustick things": Billings, *Complete Works*, p. 435.

179 exit from a kitchen fire: *Seinfeld*, season 5, episode 19, "The Fire," NBC, May 5, 1994.

179 loaf of marble rye: *Seinfeld*, season 7, episode 11, "The Rye," NBC, January 4, 1996.

179 entire publishing firm: *Seinfeld*, season 5, episode 21, "The Opposite," NBC, May 19, 1994.

179 death of a fiancée: *Seinfeld*, season 7, episode 24, "The Invitations," NBC, May 16, 1996.

179 "No hugging, no learning": At Larry David's insistence. Francis Davis, "Recognition Humor," *Atlantic*, December 1992.

180 "Well, it was nice knowing you": Arthur Marx, *Life with Groucho* (New York: Simon and Schuster, 1954), pp. 245–46.

180 "the end of the age of irony": Seth Mnookin, "In Disaster's Aftermath, Once-Cocky Media Culture Disses the Age of Irony," Inside.com, September 18, 2001.

180 "Can we be funny?": *Saturday Night Live*, season 27, episode 1, NBC, September 29, 2001.

180 the eve of September 11: The newly transplanted Wisconsinites celebrated with a party at the Bowery Ballroom, at which They Might Be Giants performed. Dylan Stableford, "*The Onion* Looks Back on 'Cathartic' 9/11 Issue," Yahoo! News, August 23, 2011, https://www.yahoo.com/tv/bp/the-onion-looks-back-on-cathartic-9-11-issue .html.

180 a comedy classic: All these stories are from the *Onion*, vol. 37, issue 34, September 26, 2001.

182 "A young healthy child": Jonathan Swift, *A Modest Proposal, and Other Satirical Works* (Mineola, N.Y.: Dover, 1996), p. 53.

182 "very fit for table": *The Works of Jonathan Swift*, ed. Walter Scott (Edinburgh: Constable, 1814), 17:315.

183 ironically pro-Soviet demonstration: Srdja Popovic and Matthew Miller, *Blueprint for Revolution: How to Use Rice Pudding, Lego Men, and Other Nonviolent Techniques to Galvanize Communities, Overthrow Dictators, or Simply Change the World* (New York: Spiegel & Grau, 2015), p. 107.

183 "This is all America's fault!": Sunghui Moon and Richard Finney, "North Korean Citizens Warned Against 'Hostile' Speech," Radio Free Asia, September 2, 2016, http:// www.rfa.org/english/news/korea/warned-09022016160227.html.

183 a too-large cookie: "Things Everybody Does but Doesn't Talk About," BuzzFeed News, February 12, 2015, https://www.buzzfeed.com/andrewgauthier/the-president-uses-a-selfie-stick. The video was (of course) a promotion for the HealthCare.gov Obamacare website.

184 "sarcasm detector": Katie Zezima, "The Secret Service Wants Software That Detects Social Media Sarcasm. Yeah, Sure It Will Work," *Washington Post*, June 3, 2014.

184 in a 2005 study: Justin Kruger and Nicholas Epley, "Egocentrism over E-Mail: Can We Communicate as Well as We Think?" *Journal of Personality and Social Psychology* 89, no. 5 (December 2005), pp. 925–36.

184 the percontation point: Keith Houston, *Shady Characters: The Secret Life of Punctuation, Symbols, and Other Typographical Marks* (New York: W. W. Norton, 2013), p. 219.

185 "The moment has come": Kurt Andersen, "No More April Fools' Shenanigans," *Spy*, April 1989.

EIGHT: MIRTH CONTROL

186 "to speak jocosely": Charles Marriott, ed., *A Library of Fathers of the Holy Catholic Church*, vol. 9, *The Homilies of S. John Chrysostom, Archbishop of Constantinople, on the Statues*, trans. W. R. W. Stephens (London: Walter Smith, 1885), p. 236.

186 "unrestrained and immoderate": *The Fathers of the Church*, vol. 9, Saint Basil, *Ascetical Works*, trans. M. Monica Wagner (Washington, D.C.: Catholic University of America Press, 1962), p. 271.

187 any "buffoonery": "Abandoned men often make use of a single light expression to try the gates of chastity," warns Jerome. "To Demetrias," trans. and ed. Philip Schaff and Henry Wace, in *Nicene and Post-Nicene Fathers of the Christian Church, Second Series*, vol. 6, *Letters and Selected Works* (New York: Scribner, 1893), p. 267.

187 the slightest *smile:* John Chrysostom, *On Virginity; Against Remarriage*, trans. Sally Rieger Shore (New York: Edwin Mellen, 1983), p. 100. See also Ingvild Saelid Gilhus, *Laughing Gods, Weeping Virgins: Laughter in the History of Religion* (London: Routledge, 1997), which was invaluable to me here.

187 condemns *eutrapelia:* Eph. 5:4.

187 "merry heart": Prov. 15:13 (King James Version).

187 Jesus doesn't laugh: Karl-Josef Kuschel, *Laughter: A Theological Reflection* (New York: Continuum, 1994), p. 43.

187 the word Aristotle used: Aristotle, *Nicomachean Ethics*, p. 33.

187 the master's "faint smile": Gilhus, *Laughing Gods, Weeping Virgins*, p. 132.

187 he's eating dates: This story doesn't have the strongest *sanad* (sourcing) of the hadith, but it is found in both the Sunni and Shia traditions.

188 Jesus's parables: Mary Douglas, "Jokes," in *Implicit Meanings: Essays in Anthropology* (London: Routledge and Kegan Paul, 1975), pp. 99–100.

188 God being sarcastic: Hershey H. Friedman and Linda Weiser Friedman, *God Laughed: Sources of Jewish Humor* (New Brunswick, N.J.: Transaction, 2014), p. 206.

188 Jonah best understood: John A. Miles Jr., "Laughing at the Bible: Jonah as Parody," *Jewish Quarterly Review* 65, no. 3 (January 1975), pp. 168–81.

188 from John 12:8: Kurt Vonnegut, *Palm Sunday: An Autobiographical Collage* (New York: Delacorte, 1981), p. 300.

188 "violet trick": Eckehard Simon, "The Rustic Muse: *Neidhartschwänke* in Murals, Stone Carvings, and Woodcuts," *Germanic Review* 46, no. 4 (November 1971), pp. 243–56.

189 Origen read: Johan Verberckmoes, "The Comic and Counter-Reformation in the Spanish Netherlands," in Bremmer and Roodenburg, *A Cultural History of Humour*, p. 80.

189 "blessed are ye": Luke 6:21 (King James Version).

189 *Rule of Saint Benedict*: Benedict, "Rule for Monasteries," in *Readings in Medieval History*, 4th ed., ed. Patrick J. Geary (Toronto: University of Toronto Press, 2010), pp. 164, 167.

189 *Duyfken and Willemynken*: Johan Verberckmoes, *Laughter, Jestbooks and Society in the Spanish Netherlands* (London: Macmillan, 1999), p. 156.

189 more than twenty times: E. K. Grootes and M. A. Schenkeveld-Van der Dussen, "The Dutch Revolt and the Golden Age, 1560–1700," in *A Literary History of the Low Countries*, ed. Theo Hermans (Rochester, N.Y.: Camden House, 2009), p. 248.

190 "Saint Nobody": We only know about Radulphus from a 1290 refutation of this "abominable sermon" by his contemporary Stephanus. Lucie Dolezalova, "Absolute Alterity in the Cult of Saints: Saint Nobody," in *Identity and Alterity in Hagiography and the Cult of Saints* (Zagreb: Croatian Hagiographic Society, 2010), pp. 89–102.

190 a 1937 broadcast: Jon Tuska, *The Complete Films of Mae West* (New York: Citadel, 1992), pp. 134–36.

190 "I believe in censorship": Nora Gilbert, *Better Left Unsaid: Victorian Novels, Hays Code Films, and the Benefits of Censorship* (Stanford, Calif.: Stanford University Press, 2013), p. 150.

191 "The *Daily Planet*": *Talking Funny*.

191 "I'd like to kiss you": *Nothing but the Truth*, Paramount, 1941. Hope's character is uncharacteristically forthright about his attraction to Goddard because he's made a wager that he can't go twenty-four hours telling the unadulterated truth about everything, essentially the same gimmick as Jim Carrey's *Liar Liar* almost sixty years later. This telling example of thinly veiled sexuality in Hays Code–era Hollywood is in Gershon Legman, *Rationale of the Dirty Joke: An Analysis of Sexual Humor* (New York: Simon & Schuster, 2006), p. 399.

192 the Old Comedy: All these examples of cheerful Attic vulgarity are from the exhaustive survey in Jeffrey Henderson, *The Maculate Muse: Obscene Language in Attic Comedy* (New Haven, Conn.: Yale University Press, 1975).

192 "his bugle of an ass-hole": *The Divine Comedy: Inferno*, in *The Portable Dante*, trans. and ed. Mark Musa (New York: Penguin, 1995), pp. 116–17.

193 Merv Griffin credited: Or so Yankovic has been told, though I'm not 100 percent sure the timeline holds up. "I Lost on Jeopardy" was released in June, and *Jeopardy!* was back on the air by September. Maybe the "Weird Al" hit helped boost viewership for the already-in-the-works revival.

194 fourth consecutive decade: The only other artists with new Top 40 hits in each of the last four decades are Michael Jackson, Madonna, and U2. Gary Trust, "U2 Joins Michael Jackson, Madonna & 'Weird Al' Yankovic with Top 40 Hot 100 Hits in '80s, '90s, '00s & '10s," *Billboard*, April 27, 2017.

194 the era of Allan Sherman: Mikael Wood, "'Weird Al' Yankovic Hits No. 1 on *Billboard* Chart with *Mandatory Fun*," *Los Angeles Times*, July 23, 2014.

194 "I once had a girl": These two lyrics are, of course, the first lines of the Dylan-influenced "Norwegian Wood," by the Beatles, and Dylan's own "Highway 61 Revisited."

195 "Single Women": *Saturday Night Live*, season 7, episode 2, NBC, October 10, 1981.

195 list of past winners: Mary Ann Madden, "Competition #940," *New York*, May 3, 1999.

196 fanciful images: "Shoveling Snow with Buddha" is in Billy Collins, *Picnic, Lightning* (Pittsburgh: University of Pittsburgh Press, 1998), p. 37. "Another Reason Why I Don't Keep a Gun in the House" and "Flames" are from Billy Collins, *The Apple That*

Astonished Paris (Fayetteville: University of Arkansas Press, 1988), pp. 27, 50. "The Lanyard" and "Litany" have both been reprinted in Billy Collins, *Aimless Love* (New York: Random House, 2013), pp. 32, 60.

196   a six-figure advance: Bruce Weber, "On Literary Bridge, Poet Hits a Roadblock," *New York Times*, December 19, 1999.

197   funny contemporary verse: Barbara Hamby and David Kirby, eds., *Seriously Funny: Poems About Love, Death, Religion, Art, Politics, Sex, and Everything Else* (Athens: University of Georgia Press, 2010).

197   "tragedy is a representation": Aristotle, *Poetics*, trans. Anthony Kenny (Oxford: Oxford University Press, 2013), p. 22.

198   Evelyn Waugh always maintained: David Wykes, *Evelyn Waugh: A Literary Life* (London: Macmillan, 1999), p. 153.

198   most successful box office genre: In terms of total box office, comedy in toto has led the box office since the mid-1990s for a total take of $43 billion domestically, even if you separate out "romantic comedy" into its own category. (Of course, this is largely because comedies are more numerous than any other movie genre except drama.) In 2017, "adventure" surpassed comedy for the first time, a result of the superhero movie boom. The Numbers, http://www.the-numbers.com/market/genres.

198   within a whisker: Paramount actually avoided the word "comedy" completely in its Oscar campaign for *The Big Short*, knowing that was the kiss of death. Glenn Whipp, "Best Picture Predictions: It's *The Big Short* for the Win," *Los Angeles Times*, February 25, 2016.

200   humor in office: Emily Antenucci and Carol Glatz, "Jokes, Quips, Wisecracks: John XXIII Lived with Keen Sense of Humor," *National Catholic Reporter*, March 24, 2014.

200   short, clever jokes: Several signs in this section are taken from Steve Paulson, *Church Signs Across America* (Woodstock, N.Y.: Overlook, 2006).

201   "number-one outreach tool": Christian Davenport, "Churches Offer Spiritual Advice in Tiny Bites, Goofy or Poignant," *Washington Post*, March 25, 2006.

201   simple slapstick idea: "Top Soccer Shootout with Scott Sterling," *Studio C* television clip, November 14, 2014, https://www.youtube.com/watch?v=8F9jXYOH2c0.

202   caffeinated sodas: BYU lifted the sixty-year Coke ban in September 2017 as this book was in its final edits, presumably just to spite me and force me to add this endnote.

202   "enough of tragedy": Horace G. Whitney, *The Drama in Utah: The Story of the Salt Lake Theatre* (Salt Lake City: Deseret News, 1915), p. 29.

NINE: A BLURRY, AMORPHOUS THUD

205   without a single member: Wayne Whipple, *The Story-Life of Lincoln: A Biography Composed of Five Hundred True Stories* (Chicago: John C. Winston, 1908), pp. 481–82.

205   ribald British jokebook: Keith A. Erekson, *Everybody's History: Indiana's Lincoln Inquiry and the Quest to Reclaim a President's Past* (Amherst: University of Massachusetts Press, 2012), p. 98.

205   battled clinical depression: Joshua Wolf Shenk, "Lincoln's Great Depression," *Atlantic*, October 2005.

206   "As a rule": *Lincoln's Inaugurals, Addresses and Letters (Selections)*, ed. Daniel Kilham Dodge (New York: Longmans, Green, 1910), p. xvii.

206 "The occasion is too serious": Ibid.

206 "as a handy peg": Carl Sandburg, *Abraham Lincoln: The Prairie Years and the War Years* (San Diego: Harvest, 1982), p. 562.

206 *rex facetus*: Simon R. Doubleday, *The Wise King: A Christian Prince, Muslim Spain, and the Birth of the Renaissance* (New York: Basic, 2015), p. 116.

206 dining and trading wisecracks: "He used to send trifling verses from court to the Scriblerus Club almost every day; and would come and talk idly with them almost every night, even when his all was at stake," Pope remembered. Joseph Spence, *Observations, Anecdotes, and Characters of Books and Men* (London: Murray, 1820), p. 167.

207 "Never make people laugh": Gilded Age diplomat and gadfly Donn Piatt claimed Corwin gave this advice to him, not President Garfield, though the latter undoubtedly makes for a better story. Donn Piatt, *Memories of the Men Who Saved the Union* (New York: Belford, Clarke, 1887), p. 95.

207 "infinite humor": *Life and Speeches of Thomas Corwin*, ed. Josiah Morrow (Cincinnati: W. H. Anderson, 1896), p. 20.

207 "How do you entertain": "Flatulence Joke Is World's Oldest," BBC News, August 1, 2008, http://news.bbc.co.uk/2/hi/7536918.stm.

208 comedians warned him: Nesteroff, *The Comedians*, p. 161.

208 Joe Kennedy tried: Ibid., p. 199.

208 "degrading to the presidency": Peter M. Robinson, *The Dance of the Comedians: The People, the President, and the Performance of Political Standup Comedy in America* (Amherst, University of Massachusetts Press, 2010), p. 133.

208 fastest-selling record: Sales figures and stories about Meader's quick fall from fame drawn from Tim Carvell, "Exactly 40 Years Ago, for a Brief Shining Moment, Vaughn," *Entertainment Weekly*, March 28, 2003.

209 complicit in murder: Newcomb, *Encyclopedia of Television*, p. 2310.

209 last-minute Plan C: Hal Erickson, *"From Beautiful Downtown Burbank": A Critical History of "Rowan and Martin's Laugh-In," 1968–1973* (Jefferson, N.C.: McFarland, 2012), p. 168.

209 "too angry": Brian Abrams, "Sock It to Me: Behind the Scenes of Richard Nixon's *Laugh-In* Cameo," Death and Taxes, November 5, 2012, https://www.deathandtaxesmag .com/190513.

210 head writer Paul Keyes: Lorne Michaels and other *Laugh-In* writers remember that the conservative Keyes was forever stripping Nixon jokes out of the show. Erickson, *"From Beautiful Downtown Burbank,"* p. 170.

210 "A few timely touches": Marshall McLuhan, *Understanding Media: The Extensions of Man* (Cambridge, Mass.: MIT Press, 1994), p. 309.

210 "She was losing popularity": Jonathan Lynn, "Margaret Thatcher Hijacked My TV Show," CNN, April 10, 2013, http://www.cnn.com/2013/04/10/opinion/lynn-yes-prime-minister-thatcher/index.html.

210 Humphrey said no: Erickson, *"From Beautiful Downtown Burbank,"* p. 167.

211 "Look," she said: "Clinton," *American Experience*, PBS, February 20–21, 2012.

212 fastest turnaround: S. Robert Lichter, Jody C. Baumgartner, and Jonathan S. Morris, *Politics Is a Joke: How TV Comedians Are Remaking Political Life* (Boulder, Colo.: Westview, 2015), p. 184.

212 "the association with jazz music": The Walters-Wicker exchange from *This Week with David Brinkley*, recorded in Joseph Hayden, *Covering Clinton: The President and the Press in the 1990s* (Westport, Conn.: Praeger, 2002), p. 20.

212 "because I'm the president": Michael Parkin, *Talk Show Campaigns: Presidential Campaigns on Daytime and Late Night* (New York: Routledge, 2014), p. 26.

212 "The separation between theater and state": Robert Klein, "This Funny Business About Comedy and Politics," *New York Times*, November 3, 1996.

213 Political candidates appeared: Lichter et al., *Politics Is a Joke*, p. 5.

213 Pryor to Louis C.K.: *WTF with Marc Maron*, episode 613, June 22, 2015.

213 blunt antijoke: Karen Tumulty and Sean Sullivan, "McConnell Responds to Obama Joke with Glass of Wine," *Washington Post*, April 29, 2013.

214 tooling around the South Lawn: *Comedians in Cars Getting Coffee*, season 7, episode 1, "Just Tell Him You're the President," Netflix, December 30, 2015.

214 "like Hitler's dream": "Brad Pitt," *Between Two Ferns with Zach Galifianakis*, Funny or Die, October 27, 2014, https://www.youtube.com/watch?v=wnF-zTrHvGs.

215 Portman was asked: "Natalie Portman," *Between Two Ferns with Zach Galifianakis*, Funny or Die, November 3, 2009, https://www.youtube.com/watch?v=jOVq_UL48o0.

215 Obama was the last: "President Barack Obama," *Between Two Ferns with Zach Galifianakis*, Funny or Die, March 13, 2004, https://www.youtube.com/watch?v=UnW3x-kHxIEQ&t=2s.

218 "the Galifianakis bump": Other experts were more measured, attributing the March uptick to the looming enrollment deadline, not the video. Philip Bump, "Bradley Cooper Did Not Save Obamacare, the Calendar Did," *Atlantic*, April 2, 2014, https://www.theatlantic.com/politics/archive/2014/04/bradley-cooper-did-not-save-obamacare-the-calendar-did/360021/.

221 his after-dinner speech: "President Obama at the 2011 White House Correspondents' Dinner," C-SPAN, April 30, 2011, https://www.youtube.com/watch?v=n9mzJhvC-8E.

221 "Trump's humiliation": Adam Gopnik, "Trump and Obama: A Night to Remember," *New Yorker*, September 12, 2015. It's worth noting that not all writers agreed with Gopnik's hindsight. Roxanne Roberts, who sat immediately to Trump's left that night, said he was a good sport and repeatedly told reporters he felt "honored" to be roasted by Obama. Roxanne Roberts, "I Sat Next to Donald Trump at the Infamous 2011 White House Correspondents' Dinner," *Washington Post*, April 28, 2016.

222 language of comedy fans: Emma Roller, "Can You Insult Your Way to the White House?" *New York Times*, June 21, 2016.

222 Trump heard a baby: Ashley Killough, "Trump: 'You Can Get the Baby Out of Here,'" CNN News, August 3, 2016, http://www.cnn.com/2016/08/02/politics/donald-trump-ashburn-virginia-crying-baby.

223 "the Austrian comedian": Heinrich Mann, *Essays und Publizistik*, eds. Wolfgang Klein, Anne Flierl, and Volker Riedel (Bielefeld, Ger.: Aisthesis, 2009), 6:80.

223 "The laughs": Jimmy Carr and Lucy Greaves, *Only Joking: What's So Funny About Making People Laugh* (New York: Penguin, 2006), p. 206.

223 a 2008 experiment: Jody C. Baumgartner and Jonathan S. Morris, "One 'Nation,' Under Stephen? The Effects of *The Colbert Report* on American Youth," *Journal of Broadcasting & Electronic Media* 52, no. 4 (December 2008), pp. 622–43.

224 an MSNBC clip: "Black Voter Flashes Pro-Trump Hat While Voting During Live MSNBC Broadcast," November 8, 2016, https://www.youtube.com/watch?v=GNIK BIEHby8.

224 "Everything is changing": *Will Rogers' Daily Telegrams*, vol. 3, *The Hoover Years, 1931–1933*, ed. James Smallwood (Stillwater: Oklahoma State University Press, 1979), p. 241.

224   46 percent of young voters: In 2008; these numbers are presumably higher today. Lichter et al., *Politics Is a Joke*, p. 34.

225   Marco Rubio stumbling: Timothy P. Carney, "With Penis Jokes and Spray-Tan Riffs, Rubio Gets in the Mud with Trump," *Washington Examiner*, February 28, 2016, http://www.washingtonexaminer.com/article/2584485.

225   more time on Trump: David Bauder, "2 Studies Point to Lack of Campaign Substance on Newscasts," Associated Press, October 26, 2016. If you include the primary season, the Tyndall Report calculated an even starker difference, with Trump scoring 2.2 times the nightly newscast coverage that Clinton did. See http://tyndallreport.com /yearinreview2016.

226   more cynical about politics: Jody Baumgartner and Jonathan S. Morris, "The *Daily Show* Effect: Candidate Evaluations, Efficacy, and American Youth," *American Politics Research* 34, no. 3 (May 2006), pp. 341–67.

227   "I leave it to": This particular joke is probably apocryphal, as it was told about other politicians, including Minnesota congressman Frank Eddy, long before being attributed to Lincoln. *Friends' Intelligencer and Journal*, January 20, 1900, p. iii.

227   "Don't buy a single vote more": Kennedy's and Goldwater's self-deprecating jokes from Charles E. Schutz, *Political Humor: From Aristophanes to Sam Ervin* (Rutherford, N.J.: Fairleigh Dickinson University Press, 1977), pp. 167–69.

227   "dispels extremely ugly matters": Cicero, *De Oratore* 2.58.

228   "We can neither confirm nor deny": Erik Wemple, "Want to Talk to the CIA? Tweet @CIA," *Washington Post*, June 6, 2014.

228   "the end of political satire": Darby Maloney and Elizabeth Nonemaker, "Aaron Sorkin: Donald Trump May Be 'the End of Political Satire,'" *The Frame*, KPCC, December 10, 2015.

228   "political satire became obsolete": Nachman, *Seriously Funny*, p. 139.

228   "Clinton was wildly generous": This quote and Clinton's late-night monologue ubiquity from Lichter et al., *Politics Is a Joke*, pp. 50–52.

229   the line was taken directly: The two versions of the answer are not verbatim, but are so close as to be hard to tell apart; Palin's confusion isn't heightened. "Katie Couric Interview," Snopes, October 1, 2008, http://www.snopes.com/politics/palin/interview .asp.

229   "How can there be mirth": *Dhammapada*, 146, as translated in Gilhus, *Laughing Gods, Weeping Virgins*, p. 132.

TEN: WE SHALL OVERCOMB

230   "Telling me that I'm obsessed": Sarah Sahim, "Hari Kondabolu: 'My Comedy Is Very American. It's Aggressive,'" *Guardian*, December 11, 2015.

230   a live comedy record: Hari Kondabolu, *Waiting for 2042*, Kill Rock Stars, 2014.

231   "clapter": Jim Downey, interviewed in Sacks, *Poking a Dead Frog*, p. 3.

233   retired from comedy almost completely: Ben Brantley, "Advice from an Authority: Laugh!" *New York Times*, December 15, 1995.

233   "Every time Congress": Ray Robinson, *American Original: A Life of Will Rogers* (Oxford: Oxford University Press, 1996), p. 267.

233   his columns: William R. Linneman, "Will Rogers and the Great Depression," *Studies in American Humor* 2, no. 2/3 (Summer–Fall 1984), pp. 173–86.

234   "Well folks, sure glad": Ibid.

235 *Captain Billy's Whiz Bang:* The publisher was claiming 1.5 million readers by December 1921, though "Captain Billy" Fawcett was a notorious exaggerator.

236 "so dark": Eastman, *Enjoyment of Laughter*, p. 353.

236 "Negro ghost story": Mark Twain, *How to Tell a Story, and Other Essays* (New York: Harper, 1909), pp. 12–13.

236 Lincoln loved minstrel shows: Richard Lawrence Miller, *Lincoln and His World*, vol. 3, *The Rise to National Prominence, 1843–1853* (Jefferson, N.C.: McFarland, 2011), p. 328.

236 the "Negro Minstrel": Rourke, pp. 78–104.

236 at least *some* of the music: Because minstrel shows also drew heavily from white Appalachian culture, this lineage isn't always clear. See, for example, William J. Mahar, *Behind the Burnt Cork Mask: Early Blackface Minstrelsy and Antebellum American Popular Culture* (Urbana: University of Illinois Press, 1999).

236 African American performers: This history is treated exhaustively in Henry T. Sampson, *Blacks in Blackface: A Sourcebook on Early Black Musical Shows* (Lanham, Md.: Scarecrow, 2014).

236 Redd Foxx single-handedly invented: Nesteroff, *The Comedians*, pp. 191–92.

237 a daredevil's leap: Jerry Seinfeld, *On Comedy*, Laugh.com, 2005.

238 "Polack jokes" boomed: Davies, *Ethnic Humor Around the World*, p. 161.

238 "A man from Abdera": Beard, *Laughter in Ancient Rome*, p. 191.

238 forty-five different regional fooltowns: Christie Davies, *Jokes and Their Relation to Society* (Berlin: Mouton de Gruyter, 1998), p. 12.

239 eat weird food: Davies, *Ethnic Humor Around the World*, pp. 276–306.

239 cannier opposite numbers: Ibid., pp. 102–30.

240 "To treat [Jewish] jokes": Ibid., p. 121.

240 women were even allowed: Graham Ley, *A Short Introduction to the Ancient Greek Theater*, rev. ed. (Chicago: University of Chicago Press, 2006), p. 49.

241 a big old phallus: Carr and Greaves, *Only Joking*, pp. 39–41.

241 Marietta Holley: Kate H. Winter, *Marietta Holley: Life with "Josiah Allen's Wife"* (Syracuse: Syracuse University Press, 1984), pp. 6, 68, 79.

241 incognito: Gwendolyn B. Gwathmey, " 'Who Will Read the Book, Samantha?': Marietta Holley and the 19th-Century Reading Public," *Studies in American Humor* 3, no. 1 (1994), pp. 28–50.

242 "Fanny Fern": Joyce W. Warren, "Fanny Fern, Performative Incivilities, and Rap," *Studies in American Humor* 3, no. 6 (1999), pp. 17–36.

242 "There is a reason": Kate Sanborn, *The Wit of Women* (New York: Funk & Wagnalls, 1885), pp. 205–6.

242 *when women are the butt:* Martin D. Lampert and Susan M. Ervin-Tripp, "Exploring Paradigms: The Study of Gender and Sense of Humor Near the End of the 20th Century," in *The Sense of Humor: Explorations of a Personality Characteristic*, ed. Willibald Ruch (Berlin: Mouton de Gruyter, 1998), p. 239.

243 a 2011 study found: Gil Greengross and Geoffrey Miller, "Humor Ability Reveals Intelligence, Predicts Mating Success, and Is Higher in Males," *Intelligence* 39, no. 4 (July–August 2011), pp. 188–92. In a similar study published the following year, men's captions were only slightly funnier—and, tellingly, participants of both genders tended to misremember the funny captions as coming from men and the unfunny ones as from women. Laura Mickes et al., "Who's Funny: Gender Stereotypes, Humor Production, and Memory Bias," *Psychonomic Bulletin Review* 19, no. 1 (February 2012), pp. 108–12.

243 that build solidarity: See, for example, Jennifer Hay, "Functions of Humor in the Conversations of Men and Women," *Journal of Pragmatics* 32, no. 6 (May 2000), pp. 709–42.

243 "It does help": Doug Hill and Jeff Weingrad, *Saturday Night: A Backstage History of "Saturday Night Live"* (New York: Beech Tree, 1986), p. 245.

243 "outright hostility to women": Megan Beth Koester, "Why It Sucks to Be a Woman in Comedy," Vice, December 3, 2015, https://www.vice.com/en_us/article/yvx49x /why-it-sucks-to-be-a-woman-in-comedy-1202.

244 "Wouldn't it be funny": All quotes about this incident are taken from Amanda Holpuch, "Daniel Tosh Apologises for Rape Joke as Fellow Comedians Defend Topic," *Guardian*, July 11, 2012.

244 her late father: *This American Life*, episode 545, "If You Don't Have Anything Nice to Say, SAY IT IN ALL CAPS," PRX, January 23, 2015.

244 online responses to West: Lindy West, *Shrill: Notes from a Loud Woman* (New York: Hachette, 2016), p. 196.

246 fear of "faggots": Murphy's consistency is remarkable: he opens both *Eddie Murphy* (Columbia, 1982) and *Comedian* (Columbia, 1983), as well as his concert film *Eddie Murphy Raw* (Paramount, 1987), with a "faggot" routine. He apologized to the gay community in 1996 for the years of slurs and AIDS jokes.

246 "with her wrists closed": *Woody Allen*, Colpix, 1964.

246 a "Nazi rally": John J. O'Connor, "Taking a Pratfall on the Nastiness Threshold," *New York Times*, July 22, 1990.

246 have it both ways: All these jokes are from Louis C.K., *Hilarious*, Comedy Central, 2011.

246 "Everyone has his reasons": *The Rules of the Game*, Gaumont, 1939.

247 after that tour: *60 Minutes*, season 37, episode 21, CBS, February 20, 2005.

247 laughed a little too hard: *The Oprah Winfrey Show*, "Chappelle's Story: Dave's Moral Dilemma," February 3, 2006.

247 "I want to make sure": Christopher John Farley, "On the Beach with Dave Chappelle," *Time*, May 15, 2005.

247 "mouth-full-of-blood laughs": Dave Itzkoff, "Sarah Silverman on Bernie or Bust, and the Joke She Didn't Tell," *New York Times*, July 26, 2016.

248 structured like this: See the work of Thomas E. Ford—for example, Ford et al., "More Than 'Just a Joke': The Prejudice-Releasing Function of Sexist Humor," *Personality and Social Psychology Bulletin* 34, no. 2 (February 2008), pp. 159–70.

248 due to cowardice: Davies, *Ethnic Humor Around the World*, pp. 227–31.

249 "Jeer pressure": Leslie M. Janes and James M. Olson, "Jeer Pressure: The Behavioral Effects of Observing Ridicule of Others," *Personality and Social Psychology Bulletin* 26, no. 4 (April 2000), pp. 474–85.

249 John Henderson: Maria Elena C. Lopez, "Student's Ordeal Will Fund College," *Tucson Citizen*, December 2, 1993.

250 "I offer no 'cheers'": Carl Rowan, "No Cheers for Blackface," *Baltimore Sun*, October 14, 1993.

252 "gay plague": Scott Calonic used the audio clip to score his 2015 documentary *When AIDS Was Funny* for *Vanity Fair*, http://video.vanityfair.com/watch/the-reagan-administration-s-chilling-response-to-the-aids-crisis.

252 analysis of survey data: Natalia Khosla and Sean McElwee, "New Research Findings: People Who Say Society Is Too Politically Correct Tend Not to Have Experienced

Discrimination," Demos, June 1, 2016, http://www.demos.org/blog/6/1/16/new
-research-findings-people-who-say-society-too-politically-correct-tend-not-have-exper.

254 "like finding out that Ke$ha": *Last Week Tonight*, season 2, episode 15, HBO, May 31, 2015.

254 they get results: Sara Boboltz, "10 Real-Life Wins for John Oliver's Longest Segments on *Last Week Tonight*," *Huffington Post*, August 12, 2015, https://www.huffingtonpost.com/entry/john-oliver-real-life-wins_us_55c8e128e4b0f73b20bal71e.

254 "Stop them damn pictures!" Garth S. Jowett and Victoria O'Donnell, *Propaganda & Persuasion*, 6th ed. (Thousand Oaks, Calif.: SAGE, 2015), p. 85.

255 what he calls "laughtivism": Popovic and Miller, *Blueprint for Revolution*, pp. 100–3, 113–14, 120–21.

255 "a laugh will bury you!": Simon Critchley, *On Humour* (London: Routledge, 2002), p. 11.

256 "President Bannon": Peter Baker, Maggie Haberman, and Glenn Thrush, "Trump Removes Stephen Bannon from National Security Council Post," *New York Times*, April 5, 2017.

256 joking about the Reich: This brief history, including the footnote, taken from Steve Lipman, *Laughter in Hell: The Use of Humor During the Holocaust* (Northvale, N.J.: Jason Aronson, 1991), pp. 25–26, 40–42.

256 "There are those who thought": *The Essential Reinhold Niebuhr* (New Haven, Conn.: Yale University Press, 1986), p. 52.

257 "Wine barrels burst": Mikhail Bakhtin, *Rabelais and His World*, trans. Hélène Iswolsky (Bloomington: Indiana University Press, 1984), p. 75.

257 revolutionaries avoided humor: As Ernst Dronke said, "If the Berliner has laughed at something, then 'it no longer exists' for him. He ignores it with equanimity." Mary Lee Townsend, *Forbidden Laughter: Popular Humor and the Limits of Repression in Nineteenth-Century Prussia* (Ann Arbor: University of Michigan Press, 1992), p. 19.

257 George Mikes claimed: George Mikes, *Humour in Memoriam* (London: Routledge & Kegan Paul, 1970) p. 98.

257 Leslie Martin speculated: Katherine Bouton, review of *The Longevity Project: Surprising Discoveries for Health and Long Life from the Landmark Eight-Decade Study*, Howard S. Friedman and Leslie R. Martin, *New York Times*, April 18, 2011.

257 Because of the jokes: Christie Davies, *Jokes and Targets* (Bloomington: University of Indiana Press, 2011), p. 251.

258 "A woman is walking": Mark Perakh, *Laughing Under the Covers: Russian Oral Jokes and Anecdotal Tales*, Talk Reason, 1998, Joke 1.20, http://talkreason.org/marperak/jokes/jokes.htm.

258 "A man calls KGB headquarters": From a file of eleven "Soviet Jokes for the DCCI" declassified by the CIA in 2013, https://www.cia.gov/library/readingroom/docs/CIA-RDP89G00720R000800040003-6.pdf.

258 "jokes are thermometers": Christie Davies, "Jokes as the Truth About Soviet Socialism," *Folklore* 46 (2010), pp. 9–34.

258 "Controlling a culture": Hilary Lewis, "Jon Stewart Talks Media's Role in Election Outcome, How to Combat Spread of Fake News," *Hollywood Reporter*, December 2, 2016.

259 "As for jest": "Of Discourse," *The Works of Francis Bacon* (New York: R. Worthington, 1884), 1:40.

259 Cicero and Castiglione: Jan Bremmer and Herman Roodenburg, *A Cultural History of Humour* (Cambridge, UK: Polity, 1997), p. 4.

259 "You have a mangrel": Mark Twain, *The Mysterious Stranger and Other Stories* (Mineola, N.Y.: Dover, 1992), p. 117.

ELEVEN: NEW TIRYNTHA

260 "Humour is the great thing": Mark Twain, "What Paul Bourget Thinks of Us," in *The Writings of Mark Twain*, vol. 22, *Literary Essays* (New York: Harper & Brothers, 1899), p. 163.

260 Bill Haverchuck: This wasn't intended to be the next-to-last episode, but NBC dropped three episodes from the show's network run. They finally aired that fall on Fox Family, long after the show's cancellation. *Freaks and Geeks*, episode 14, "Dead Dogs and Gym Teachers," NBC, October 10, 2000.

261 digital editing: Adam McKay interviewed in Sacks, *Poking a Dead Frog*, p. 129.

263 "Are we paying more bucks": Malcolm Kushner, "More Bucks for Less Yucks: Cost of Laughing Index Up Again," Huffington Post, March 31, 2017, https://www .huffingtonpost.com/entry/more-bucks-for-less-yucks-cost-of-laughing-index-up _us_58de8e4de4b0d804fbbb7264. In fairness to Kushner, maybe an intern wrote the headline.

263 "Everything's been done": Stephen Merchant interviewed in Sacks, *Poking a Dead Frog*, p. 402.

263 "a grave, twenty-three inches long": Don Marquis, *The Annotated Archy and Mehitabel* (New York: Penguin, 2006), pp. xxx–xxxi.

264 "went temporarily 'joke-blind'": Carr and Greaves, *Only Joking*, p. 80.

264 "If I laugh": Byron, *Don Juan*, canto 4, st. 4.

265 "I have more faith": Elie Wiesel, *Night* (New York: Hill and Wang, 2006), p. 81.

265 "the currency of hope": Lipman, *Laughter in Hell*, p. 10.

265 popular running gag: Viktor E. Frankl, *Man's Search for Meaning* (Boston: Beacon, 2006), p. 44.

265 the Ik people: Colin M. Trumbull, *The Mountain People* (New York: Touchstone, 1987).

266 strange story of Tiryntha: Stephen Halliwell, *Greek Laughter: A Study of Cultural Psychology* (Cambridge, UK: Cambridge University Press, 2008), pp. 155–57.

266 "They perceived": Athenaeus, *The Deipnosophists; or, Banquet of the Learned*, trans. C. D. Yonge (London: Henry G. Bohn, 1854), 1:410.

266 "I'm not ready": Nesteroff, *The Comedians*, p. 348.

267 Queen Elizabeth's eventual death: "BBC Staff Are Trained on Correct Way to Announce Death of Queen in Bid to Avoid Another Embarrassing Gaffe," *Daily Mail*, October 30, 2011. This follows the precedent from George VI's death in 1952. In 2017, the *Guardian* reported that the BBC might not even go that far this time, nixing political satire but not necessarily all comedy.

270 "The failure mode of clever": John Scalzi, "The Failure Mode of Clever," Whatever (personal blog), June 16, 2010, https://whatever.scalzi.com/2010/06/16/the-failure-state-of-clever.

271 "whose first object in life": Jane Austen, *Pride and Prejudice* (London: Penguin, 2003), p. 56.

271 "something like a momentary anesthesia": Bergson, *Laughter*, p. 5.

272 "If, after hearing my songs": *Songs & More Songs by Tom Lehrer* liner notes, Rhino, 1997.

272 hijackers took over: As remembered by Funt's daughter Juliet on "Smile My Ass," *Radiolab*, WNYC, October 6, 2015.

272 "When a man once": Josh Billings, *Everybody's Friend; or, Josh Billing's Encyclopedia of Proverbial Philosophy of Wit and Humor* (Hartford, Conn.: American, 1874), p. 552.

INDEX

305